Beyond
the Waste Land

Beyond
the Waste Land

*A Democratic Alternative to
Economic Decline*

Samuel Bowles
David M. Gordon &
Thomas E. Weisskopf

ANCHOR PRESS/DOUBLEDAY
GARDEN CITY, NEW YORK 1983

Library of Congress Cataloging in Publication Data
Bowles, Samuel.
Beyond the waste land.
Includes index.
1. United States—Economic conditions—1971–   .
2. United States—Economic policy—1981–   .
3. Economic policy.   I. Gordon, David M.   II. Weisskopf,
Thomas E.   III. Title.
HC106.8.B68   1982   338.973
ISBN: 0-385-18345-3
Library of Congress Catalog Card Number 82–45514

To our parents
Dorothy Stebbins Bowles and Chester Bowles
Margaret S. Gordon and the late Robert Aaron Gordon
Ellen Weisskopf and Victor Weisskopf

whose hopes for a just and democratic society
are reflected in these pages

ACKNOWLEDGMENTS

We are grateful to our friends, colleagues, critics, and students for their contributions to this book. Lynn Eden, Diana R. Gordon, and David Plotke read the entire manuscript with great care and suggested countless improvements. Dan Clawson, Gerald Epstein, Aylette Jenness, Les Leopold, Michael Merrill, Tony Mazzocchi, Michael Reich, Barbara Richards, and Sam Rosenberg offered helpful comments on substantial portions of the book. Michele Naples and Juliet Schor shared their invaluable insights in helping us model some essential dimensions of labor relations. Ian Begg, Stephen Cohn, Susan Contratto, Sheldon Danziger, Gerald Duguay, James Medoff, Tom Michl, Paul Newlin, Leonard Rodberg, William G. Shepherd, and Walter Weisskopf generously shared their expertise in particular fields. Peter Alexander, Reza Bahar, Clare Battista, Suzanne Bergeron, Caren Grown, Monty Graham, David Kitchen, Judith Knight, Rob Parenteau, Jessica Payne, Danny Popkin, and Howard Shapiro provided essential research assistance.

Our ideas have been greatly influenced by what we have learned from our fellow staff members at the Center for Popular Economics (Amherst) and the Institute for Labor Education and Research (N.Y.)—and from the labor, community, feminist, minority, and other activists brought together by these institutions. Comments by participants at the 1982 summer conference of the Union for Radical Political Economics—particularly Marilyn Power and Bob Sutcliffe—resulted in many improvements. We also owe a profound, much more general intellectual debt to our fellow members of the Union for Radical Political Economics.

Unpublished data and other invaluable assistance were made available by the research and statistical staffs of the Organization for Economic Cooperation and Development, the U.S. Bureau of

Labor Statistics, the Bureau of Economic Analysis of the U.S. Department of Commerce, the President's Council of Economic Advisers, and the Edison Electric Institute. Staff at the Institute for Labor Education and Research also provided valuable support services. We would also like to thank the staff of the University of Massachusetts Library.

Howard Saunders generously helped with the design of the tables and graphs, while Joe Pomar and the staff of U.S. Lithograph skillfully crafted the final products.

The project originated in a mandate and a small travel grant from the Progressive Alliance, a coalition of progressive labor unions and other organizations and activists. We owe special thanks to Bill Dodds and Ed James for their foresight and patience in shepherding that early relationship.

We are particularly grateful to Felecia Abbadessa and Peyton H. Moss, Jr. of Doubleday Books for their help and support. Phil Pochoda, our editor at Doubleday, played a crucial role by keeping us on track, reminding us that communication of our ideas was at least as important as their conception.

CONTENTS

Appendixes

LIST OF FIGURES

Beyond
the Waste Land

1

THE SLACK ECONOMY AND THE ZERO-SUM ILLUSION

I would direct a question to those who have already indicated an unwillingness to accept |our| plan: Have they an alternative which offers a greater chance of balancing the budget, reducing and eliminating inflation, stimulating the creating of jobs and reducing the tax burden? And, if they haven't, are they suggesting we can continue on the present course without coming to a day of reckoning?

—Ronald Reagan, message to Congress,
February 1981[1]

Voters wanted a change in 1980. The economy was a prism for their frustrations. By the end of 1980, a poll commissioned by the New York Stock Exchange showed that
- 77 percent of adults agreed that the U.S. economy was "seriously off on the wrong track";
- 72 percent cited economic problems as the "most important we face as a nation and as individuals";
- 61 percent concluded that the economy was in "a real crisis"; and
- 52 percent believed that it was "very likely" or "somewhat likely" that we would face a major depression within the next two or three years.[2]

Our honeymoon with supply-side economics in the next two years did little to allay these concerns. While an eager public has waited for the President to pull economic recovery out of his hat, many more people experienced crunching economic dislocation and insecurity. "Ask yourself," Reagan suggested during his presidential debates with Jimmy Carter, "if you are better off than you were four years ago." Democrats gleefully recalled this challenge during the 1982 congressional elections. According to polls conducted in mid-1982, most voters felt that the Reagan program had hurt the economy. And when they reached the polls, many of these voters vented their resentments. According to a New York *Times*/CBS News exit poll during the November 1982 elections, "the great majority of voters saw yesterday's Congressional elections as a referendum on President Reagan's economic program. . . ." Democrats made substantial electoral gains, and the *Times*/CBS poll concluded that the voters "who provided the swing from 1980" were those "who tended to view the election as a referendum on Mr. Reagan and who told poll-takers that unemployment was the main factor deciding their vote." Two years of the conservatives' slash-and-burn approach to economic recovery had left a charred terrain. Many opponents of Reaganomics followed the theme advanced by Richard Celeste in his successful campaign for the Ohio governorship: "Send the President a message from the heartland of America—give us back our jobs."[3]

While liberals had good reason to be pleased with the electoral reaction against the President, however, they have provided remarkably little coherent alternative to Reaganomics, offering more of an echo than a choice. Most Democrats have raced to outbid Republicans in granting tax concessions to the corporations and the wealthy. Some have criticized the "trickle-down" distributions of tax-and-expenditure benefits—inveighing against the injustice of business tax privilege, social-spending cuts, and soaring military expenditures—but none have provided coherent proposals for resolving our current economic problems. Where is the liberal program for reviving the U.S. economy?

"Have they an alternative?" Reagan asked of his critics at the beginning of his administration. The silence has been deafening. And the silence has helped foster a growing fatalism and apathy about the possibilities for progressive economic change. Without clear choices, political disaffection has spread.

The uncontested reign of probusiness prescriptions has stemmed largely from the unchallenged sway of probusiness diagnoses. The prevailing economic wisdom has insisted on a trickle-down approach to economic recovery. It advocates a transfer of wealth from the needy to the powerful in order to fuel the engines of expansion. Trickle-down economics builds upon a fundamental premise—that the key to economic growth is expanding the stock of machinery and other productive equipment. This premise may be termed the *capital-shortage* explanation of economic decline: the economy has grown less rapidly as a result of sluggish capital formation. The solution is clear: put more money in the hands of the rich so that they can invest and expand the productive capacity of the nation.

The capital-shortage explanation reflects the logic of the "zero-sum" approach to economic recovery.[4] If the current economic crisis results from a shortage of capital, its necessary solution is belt tightening all around—for workers, students, the poor, the elderly, and the unemployed. Wall Street executive and former secretary of commerce Peter G. Peterson underscored this conclusion in January 1981:

We have chosen to consume, not invest. . . . The only way to afford and enjoy the future is to invest in it. . . . Unless a nation pays the dues required for economic progress, its politics becomes a mean contest over scarce resources. . . . Unless we start saving for the future, . . . our children and grandchildren will inherit a harsh and illiberal society. . . . Where are we to find the resources for a Decade of Investment? Whose consumption is to be cut?[5]

We reject this zero-sum logic. As an account of economic decline in the United States, the capital-shortage argument is contradicted by the most elementary facts about investment over the past two decades. The U.S. economy is a *slack economy:* there are huge stocks of available resources—buildings and machines and people and dollars—which could be used for investment and growth. We forgo billions of dollars of potential output as a result of costly conflicts between corporate hierarchies and resentful workers. We enjoy much lower standards of living than we might because of wasteful and often dangerous products and government expenditures. We need to reclaim the waste land, not reduce our own consumption.

Flawed analysis, not surprisingly, leads to misguided policies. As a prescription for America's economic problems, the trickle-down strategy is not only mean-spirited; it is more likely to cripple our economy than to revive it. Relying on a blanket scapegoating of government programs, the probusiness approach insists upon "free-market solutions" to our economic problems. But the logic of the free market—that profitability is an accurate guide to economic welfare and an irreplaceable stimulus to economic growth—is much more a part of the problem than a key to its solution.

We do not suggest replacing one simplistic slogan with another; we are no more inclined to "leave it to Uncle Sam" than we are to rely on "free enterprise." We believe in neither the "free market" nor centralized bureaucratic remedies for our economic ailments. We propose a democratic alternative to trickle-down economics. We base our economic proposals on the harsh facts of economic decline and the high hopes and humanitarian values of the vast majority of people in the United States.

Our democratic alternative builds on four major arguments:

First, the problems facing the U.S. economy may be traced to the costs of maintaining a faltering system of private corporate power, not to a failure of technique or a dearth of productive machinery.

Second, as a result, the U.S. economy falls far short of its productive potential, squandering time, energy, and natural resources on a monumental scale.

Third, the key to economic recovery is lifting this colossal waste burden. The dismal science insists that there is no such thing as a free lunch, but this "law" is based on the zero-sum illusion. If we stop wasting and misusing productive resources, we can make our lunch and eat it too.

Fourth, we cannot end this costly homage to the system of private corporate waste by handing over a blueprint to Washington's policymakers. We will require sustained popular mobilization for a democratic alternative. A practical program for a democratic economy can spur that mobilization.

MORE THAN MACHINES

Conventional economists believe that economic growth depends primarily upon the rate of capital formation and the rate of technical progress: more and better machines will guarantee a higher standard of living. But this approach is fundamentally misleading, and about as illuminating of economic behavior as the Newtonian model would be for comprehending the success or failure of marital relationships.

We begin with an understanding that the economy is people, that its basic relationships are social relationships. It should not be necessary for us to affirm this obvious point. But, as Harvard sociologist Daniel Bell notes, the mainstream economic model "is that of classical mechanics."[6] The economics profession has adopted the view that the economy runs like a machine, a clockwork mechanism in perpetual synchrony.

This is more than an ugly metaphor. It is a mode of thought which expunges concern for what people are like and what people want. We make use, instead, of a *social model* of the economy, the basis for an approach we call *democratic economics*. We shall show that what people are like, what they want, how they relate to each other, and how their aspirations are thwarted, diverted, or mobilized are all fundamental determinants of the rate of economic progress.

We provide a clear comparison of these alternative economic views by focusing on the causes of the slowdown of productivity growth in the United States. By their own admission, mainstream economists have floundered in studying the productivity slowdown; Commerce Department economist and leading productivity export Edward Denison reports that the productivity problem is, "to be blunt, a mystery."[7] The capital-shortage theory accounts for remarkably little of the slowdown in productivity growth in the United States.

Our alternative explanation focuses on power relationships in the postwar U.S. economy. We refer to this analysis as the *costs-of-corporate-power* model. The rate of productivity growth fell, we argue, because people increasingly balked at the tasks and roles upon which prosperity in the postwar corporate system depended. The result was a stalemated economy in which the costs of goading reluctant participants drained more and more out of the system.

Coal mining provides a simple example. Productivity growth essentially stopped: in the late 1960s and early 1970s there was a marked decline in the average number of tons of coal mined for each hour worked by a coal miner. This decline cannot be explained by a shortage of machinery, however, since capital equipment per worker in coal mining was one third higher in 1973 than in 1966. Social factors provide a much more promising explanation—the miners' rejection of unsafe working conditions, the coal-mine operators' stonewalling on the safety issue, and the subsequent breakdown of labor-management relations.[8]

This example reflects the entire postwar experience. The *postwar corporate system,* as we shall call it throughout the book, was based upon relations of domination and subordination, forged into an inflexible and hierarchical structure of private privilege. U.S. corporations achieved their power in the world economy shortly after World War II—but only at the expense of European and Japanese companies, Third World countries, and many people in the United States. This particular structure of domination was likely to last only as long as corporations could sustain it against challenges from below.

They could not do so for long. European and Japanese corporations regrouped; international competition eventually intensified. Third World people rebelled; the erosion of U.S. domination in the Third World was signaled by both the defeat of the U.S. military in Vietnam and the burgeoning market clout of the OPEC nations. At home, the capitalist order also began to crack, as minorities, the elderly, women, and organized workers demanded better terms in the distribution of prosperity's bounty. Both at home and abroad, the tasks of preserving the postwar corporate system grew more and more arduous. The costs of maintaining private power and privilege ultimately overtaxed the resources and flexibility of the U.S. capitalist economy.

The breakdown of the world monetary system is one of many illustrations of this institutional erosion. Carefully constructed during the closing months of World War II, the Bretton Woods system, as it was known, had secured international monetary stability on terms highly favorable to U.S. business. As international competition intensified and U.S. overseas military expenditures mounted, however, balance-of-payments deficits strained the system's mechanisms and eroded U.S. bargaining leverage. The Vietnam era compounded these strains. Patchwork efforts failed, and the U.S. government was eventually forced to break the pledge of dollar–gold conversion upon which the system rested. The Bretton Woods system collapsed in 1971.

Neither corporations nor the government fiddled while Rome burned, of course; both acted strenuously to prevent institutional erosion and to restore the relations of power and privilege upon which the postwar corporate system rested. Corporations moved more and more aggressively against organized labor and government restraints, seeking more effective ways to moderate worker resistance and citizen demands. While they awaited the results of these efforts, they poured more and more of their cash into mergers and speculation. The federal government simultaneously adopted growth-restricting fiscal and monetary policies in order not only to combat inflation but also to help restore discipline to the labor market. High unemployment would impose some stringent personal costs on the disadvantaged, to be sure, but it would also serve the more pertinent objective of reviving corporate control at the workplace. The Great Repression—as many have labeled the dominant approach to economic policy since 1973— aimed to influence people, not to win friends.

However unfamiliar to mainstream discussion, this analysis is not born of wishful thinking and populist illusion. As we shall show, *the costs-of-corporate-power model statistically accounts for almost all of the slowdown of productivity growth in the U.S. economy.* Given our evidence, the analytic shoe is now on the other foot. The burden of proof has shifted to the prevailing wisdom.

This account of the rise and demise of the postwar corporate system, resting on substantial historical and quantitative evidence, may suggest to some readers that we are implicitly "blaming the victims" of corporate domination for their untimely efforts to upset the business apple cart. Our analysis carries neither this intention nor its implication. We blame a *system of domination,* not its victims, for the heavy toll it exacted and the virtually inevitable rebellions which it prompted. Those who are currently asking the vast majority of U.S. workers and citizens to pay the price of economic recovery are asking for a repeat of an earlier and still-lingering history of institutional friction and erosion. The costs of corporate power have produced our current tragedy; further enhancement of that power would be worse than farce.

THE SLACK ECONOMY

Increasingly prevalent since the mid-1970s, the capital-shortage analysis has consistently prescribed short-term sacrifices in living standards in order to free up resources for higher investment. Munificence in defense of profits was surely no vice. "An economy that does not form enough capital to cover its future costs," as management consultant Peter Drucker has warned, "is an economy that condemns itself to decline and continuing crisis. . . ."[9]

Many will recognize this argument as the classic "guns-vs.-butter" trade-off of textbook economics—applied in this case to consumption vs. investment. You can't get something for nothing. To complain about it is to object to the laws of arithmetic. Right?

Wrong. There is a hidden assumption in the logic of those who endorse the zero-sum affirmation of inevitable trade-offs. They assume that nothing is currently wasted, that no productive inputs are currently lying fallow, that we are presently taking maximum advantage of the human and other resources applied in production. If there is widespread waste through either neglected or misused resources, however, the zero-sum logic fails. Not because two plus two equals five, but because more investment *and* more consumption are possible if we can make better use of our productive capacity. You can get something for nothing if you stop wasting resources.

The auto industry provides a graphic example of the waste burden in our economy. A quarter of a million unemployed automobile workers have been told that their layoffs are necessary to revive the industry. But much of the current competitive plight of the U.S. auto industry results from the waste built into the structure of the industry itself. For every worker engaged in the production of cars and trucks and buses, there are nearly two additional employees engaged either in supervising the productive workers or in selling cars. Car dealers and their employees alone outnumber production workers in the auto industry by a considerable margin.[10] Those salaries impose a burden borne by workers and consumers alike.

The cars themselves embody additional waste. During the halcyon days of the 1950s, according to a study by three highly respected economists, 25 percent of the cost of the average U.S. car and 20 percent of the cost of the gasoline needed to run it were attributable to annual style changes, to increases in horsepower and weight, and to advertising.[11] The growing popularity of foreign imports—at first primarily the VW bug—showed that many customers preferred simplicity and economy to the costs of redundant horsepower and annual cosmetic model changes. The auto industries dallied for years. Once they responded, they changed their models hastily and wastefully. Documents obtained during the Ford Motor Company Pinto trial reveal that the company knowingly sold cars whose gas tanks would explode if the cars were rear-ended. (Ford even calculated the likely number of deaths which would result, but—at eleven dollars per tank—the costs of repairing the fault were not thought to be cost-effective.[12]

If we preserve this structure in the auto industry, with its top-heavy management and shortsighted planning, others must certainly sacrifice in order to revive its fortunes. But if we lift the waste burden by pushing for lower administrative costs and more rational industrial planning, we can free up resources to help make both auto production and transportation systems much more efficient. Preserving the current rules imposes the zero-sum logic. Changing those rules would create many additional degrees of freedom, providing plenty of extra margin for both consumption and investment.

The auto industry is hardly unique. We argue that *waste pervades our economy,* a ubiquitous consequence of the priorities and power structure of the postwar corporate system. We point to waste on both the "demand side" and the "supply side" of the economy.

Demand-side waste results from a failure to operate the economy at full employment and full capacity; resources lie idle which could be put to productive use. While the Great Depression of the 1930s focused urgent attention on this source of waste, many mainstream economists are currently inclined to deny the existence of serious involuntary unemployment—ascribing joblessness to the necessary frictions and discipline of a "free" labor market. They refuse to consider simple steps which would make fuller use of our resources because they refuse to countenance the coordination and planning such steps would involve. We disagree. We think that full employment is possible, and we will show how the current burden of unemployment and resource underutilization can be lifted.

Supply-side waste is inefficient use of the labor and resources which are employed. We argue that it results from the imperatives of maintaining a system of private corporate power. Inefficient production results from labor-management conflict. Inefficient use of labor and wasted intellectual resources result from racial, sexual, and other forms of discrimination and from inequality of educational opportunity. Environmental destruction and community decay result from the inability of our economy to value the things that money cannot buy. Product waste results because some products are able to earn a profit even though they do not meet most people's needs. Supply-side waste—spurred by costly efforts to shore up the postwar corporate system—has recently brought us, among other bequests, the burgeoning costs of supervising and monitoring workers; the growing corporate resources diverted to legal counsel, financial speculation, and advertising; the rising costs of environmental cleanup and occupational illness; and the soaring expenses of a defense establishment nearly out of control.

Most economists and public officials claim that these are necessary (if regrettable) expenses. We argue that they are necessary only because we continue to play by the corporate capitalist rules of the game.

These criticisms seem cosmic, but they can also be grounded in concrete applications to our own economy. We provide a conservative quantitative estimate of the *waste burden* in the U.S. economy which has resulted from the rise and decline of the postwar corporate system. We show that our economy in 1980 was afflicted by something like $360 billion in demand-side waste and

$840 billion in supply-side waste. Useful output could have been more than $1.2 trillion higher than it was in 1980, the equivalent of 49.6 percent of useful national product in that year.

BEYOND THE WASTE LAND

The enormous size of the waste burden in our economy implies that we need not *necessarily* solve the current economic crisis through a redistribution of resources from consumption to investment, much less from the poor to the rich. We could, instead, pursue a transformation of a slack economy into an economically productive and socially more rational system. When there is so much slack in the economy—as a result of unutilized or misutilized resources—*there can be such a thing as a free lunch*. Mainstream economists take for granted the current social, legal, and economic organization of production and distribution. The possibility of a free lunch depends precisely on the development of alternative methods of mobilizing and utilizing our economic resources. It depends on a new set of priorities and a new way of doing business. It depends, in short, on our willingness and our ability to change the rules of the postwar corporate system.

Many will wonder about the coherence and practicability of alternatives to the present economic system. Do we really have any choice? Can we really pursue less wasteful economic structures? And can we pay for them?

We propose at the end of this book a twenty-four-point Economic Bill of Rights—a popular economic program that offers the possibility of a successful and democratic recovery of the U.S. economy in the 1980s. Our program holds promise, we argue, precisely because it addresses the basic sources of waste in our corporate capitalist economy. *Without* attention to these sources of waste, any economic program runs the risk of political divisiveness and economic irrelevance. *With* careful attention to the principal economic sources of waste, a democratic program for economic recovery can open up vast opportunities for rapid economic revival serving decent human priorities. By changing the way we run our economic lives, it can transcend the distasteful trade-offs which insist that someone's gain must always be someone else's loss.

This economic promise has clear historical precedent. More guns does not mean less butter unless both guns and butter are being produced efficiently and in ways which fully employ available inputs. The U.S. experience during World War II shows what can happen when this is *not* the case. Billions of dollars were poured into the U.S. war machine between 1939 and 1945—at least the equivalent of the kind of investment offensive for which corporations now call—but *consumption was not sacrificed.* Quite the contrary. Per capita real personal consumption increased by 11 percent between 1939 and 1945 despite the massive military buildup.[13] We got more guns *and* more butter per capita in the 1940s than in the 1930s. The reason is clear: all of the available inputs were put to use in the wartime economy and, equally important, the rate of productivity growth increased.

The key to a *peacetime* free lunch is similarly a coordinated effort to lift the current waste burden and to move beyond the slack economy.

• We can stop throwing away talent. We need policies explicitly aimed at full utilization of available resources—labor, knowledge, and physical resources—and at the moderation of economic frictions, including inflation, which such policies would initially encounter.

• We can stop putting working people down. We need new ways of organizing the work process which respect workers' dignity, reward their labor fairly, and tap their capacities instead of inviting their resistance.

• We can stop the outpouring of junk. We need a general method of resource allocation and decision-making which directs production *toward* essential human needs and *away from* the luxury wants and wasteful or dangerous projects, including military and nuclear spending, which currently clutter corporate and government drawing boards.

• We can stop the pillage of nature and the decay of community life. We must move toward economic decision-making which incorporates all relevant decision impacts—on our communities, our families, our natural environment—and goes beyond those narrower considerations which guide the calculus of private profit.

Our Economic Bill of Rights outlines a detailed, concrete, and practical economic program which, in our view, would move us toward each of these critical objectives. The program is sufficiently concrete that much of it could be implemented soon, if the political will could be mobilized. Its substantial costs would be covered by the returns to lifting the waste burden of the slack economy; as we show in detail in Appendix E, the resources now being wasted would provide more than enough to finance it. And the twenty-four points of our program are not politically outlandish. Some of what we propose is already on the books in at least some states. Many of our planks have actually been implemented somewhere—either in the U.S. or in countries whose economies and social systems are not so different from our own. In every case where there are relevant public-opinion-poll results, a solid majority supports the directions in which our specific proposals point.

We are convinced that a more democratic and egalitarian economy will work better, not worse, than our present system. The kind of economic program we propose would help promote higher living standards for all but a tiny minority. The underlying logic is simple enough: a more democratic and egalitarian economy will work better because the vast majority of people in the United States want it—and because it makes more economic sense to build an economy around what people want than to bear forever the costs of thwarting people.

THE POLITICS OF A DEMOCRATIC ALTERNATIVE

We do not intend to mail our program for economic revival to Washington, D.C., in the hope that it will be implemented tomorrow. We do not anticipate that our present political leadership—either in the White House or on Capitol Hill—will jump at the chance to implement the programs we outline in our closing chapters. They will need to be pushed.

We direct our ideas, instead, to those who have not had a hand in formulating economic policy and who more often than not have been the losers, the targets, and the victims of the economic policy-making establishment. We have developed the program outlined in this book through conversations, debates, and common political work with hundreds of grass-roots political activists: labor union officials and members, neighborhood organizers, environmentalists, feminists, minority activists, gay advocates, peace mobilizers, and others. For our program to have effect, it must be read, discussed, debated, and developed—not in corporate boardrooms, congressional chambers, or the Oval Office, but in union halls and churches, in kitchens and dormitories, in bars and workplaces across the country.

Our first objective is therefore education and mobilization, not implementation. Nothing that we propose will foster a viable economic recovery unless the vast majority of people in the United States are awakened to the economic feasibility of a program which works because it puts ordinary people in the driver's seat. With such an awakening, sustained popular mobilization can move us rapidly toward a democratic recovery.

But there is more to the politics of this democratic alternative than personal preferences about who should hold the steering wheel. The political stakes are high, and the political implications of alternative approaches to economic revival are critical.

The stakes are high, in large part, because our economy is changing—whether we like it or not. Conservatives have called for wholesale dismantling of social programs and, to a large degree, the limitation of union rights. Some corporate leaders have called for less democratic and more centralized decision-making in both the private and the public sectors.

Economic and political restructuring is on the agenda. It is no longer a question of the status quo vs. its critics. The character of the current economic impasse impels all participants in the debate toward institutional transformation. In what directions should we move? Whose interests should be served?

As one approach to such institutional transformation, trickle-down solutions pose potentially serious threats to our democratic rights and processes. They pit the short-run interests of most people in the United States against the richest families and largest corporations whose savings and investments have been designated as the motor of economic recovery. They are also likely to feature, in the interest of profits, renewed efforts to consolidate and intensify management control over labor. Further, by insisting on profits as the final arbiter of economic and social value, they are prepared to sacrifice occupational health, consumer safety, and environmental balance wherever and whenever pursuit of these objectives obstructs profits. The bottom line is measured in dollars and cents.

Under conservative economic policies, the near future will witness many more losers than winners. Trickle-down solutions will therefore require that more and more people be excluded from economic decision-making—simply to protect Robin Hood-in-reverse redistributive policies from the long winters of popular discontent. We have already seen this dynamic in scattered political efforts to curtail the popular accountability of government bodies—as in New York City, with the Emergency Financial Control Board established in 1975. Projected into the future, this exclusionary imperative will potentially undermine the democratic process in the United States.

The politics of our alternative program differ dramatically. Democratic procedures are both the engine *and* the rudder of its economic strategy. The economic viability of the program we outline will not be undermined by democratic and cooperative methods of decision-making. Quite to the contrary, our program depends on those methods for its direction *and* for its capacity to promote the growth of productivity in our economy.

Many have recently despaired about the fate of their humanitarian impulses and democratic values. Our analysis and program should help rekindle their faith. The "trade-off" between material security and a decent society is not a law of economics. It is a veil of privilege. There is an alternative which both points toward rapid recovery *and* supports traditional values of democracy, equality, and community. Democracy is the key to moving beyond the waste land.

I

Anatomy of a Crisis

Different programs for economic recovery build from different analyses of the sources of economic crisis. The capital-shortage view argues that economic decline has been conditioned primarily by a squeeze on capital investment in productive buildings and equipment. Conservative attacks on the government insist that public taxes and regulation have strangled private initiative. Our own analysis argues that economic crisis has resulted from the huge and mounting costs of maintaining the postwar corporate system in the U.S. economy.

It is impossible to debate the merits of alternative programs without first comparing alternative analyses of the problems those programs seek to resolve. The following six chapters provide that comparison. Mainstream explanations of the current crisis fare badly. Neither historical nor empirical evidence provides them much comfort. Our costs-of-corporate-power analysis offers much clearer guidance to the sources and trajectory of economic decline. It is time to abandon the conventional wisdom.

2

THE ARITHMETIC OF ECONOMIC DECLINE

The economy is basically healthy: the problems we have now are less economic than emotional.
—Chief economist, Bank of America, 1977[1]

Things are going much better in the economy than most people realize. It's our attitude that is doing poorly.
—Chair, Federal Reserve Board, 1978[2]

Most people in the United States now recognize that our economy is a mess. Some still believe that quick fixes and magic potions will be enough, that a few tax cuts here and a little exhortation there will turn the economy around. Others believe that the economy could return quickly to full health if only the government would get off its back. Increasing numbers of people are prepared to make more significant changes in economic organization to resolve our most critical problems—which helps explain why so many were prepared to countenance the supply-side juggernaut in 1981.

These varying attitudes reflect major uncertainty about the proper diagnosis of our economic disease. Some, pointing to the continued rise in per capita gross national product, deny the existence of serious economic problems altogether. Others, pointing to bad harvests and soaring oil prices since 1973, concede the reality of the crisis but nonetheless attribute it to accidental external events of relatively little enduring importance. Still others suggest much deeper causes requiring much more fundamental solutions.

Standard measures of economic performance can help us choose among such conflicting views. The data suggest a stark conclusion. Two results are most important. First, our economic fortunes began to decline *in the mid-1960s;* the deterioration of the U.S. economy has been unfolding for at least a decade and a half. Second, that deterioration has continually intensified ever since: far from receding, our problems have persisted and deepened.

These factual conclusions are not simply fodder for triviamongers and number crunchers. They carry profound implications for debates about program and strategy: Our problems are long-standing and fundamental. Those who attach later dates to the onset of decline are likely to miss the first moments of reversal and, as a result, the first causes of economic deterioration. Those who regard our current problems simply as cyclical downturns or the result of accidental jolts to a healthy economy are likely to prescribe Band-Aids for much more fundamental ailments. The persistence and severity of our economic problems should persuade us that those problems stem from structural faults in the foundations of the postwar corporate system. They are not temporary aberrations. They will not disappear by themselves. They require fundamental structural solutions.

HOW RECENT?

Few would disagree that there has been a turning point at some time during the past decade or two. The history of the United States economy (as well as the world economy) appears to encompass two fundamentally different periods since World War II.

The first, beginning shortly after the war and continuing at least through the early 1960s, created "boom" conditions for most people in the United States. There were obvious flaws in the vessel of expansion: Many continued to have difficulty finding a steady job, even in conditions of relatively full employment. Income inequalities persisted—between rich and poor, men and women, whites and blacks—and some even widened. Working conditions were often unhealthy, public services were often inadequate, and economic priorities were often inappropriate to meet people's real needs. As John Kenneth Galbraith argued in the late 1950s, the "affluent society" was far from perfect; Michael Harrington's *The Other America* was the flip side of postwar prosperity.

Yet, in spite of these continuing problems, there was a real sense in which the economy was working. Total output and total income were growing so rapidly that most people in the United States could realistically anticipate a brighter economic future. The expanding pie helped moderate some of the tensions inherent in an unequal society and cushioned the blows of misplaced priorities and irrational economic allocations.

Those years of optimism now seem like the distant and receding past. Economic welfare has been stagnating or declining for large proportions of the U.S. labor force and U.S. households. Economic anxiety has been spreading like the plague—infecting more and more of us, reaching from Wall Street to Main Street. "It would be necessary to go back to the 1930s and the Great Depression," pollster Daniel Yankelovich concludes, "to find a peacetime issue that has had the country so concerned and so distraught."[3]

How do we measure this reversal of economic fortunes? And when did this reversal begin?

Inflation and unemployment are the symptoms of economic deterioration to which economists and the media have devoted most of their attention. In order to clarify the timing of the decline in these familiar terms, we present the basic data on inflation and unemployment in Figure 2.1.[4]

The top panel plots the annual rate of inflation over the postwar period, using annual percentage changes in the consumer price index as a measure of price inflation. From the early 1950s through 1965, the annual rate of price increase fluctuated around an average of 2 percent. It neither showed a noticeable tendency to rise nor displayed sharp fluctuations; indeed, the most striking feature of the first part of the graph is the *growing stability* of a relatively low inflation rate through the early 1960s.

From the mid-1960s to 1981, however, the rate of inflation increased dramatically—climbing to double-digit levels from 1979 to 1981. Each of its peaks was higher than the previous business-

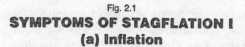

Fig. 2.1

SYMPTOMS OF STAGFLATION I
(a) Inflation

average annual % change in Consumer Price Index

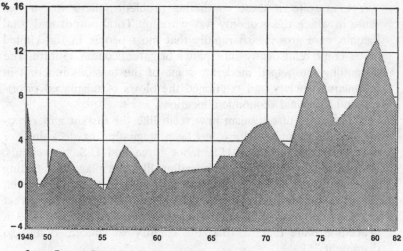

Source: Economic Report of the President, 1982, B-55

(b) Unemployment

average annual % of civilian labor force

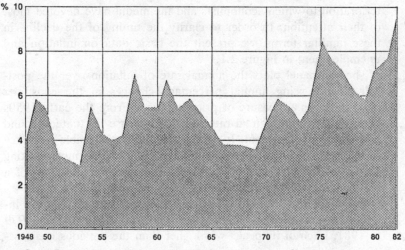

Source; Economic Report of the President, 1982, B-29

cycle peak, and each of the troughs was higher than the rate of inflation in the previous trough. The acceleration of inflation began well before OPEC got its act together in 1973.

The rate of inflation dropped significantly in 1982—thanks in large part to the highest unemployment rates since the Great Depression. Even with more than 10 million jobless, however, inflation was still more severe in 1982 than it was in 1976, the previous cyclical low in the inflation rate. This can hardly be considered a permanent cure for the accelerating inflation shown in Figure 2.1, since the pattern of higher inflation rates at each cycle trough has continued. And who knows how many more million unemployed must lose their jobs before such hard-times strategies could permanently reverse the inflationary dynamic? (We return to this question in Chapter 9.)

The bottom panel of Figure 2.1 provides official government data on the rate of unemployment. Unemployment is itself subject to sharp cyclical fluctuations, but it is evident from the graph that joblessness began to move significantly upward from the late 1960s through the 1970s and into the 1980s. The data for 1948 to 1965 show no obvious trend. After the mid-1960s, as with the inflation data, each peak is higher than the previous one and each trough is higher than the previous trough as well.

Dismal though they are, these data on unemployment disguise much of the problem. Women, minority workers, and teenagers all experience higher rates of unemployment; their relative disadvantages in the labor market, by this measure, have been intensifying throughout the years of economic decline. Equally important, the official overall unemployment rate excludes many in the labor force who nonetheless have serious employment problems —those who have grown discouraged and abandoned their search for work and those who want full-time work but must settle reluctantly for part-time jobs. The official data further understate the extent of joblessness, as well, because they measure unemployment only at a particular moment. In 1981, for example, unemployment was recorded at 8.3 million persons but the Bureau of Labor Statistics estimates that 23.4 million were unemployed *at some time or another* during the year.[5]

Those who were able to find and hold jobs were more fortunate, of course, but they hardly escaped the effects of economic decline. Roughly 90 percent of U.S. households depend on wage and salary income for their survival.[6] For this vast majority, two principal trends determine the level of income available to their households: take-home pay per hour of work and the total hours worked to support household members. What has happened to hourly earnings, and what has happened to hours worked?

Figure 2.2 presents some basic data on both earnings and hours for the postwar period. Viewed together, the two panels provide a quick summary of the fate of working people in the United States.

The top panel presents data on the average production worker's take-home pay—or *real spendable hourly earnings*.[7] (Production workers comprised 81.3 percent of total employment in 1980 and represent that group in the labor force which is most clearly dependent on wage and salary income.)[8] Spendable hourly earnings measure the average worker's hourly wage and/or salary income plus other compensation—for example, medical benefits—minus personal income taxes and Social Security taxes. These earnings are expressed in constant (1977) dollars in order to adjust for the effects of inflation on the cost of living. The graph charts the level of average real hourly spendable earnings in the United States from 1948 to 1981.

The data show a clear pattern: The average worker's real after-tax pay grew rapidly through the mid-1960s. Its growth then slowed, with some fluctuations, until 1978, and then declined precipitously after 1978. By 1981, average real after-tax hourly earnings had fallen back to their lowest levels since 1961, twenty years earlier. Average annual growth in real spendable earnings was 2.1 percent from 1948 to 1966, slowed to 1 percent between 1966 and 1973, and then dropped by 1.9 percent a year from 1973 through 1981.

The bottom panel presents Commerce Department data on average annual *hours worked per capita* by the U.S. population. This measure reflects the total amount of labor which U.S. households committed to the economy in order to support themselves and their dependents. The data on hours almost exactly mirror the top panel on earnings. Average hours per capita declined fairly steadily until the early 1960s—as workers and households were able to take advantage of rising wage and salary income. They rose in the mid-1960s as the growth of real earnings began

Fig. 2.2

SYMPTOMS OF STAGFLATION II
(a) Real Spendable Hourly Earnings

production workers' (after-tax) hourly earnings in $1977

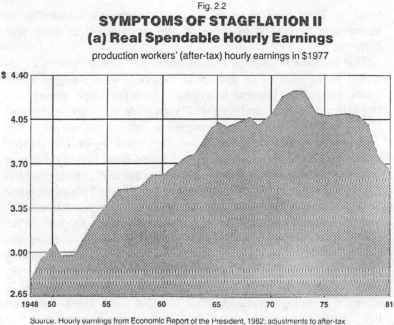

Source: Hourly earnings from Economic Report of the President, 1982; adjustments to after-tax
earnings from S. Bowles, D. Gordon, and T. Weisskopf, "A Continuous Series on 'Real
Spendable Hourly Earnings'," Technical Note, Economics Institute of the Center for Democratic
Alternatives, 1982

(b) Hours Per Capita

average annual hours of work (excluding unpaid family labor) per capita

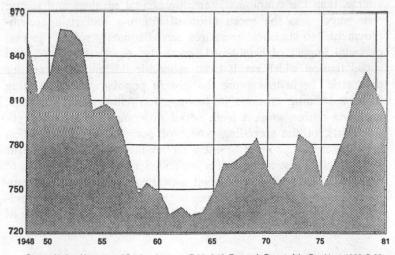

Source: National Income and Product Accounts, Table 6.13; Economic Report of the President, 1982, B-28.

to slow. They have risen most rapidly since the mid-1970s as households have tried to stave off the squeeze of declining real earnings.[9]

This increase in average annual hours per capita reflects an increase in the number of household members working outside the home, and not an increase in average hours per week. Faced with stagnating and then declining real spendable earnings, additional family members, particularly married women, have sought work. The percentage of the adult population working or looking for work outside the home—a figure which had been roughly constant over the postwar period—began to rise in the mid-1960s, climbing from 59 percent in 1966 to 64 percent in 1981.[10] This extra labor helped sustain total household earnings, making possible continued increases in household consumption levels. As the 1970s progressed, *Business Week* noted, it became more and more important to take into account "the sweat that goes into producing [household] income."[11] "Everybody is working harder to maintain their standard of living," University of Massachusetts economist Leonard Rapping concludes, "but most of them are not making it."

Figure 2.2, in short, tells a familiar story. Since the mid-1960s, through both the stagnation in real spendable earnings and the added hours necessary to compensate for that stagnation, working households have felt the pinch. There is more to the crisis, of course, than the symptomatic erosion of real earnings and leisure time, much less the acceleration of inflation and rising unemployment. No statistical measures can adequately reflect the real personal impact of heightened insecurity, personal anxiety, and social tension which result from economic decline. Nor can our data series begin to capture the loss in popular power resulting from continuing erosions in labor union vitality and leverage, declining citizen support from social programs and personal entitlements, or the spreading power of corporate political action committees (PACs) and business money in electoral politics. But even simple statistical measures are sufficient to shift the terms of discussion. According to relevant measures and available government data, our economic fortunes began to deteriorate in the mid-1960s, not later. We have now experienced almost two decades of economic decline.

HOW DEEP?

We have focused on aspects of economic decline which people have experienced more or less directly. But in order to assess the depth of our economic problems, we must move from measures of personal distress to more fundamental indicators of basic economic performance.

Periods of Growth and Decline. The first task is to distinguish between the short-term business cycle and more persistent trends in the economy. As the graphs in Figures 2.1 and 2.2 show, most indicators of economic distress move up and down over the business cycle, riding the roller coaster of expansion and contraction every few years. If we want to probe the depth of the current economic crisis, we should make comparisons which avoid confusing short-term movements with more persistent trends.

One common method of controlling for short-term oscillations concentrates on *comparable stages* of successive business cycles. If we compare rates of growth from one business-cycle peak to another, for example, we can highlight the economy's performance between years when it is at the same stage of each cycle.

In the discussions which follow, both in this chapter and in subsequent analysis, we use this standard peak-to-peak method of controlling for the effects of the short-term cycle. We identify the business-cycle peak years by looking at the ratio of actual gross national product (GNP) to the corresponding "potential" GNP; potential GNP is an estimate of what the economy was capable of producing with what is somewhat arbitrarily termed "full utilization" of available resources. The ratio of actual to potential GNP reaches a cyclical peak at the stage of an expansion when the economy's productive potential is most *fully* utilized.

By this measure, there were seven business-cycle peaks in the postwar period up to the 1980s: 1948, 1951, 1955, 1959, 1966, 1973, and 1979. Since everyone seems to agree that the boom period lasted at least until 1966, we study the economy's performance during the years of stable prosperity by examining the *entire* period from 1948 to 1966, ignoring the several short-term cyclical fluctuations in between. Then, in order to sharpen our focus on the contours of subsequent decline, we consistently compare two stages of deterioration: from the cyclical peaks of 1966 to 1973 and 1973 to 1979.

Much of our analysis will focus, in short, on data for just three key periods between bench-mark years: the boom period, from 1948 to 1966; the first phase of decline, from 1966 to 1973; and the second phase, from 1973 to 1979. Where possible, we will also introduce data for more recent years, although economists cannot yet agree on whether or not the sustained decline since 1979 was punctuated by a feeble cyclical peak in 1981.

Measures of Growth and Decline. Our second task is to choose an indicator of the economy's overall performance. Economists often focus on "per capita GNP"—a society's gross national product divided by its total population. The rate of growth of per capita GNP, adjusted for inflation, is thought to reflect the rate of improvement in the average citizen's well-being. For reasons which we discuss in detail in Appendix A, we prefer an alternative measure which we label "hourly income"—real net national income per hour of work.

Hourly income differs from per capita gross national product in three respects: (1) in accordance with widely accepted economic reasoning, it removes from gross national product the amount spent on "depreciation," that is, the output needed to replace deteriorated structures and equipment; (2) it adjusts for inflation with a price index reflecting changes in the prices of *purchased* rather than *produced* commodities, allowing us to take into account changes in international terms of trade; (3) it substitutes total hours of work for total population as the standard against which real income should be measured.

None of these modifications is particularly controversial, but the third one—dividing by hours of work rather than population—is quite important. Many agree that the current problems of the U.S. economy involve its productive capacity and efficiency. By focusing on *hourly* income, we can sharpen our attention on the standard of living we attain *in return for the amount of work we must perform to achieve that standard of living.* Increases in per capita GNP may not be desirable if we must work too many additional hours to achieve them. And, as we have already seen, hours of

work per capita have been rising dramatically, accounting for a
substantial portion of recent increases in per capita GNP.

Figure 2.3 presents data on the average annual rates of growth

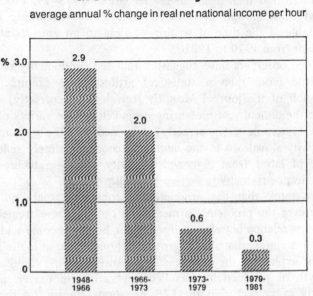

Fig. 2.3
Growth of Hourly Income
average annual % change in real net national income per hour

Source: National Income and Product Accounts; see Appendix A.

of *hourly income*. We present data for our three main periods of
comparison and for the most recent available trends from 1979 to
1981. These data confirm the impressions we have already
formed: hourly income grew rapidly from 1948 to 1966; slowed
noticeably from 1966 to 1973; and declined even more dramatically from 1973 to 1979. Hourly income essentially stagnated between 1979 and 1981. (Final figures were not available for 1982
at the time of writing, but they will almost certainly show even
further deterioration when they arrive.)[12]

There is one obvious source of these dramatic declines in
hourly income—the slowdown in the rate of growth of *productivity* (that is, real output per hour of work).[13] Hourly *income*
did not grow as fast after the mid-1960s largely because hourly

output—another term for productivity—did not rise as rapidly as
during the two decades following World War II. Using the same
bench-mark years, we find that the average annual rate of growth
of hourly output in the private-business economy of the United
States slowed from 3.2 percent in 1948–66 to 2.3 percent in
1966–73 and then again to .8 percent in 1973–79. Productivity
growth has slowed even more since 1979—according to data
available at the time of writing—falling to an annual rate of .4
percent from 1979 to 1981.[14]

Some observers have suggested that the productivity slowdown
is little more than a statistical artifact. For example, Harry
Magdoff of the journal *Monthly Review* has (correctly) emphasized the difficulty of measuring output in a wide variety of industries. Others have (incorrectly) supposed that the measured productivity slowdown in the aggregate economy simply reflects the
shift of labor from higher-productivity goods-producing sectors
into lower-productivity service-providing sectors.

We think that the productivity problem is real and severe.
Whatever the problems in measuring output, the extremely close
correspondence between our series for hourly income and hourly
output suggests that slower growth in hourly output is the likeliest
factor explaining the more easily measured income trends. Slower
growth of productivity has been pervasive, moreover, affecting
nearly every sector in the U.S. economy. Figure 2.4 shows the
trends in hourly output growth for eleven separate industries covering the full breadth of the economy. Almost all of the sectors
show the same two-step decline we have already seen for the total
private business economy. The most important exception to this
pattern is manufacturing, which did not begin to experience the
productivity slowdown until 1973–79. But this exception largely
reflects the unusually rapid rate of capital investment in manufacturing during the Vietnam years. And the general pattern in Figure 2.4 seems clear enough. It is hard to write off the general
overall decline in productivity growth as a statistical mirage.[15]

Deterioration. Some may not find the drop in hourly-income
growth from 1948–66 to 1966–73, as shown in Figure 2.3, to be
particularly striking; it is certainly true that the later drop to
1973–79 is more substantial both absolutely and relatively. But
this is not the relevant standard of evaluation. The slowdown in

hourly-income growth in 1966–73 would be extremely important *if* it created stresses and strains which the economy was unable to overcome and thereby led to even more severe problems in subsequent years. And this is exactly what happened. We present a detailed discussion in later chapters of such connections between the first and second phases of economic decline. An example at this point may help to clarify our argument.

When the postwar corporate system was working well, at least from the viewpoint of corporations, profitability recovered from short-term recessions and achieved levels more or less comparable to its prerecession peaks. Despite the depths of the 1957–58 and 1960–61 recessions, for example, the after-tax rate of corporate profits was far higher in 1965 than it had been in 1955, before those two recessions.

After 1966, however, corporate profitability did not recover from the stresses of economic downturn. After the recession of 1969–70, the after-tax profit-rate peak in 1972 was one third lower than it had been in 1965. After the recession of 1974–75, once again, the after-tax profit-rate peak in 1977 had fallen below its 1972 peak.[16]

Fig. 2.4

The Productivity Slowdown

average annual rates of productivity growth by industry

Industry	1948-1966	1966-1973	1973-1979
Agriculture (3.3%)	4.9	3.1	2.5
Mining (2.9)	4.4	2.1	-5.2
Construction (4.8)	2.8	-1.0	-2.8
Manufacturing (24.0)	2.9	3.3	1.5
Utilities (2.5)	6.3	3.3	1.0
Transportation (3.8)	3.4	2.2	1.2
Communications (2.6)	5.3	4.8	6.0
Trade (16.6)	2.9	2.6	0.8
Finance & Real Estate (14.8)	2.0	0.5	0.6
Other Services (12.8)	1.3	1.5	0.4
Government (11.8)	0.2	0.7	0.4

Source: U.S. Department of Commerce. Figures in parentheses after each industry are % of gross domestic product represented by each industry in 1979.

This observation echoes our earlier comments on Figure 2.1. There we noted that with each successive business cycle since 1966, rates of inflation and unemployment have become worse. The pattern of deterioration of profitability is parallel: it has declined from cycle to cycle since the mid-1960s. Operating through its normal cyclical mechanisms, *the economy has been unable to reverse this process of decline by itself.*

Domestic and International Decline. This pattern of economic deterioration has affected not only the U.S. economy but also the world economy.

The domestic dimensions of the crisis have become painfully familiar by now. The U.S. economy has lost much of its initial competitive advantage, falling from its lofty pinnacle in the earlier postwar decades. In 1951, for example, the U.S. economy accounted for 30 percent of the world trade of the sixteen leading industrial nations; by 1971, the U.S. share had fallen to 18 percent.[17]

Even more dramatically, the U.S. economy has taken a nose dive in the international rankings by per capita gross domestic product. The United States, as we were frequently reminded, was numero uno in 1950, in 1960, and again in 1970—still over 20 percent ahead of its nearest competitor. By 1980, the original land of plenty had dropped to number eleven (not counting the oil-rich Middle Eastern states), trailing Switzerland, Sweden, Norway, Germany, Denmark, Luxembourg, Iceland, Finland, the Netherlands, and Belgium in that order.[18]

Despite these relative advances, however, other countries have been suffering economically as well. All of the advanced countries have experienced significant declines in the growth of output and productivity. Even Japan, that economic wonder held up for all to emulate, has been growing less than half as rapidly since the early 1970s as it did during the 1950s and 1960s.

This worldwide character of the economic crisis serves as a potent reminder of the complexity of its causes. When and if we in the United States begin to move toward promising economic solutions, we must be certain to review their international implications. The U.S. economy, despite its great internal resources, is tightly bound to the world economy. We can gain much greater control over our own economic destinies, but we cannot afford to neglect the impact of our own actions on the rest of the world and, in turn, the effects of international trends on our domestic margin for maneuver.

Short Memories

It is unfortunate, perhaps, that so few economists and policy makers still remember the interwar years—the years of persistent instability from the 1920s through the Great Depression. Many of us learned our practical economic lessons during the period of unprecedented boom and social progress from World War II through the mid-1960s. We came to take expansion for granted, regarding rapid economic growth, relative social harmony, and continuing political stability as the expected norm. There were occasional recessions, to be sure, but the steady waves of expansion carried us over and beyond their troughs to new highs.

We must discard such rosy expectations. The 1950s and the 1960s will not provide a fruitful model for the coming decade or two. The 1920s and 1930s, with their economic gyrations, political instability, and social unrest, may well be more pertinent. We have not experienced the soup lines and massive unemployment of the Great Depression, of course, and the impact of decline has been much more varied and diffuse than it was during the 1930s. But institutional sclerosis and continuing economic instability indicate that we are in an economic crisis nonetheless.

Others, apparently, have reached similar conclusions. Few used to speak about "capitalism" during the boom years because most took "capitalism" for granted. The word has since been readmitted to polite company. Magazines ask, "is Capitalism in trouble?" Business executives worry out loud about its future. More than three fifths of those polled in 1980, as we noted at the beginning of Chapter 1, agree that the economy is in "a real crisis."

Economic decline has continued for nearly twenty years. It is time for both analysis of its causes and programs for revival to catch up with the true dimensions of the crisis.

3

BEYOND SCAPEGOATS

It's like the old saying, "Don't ever have a political philosophy
that can't fit on a bumper sticker."
—Local politician on the economy
in 1980 campaign[1]

It will be easiest to present our own analysis of economic decline
if we first clear the decks of other, less promising explanations.
We first consider a number of relatively superficial explanations
of the current economic crisis, analyses which sacrifice complexity for the reassurance of blaming a single major culprit as the
source and cause of all our economic problems. We then turn to
a more significant and ultimately more dangerous analysis: the
capital-shortage theory of economic decline, which underlies all
of the trickle-down approaches to economic recovery.

We subject each of the competing theories to the test of empirical evidence.* None, we conclude, provides an adequate basis for
understanding the onset and persistence of economic deterioration in the United States. While some of the theories refer to
important strands of spreading instability, none is sufficient by itself to explain what went wrong. In every case, these explanations
are inadequate because they fail to account for either the *timing*
or the basic *character* of the decline of the U.S. economy. Programs for recovery based on these flawed diagnoses are as likely
to aggravate our economic plight as to relieve it.

* We concentrate in this chapter on these theories as *explanations of
economic decline*. We return to related arguments in Chapters 8 and 9
when we evaluate the promise of *strategies for recovery* which depend to
some degree on these analyses.

SIMPLE CULPRITS

Five single-factor theories have dominated discussion in one or another arena. Each of these theories targets a particular object of blame. While many proponents of these explanations understand that no single factor alone can account for everything that has plagued the U.S. economy, these single-factor analyses are often presented *as if* they were all we needed to know about our economic problems.

Those who wish capitalism well have tended to point the finger at some external disturbance, hoping to shield the operations of capitalism itself from critical scrutiny. Two prominent theories blame (1) OPEC and (2) the government for our problems. These two analyses resemble the "outside-agitator" theory of social unrest.

Others have tended to blame their opponents in the political economy; unlike the outside-agitator explanations, these theories focus on the internal operations of the private economy. Many in business have pinned the blame on (3) labor, arguing that its wage gains have outstripped productivity growth, consequently squeezing corporate profits and triggering the deterioration in U.S. international competitiveness. Others, inclined in more populist directions, have tended to blame (4) excess corporate profits; and/or (5) growing monopoly power for declining efficiency and rising inflation.

In every case, it turns out, simplicity of analysis contributes little to the task of constructing an adequate understanding of economic decline.

Blaming OPEC

It is almost taken for granted that the U.S. economy began to falter when OPEC countries jacked up their prices in 1973. As the Business Week Team, writing about reindustrialization, observes, "the world changed drastically in 1974, when the Organization of Petroleum Exporting Countries (OPEC) quadrupled oil prices. . . . And only when we separate the data into pre-OPEC and post-OPEC periods can the real extent of the damage to the U.S. standard of living be assessed."[2]

There is no doubt that dramatic increases in the price of imported oil since 1973 have delivered a harsh blow to the U.S. economy and its consumers. But these price increases can hardly account for our present economic problems.

The first problem with the blame-OPEC analysis involves *timing:* U.S. Department of Energy data indicate that the average real domestic price of oil declined or remained constant over most of the postwar period.[3] This index of energy cost did not begin its increase until 1973, substantially *after* the process of economic deterioration had already begun.

The second problem involves the *source* of the energy price increases. Even after 1973, only part of the increase in domestic energy costs can be attributed to the greed and shenanigans of OPEC. The 1980 *Economic Report of the President* provides one example:

Gasoline prices at the pump rose 35 cents per gallon over the 4 quarters of 1979. . . . Approximately 14 cents of this increase stemmed from higher prices for imported crude oil and products [or only two fifths of the total increase], and 11 cents came from widening gross margins of refiners, retailers and distributors. About 10 cents resulted from higher domestic crude oil prices, only a part of which was due to decontrol.[4]

In this case, in short, only 40 percent of the increase in energy prices resulted from foreign price hikes.

Third and most important, even after 1973 energy-price increases—from *all* sources, both domestic and foreign—explain but a small portion of the symptoms of economic deterioration. The price hikes were themselves gigantic, but their economic *impact* was surprisingly small.

One study, by Yale economist and former presidential economic adviser William Nordhaus, examined the impact of the 1973–74 oil-price increases on all the advanced countries for the period from 1973 to 1979.[5] Comparing their performance with the previous ten years, Nordhaus concluded that the oil shock accounts for no more than

- 6 percent of the decline in the average growth rate of GNP;
- 11 percent of the increase in the rate of inflation;
- 10 percent of the increase in the unemployment rate; and
- 6 percent of the decline in the rate of productivity growth.

While this analysis is not directly applicable to the United States alone, a 1981 Congressional Budget Office study suggests that Nordhaus' findings *overstate* the OPEC impact on the U.S. as a result of the relatively greater dependence of Europe and Japan on imported oil.[6]

Further studies confirm these impressions of limited impact. An analysis by three economists at the U.S. Bureau of Labor Statistics provides what they consider to be a "large" estimate of the effect of the energy-price increases (without indicating how much of this effect is due to OPEC).[7] They conclude that labor productivity in manufacturing would have risen only .18 percentage points more rapidly between 1973 and 1978 if the relative price of energy had not changed; this amounts to only 6 percent of the average annual growth in manufacturing productivity from 1948 to 1966. And energy-price increases certainly had even less impact on the U.S. economy in sectors outside manufacturing which are less heavily dependent on energy inputs. In general, according to a careful study by M.I.T. economist Ernst Berndt, "energy prices are unlikely to have played a major direct or indirect role in the 1973–77 productivity slowdown. . . ."[8] Our problems go much deeper than the price of a barrel of oil.

Blaming the Government

Conservatives have made an art form out of their attacks on big government. William E. Simon, leading conservative spokesman and former secretary of the treasury, offers typical hyperbole in his book *A Time for Action:*

Most efforts to describe the size and workings of government these days remind me of the blind men trying to describe an elephant by feeling different parts of it—and having no idea of the total immensity

of the subject. The only change I would make in this image would be
to substitute a brontosaurus for the elephant. The federal government
is so huge that nobody, including the people supposedly in charge of
it, knows how big it really is. . . .

But because of this very immensity, it is essential that we make an
effort to grasp the scope and nature of government activity. Unless we
understand what it is doing to our economy, . . . the very hugeness
we don't understand will eventually crush us.[9]

These conservative critics of the public sector do not refer to
the massive military budget, of course, nor to the considerable
government subsidies to private business. They concentrate, instead, on three principal targets: taxes on both business and individuals; government regulation—particularly by the Environmental Protection Agency (EPA) and the Occupational Safety
and Health Administration (OSHA); and social-welfare programs.

We will deal with each of these specific arguments in turn, but
it is important to consider the general logic of the blame-government argument first. The basic point has echoed through
continual and sometimes deafening repetition: where government
involvement in the economy is greater, other relevant considerations being equal, conservatives argue that the rate of economic
growth will be lower.

The first test of this proposition is the most encompassing: has
total government spending increased more rapidly as the economy
has declined, choking out the private sector with the spreading
weeds of government activity? Figure 3.1 shows the share of total
federal, state, and local government expenditures in GNP for our
familiar bench-mark years, 1948, 1966, 1973, and 1979. It appears from the graph that government spending increased much
more rapidly during the boom years than during the two phases
of economic decline. Simple arithmetic confirms this visual impression. From 1948 to 1966, the government-spending share of
GNP increased by an average of 2.5 percent a year. From 1966
to 1973, this relative growth in the government-spending share increased by only 1.2 percent a year. By the second phase of crisis,
from 1973 to 1979, the growth of the share of total government
spending had virtually ceased, increasing at only .3 percent per
year. The conservatives find little support from this measure; the

growth of the public sector was most rapid when the economy
was booming and slowed during the successive phases of decline.

This comparison is not yet sufficient to dispel the conservatives'
attack, of course; they might still argue that government spending
was too high in any case and that the early growth of the public
sector helped sow the seeds of subsequent decline.

Fig. 3.1
Rising Government Spending?
federal, state, and local government expenditures as % of GNP

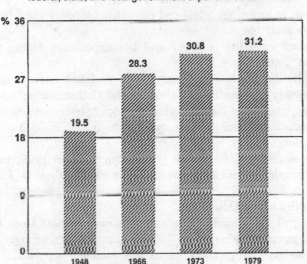

Source: Economic Report of the President, 1982, B-75, B-1

We cannot replay history, unfortunately, so we cannot actually
judge how the U.S. economy might have fared during the postwar
period if public spending had grown less rapidly. We can make
some fruitful international comparisons, however, since the conservative argument would imply that the U.S. economy fared less
well than some of its competitors because the burden of the public sector was too great.

We begin this comparison by looking at the experience of
Sweden, which for many has become virtually synonymous with
the welfare state, high taxes, and burdensome government inter-

ference. We do not propose Sweden as a model for the United States. We ask simply, has big government in Sweden shackled the Swedish economy?

From the Great Depression until the mid-1970s, the governing political coalition in Sweden instituted many government policies designed to achieve full employment, a high level of social services, and greater social and economic equality. According to official international data, it made considerable progress toward these objectives:

- Income inequality in Sweden was, by the mid-1970s, lower than in any other advanced capitalist economy for which data are available;
- Infant mortality is lower and life expectancy higher than in the United States;
- Pollution levels (both per capita and per energy unit consumed) are roughly half those in the United States;
- The fraction of Swedish gross national product devoted to education is more than a quarter higher than in the United States; and
- Even during the stagnant years from 1973 to 1979, the average rate of unemployment in Sweden—adjusted for comparability to U.S. figures—was just under 2 percent, less than a third of the U.S. levels.

Many of these achievements have flowed in part from the size of the government's role in Sweden: taxes consume over half of the Swedish GNP, compared to less than a third in the United States.[10]

Did this ample public provision for social needs in Sweden cramp the satisfaction of private wants? Quite the contrary. The Swedes began the postwar period with substantially lower living standards than those in the United States. Now, measured by gross national product per capita (in current dollars), the standard of living in Sweden is roughly 30 percent higher than in the United States.[11]

This rapid growth was reflected in the economic conditions of Swedish workers. According to the U.S. Bureau of Labor Statistics, Swedish workers' hourly wages in 1950 averaged 60 percent lower than U.S. workers'; in 1980, they had risen to 46 percent higher. Average weekly hours for Swedish manufacturing workers

declined by nearly 30 percent from 1950 to 1980, while U.S. industrial employees work almost exactly as many hours per week
today as they did thirty years ago.[12]

The secret to these rising wages and shorter working hours lies
in rapid productivity growth: output per worker-hour in Swedish
manufacturing grew twice as fast over the postwar period as in
the United States.[13]

The Swedish example does not appear to be unique. Many of
the advanced countries which grew most rapidly during the postwar period had very active public sectors. Conservatives charge
that a bloated public sector shackles the efficiency of the private
sector, creating a drag on efficiency and productivity growth. But
Figure 3.2 suggests just the opposite. In the graph, we compare
the average growth of manufacturing productivity between 1960
and 1979 with the average level of social-welfare expenditures
(as a fraction of the gross domestic product [GDP]) during that

Fig. 3.2

Government Spending and Productivity Growth

International comparison of hourly output growth in manufacturing
and social-welfare spending as % of gross domestic product, 1960-79

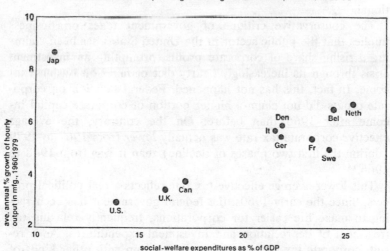

Source: Hourly output data from U.S. Bureau of Labor Statistics, unpublished data, 1982; social-
welfare expenditures include health, education, and income support payments—from
OECD, National Accounts, 1982, Vol. 2, and unpublished data. Figures on social spending
are averages of levels in 1960 and 1979.

same period for eleven advanced countries. With the obvious exception of Japan (which we discuss in detail in Chapter 9), there is a surprisingly close positive relationship among these economies: those with the highest levels of social spending also enjoyed the most rapid productivity growth.

We do not believe for a moment, we rush to add, that these comparisons establish a *causal* relationship between active governments and economic success, since we think that the sources of economic growth are much more complex than such simple causal relationships would imply. We present the data for a much simpler purpose: to counsel skepticism toward persistent scapegoating of the public sector as the source of economic decline in the United States. Neither for the United States nor in international comparisons, at the aggregate level, can the conservatives find any statistical support for their attacks: "big government" does not appear to cause economic stagnation.

What about more specific charges? We turn now to arguments focusing on "overtaxing," "overregulation," and "extravagant" welfare programs. These charges fare no better.

Taxation. Have business taxes stifled private initiative? We can make two kinds of comparisons, one domestic and one international.

The conservative critique of government taxes on business implies that the public sector in the United States has been claiming a rising share of corporate profits, prompting an investment crisis through its increasingly hearty diet of taxes on business income. In fact, this has not happened. Federal taxation on corporate profits did not claim a higher portion of corporate capital income after 1966 than before. On the contrary, the average effective corporate tax rate was actually *lower* from 1967 to 1979 (during the first two phases of decline) than it was from 1948 to 1966.[14]

This lower average effective tax rate reflects a real political process. Since the early 1960s, the federal government has been racing to make life easier for corporations, frequently relaxing tax treatment of depreciation and investment expenditures. As a result, corporate tax revenues have not kept up with other kinds of tax receipts; corporate income tax proceeds fell from 22 percent of all federal receipts in 1966 to only 15 percent in 1979.[15] It is hard to claim that the government has made life tougher for business during the years of deterioration.

International comparisons tell the same kind of story. The conservative assault on government business taxation suggests that corporations invest less in the United States (as a proportion of total GNP) because U.S. business taxes are more burdensome. This is simply not the case. We can compare the intrusiveness of business taxes in the United States with the situation in Japan, Germany, France, the United Kingdom, and Canada, all of which feature a higher share of investment out of GNP than the United States. In the late 1970s—before the 1981 business-tax giveaways under the Reagan administration:

- Business taxes as a percentage of total tax revenues were lower in the United States than in any of the other five countries.
- Marginal tax rates on business income were lower than in any country but Japan.
- The rate of tax subsidy of nonresidential fixed investment was more generous in the United States than in any of the other five.
- Only Canada provided a more generous allowance for depreciation of fixed investments over the first seven years of an asset's lifetime.[16]

A related tax argument is that high levels of personal income taxes have sapped the motivation of employees and entrepreneurs. Available international data suggest that this charge is unfounded. Several countries, including the Netherlands, Germany, and Denmark, have relatively high rates of direct taxation of personal income compared to the United States, while several other countries, including Japan, Italy, France, and Belgium, have relatively low rates of personal taxation.[17] All have experienced much more rapid growth in productivity than the United States, despite these wide variations in taxation of personal income; the variations in tax burden appear to make little difference.*

Regulation. Like the OPEC alibi, the overregulation argument

* We examine the supply-side claim that reduced personal taxes would unleash surges of personal work effort in Chapter 8; that promise has no more basis in fact than the analysis which blames "overtaxation."

trips on the simple matter of timing. The major targets of the overregulation theory, EPA and OSHA, were not inaugurated until 1971. According to Commerce Department economist Edward Denison, their impact on the economy, however one estimates that impact, did not become significant until 1975. But the economy's decline began much earlier—almost ten years before these new regulations became important.

There has undoubtedly been a negative impact on the net revenues of some industries—mining, several manufacturing industries, and electricity generation among them. These effects are designated as "productivity declines," however, only by equating marketed output with the social contribution of the industry. The sharp decline in the measured productivity of the underground bituminous coal mining industry, for example, was associated with a dramatic reduction in the number of mine deaths. The decline in productivity in electricity generation is to some extent explained by the costs of cleaning up the air—which, because it bears no price, is not counted as productivity. Once one begins to incorporate estimates of these benefits into assessments of the impact of government regulation, reasonably cautious estimates suggest that the benefits far outweigh the measurable costs.[18]

Even if one ignores net social benefits for the moment, more-

Fig. 3.3
Government Regulation and Productivity Growth

Changes in the Regulatory Environment, 1973-79 compared to 1948-66	The Extent of Productivity Slowdown, 1973-79 compared to 1948-66[a]	
	Worse than Average	Better than Average
More Regulation	Mining (−9.6%) Utilities (−5.3)	Manufacturing (−1.4)
No Change	Trade (−2.1)	Communications (+0.7) Other Services (−0.9)
Less Regulation	Agriculture (−2.4) Construction (−5.6) Transportation (−2.2)	Finance & Real Estate (−1.4)

[a]The extent of productivity slowdown is the average annual rate of productivity increase over 1973-79 minus the annual rate of productivity increase over 1948-66. For source, see Fig. 2.4.

over, it appears that regulation has had little aggregate effect on either inflation or productivity. The Council on Wage and Price Stability estimated in 1979 that all government regulations, both social and economic, added only about .75 percent per year to consumer prices—only 6 percent of the overall inflation rate in that year. Looking at productivity, similarly, Data Resources Inc. estimates that environmental regulations after 1970 have reduced the annual rate of productivity growth by no more than .1 percent.[19]

A careful industry-by-industry examination of the productivity slowdown confirms our skepticism concerning the antiregulation position. The overregulation complaint suggests that industries experiencing increased regulation would show stagnant productivity growth, while industries recently experiencing deregulation would show more rapid productivity growth. We display in Figure 3.3 the information necessary to make this comparison. The chart arrays industries in a matrix according to an admittedly rough assessment of their recent regulatory experience *and* their recent productivity record. If the conservatives were correct, industries should be concentrated in the top left and bottom right cells; those with *increased* regulation should have *worse*-than-average productivity performance while those with *decreased* regulation should show *better*-than-average productivity growth. But the chart shows no consistent pattern at all. As many industries which have recently experienced deregulation display tepid productivity growth (agriculture, construction, and transportation) as those which have experienced heightened regulation (mining and utilities). Only one of the recently deregulated industries, indeed, managed to achieve a better-than-average productivity-growth performance during the period covered. (The fact that the communications sector was the only industry with an *increased* rate of productivity growth in 1973–79 cannot be attributed to deregulation, since more lenient treatment of the communications sector came into effect only in the late 1970s.)

If deregulation did not lead to relatively more rapid growth in the 1970s, in short, why should we expect that it will boost the economy in the 1980s?

Welfare. The welfare state is blamed for everything from the decline of motherhood to suicide. (We cannot resist observing that the suicide rate is higher in free-market Switzerland than in welfare-state Sweden; it is twice as high in exemplary Japan as in notorious Britain.[20]) Much more seriously, the welfare state is often blamed for a major part of the present economic stagnation.

Figure 3.2, which we have already considered in the discussion of general attacks on big government, should be enough to allay most of this criticism. But the countries in that graph represent a wide variety of approaches to government spending. We can look more closely at the most ambitious welfare states for a check on the more inclusive comparisons of Figure 3.2. Among the major industrialized capitalist nations, the three with the highest average ratios of social-welfare expenditures to gross domestic product in the 1960s and 1970s were the Netherlands (25.3 percent), Belgium (24.4 percent), and Sweden (24.2 percent).[21] Conservatives would surely expect that these economies would have gagged on their own social-welfare spending, exhibiting much poorer economic performance than the United States (which allocated only 13.9 percent of its gross domestic product to social-welfare expenditures in the same period).

Figure 3.4 provides some data which graphically confound the conservative expectations. It shows that these three welfare states

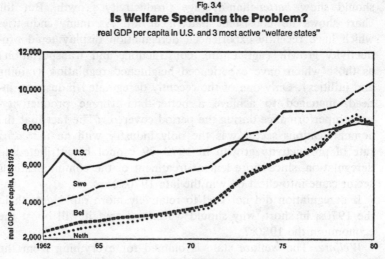

Fig. 3.4
Is Welfare Spending the Problem?
real GDP per capita in U.S. and 3 most active "welfare states"

Source: OECD National Accounts, Vol. 1, pp. 82, 88. GDP is expressed in current prices and exchange rates deflated by the U.S. implicit price deflator for GDP (1975 prices).

considerably outpaced the United States in the growth of per capita output. These economies do not appear to have been snarled in their safety nets, no matter how much protection from economic insecurity those nets provided.

Blaming Workers

Conservatives are less willing to air their charges against labor, since it is poor politics to blame the vast majority of workers for the hardships they themselves are now suffering. But the charge is heard nonetheless. At least implicitly, the blame-workers theory underlies the escalating corporate demands for wage-and-benefit concessions throughout U.S. industry.

Have high and rising workers' wages caused the deterioration of the U.S. economy?

We saw in Figure 2.2 that the growth of production workers' real spendable earnings slowed down in the mid-1960s and actually fell in the 1970s. During the boom, the U.S. economy had no trouble providing workers with rising real wages; during the crisis, real wages have virtually stagnated. If rising real wages cause problems for the economy, the problems should have been greater before than after the mid-1960s.

But many U.S. companies nonetheless appear to argue that workers' wages and bargaining strength have driven them out of competition with other advanced economies, that workers will need to make significant give-back concessions on both wages and benefits if the U.S. economy is going to survive.

Figure 3.5 provides some data which are useful for evaluating this charge. It compares average hourly compensation among ten leading industrialized countries for the period 1975–81. It substantially undercuts the corporate charge about wage disadvantages. Industrial workers' wages in the United States are on average comparable to those elsewhere, lower than some and higher than others.

Nor can one easily support the occasional corporate charge that U.S. workers have gained too many perquisites. We can compare the benefits and rights of U.S. workers in large corporations with those of comparable workers in Germany, France, Japan, Sweden, the Netherlands, and the United Kingdom. U.S. workers are the only group who are not guaranteed advance notification before plant shutdowns, one of only two of the seven country groups with no rights of worker representation in management, the sole national labor force not to enjoy guaranteed sick leaves (not including disability insurance), and the only one to have no rights of continued income upon employer insolvency. By these measures, U.S. workers are the orphans of the advanced capitalist world.[22]

Fig. 3.5
U.S. Wages Too High?
average hourly compensation in manufacturing, $U.S., 1975-1981

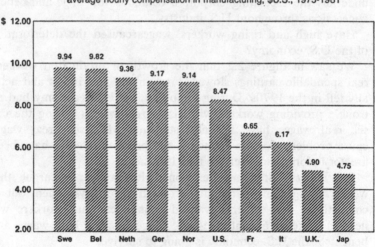

Source: U.S. Bureau of Labor Statistics, "Hourly Compensation Costs..., 33 Countries, 1975-1981," April 1982. National currencies converted to U.S. dollars at current exchange rates and averaged over the six-year period.

Still, what really counts for corporate executives is not just the level of workers' wages and benefits but also the corresponding level of workers' productivity. Even if the growth of U.S. workers' real compensation has slowed down appreciably since the mid-1960s (and U.S. workers are no longer better off than their foreign counterparts), the real cost of labor to business may have risen if productivity growth was even slower. For when workers' hourly compensation grows faster than the corresponding hourly output (both measured in real terms, using the same output price deflator), then the share of labor compensation in overall income rises and the share of profits is squeezed. Could it be that rising real labor costs have thus been cutting into U.S. corporate profitability?

Our first approach to this question involves some comparisons of unit labor costs on an international basis. According to a U.S. Bureau of Labor Statistics study of the period from 1960 to 1980, the rate of growth of unit labor costs in U.S. manufacturing was *lower* than in any of the capitalist countries in Europe, in Canada, or in Japan. Measured in dollars, unit labor costs in Europe, Canada, and Japan rose at roughly twice the rate as in the United States. Given these data, the declining competitiveness of U.S. business can hardly be blamed on relatively rising costs of labor in the United States.[23]

But could corporations' domestic problems stem from rising labor costs? To answer this question, we have calculated the rate of growth of the share of production-worker total compensation (including employer-paid Social Security taxes and other such fringe benefits) in nonfarm private-business income between each of our bench-mark years. From 1948 to 1966, this labor share fell at an average annual rate of .43 percent per year. From 1966 to 1973 it increased at a rate of .77 percent, and from 1973 to 1979 it declined again at a rate of .25 percent.[24] The evidence thus indicates that U.S. corporations benefited from a declining labor share during the boom and then suffered from a rising labor share during the first—but not the second—phase of the crisis.

Does this evidence then lend credence to those who would blame labor for our economic misfortunes since the mid-1960s? Certainly corporate profitability was squeezed by rising labor costs from 1966 to 1973. But how did lower corporate profits in this period cause general economic deterioration? The blame-labor school argues that low profitability reduces business investment and consequently hampers productivity growth. However, as we shall demonstrate in our analysis of the capital-shortage theory, there was no dearth of investment in the U.S. economy until the second phase of the crisis after 1973—when profits were no longer being squeezed by rising labor costs. Certainly there was a slowdown in productivity growth in the first as well as the second phase of the crisis, and each of these slowdowns contributed significantly to the overall deterioration of the economy. But in the first case a rising labor share did not inhibit productivity-enhancing investment, and in the second case the share of labor fell. We can hardly blame a wage squeeze on profits for the deteriorating performance of the U.S. economy.

Blaming Excess Profits

Those who are the least inclined to blame our problems on workers' wages are often most inclined to blame them on excess corporate profits. As profits have risen, according to this favorite populist argument, wages have declined, reducing demand for consumption goods and consequently causing inadequate aggregate demand, low levels of capacity utilization, and sluggish economic growth. Inadequate demand may help explain some of the economic doldrums of the late 1970s and early 1980s, as we shall see in Chapter 5, but it cannot account for either the origins or the early course of the crisis. Nor can the demand problems later on be attributed to rising profits.

Figure 3.6 presents data on the nonfinancial corporate rate of profit for the same bench-mark business-cycle peaks that we have used in earlier comparisons. It is hard to find evidence of soaring profits. The rate of profit reached its peak in 1966 and has remained far below that level ever since.

The rest of the blame-profits argument also fails to find support in the data. Consumer demand, far from lagging, has been the most buoyant component of aggregate demand since the early 1970s.[25] Lower levels of utilization during the 1970s, as we shall show in detail in Chapter 5, did not result from a squeeze on consumption—as this argument would suggest—but from consistent government policies to restrict the growth of the economy. Declining growth and stagnant incomes flow from much more complicated institutional forces, we shall see, than a simple and steady rise in the share of profits in national income; the profit share simply did not increase during the period of economic deterioration.

Blaming Monopoly

Business monopoly is often blamed for accelerating inflation and the general deterioration of the U.S. economy, particularly by those of a populist inclination. There is no question that many important industries in the United States are quite monopolistic—dominated by a few large corporations. But both the logic and the facts of the monopoly argument are flawed.

A familiar textbook model—one which ignores technical change, product innovation, and other such important factors

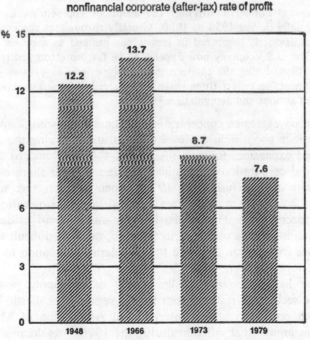

Fig. 3.6
Rising Profits?
nonfinancial corporate (after-tax) rate of profit

Source: Profits include net interest income; profit data from National Income
and Product Accounts, Table 1.13 and fixed capital stock series from
Bureau of Economic Analysis.

affecting prices—can easily demonstrate that monopolies will charge *higher* prices than firms in competitive industries. *Even if* this model faithfully replicated the realities of our economic life, all that one could safely conclude is that inflation—that is, an *increase* in prices—would result from an *increase* in the degree of monopoly.

But there is little evidence of such an increase in the degree of monopoly over the period of accelerating inflation and economic decline since the mid-1960s. A recent study by University of Michigan economist William G. Shepherd, a leading scholar on the structure of U.S. business, suggests that a combination of increased foreign competition, government deregulation, and some intensification in antitrust policy has actually *reduced* the degree of concentration and has *increased* competition in the U.S. economy. His conclusion:

The general finding is striking: the scope of competition increased substantially during 1958 to 1980, virtually throughout the economy. A trend formerly measured in inches has jumped to a much higher level. The U.S. economy now appears to be far more competitive than at any time during the modern industrial period. . . . Most of the shift appears to reflect three main causes: rising import competition, antitrust actions and deregulation.[26]

Data on aggregate concentration are consistent with Shepherd's conclusions about industry-level concentration. During the period of rapid expansion, through the 1960s, the two hundred largest industrial corporations dramatically increased their share of total corporate assets. During the 1970s, when inflation was accelerating, the asset share of the two hundred largest corporations actually decreased.[27] There was, by this measure, no evident increase in monopoly power. Prices soared, but it is difficult to find evidence that we can attribute that accelerating inflation to growing monopoly power.

Some have stressed the significance of monopoly power in specific sectors, as distinct from the aggregate level. Leslie Nulty, research economist at the International Association of Machinists, has argued that inflation during the 1970s was dominated by price increases in the "necessities"—in the sectors producing the goods and services most essential for basic survival, especially including food, energy, housing, and health care.[28]

Nulty is right that these sectors have witnessed unusually high levels of inflation. But these sectors are a mixed bag in terms of trends toward corporate concentration. Most of the centralization of power in the food industry came early, during the first two decades after World War II. Energy corporations clearly applied their concentrated power to push up fuel prices after 1973, but the housing sector has never been unusually concentrated, either during the boom years or since. Rising prices in the health-care sector reflect a combination of demand push since Medicare in the mid-1960s and the shift of health care from practitioners to hospitals.

Equally important, recent trends in industries such as auto and steel demonstrate how ineffective concentrated industrial power can be in the face of concerted international competition. For all of the monopoly behavior of the Big Three in auto and the Big Eight in iron and steel, their fortunes have waned during the late 1960s and the 1970s. They are not good examples of monoliths with growing leverage over their economic destinies. Growing imports from worldwide competitors have demonstrated that even those industries which are highly concentrated *domestically* operate in a highly competitive international environment.

Taken together, these pieces of evidence do not provide support for the view that we can blame our deepening economic problems on growing monopoly power. We don't care for monopoly power any more than Ralph Nader does, as later chapters will make perfectly clear, but we conclude that one should look elsewhere for an adequate explanation of U.S. economic decline.

A CAPITAL SHORTAGE?

Many mainstream observers and trickle-down advocates have recognized the weakness of single-factor theories of stagnation and decline. They have become increasingly attracted instead to the capital-shortage theory, which incorporates the blame-labor, blame-government, and blame-OPEC views into a general analysis of the inadequacy of resources available for capital formation. We must all tighten our belts, according to this widely accepted analysis, so that investment may carry us back to prosperity on a tidal wave of expansion.

This is not just vintage Reagan. We had been getting the capital-shortage message well before the supply-siders took Washington, D.C., by storm. The basic idea began to germinate in the mid-1970s. *Business Week* magazine began to fret about capital shortage in 1974. "Some people will obviously have to do with less . . . ," they argued in a special editorial. "Yet it will be a hard pill for many Americans to swallow—the idea of doing with less so that big business can have more."[29] As the 1970s unfolded, the economic prescriptions became more self-assured. "We can speed up the growth of the economy," Herbert Stein, chair of the President's Council of Economic Advisers under Nixon and Ford, argued in 1979, "but not without a period of less private consumption and less public expenditure."[30]

The conservative political ascendancy in the early 1980s did not change the basic tune but merely amplified it. Liberals have been equally munificent in their concern for the wealthy—not, one must suppose, because they are fond of the plutocratic elite but more simply because they have been equally accepting of the capital-shortage view of stagnant growth. As far as one can ascertain from public policy discussion, C. Jackson Grayson, chair of the American Productivity Center, concludes, there has been an "almost single-minded preoccupation by members of the administration, economists and managers with capital investment as *the* key to our economic recovery."[31]

The capital-shortage theory identifies the slowdown in the rate of productivity growth as the principal source of our economic problems, and explains it in three simple steps:

1. The productivity slowdown has resulted primarily from *insufficient capital investment in buildings and machines.*

2. The rate of investment has been held back by a *shortage of capital funds* reflected in shrinking profits and meager savings.

3. This shortage of capital funds has itself resulted from a *squeeze on capital income*—due to rising income claims by workers, the government, and foreign suppliers, especially OPEC.

This sequence of arguments implies that we cannot solve our current economic problems without *reductions in personal consumption, reductions in government spending, and renewed in-*

centives to both savings and investment. There are no other promising paths to economic recovery. We must do what we must do.

Before we rush to volunteer our own consumption to rescue beleaguered corporate investors, let us examine more closely the content of the capital-shortage theory. *Capital* is a tricky word, liable to assume a variety of meanings in different contexts. In the capital-shortage theory, *capital* takes on two distinct meanings.

First, capital-shortage theorists argue that the U.S. productivity slowdown has resulted from a corresponding slowdown in the rate of capital formation. Here, the word capital denotes *capital goods*—machines, plants and equipment, factories, offices, and stores. The link between capital formation and productivity is captured by the ratio of the stock of capital goods to hours worked, or the *capital intensity* of production. If there are fewer capital goods available per hour of work, then any economist or business executive would expect less output to be produced per hour.

The second critical hypothesis in the capital-shortage theory involves the *sources* of the fall in the rate of capital formation. Now capital takes on a different meaning—representing the resources potentially available for capital formation, or *investable resources*. Capital-shortage theorists argue that the rate of capital formation has fallen because so large a part of the national product is claimed for other uses—such as personal consumption and government expenditure—that there is not enough left for purchase of real capital goods. People are consuming too much; governments are spending too much—these claims on goods and services have been "crowding out" the efforts of businesses to invest in capital formation. The shortage of capital—in this sense of investable resources—becomes manifest through rising costs of both capital equipment and investment funds; with so much demand for and such shrunken supplies of investable resources, starved investors bid up the cost of investable funds. The real cost of borrowing soars.

For the capital-shortage theorists to be right, in short, we must find evidence of *both* (1) a slowdown in the rate of growth of capital intensity, and (2) a decline in the availability of investable resources. If the first does not occur, there is no capital-shortage problem. If the first occurs but the second does not, then the investment slowdown has some other cause than a shortage of investable resources. In that case the problem would be the incentive to invest; we would not need to transfer resources from our pockets to investors' accounts; rather, we would need to do something about the failure of those with surplus savings to channel them toward the kinds of productive investment we need.

The first flaw in the capital-shortage logic is that its timing is wrong. Figure 3.7 presents data on two relevant measures of the

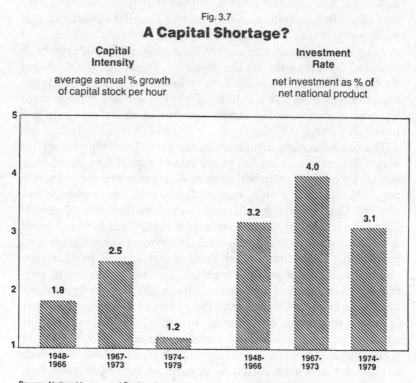

Fig. 3.7

A Capital Shortage?

Capital Intensity	Investment Rate
average annual % growth of capital stock per hour	net investment as % of net national product

Source: National Income and Product Accounts and unpublished data from Bureau of Economic Analysis. Capital stock is for nonfarm-business sector; investment rate measures net fixed nonresidential investment.

rate of capital formation. The left-hand bars trace the growth in capital stock per hour, or *capital intensity,* in the nonfarm-business sector. Despite the fact that productivity growth began to fall from 1966 to 1973, the growth of capital intensity actually increased during the same period; the capital-shortage view, as we have already seen, would have predicted a decline in the growth of capital intensity as a cause of declining productivity growth.

The right-hand bars provide data on the rate of fixed nonresidential investment as a share of GNP. This measures the share of total available resources devoted to productive investment. As with capital intensity, the numbers move in the wrong direction during the first phase of the crisis: the rate of investment was significantly *higher* during this period than it had been during the two decades following the Second World War; according to the capital-shortage view, it should have been lower.

Only by the second phase of the crisis, from 1973 to 1979, did capital intensity begin to slow its growth and the investment rate decline. The fall in investment was therefore not a cause, but more likely an effect, of the deterioration of the economy after 1966.

Second, even after 1973, there is little evidence to support the capital-shortage argument that business investment was squeezed by workers, government, OPEC, or other claims on available investable resources. The years from 1974 to 1979 were characterized by relatively low levels of capacity utilization in manufacturing and in the economy as a whole.[32] In this period of idle workers and idle factories, it would not have strained available resources at all to produce more capital goods. We weren't using the resources at hand; the problem was economic torpor, not a squeeze on available investable resources.

Evidence on the cost of acquiring funds for investment confirms this impression. We have already noted that a capital shortage should *push up* the cost of capital as investors scramble for scarce investable resources. The data suggest exactly the opposite trend.

One indicator is the "cost of capital"—the true cost to business of using the services of the capital stock. An increase in the cost of capital suggests that investable funds are in scarce supply, while a decrease suggests the opposite. According to figures compiled by Stanford economist Peter K. Clark, the cost of capital equipment was considerably *lower* in the 1970s than it had been in the 1950s or the 1960s, suggesting a capital surplus in the later

Fig. 3.8
Cost of Capital
real rate of interest for financing capital equipment

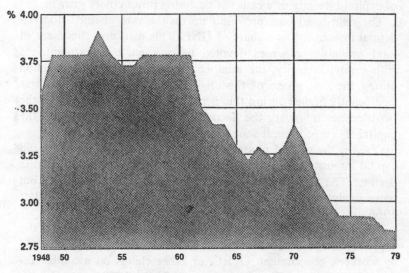

Source: Unpublished data provided by Peter K. Clark

period.[33] Figure 3.8 shows these data for the postwar period, demonstrating the significantly lower levels of the cost of capital after the early 1970s.

Evidence on the cost of borrowing investment funds shows a similar pattern. If there were a shortage of resources available for investment, the real interest rate—the true cost of borrowing funds for investment purposes—would be relatively high. But a study for the National Bureau of Economic Research by Frederic S. Mishkin has found that the real interest rate fell from the 1950s and 1960s to the 1970s; it was positive throughout the period from 1953 to 1973 and actually turned negative from 1973 to 1979 as inflation outpaced nominal interest rates.[34]

This suggests that there was a surplus of potential investable resources, not a shortage.

One supporting piece of evidence comes from what little we know about corporate speculation during this period. There were enough funds available to corporations, for example, to finance roughly $100 billion of stock tender offers between 1975 and

1980.[35] And by 1980, according to the best available estimates, funds in the neighborhood of $1.5 trillion were floating around "Eurodollar" markets in Europe, available at a moment's notice for domestic investment.[36]

Much more important support for this suspicion comes from available data on *potential* investment—on the levels of investment which would have been possible had the economy been operating at closer to full capacity during the 1970s. Had available funds been applied to investment, the economy could readily have produced the necessary capital goods—machinery and structures —without sacrificing production in other areas.

We can see this from data on the economy's potential output during the 1970s. During the period of the investment slowdown after 1973, demands for goods and services by consumers and the government fell far short of the economy's productive capacities. Higher levels of investment demand would not have drawn resources away from the production of consumer goods and government services; instead, they would have put unemployed workers to work and set in motion the wheels of idle plants and machinery.

The Commerce Department estimates that an average of 18 percent of existing durable-goods manufacturing capacity was unused during the period of initial investment slowdown from 1974 to 1979. During the same period, an average of 6.6 million workers were unemployed. Had the economy merely achieved the relatively slack level of 4 percent unemployment over this period, net domestic investment could have risen to substantially more than double its actual levels without diminishing any other claims on output.[37] Investment could have flourished if the economy had not been suffering the doldrums of recurrent stagnation. Investment was not squeezed by rapacious consumers and government bureaucrats; it was starved by an economy operating far below its potential.

There were investable resources available both actually and potentially, in short, but less and less incentive for businesses to devote those funds to new capital formation. The capital-shortage theory neither explains this lagging investment incentive nor finds support for its own empirical claims.

WHAT NEXT?

Although you might not know it from popular discussion of our economic problems, these conclusions about the capital-shortage theory are actually familiar to many mainstream economists. They have been unable to illuminate the productivity slowdown through the capital-shortage lens. One careful study by Yale economist William D. Nordhaus, reviewing "consensus" estimates from a wide variety of other studies, attributes only about 12 percent of the drop in productivity growth to a decline in the rate of capital formation.[38] More recent studies "confirm the conclusions of other researchers," in the words of leading Brookings Institution economists William Brainard and George Perry, "that conventional measures of the business capital stock do not suggest [that] a capital shortage is the cause of the poor performance of productivity."[39]

If there is so little evidence for this explanation, why does it continue to dominate discussions of the sources of economic decline?

Taking a relatively cynical view, one could simply conclude that some economists, most politicians, and almost all of the media have bought the corporate line, falling in behind corporate pleas for better treatment and higher profits. But there is a more charitable interpretation. Given that simple scapegoating explanations have obvious flaws, we can surmise that many have proposed or accepted the capital-shortage theory because no other convincing explanation has been put forward.

We develop a more promising explanation of the U.S. economic crisis in the following four chapters. Our conclusions in this chapter point to some of the requisites of a more useful approach:

- We must develop an analysis that explains the sources of our economic problems from the very *beginning* of the deterioration of the economy in the mid-1960s.
- We must resist the temptation to point the finger at particular actors in the economic arena or to look for a single prime

scapegoat; the roots of the crisis appear too complex to permit such easy modes of explanation.
- We must recognize that economic deterioration has been pervasive, hitting both profits and wages, affecting nearly every sector of the economy; the crisis has been both broad and deep.
- We must develop, in sum, an analysis that is rooted in forces as fundamental and systemic as the process of economic decline itself. Nothing less will do.

4

THE RISE AND DEMISE OF THE POSTWAR CORPORATE SYSTEM

Truman had been able to govern the country with the cooperation of a relatively small number of Wall Street lawyers and
bankers. By the mid-1960s, the sources of power in society had
diversified tremendously, and this was no longer possible.
— Samuel P. Huntington, report
for the Trilateral Commission[1]

Between the fall of Vietnam and the fall of the Shah of Iran, the
U.S. has been buffeted by an unnerving series of shocks that signal an accelerating erosion of power and influence. Although the
shocks themselves have occurred primarily in the military and
foreign policy arenas, they have deep-seated economic and monetary roots.
— "The Decline of U.S. Power,"
Business Week, 1979[2]

During the Great Depression and World War II, many U.S. corporate leaders wondered, as one business-magazine editor wrote
in 1940, "whether the American capitalist system could continue
to function."[3] Their fears proved to be short-lived. By the late
1950s, the Age of Affluence was upon us and the End of Ideology
was at hand. The U.S. government and U.S. corporations now
presided over a world trading system whose scope and fluidity
was without historical precedent. The view from the top was
resplendent. "World opinion? I don't believe in world opinion,"
financier and presidential adviser John J. McCloy announced in
1963. "The only thing that matters is power."[4]

This resurgence of U.S. corporate capitalism did not fall from the sky. It was nurtured through a profound alteration of the earlier capitalist order. The institutional changes which emerged after World War II created a new economic landscape. The U.S. economy was still capitalist, but it was a different kind of capitalism. Its institutional topography had changed.

We call this new institutional structure the *postwar corporate system*. It worked because its major institutions fit together, combining to support the central corporate empire like a set of flying buttresses in a Gothic cathedral. The system had an internal coherence, gradually emerging through the years of upheaval and reconstruction during the 1930s and 1940s. "The structure was not completed until after World War II," economist Robert L. Heilbroner has recently written. "Only then did it become widely recognized that a new form of capitalism had come into being. . . . It was widely hailed as the purified descendant of the 'bad' capitalism that had led us into the Great Depression, which would never be allowed to happen again."[5]

Many analysts have simplified the character of this new system of corporate power, emphasizing one or another single dimension of transformation. Some emphasize the much greater role of the government, calling it the "welfare state" or the "mixed economy." Others have focused on its international dimensions, concentrating on the American Century or its "neo-imperialist" relations. Others have pointed to the rise of industrial unions as its central distinguishing feature.

We argue that the postwar corporate system rested upon not one but three principal buttresses of private power. Each involved a particular set of institutionalized power relations. One involved U.S. capital's dealings with foreign competitors and suppliers. A second featured new and much more structured relationships between corporations and a substantial segment of the work force in the United States. A third managed the continuing domestic conflicts between the business quest for profits and popular demands for the social accountability of business. Each of these three new institutional relations became structures of domination, ensuring for a while the unchallenged preeminence of private corporate power and privilege. Each worked, as well, to moderate the tensions which hierarchical systems always produce. The success of each of these three institutional compromises contributed, in the end, to high rates of corporate profit and a rapid growth of hourly income. The postwar corporate edifice worked as long as each of its institutional buttresses held firm.

These structures of domination did not hold forever, however. Challenges to the power of U.S. corporations soon emerged along each of the three institutional dimensions. These challenges led to a realignment of political and economic power. This realignment reduced the effectiveness of U.S. corporate power, raising the real costs of imported materials and labor for U.S. corporations, reducing their ability to burden the domestic citizenry with the social costs of private capitalist development and slowing the rate of productivity growth. With this realignment, U.S. corporations suffered a sharp reverse on the front that most concerns them: their profitability fell.

Capitalism had not collapsed, to be sure; large corporations still held enormous power. But the particular structure of domination which had permitted rapid growth for twenty years had begun to erode. It no longer worked smoothly or effectively. Although worker, Third World, and popular resistance to business offensives now seem muted, they played a crucial role in the early erosion of the postwar corporate system. The resulting institutional disintegration produced economic decline.

We develop this model of economic decline in three stages in this chapter. We begin by tracing the construction of the three principal institutional buttresses of the postwar corporate system, emphasizing the relations of domination threaded through each. We then examine the erosion of each of these three postwar structures, focusing on the internal sources of their eventual demise. We close with an analysis of the rise and decline of U.S. corporate profitability. Although the profit rate does not measure economic well-being in general, we focus on it because it provides a good measure of the vitality of the postwar corporate system. We show the links between the three dimensions of institutional erosion and the increasingly anemic condition of corporate balance sheets. We save for the following chapter a discussion of how this institutional disintegration led to our economic crisis, shedding light on the twists and turns of U.S. macropolicy and on the new and puzzling phenomenon of "stagflation."

THE LOGIC OF THE POSTWAR CORPORATE SYSTEM

Each of the three principal institutional structures of the postwar corporate system involved complex constellations of power relationships. These structured relations can easily sound abstract, devoid of the tugs and pulls of individual historical actions. But the rise and demise of the postwar corporate system were the product (often unintended) of the projects and struggles of real people trying to cope with changing circumstances. To suggest some of the human drama underlying our institutional account, we begin the first three sections on postwar structures with a set of illustrative vignettes contrasting the early period of institutional ascendancy with the subsequent period of decline.

Postwar Structure I: Pax Americana

In the beginning:
Economists, bankers, and diplomats converged on Bretton Woods, New Hampshire, in 1944 to shape a new international monetary order. John Maynard Keynes, the great British economist, envisioned an international bank which would act as "a genuine organ of international government."[6] The U.S. representatives, however, insisted on effective control over the International Monetary Fund and the World Bank which emerged from the conference—installing the dollar as the key currency in the new international monetary system. "Keynes himself agreed to these changes only with the greatest reluctance," political scientist Alan Wolfe has written about the final moments of the conference, "knowing that Americans had the power in these matters and that the choice was between a fund on American terms or no fund at all."[7]

Congress still needed to approve the agreements, and the isolationists wanted no part of it. It was easier to win acceptance than expected, however, because the U.S. representatives had so thoroughly dominated the formation of the Bretton Woods Agreement itself. "The

Congress would be given assurances," historian Richard Gardner concluded, "that the fund would operate in accordance with the national
interests of the United States."[8] After approval, symbolically, the U.S.
government insisted successfully that the new institutions' head-
quarters be located in Washington, D.C. This sealed the fate of the
new monetary system. "This decision," added Gardner, "was an important victory for the idea of close national control of the Bretton
Woods institutions."

And then:

On August 15, 1971, President Richard Nixon appeared before a
startled television audience to announce his "New Economic Policy."
Among other bombshells, the U.S. government was to devalue the dollar and end the fixed-rate convertibility of dollars to gold at thirty-five
dollars an ounce. The Bretton Woods system had been dying for
years. The President's unilateral pronouncement put the final nail in
its coffin.

In the beginning:

In August 1953, the U.S. Central Intelligence Agency overthrew
Iranian Prime Minister Mohammed Mossadegh after diplomatic
efforts had failed to secure reversal of his nationalization of the
Anglo-Iranian Oil Company.

Kermit Roosevelt, the CIA operative who engineered the coup, has
provided a detailed description of the operation, which was called
"AJAX":[9]

> What AJAX was intended to be was a co-operative venture. It al-
> lied the Shah of Iran, Winston Churchill, Anthony Eden, and
> other British representatives with President Eisenhower, John Fos-
> ter Dulles, and the U.S. Central Intelligence Agency. The alli-
> ance was to be formed for the purpose of replacing an Iranian
> Prime Minister, Dr. Mohammed Mossadegh.

The Shah, according to Roosevelt's report, was extremely grateful.
He later told Roosevelt, " 'I owe my throne to God, my people, my
army, and to you.' By 'you' he meant me and the two countries, Great
Britain and the U.S., I was representing. We were all heroes."

Ten thousand miles away, in June 1954, the U.S. government
planned and executed a successful coup against Guatemala's democratically elected president, Jacobo Arbenz. (Kermit Roosevelt had
been asked to arrange this coup as well, but he had declined.) It acted
at the request of the United Fruit Company. Arbenz had offended
sensibilities by expropriating a portion of United Fruit's land—after
the company had turned down his offer to pay the company what it

had claimed the land was worth for tax-assessment purposes. (United Fruit later insisted it was worth twenty-five times as much.)

The coup was carried out under the cover of U.S. pilots flying P-47s and other aircraft. The day before Operation Success was scheduled to begin, the U.S. ambassador in Guatemala City, a West Point dropout named John Peurifoy, told his colleagues, "Well, boys, tomorrow at this time we'll have ourselves a party."[10]

As the coup gained ground, President Arbenz made a final report over a radio heavily jammed by the CIA:

> Our crime is having enacted an agrarian reform which affected the interests of the United Fruit Company. . . . Our crime is our patriotic wish to advance, to progress, to win economic independence to match our political independence. We are condemned because we have given our peasant population land and rights.

And then:

Kermit Roosevelt published his true-life-spy's account of AJAX in 1979, just in time to ride the public fascination with Iran following the successful revolution against the Shah and the eventual incarceration of the U.S. hostages. Iran had already prospered from the OPEC oil-price hikes six years before, which produced a more massive resource transfer to Iran than Dr. Mossadegh could ever have imagined.

Rebellion crested in Central America during the same years. Sandinistas seized state power in Nicaragua. Rebels mounted a serious insurrection in El Salvador. And the autocratic regime in Arbenz's Guatemala rested on shifting sands, fearing a spreading guerrilla war.

Neither an AJAX nor an Operation Success was able to come to the rescue. By the early 1980s, such rescue operations were visions of Christmas past. The New York *Times* concluded in June 1982 that "the prospects of spreading revolutions and war in Central America and the Persian Gulf have not receded . . . Few in or outside the Reagan Administration maintain that the United States has the power to actually control these events."

The United States emerged from World War II as the world's dominant economic and military power. No European ally, much less the defeated Germans and Japanese, could challenge the preeminence of the United States. U.S. economic dominance was formalized by the Bretton Woods agreement, which established the new rules of the game for the capitalist world economy. The dollar was king, Wall Street replaced the City of London as the world's financial center, and the International Monetary Fund and the World Bank set up shop within a stone's throw of the White House.

In subsequent years, the United States assured a stable climate within which capitalist trade, investment, and output could grow rapidly throughout much of the world. Insistent U.S. leadership helped to lower tariffs and other barriers to trade. Marshall Plan aid to devastated European economies facilitated their economic recovery. U.S. direct private investment abroad contributed as well to the reconstruction and development of capitalist enterprise in many parts of the world.

Altruism and self-interest worked hand in hand. The dollars pumped into the world system by U.S. investment and foreign aid quickly returned through growing demand for U.S. exports. Booming foreign markets and stable world market conditions raised both corporate profits and private business expectations; this stimulated high rates of U.S. capital investment at home as well as abroad. Domestically, U.S. corporate leverage in international markets helped promote high rates of growth and capacity utilization in key industries such as steel and auto. Internationally, the real value of U.S. direct long-term investments abroad grew at a blistering 8.8 percent average annual rate from 1948 to 1966, well over twice the rate of growth of U.S. gross domestic product.[11] The main features of this world economic dominion reinforced each other.

Two additional benefits flowed to U.S. corporations:
- U.S. capital gained access to foreign raw material and energy supplies on increasingly favorable terms. The real cost of imported raw materials—that is, their price relative to the prices received by U.S. producers of finished goods—fell until the mid-1960s.[12] Cheap energy helped to promote the spread of automobiles and suburban housing throughout the postwar boom.
- U.S. sellers sold in a seller's market and U.S. buyers bought in a buyer's market. Between 1951 and 1966, the U.S. terms of trade—the average price of exports relative to the average price of imports—improved by 24 percent.[13]

None of these advantages emerged through private initiatives alone. The U.S. decisively abandoned isolationism to adopt an in-

creasingly interventionist international stance. As with other empires, private gains—from international trade, the mobility of
U.S. capital, and the central world financial role of Wall Street—
were based on a confluence of economic and military power. U.S.
ascendancy rested on two pillars. U.S. technology—the impres-
sive machinery with which U.S. workers turned out products
"made in America"—and the huge productivity advantages of
U.S. workers combined to form the first. Aggressive political support of foreign investment and imposing military power joined to
provide the second.

One of the most important government supports of foreign investment resulted from tax-code revisions. U.S. corporations were
allowed to credit, rather than deduct, foreign tax payments
against their domestic income tax obligations. They were also
permitted to postpone tax payment until actual repatriation of
profits earned overseas. All the while, they could juggle their internal accounts to take advantage of international differences in
business-tax rates; this practice has been dubbed *transfer pricing*.
By 1972, as a result of these numerous tax advantages on overseas investment, U.S. corporations paid only $1.2 billion in taxes
on foreign earnings of $24 billion—an effective tax rate of just 5
percent.[14]

Military expansion was at least as important. The U.S. military
had demobilized after World War I, but no such dismantling followed World War II. Ten years after the Treaty of Versailles in
1919, the combined Navy and War Departments' budgets constituted three quarters of 1 percent of U.S. GNP, an amount equal
to only 8 percent of gross private fixed nonresidential investment.
In 1955, military expenditures represented 10 percent of U.S.
GNP, an amount actually greater than gross private fixed nonresidential investment.[15] Military expenditures have continued to
constitute a significant fraction of GNP ever since.

Drawing from a varied tool kit, the U.S. government built the
military, economic, and political machinery to police much of the
world. Employing dollar diplomacy, CIA intervention, and occasional Marine landings, the United States blocked most challenges
to the new order by populist, nationalist, and socialist movements. Dr. Mossadegh and President Arbenz suffered because
they had dared not to play by the rules. President Kennedy

affirmed these rules of the private-public partnership at the beginning of his administration, addressing a group of executives: "Our [national] success is dependent upon your profits and success. Far from being natural enemies, government and business are necessary allies. . . . We are anxious to do everything we can to make your way easier."[16]

Postwar Structure II: The Limited Capital-Labor Accord

In the beginning:
Immediately after World War II, corporations were wringing their hands over what one government agency called "the most concentrated period of labor-management strife in the country's history."[17] They desperately sought some kind of accord with the new and militant industrial unions.

The mine workers' union provides one clear example of the success of this effort. In 1956, United Mine Workers president John L. Lewis, once the very symbol of hell-raising union militance, congratulated the union's national convention:

> It augurs well for the future. For six years now there have been no major stoppages in the industry and for an indefinite period into the future that will continue, providing the leaders in industry on both sides continue to exercise that discretion in judgment which they have now exhibited that they possess.[18]

As respected Princeton labor economist Richard Lester observed about the mine workers, "The union has been bearing down on any unauthorized strikes with fines and threats of expulsion of individual members. In contrast, during the 13 years ending with 1950, national stoppages took place on the average every 18 months."[19]

And then:
By the late 1960s, rank-and-file miners were agitating against autocratic union rules and unsafe mining. Unauthorized strikes began to proliferate. The corporate-union accord could not contain worker rebellion. In 1969, a black lung wildcat spread to 45,000 miners in Ohio, Pennsylvania, and West Virginia. In 1975, 62,000 miners struck to protest safety violations and delays in the administration of the grievance procedure. The protests continued. Roderick Hill, president of the Peabody Coal Company, complained in the mid-1970s about

the "labor disruptions, wildcats, absenteeism and declining productivity in the coal industry."[20] According to three Harvard economists who studied the precipitous decline in net tons of coal mined per worker-day from 1969 to 1977, "deterioration in industrial relations in the coal industry is a major cause of the observed downward trend in productivity."[21]

In the beginning:

Blacks' hopes were raised during World War II. But reality began almost immediately to provide a bitter antidote.

The fate of the tobacco workers' union was typical of black experience in the South.[22] The Tobacco Workers Organizing Committee (TWOC) had concentrated on organizing black workers during World War II. Forging an alliance among black and white workers, the TWOC was able to win certification in R. J. Reynolds' Winston-Salem plants in December 1943. As one organizer recalls, "The people realized something they had never thought of before: we hold the strength in our hands to stop this company. They had allowed that company to ride over them roughshod all those years."

But times changed after the war. A historian recounts the union's experience:

> Reynolds bitterly fought every attempt by its workers to build democratic organizations in the factories and in the community. Traditional South racial animosities in the community were heightened to turn white workers against the predominantly black union; automation was used to lay off union members. Finally a prolonged "red-baiting" campaign attempted to divide the union leadership from the workers. In the midst of these attacks, intensified by the national cold-war atmosphere, the union narrowly lost an NLRB certification vote in 1950.[23]

North of the Mason-Dixon line, the limits were imposed more subtly. Most blacks were confined to low-wage jobs with little hope of advancement. The ghettos began to feel like dead-end alleys, confining and claustrophobic. Claude Brown recalled the spreading sense of despair in his best-selling book, *Manchild in the Promised Land:*

> There was a tremendous difference in the way life was lived up North. There were too many people full of hate and bitterness crowded into a dirty, stinky, uncared-for closet-size section of a great city. . . .
> The children of these disillusioned colored pioneers inherited the total lot of their parents—the disappointments, the anger. To

add to their misery, they had little hope of deliverance. For where
does one run to when he's already in the promised land?[24]

And then:

The civil rights movement ignited the South in 1960–63. Spurred by
its successes, blacks in northern ghettos erupted against their own,
more "invisible," kind of confinement.

The explosion in the Watts section of Los Angeles in August 1965
was typical—if also surprising because Watts did not "look" like
Harlem or the South Side of Chicago. Federal troops were necessary
to quell the uprising. There was an estimated $40 million in property
damage.[25]

The disorder had begun in protest over police treatment of two
young brothers. One, Marquette Frye, was clear about the sources both
of his own resistance and of the anger which immediately exploded.
He reported in late 1965:

> . . . I never felt I had security; I didn't feel I should get married
> until I got a better job. . . . I would answer an ad, fill out an ap-
> plication, then never hear from the people when they saw I was
> colored. I looked for work, but I just didn't get the jobs.
>
> In this neighborhood, there is nothing for a young man to do.
> So you just stand around. And when you stand around, the next
> thing you know there come the police to roust you. . . . When
> you're pushed, for no reason, you're going to push back. . . .
>
> Never again, never again in this neighborhood will any young
> men, like my brother and me, stand by and take abuse.[26]

With spreading disorder in urban ghettos, business profits from
a submissive and isolated minority work force became more and
more vulnerable. And the fiscal costs of pacifying this mounting
rebelliousness—through the War on Poverty and other Great Society Programs—began to soar.

International domination alone could not guarantee prosperity.
The limited truce between corporations and labor was a second
essential element of the postwar corporate system.

The capital-labor accord was not as formal as the Bretton
Woods Agreement. It did not include all sectors of the U.S. labor
force. But it did guide production in the postwar period, building
upon a tacit agreement between corporate capitalists and the organized labor movement.

The accord required a purge of militant unionists from leadership positions in the late 1940s, and the passage of legislation, especially the Taft-Hartley Act of 1947, which limited union actions. Weakened by both McCarthyism and restrictive legislation, unions moved toward a clear *quid pro quo* with large corporations. Corporations would retain absolute control over the essential decisions governing enterprise operations—decisions involving production, technology, plant location, investment, and marketing. This set of corporate prerogatives was codified in the "management rights" clauses of most collective bargaining agreements. In return, unions were accepted as legitimate representatives of workers' interests. They were expected to bargain on behalf of labor's immediate economic interests, but not to challenge employer control of enterprises (much less the legitimacy of the capitalist system itself). Unions would help maintain an orderly and disciplined labor force while corporations would reward workers with a share of the income gains made possible by rising productivity, with greater employment security, and with improved working conditions.

There *were* productivity gains, and they were shared. The real value of the spendable hourly earnings of production workers rose at an annual average of 2.1 percent from 1948 to 1966—fast enough to double once every generation if the pace had continued. Job security also improved; the aggregate unemployment rate dropped to 3.8 percent by 1966, roughly one quarter of its average levels during the 1930s. Working conditions also improved; the industrial accident rate declined by nearly one third from 1948 through the early 1960s.[27]

If these realized promises were the carrot inducing labor accommodation, the continuing threat of cyclical unemployment was the stick sustaining capital's take-it-or-leave-it offer. Four cyclical downturns between the late 1940s and the early 1960s periodically boosted unemployment rates and reminded workers that they should be grateful to have a job.

Carrots and sticks combined to effect a steady movement toward labor cooperation. Negotiated union contracts, as in both steel and auto, were increasingly likely to include clauses restricting or prohibiting strikes. Strike activity itself dropped sharply: the proportion of work time idled because of strikes fell from an average of .54 percent in the first postwar business cycle (1946–48) to .22 percent in the next four cycles (1949–66).[28]

Corporations had agreed to cooperate with the unions they had battled only fifteen years before, and they reaped the dividends of restored control over production. As *Fortune* magazine noted about the first "productivity bargaining" agreements between General Motors and the United Automobile Workers Union in 1948 and 1950, "GM may have paid a billion for peace [but] it got a bargain. General Motors has regained control over . . . the crucial management functions."[29]

In order to take full advantage of this restored control, corporations dramatically expanded their supervisory apparatus. They developed systems of closely monitored bureaucratic control, applying sophisticated new methods for keeping track of employees' output, screening for favorable personality characteristics, and inducing worker effort through differentiated incentives, promotional rewards, and wage supplements. All of this took personnel —the managers and supervisors who watched over this system of bureaucratic control. One of the most rapidly expanding occupations between 1950 and 1970 was a relatively new category called labor-relations personnel. Overall, the resources devoted to managerial and supervisory personnel climbed significantly. Between 1948 and 1966, for example, the ratio of supervisory to nonsupervisory employees in the private business sector increased by nearly 75 percent—from roughly thirteen supervisory employees per one hundred nonsupervisory employees to more than twenty-two. By the late 1960s, nearly twenty cents of every dollar of revenue paid to the private business sector covered the salaries of managerial and supervisory personnel.[30] Some of these employees were designated as supervisory workers simply in order to exclude them from collective bargaining units and narrow unions' base of operations. But most had real managerial and supervisory functions. Both tendencies resulted in an expanding bureaucracy beyond production workers' control. The internal costs of the postwar corporate system rose steadily.

While the accord benefited some workers, it excluded others.

Unorganized workers, women, and minorities could not easily gain access to the bountiful garden of productivity dividends. The wages of workers in the "core" sector of industry outstripped those of workers on its periphery. Income inequality among wage and salary earners increased through the 1960s.[31] This growing segmentation of labor helped divide labor and strengthen corporate bargaining leverage. The limited capital-labor accord worked as long as these divisions remained firm. When the excluded began to knock at the garden gate, the terms of the accord would be jeopardized.

Postwar Structure III: The Capitalist-Citizen Accord

In the beginning:
    Operating under the banner of the "peaceful atom," a tight circle of cold warriors, government scientists, and giant corporations—chiefly including General Electric and Westinghouse—established the nuclear power industry in the mid-1950s.[32] Through institutions such as the Atomic Energy Commission and the Joint Committee on Atomic Energy of the U.S. Congress, they exercised virtually unchallenged sway over its directions for two decades. "The 1946 Atomic energy legislation established," according to a retrospective account by Harvard Business School professor Irwin Bupp, "a perfectly insulated, self-perpetuating organization with plenary powers. . . . The Joint Committee's role . . . is a textbook illustration of how to guarantee the triumph of special interest over public interest."
    Exhibiting the optimism which came to characterize the nuclear establishment in the 1950s, Atomic Energy Commission head Lewis Strauss exulted, "It is not too much to expect that our children will enjoy in their homes electrical energy too cheap to meter." By 1962, the AEC was predicting on-line user charges in 1980 which were only 40 percent of the best prevailing rates in the early 1960s. When nuclear power plant construction costs seemed to be falling below early expectations in the mid-1960s, the battle for nuclear power seemed to have been won. An AEC report concluded, "Nineteen sixty-six will be remembered as the year in which the atom became economically competitive." *Fortune* magazine added, "The unmistakable message . . . [was that] coal and atomic energy competed head on . . . and

atomic energy won decisively." Reactor sales skyrocketed to an average of 25 per year over the 1969 to 1974 period.

In the end:

There had always been opposition to the development of nuclear power. The auto workers' union had early sought an injunction against the Fermi I reactor in Detroit, for example, and intensified its struggle after the partial meltdown at Fermi in 1966.[33]

But the political, legal, and regulatory environment first began to shift substantially in the late 1960s and early 1970s. The Freedom of Information Act helped to erode the monopoly on nuclear information, as did a series of defections of AEC and nuclear-industry scientists and engineers. The Water Quality Improvement Act of 1970 and the National Environmental Policy Act posed additional legal challenges to the nuclear industry. Growing opposition to nuclear power led to the abolition of the AEC in 1974 and of the Joint Committee on Atomic Energy in 1977.

Massive political mobilizations at New Hampshire's Seabrook plant and elsewhere began to force the redesign of safety features of the plant. Energy economist and nuclear power specialist Stephen Cohn concludes:

> . . . the most important effect of the anti-nuclear movement in the regulatory area was its success in forcing the nuclear industry to bear more of the costs of its negative externalities. The bulk of the increase in nuclear plant capital costs . . . (1971–1979) and more than one cent kilowatt hour increase in generating costs can be attributed to this internalization.

The costs of making nuclear power even a little safer mounted as knowledge of the safety hazards accumulated. Costs per kilowatt-hour in nuclear plants coming on line in 1980 were two and one half times higher than the AEC's 1962 prediction even after subtracting the effects of general inflation. Rising costs made nuclear generation look like an increasingly poor investment. Wall Street finally turned off the tap. Consumers and voters also balked at paying for the increased costs years before the plants were due for completion. Cancellations of nuclear-reactor orders have outnumbered new orders in every year since 1975. The "energy of the future" was beginning to look like a fuel of the past.

The Depression generated more than labor struggles. Millions also battled for tenant's rights and public housing, for social security and public assistance, for protection against the vagaries of life in capitalist economies.

These demands were hardly new, but the state had not heeded them in earlier periods of crisis and instability. The "free-enterprise" system had forced people and businesses to fend for themselves. The government had kept its hands off, refusing to cushion the jolts of the roller-coaster ride.

But now these demands were at least partly accommodated. The state began trying to smooth the rough edges of the market economy without compromising the reign of profits as a guide to social priorities. The Social Security Act of 1935 and the Employment Act of 1946 represented two important milestones along the way.

Three aspects of the expanded state role were crucial.

First, the government sought to reduce macroeconomic instability, hoping to avoid the kind of economic downturn which had threatened the survival of all the leading capitalist economies in the 1930s. The government did not move in practice to eliminate the capitalist business cycle altogether, much less to provide for continuous full employment, since periodic contractions help to limit the power of labor and to purge the economy of weak and inefficient firms. (The former concern motivated the ferocious business opposition to the original ambitious, truly full-employment versions of the Employment Act of 1946.) Macro-policy eventually sought much more modestly to moderate and guide the cycle, not to eliminate it, in the interests of political stability and profitability.

From the late 1940s to the mid-1960s, this effort succeeded. This was due partly to deliberate government stabilization policy and partly to the "automatic stabilizers" built into the postwar U.S. economy. (These latter include the progressive income tax and unemployment insurance, which tend automatically to reduce aggregate demand when the economy heats up and to stimulate demand when it cools.) The huge military buildup in the early 1950s also provided a fortuitous boost to aggregate demand after the initial postwar expansion ran out of steam in 1949, and high levels of military spending subsequently provided a solid base of demand stimulus that would help to prevent any recession from developing into a major downturn. The results were felicitous: the first five postwar business-cycle recessions were more than two thirds less severe—measured by the magnitude of their average-output slowdown—than business cycles during the comparable period of expansion after the turn of the century.[34]

Second, direct public expenditures supporting business increased substantially at all levels of government—federal, state, and local. Government contracts provided guaranteed markets for many major corporations, especially in military production, while government subsidies favored many private businesses, particularly in nuclear power and agriculture. Even more important, government expenditures on transportation, communications, and other infrastructural facilities, as well as on education and research, lowered the costs of business for almost all private firms. Some of the resulting economic benefits were passed on to consumers through lower prices, but firms also profited from this public largess.

Finally, the state committed itself to at least a margin of economic security for all Americans, whether aged, unemployed, or simply poor. As with the case of the "full-employment" objective, the social-insurance objective was tempered in practice by the need to preserve the effective disciplinary force of competition in low-wage labor markets. Yet over most of the postwar period, up to 1966, unemployment insurance coverage grew, the size of the weekly unemployment check relative to workers' take-home pay increased slightly, and the sum of social-insurance programs, education, health, and general assistance inched upward as a fraction of gross national product. These programs provided real benefits to many people but were nonetheless contained within the larger framework of capitalist priorities. For example, the distress of unemployment was reduced only by limited cash transfers to those who lost their jobs, not by structural changes guaranteeing everyone a job on a continuous basis. The plight of the elderly was addressed not by programs integrating them into useful social roles, but only by cash transfers to enable them to survive in the market economy.

This part of the capitalist-citizen accord, in short, involved a delicate dynamic. The new state role was constrained not to compromise the basic profitability of corporations while creating a new and significant relationship between the state and its citizens. "The emergence of the welfare state was a momentous development in American history," as social-welfare analysts Frances Fox Piven and Richard A. Cloward conclude. "It meant that people could turn to government to shield them from the insecurities and hardships of an unrestrained market economy."[35] The balancing act worked through the early 1960s, and the stability and legitimacy of the capitalist regime was bolstered as a result.

THE EROSION OF THE POSTWAR CORPORATE SYSTEM

These institutional foundations of corporate power and privilege promoted prosperity for twenty years. They worked because they secured the dominance of a private profit-making, capital-accumulating logic over the economy as a whole. They worked, but they were also vulnerable. Conflicts eventually emerged from *within* each of these three relations of power and privilege, challenges rooted in the spreading refusal by foreigners, U.S. workers, and U.S. citizens to accept the subordination required by the structure of the postwar corporate system.

Erosion I: The Decline of U.S. International Domination

U.S. corporations faced growing challenges in both the First and the Third worlds. These challenges substantially weakened the international position of U.S. capital. By the mid-1960s, the structure of Pax Americana was tottering.

One of the guiding principles of the postwar system had been the economic reconstruction and revival of war-torn Europe and Japan. U.S. aid for this purpose seemed necessary both to reverse the spread of anticapitalist movements abroad and to stimulate demand for U.S. exports. The phenomenal economic success of postwar Japan and most of Europe clearly helped pull the rug out from under left-wing labor movements in these countries, but

Japanese and European economic growth also created a major competitive challenge to the United States in the world market and eventually led to a massive penetration of U.S. domestic markets.

In 1955, U.S. merchandise exports accounted for 32 percent of the merchandise exports of the major capitalist economies. By 1971, the U.S. share had fallen to 18 percent. Imports had remained a low and constant or declining share of gross domestic product over most of the postwar era. Around the mid-1960s, import penetration suddenly escalated. Between 1960 and 1970, imports rose from 4 percent to 17 percent of the U.S. market in autos, from 4 to 31 percent in consumer electronics, from 5 to 36 percent in calculating and adding machines, and from less than 1 percent to 5 percent in electrical components.[36]

A measure of the importance of imports in the whole of domestic production is presented in Figure 4.1. Aggregate import pene-

Fig. 4.1
Import Competition
imports as % of U.S. gross domestic product

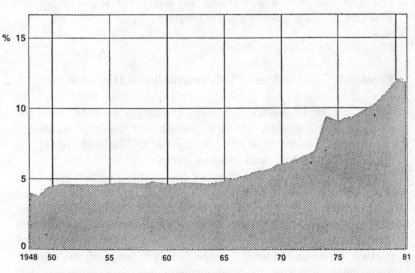

Source: Economic Report of the President, 1982, B-1, B-8.

tration began to increase precisely in 1965, and it accelerated in the 1970s.

It seems likely that the decline in U.S. competitive strength was attributable, at least in part, to the size and relative importance of the U.S. military machine. The military role of the United States was indispensable in helping to police the postwar international system, but it also constituted an enormous drain on the productive capacity of the United States. Figure 4.2 illustrates the com-

Fig. 4.2

World Trade Shares and Military Spending

international comparison of percentage gain (+) or loss (−) in world trade shares with military spending as % of GDP, 1960-1960

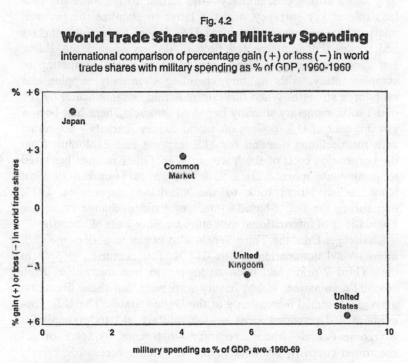

Source: OECD, National Accounts; Stockholm International Peace Research Institute, Yearbook, 1975, 1981.The "world trade share" is a country's total exports of goods and services expressed as a percent of total exports of the member nations of the OECD. Changes in this trade share are calculated for 1961-71.

petitive drag induced by military spending. Among the four major economic units of the advanced capitalist world system during the 1960s—the United States, Great Britain, the Common Market countries, and Japan—there was an almost perfectly negative correlation between the growth of export shares and the rate of military spending during the decade of the 1960s. Because the United States and the United Kingdom were devoting substantially higher proportions of aggregate domestic product to military spending, they had significantly less available to devote to productive capital formation.

Could this drain have been avoided? In retrospect we can see that the Bretton Woods system required *both* a strong U.S. economy *and* a strong U.S. military—the former to reinforce the dollar's role as key currency, and the latter to stabilize the political relationships necessary to enforce U.S. access to foreign markets and secure the uninterrupted flow of dollars around the globe. But these requirements turned out to be as much competing as complementary, with military spending eventually sapping the economy's strength. When this contradiction became acute, by the mid-1960s, monetary stability began to unravel. There had been a growing glut of U.S. dollars on world money markets—beginning with the declining demand for U.S. exports and exploding from the burgeoning costs of the Vietnam War. Other nations hesitated to accumulate more dollars. Gold began to pour out of Fort Knox. When Nixon took to the television cameras in 1971, renouncing the dollar-based system of fixed exchange rates, the foundations of international monetary stability were shattered.

Challenges from the Third World also began to undermine U.S. international domination in the 1960s. For centuries, people in the "Third World" had been struggling to free themselves from colonial domination. It was hardly surprising that these liberation movements aimed increasingly at the United States. The U.S. government had provided most of the military aid to procapitalist governments and—where necessary—intervened by force or orchestrated coups to promote favorable foreign access for private capital. U.S.-based multinational corporations had led the penetration of Third World societies, scooping up resources and overturning traditional societies. More and more, the U.S. government and U.S.-based multinationals drew the sights of liberation rifles —whether fired for purely nationalist or explicitly socialist purposes.

The U.S. government initially had little difficulty suppressing such challenges; the ousters of Mossadegh and Arbenz came easily. But the failure of the Kennedy administration to overthrow Castro in the 1961 Bay of Pigs invasion, and especially the long and humiliating failure to stem the revolutionary tide in South Vietnam, marked a significant and escalating erosion of the U.S. government's capacity to "keep the world safe" for private enterprise. The United States could no longer throw its weight around so effectively.

A final significant challenge in the world economy came from exporters of raw materials, primarily in Third World nations. This development did not involve a direct political challenge to the reign of private corporate power. It reflected a narrower economic demand for greater national control over natural resources and for a larger share of the global economic pie.

By the late 1960s, the time for such demands was ripe: rivalry among the advanced countries had increased, U.S. military capacities were strained while countervailing Soviet power had grown, and pressure on worldwide resource supplies had begun to increase. The economic bargaining power of some of the Third

Fig. 4.3

The U.S. Terms of Trade

ratio of export price deflator to import price deflator

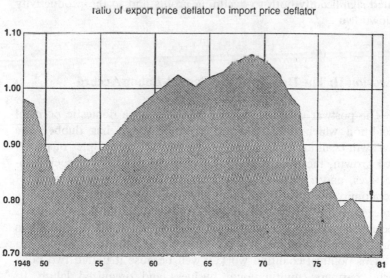

Source: Economic Report of the President, 1982, B-3

World raw-material-exporting nations increased substantially. The OPEC cartel was the most visible and important example. In conjunction with multinational petroleum companies, it succeeded in shifting the terms of the oil trade sharply against the oil-importing nations, first in 1973 and then again in 1979.

All three of these international challenges—from the advanced economies, from Third World rebellions, from raw-materials exporters—combined to diminish U.S. international power. One of the best indicators of this effect is the U.S. terms of trade, or the ratio of prices of U.S. exports to prices of U.S. imports. The higher the terms of trade, the greater the quantity of goods and services that can be purchased abroad by a unit of real output produced in the U.S. economy. Figure 4.3 presents the basic movements of the U.S. terms of trade. After an initial decline to 1951, the U.S. terms of trade improved steadily until the late 1960s—a clear summary indicator of the fruits of Pax Americana. The terms of trade reached their peak in 1969. They then turned sharply downward in the 1970s, notably before the impact of the OPEC price hike in 1973. This decline in the terms of trade was felt acutely in the domestic economy, as we shall see when we turn to our more quantitative analysis, and it contributed significantly both to declining profits and to the productivity slowdown.

Erosion II: The Demise of the Capital-Labor Accord

The postwar corporate system rested upon a domestic political coalition which political scientist Alan Wolfe has dubbed the "growth coalition."[37] It was united around the principles of profit-led growth, the priority of profitability in establishing social objectives, and a mutual nonaggression pact in the distribution of economic bounty. (This last principle essentially involved a freeze of the distributive shares with which coalition members began, continuing the distribution of the dividends of growth in those relative proportions.)

This political coalition worked well because it united two powerful partners: multinational business and organized labor. Its politics turned out to be complex, however, because it included neither *all* capital nor *all* labor. The coalition was broad enough to be electable and narrow enough to allow significant spoils to its constituent members—often at the expense of excluded elements in the United States. But its limited scope continually risked the rebellion of the excluded.

Through the 1960s, the exclusion of small capital was both obvious and effective. Small business had been lukewarm, at best, to the initial terms of the accord—particularly toward its accommodation of labor. But these constituent groups, like the left in the labor movement, suffered serious political defeats in the immediate postwar period: the Republican Party rejected isolationism (in favor of free trade), traditional conservatism (in favor of the accord with labor), and Robert Taft (in favor of Dwight D. Eisenhower and the Eastern, liberal wing of the party which supported him). The ideological and programmatic centers of the business community shifted to the Council on Foreign Relations and the Committee on Economic Development, which was an early pro-Keynesian advocate, and away from the National Association of Manufacturers. Small business continued to grow weaker economically, as both corporate concentration and the rate of small-business failures increased. Small enterprises were hardly in a position to challenge the central powers of the coalition.

The exclusion of many workers proved much more problematic, much earlier. While nonunion labor benefited substantially from the spillover effects of union political and economic victories, they were clearly not part of the coalition. Their exclusion had two critical consequences—for organized labor and eventually for the postwar accord itself.

From the side of organized labor, its narrow scope ultimately proved its undoing. Close to 40 percent of the wage-labor force worked in what many economists call "secondary jobs," which provided much less favorable opportunities for wage gains and stable employment than primary jobs. Women, minority, and younger workers disproportionately filled these secondary jobs. As a result of the effectiveness of the accord between large corporations and organized labor, the wage gap between "core" and "peripheral" sectors—between those industries most and least benefiting from the accord—widened steadily through the postwar period, increasing (according to our estimates) by 15 percent from 1948 to 1966.[88] This resulted in widening income inequality by race and sex. Figure 4.4 provides a composite index of the degree of income advantages for white male over female and black male workers. As the graph shows, this measure of income inequality increased substantially through the 1960s. Unemployment disadvantages by race and by sex also widened significantly.[89]

Fig. 4.4
Earnings Inequality
ratio of white male earnings to female and black male earnings

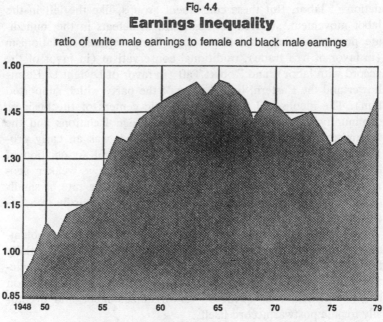

Source: Current Population Reports, Series P-60, No. 129. The index of earnings inequality is the weighted ratio of male earnings over female earnings and non-white male earnings, respectively weighted by the share of non-white males and females in total employment.

The net effect for the labor movement was a significant narrowing of its reach. Labor-union membership, which had soared from the mid-1930s through the late 1940s and early 1950s, fell dramatically from its postwar peaks, dropping from 35 percent of the nonagricultural labor force at the time of the AFL–CIO merger in 1954 to only 28 percent in 1966.[40] Eventually, organized labor felt the effects of this decline through erosion of its bargaining power.

The consequences for the postwar accord were just as serious, beginning to backfire in the late 1950s and early 1960s. Protest against the racism, sexism, and distributive injustice of the growth coalition emerged through four different but effective movements: the civil rights movement, the welfare rights movement, the organization of the elderly, and the women's movement. These movements all led to government efforts at accommodation, cumulating with accelerating force in the mid-1960s through Medicare and Medicaid, the Great Society legislation producing the Voting Rights Act and the poverty program, the expansion of public assistance, and spreading attention to affirmative action and equal rights. Many of these programs cost money, and their growing costs reflected the mounting and increasingly expensive requirements of containing resistance to an unequal distribution of power and privilege. These were real economic gains won by mass movements, and they tended increasingly, as we shall see throughout these chapters, to undermine the structure of the postwar corporate system.

These represented challenges from *outside* the capital-labor accord. Yet the accord began to encounter increasingly serious resistance from the predominantly unionized workers *within* the coalition as well. Several factors contributed to the growth of discontent and recalcitrance among these "primary" workers.

The first involves an apparent shift in attitudes and focus. Rising real wages, heightened job security, and improved working conditions were increasingly taken for granted—as memories of the Depression receded and young workers replaced those who had struggled through the 1930s. This decline in *material* insecurity apparently led to greater concern about occupational health-and-safety issues, influence over workplace decisions, and opportunities for meaningful and creatively challenging work.[41] These spreading concerns could conceivably have been accommodated, but they tended to run up against the vast apparatus of bureaucratic control. The increasing intensity of supervision worked well for those workers who understood and still believed in the terms of the initial bargain, but it was less and less likely to remain effective when it confronted a labor force which—by age, education, and temperament—was increasingly resistant to arbitrary authority. Even among blue-collar workers, rank-and-file movements in the United Auto Workers, the United Steel Workers, the United Mine Workers, the Teamsters and several other important unions all challenged authoritarian and business-oriented leadership, often seeking to bring the issues of union democracy, racism, and job safety to the fore.

These sources of erosion were complemented by another and clearly critical problem for capital: the declining effectiveness of the traditional source of capitalist leverage over the work force, the threat of unemployment. This threat is based on two simple facts of life in a capitalist economy: workers depend on getting jobs in order to live, and a significant number of workers at any time are stuck without a job.

Two developments in the postwar period reduced the effectiveness of this threat. First, the unemployment rate was relatively low, by historical standards, throughout the period, and it fell to unusually low levels in the mid-1960s. Second, the social programs won by popular struggles in the 1930s—social insurance, unemployment compensation, and others—were gradually extended during the 1940s and 1950s and then, under the pressure of the initiatives of the "excluded," they were greatly expanded and augmented by new programs such as Medicaid, Medicare, food stamps, and Aid to Families with Dependent Children (AFDC). The combined effect of all these programs was to provide some cushion for those laid off from work.

To document this phenomenon and to assess its relative impact, we have combined the two effects—lower unemployment and the cushion provided by social programs—into a single measure of the "cost of losing your job."[42] Our measure represents the average number of weeks' worth of overall income lost by a worker who is laid off. It varies with both the likelihood of remaining without a job for a long time—as when unemployment rises—and with the relative income lost when a worker is unemployed. The higher this measure, the greater the cost of job termination and the greater the potential corporate leverage over their workers.

We show the postwar changes in this "cost of losing your job" in Figure 4.5. Because the measure is quite sensitive to the fluc-

Fig. 4.5

The Cost of Losing Your Job

average number of weeks' earnings lost by a worker laid off

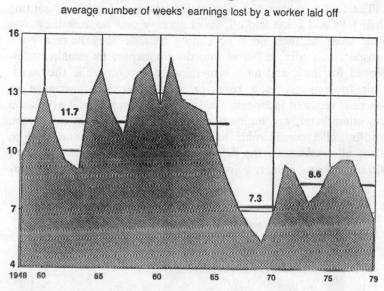

Source: J. Schor and S. Bowles, "The Social Wage and the Labor Process: Measuring Some Influences on Worker Resistance," unpublished paper, 1982, horizontal lines are period averages for 1948-66, 1967-73, and 1974-79.

tuations of the business cycle, we have superimposed the average rates for the boom period (1948–66) and the first two phases of the crisis (1966–73 and 1973–79). The shape of the graph makes evident that the cost of job loss was highest during the boom and significantly lower during the first phase of the crisis. It did rise again by the second phase, but remained on average well below its boom level. Moreover, the modest recovery from 1973 to 1979 was accomplished only by the deliberate creation of widespread unemployment. We will discuss the consequences of this "Great Repression" in the next chapter.

Measured by the cost to workers of losing their job, employers' leverage over workers declined by more than a quarter from the boom period to the first phase of crisis. This was bound to loosen their hold over labor and undermine their ability to maintain the profitability of production.

There are several indications that workers began to take advan-

tage of this reduced corporate leverage. We focus here on two
kinds of evidence.

The first considers the relative frequencies of workers quitting
their jobs and being laid off. Workers may quit because they hate
their work or their boss, or simply because they have a good
prospect of finding a better job, do not expect to remain unemployed for long, and have something to live on while they wait.
Quit frequencies, as a result, reflect either job resistance or
workers' sense of independence from their employers. Layoffs, on
the other hand, are imposed upon workers by their employers;
layoffs inflict considerable losses on some workers and tend to
place all workers on the defensive. The left-hand bars in Figure
4.6 show data on the ratio of quits to layoffs (averaged over post-

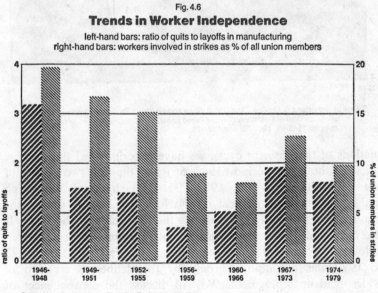

Fig. 4.6

Trends in Worker Independence

left-hand bars: ratio of quits to layoffs in manufacturing
right-hand bars: workers involved in strikes as % of all union members

Source: Handbook of Labor Statistics, Tables 54, 150, 151

war business cycles to remove short-run fluctuations). These bars
show that workers lost ground considerably during the first two
postwar decades, through the early 1960s, but were then able to
recover some freedom of maneuver after 1966.

The second indicator involves the frequency of strike activity.
We have already noted that strikes declined during the postwar

boom itself. The right-hand bars in Figure 4.6 show the number of workers involved in strikes as a percentage of all trade union members—the group of workers most likely to engage in strike activity. This measure of strike frequency follows the quits-to-layoff ratio very closely; it provides yet another measure of workers' growing sense of independence from employers during the first two postwar decades, and it shows again a sharp discontinuity after the peak of the postwar boom in 1966.

It appears, on the basis of these several indicators, that the effectiveness of corporate control over labor was beginning to decline after the mid-1960s—as a result of both friction within the bureaucratic shell and the increasingly muted effect of the unemployment threat. Workers were not staging a political revolt against the capitalist system, to be sure, but many were becoming restive with bureaucratic control and many were beginning to experience—and undoubtedly to appreciate—much greater protection from insistent corporate discipline.

This erosion of corporate leverage was bound to reduce employers' ability to push for greater work intensity and to hold down wages. When real output per worker-hour does not grow as rapidly as real compensation per hour, the real cost of labor to capital begins to rise. And this will tend, in turn, to increase the share of labor and reduce the share of capital in overall income. If the capital-labor accord was beginning to erode after 1966, we would expect it to have contributed to a simultaneous decline in corporate profitability. And this, as we show in the last section of this chapter, is exactly what happened.

Erosion III: Challenges to the Logic of Profitability

The postwar corporate system rested centrally on the premise "If it's profitable it must be desirable." The third critical fracture in the postwar edifice resulted from a widespread challenge to this principle.

At the beginning of the postwar period, the major decisions of economic life—concerning technology, product design, industrial location, occupational safety and health, and environmental balance—had been relegated to the market. Despite the more active intervention of the state, its economic intrusions did not affect the basic logic of profitability in the private sector. When Eisenhower's secretary of defense, Charles Wilson, suggested, "What is good for General Motors is good for the country," most people thought Wilson to be merely impolitic, not wrong.

But the bottom line was not to continue unchallenged for long. Beginning with occupational health-and-safety campaigns in the Oil, Chemical, and Atomic Workers Union and in the United Mine Workers, and equally with Ralph Nader's effective public mobilization around issues of consumer safety and product design, fueled by the notorious Pinto exploding-gas-tank scandal, sustained by Love Canal and the periodic burning of the Cuyahoga River, a wide variety of movements emerged to challenge the hallowed identity of private greed and public virtue. The oldest of these movements—conservation—enjoyed a veritable rebirth and transformation in the late 1960s and early 1970s, sparking a series of popular and often militant campaigns demanding environmental protection, alternative energy sources, and a halt to nuclear power.

Although these movements were largely disconnected and focused on single issues, they had the combined effect of challenging the basic logic of capitalist profitability. On issue after issue, they raised doubts about the primacy of private profitability in determining resource allocation and economic decision-making.

By the early 1970s, these several insurgencies had won a series of major legislative and legal victories, creating a sequence of agencies with major responsibility for corporate regulation—the National Highway Traffic Safety Commission (1970), the Occupational Safety and Health Administration (1970), the Environmental Protection Administration (1970), the Consumer Product Safety Commission (1972), the Mine Enforcement and Safety Administration (1973), and several others. Later in the decade, the environmental movement made further advances through its challenge to the safety hazards of nuclear power generation.

Though new social mores were important in this process, these movements did not arise solely or even primarily through changes in people's values. In many cases, they resulted much more simply from defensive and protective reactions against the rising and increasingly serious hazards of life in the postwar regime: the spread of lethal products on the market, urban air pollution, the threat of radioactive pollution, increasingly hazardous working conditions. In manufacturing, for example, the accident rate began to rise sharply after 1963–65, having fallen from its wartime highs through the 1950s; by the early 1970s, it had surpassed its early postwar levels and by the late 1970s it had risen substantially above even its World War II peaks.[43] The Mine Safety Act of 1969 was passed in the wake of the terrible 1968 Mannington Mine disaster, which that year brought coal-mine fatalities (per million man-hours worked) to a postwar peak.[44] Faced with these threats, people had no choice but to react.

One of the clearest consequences of these challenges to profitability was the rapidly rising costs of "nature-based inputs"—agricultural products, fuels, and other raw materials.[45] Many have attributed these rising costs to a "running out of nature," an issue about which we remain agnostic. It is much more likely, we think, that the rapid increases in various crude-materials prices after the mid-1960s were the result of a wide variety of contradictions within the postwar corporate system—due both to declining U.S. international domination and to spreading challenges to the logic of profitability.

The electricity-generation industry provides a particularly interesting case study of these interactions. Electricity prices fell sharply from 1948 to 1966, dropping from 1.01 cents per kilowatt-hour to .89 cents per kilowatt-hour. Prices then began to rise, increasing to 1.17 cents in 1973 and 2.83 cents in 1979.[46] Relative to the movement of all producer prices, electricity prices fell by nearly 30 percent during the boom years, grew at the same rate during the first phase of crisis, and then increased substantially during the second phase of crisis. What explains these shifts in the relative cost of electricity?

It seems likely that the initial increase in prices after the mid-1960s resulted primarily from a simple burst of energy demand—a lagged reaction to the continually cheaper electricity prices over the previous fifteen years. (The use of energy grew at over 3 percent annually from 1965 to 1972, after growing at just over half a percent annually from 1950 to 1965.)[47] After 1973, however, three important developments, reflecting both international and domestic challenges to the postwar corporate system, combined to push electricity prices nearly through the roof.

The first, of course, was the sharp increase in oil prices after 1973, which greatly raised the cost of generating electricity in oil-fired plants. This, as we have already argued, was a reflection of declining U.S. international domination.

The second development involved mining. Changing relative prices dictated a shift away from oil fuel to relatively cheaper coal inputs. But this shift was impeded both by growing environmental restrictions on coal burning and strip mining, on the one hand, and by a sharp drop in coal output per miner-hour, from 19.3 tons per worker-day in 1968 to 14.26 tons in 1979, on the other.[48] This officially designated "productivity" decline, we have argued, stemmed primarily from a breakdown in labor relations in the mines—as wildcatting miners refused to work in unsafe mines. (Fatalities in the mines dropped even more dramatically, from 311 in 1968 to 106 deaths in 1978. Expressed in tons of coal per lost miner—a meaningful measure from the viewpoint of workers in a hazardous industry—"productivity" more than doubled over three years!)[49]

The third factor involved nuclear power—the other major alternative source of electricity-generating fuel. As we have already seen in our earlier vignette, nuclear-power advocates had, prior to the mid-1970s, secured government subsidies and lavish financial backing. By the mid-1970s, however, the antinuclear movement was inflicting major legal and political setbacks on the "fuel of the future." Costs ballooned uncontrollably and reactor sales skidded to a halt. Electricity consumers needed relief, but nuclear power no longer provided any help at all.

Taken together, these international, ecological, and political factors account for the skyrocketing price of electricity. That example, though quite specific, nonetheless illustrates the general effects of the challenge to corporate profitability. U.S. capital was able to reap substantial advantages from the corporate-citizen accord for two decades. A wide variety of challenges to U.S. international domination and the logic of profitability eventually dried up those opportunities for advantage. The contradictions of the postwar corporate system blew up in the collective corporate face.

THE CONSEQUENCES OF EROSION: DECLINING PROFITABILITY

The average rate of profit (after taxes) is a good barometer of capital's success in maintaining its power and privilege, for the after-tax profit rate is influenced by the terms on which capital deals with the other major actors on the economic scene—labor, foreign suppliers, and the domestic citizenry (mediated by various levels of government). There are also, to be sure, technical determinants of the profitability of business operations, such as the state of technical knowledge and the abundance or scarcity of the natural environment. But much depends on the outcome of the continuing struggle over the production and distribution of the economic surplus generated by productive activity. Capital's success will vary with its ability to control labor, raw materials costs, and the impact of government—all in relation to the revenues that it realizes from the production and sale of goods and services.

We present two measures of corporate profitability in Figure 4.7. We chart (with the solid line) the after-tax rate of profit commanded by U.S. capitalists on their domestic nonfinancial corporate business operations. We also chart (with the dotted line) another common measure of corporate profitability: "Tobin's Q," named after 1981 Nobel Prize winner and Yale economist James Tobin. While the profit rate reflects *actual* returns on current operations, Tobin's Q reflects capitalists' evaluation of the business climate and their profit *expectations*.[50]

Figure 4.7 provides graphic evidence of the sharp deterioration in capital's fortunes during the first two phases of economic decline. Both the after-tax profit rate and Tobin's Q rose substantially during the boom years, peaking in 1965, and then plunged to about half of their peak levels within the next decade. Although corporate profitability staged mild upturns after the recessions of 1969–70 and 1974–75, these upturns were limited in duration and magnitude; they did little to offset the dominant downward trend from the mid-1960s through the early 1980s.

Fig. 4.7
Corporate Profitability
after-tax rate of profit and "Tobin's Q" for nonfinancial corporate business sector

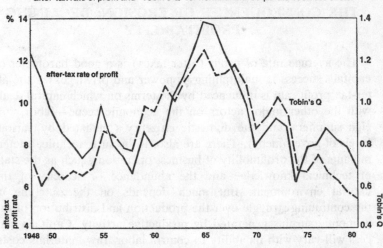

Source: See Fig. 3.6 for after-tax rate of profit. For Tobin's Q, Economic Report, 1982, B-88, and see Appendix C.

Can our analysis of the postwar corporate system explain this evident decline in corporate profitability? We have been able to develop a statistical model with accounts for almost all of the annual movements in both the after-tax profit rate and Tobin's Q; it accounts for 78 percent of the annual variation in the former and 88 percent of the annual variation in the latter.* This model includes measures which reflect the dynamics of *each* of the three principal structures of the postwar corporate system in the United States. The rise and demise of Pax Americana is captured by the U.S. terms of trade. The relative leverage which employers are able to exercise over their employees—and thus the relative effectiveness, from the corporate vantage point, of the postwar capital-labor accord—is measured by the "cost of losing your job" variable we introduced earlier. An index of the relative cost of crude materials reflects the combined effects (as illustrated in our discus-

* The statistical methodology required for this kind of analysis is introduced in our discussion of productivity in Chapter 6; the specific variables and methods we used are further detailed in Appendix C.

sion of electricity prices) of trends in U.S. international dominance and the state of the corporate-citizen accord.

These variables have significant effects on both measures of corporate profitability. Much more strikingly, movements in these three variables almost fully explain declining corporate profitability after 1966. Our three measures of the erosion of the postwar corporate system account for 77 percent of the drop in the after-tax rate of profit from 1966 to 1979 and 85 percent of the plunge in Tobin's Q over the same thirteen years. The data thus confirm our institutional account. The postwar corporate system worked for capital as long as its several institutional relations of domination were effectively unchallenged. Once people began to challenge those power relations both at home and abroad, corporations could no longer enjoy the booming profits to which they had grown accustomed. And, as we shall see, the erosion of the system led inevitably to economic decline.

We have sketched the rise and demise of the postwar corporate system. Its demise was marked by a sharp drop in corporate profits. It would have been astonishing if corporations had not fought back—both on their own and through their influence over government policy. They did—and with increasing ferocity. They failed, in the end, to restore the postwar corporate system because it proved impossible to suppress the various strands of foreign and domestic resistance. As we shall presently see, the corporate counterattack only succeeded in exacerbating the crisis.

We have written here about institutions and power relationships, about system construction and erosion. Mainstream economists and the media focus on the movement of more conventional economic measures—such as inflation, unemployment, and the growth of productivity. Can our institutional account of the fate of the postwar corporate system and the decline of corporate profitability shed light on the behavior of these more familiar macroeconomic variables?

We turn in the next two chapters to this question. We show that our institutional history of the crisis explains both the puzzling phenomenon of "stagflation" and the widely noted slowdown in productivity growth.

5

THE MISSED RECESSION,
THE GREAT REPRESSION,
AND SPIRALING STAGFLATION

How to describe the underlying condition of the American economy. . . . Is this, then, a depression we are in? Looking backward the term seems too strong. The economy has been stagnating, not collapsing. If the roof were to fall in later this year or next it could become a depression, but the odds are still against it.

Call it a repression—a chronic state of underemployment and industrial slack that has dogged the economy for the greater part of the past decade, a condition brought on by repressive actions by governments in the industrial world. . . .

When did this Great Repression begin? Since history is a seamless web it is hard to date it precisely. But the escalation of the Vietnam war in 1965 and 1966 seems the logical point. . . .
—Leonard Silk, the New York *Times,* March 1982[1]

During the first phase of economic decline, from 1966 to 1973, few perceived the systemic character of the erosion of the postwar corporate system. Responses were phlegmatic and haphazard.

By the early 1970s, however, corporations were beginning to recognize the threat to their own power and privilege. Many corporate leaders, aided by their friends in government, mounted an aggressive counterattack, seeking to block the spreading challenges to the corporate regime. They failed. Despite the power of their counteroffensive, they achieved no better than a political standoff.

But this counteroffensive did succeed in stalling the encroachment on corporate prerogatives. The stalemate continued through the second phase of decline, from 1973 to 1979. The U.S. economy entered its trench-warfare stage. The casualties mounted on all sides.

In this chapter we show how the erosion of the postwar corporate system and corporate efforts to revive it generated increasingly severe "stagflation"—the coincidence of rising unemployment and rapid inflation. To understand this process we will need to examine the twists and turns of U.S. government macropolicy as the postwar system entered its period of decline.

THE MISSED RECESSION

We now know that by the mid-1960s economic crisis was around the corner. But such premonitions would have seemed ludicrous in 1964 or 1965. We were then riding the crest of the most successful economic expansion since the recovery from the Great Depression.

The boom was sustained by a surge of investment: real gross private fixed investment, which had hardly risen at all between the business-cycle peaks of 1955 and 1959, increased rapidly from $101 billion in 1959 to $146 billion in 1966 (in 1972 dollars).[2] The "new economists" of the Kennedy and Johnson administrations sought to sustain the investment boom with generous tax favors—including both accelerated depreciation allowances (beginning in 1961) and the investment-tax credit of 1963. The result was a substantial reduction of the corporate profit tax burden; the effective rate of federal taxation on corporate profits dropped from 48 percent in 1959 to 40 percent in 1966. The magnitude of this tax subsidy was substantial: it amounted to a transfer of about 1 percent of U.S. GNP from government to business.[8]

As the rate of business taxation fell, the pressures on government expenditure mounted with the escalation of Lyndon Johnson's two wars: the war in Vietnam and the War on Poverty. By 1966, Vietnam War costs, according to the Defense Department's estimate of the "incremental" costs of the conflict, constituted almost 1 percent of the gross national product. The additional eco-

nomic burden of this war would average 1.9 percent over the next
seven years.[4] The War on Poverty was also expanding rapidly:
social-welfare expenditures—health, education, social insurance,
and income support—rose by a half of a percent of GNP from
1964 to 1966 and then by several more percentage points over
the rest of the 1960s.[5]

These parallel expansions of government expenditures reflected
the mounting pressure—both domestic and international—against
the postwar corporate system. The force of this pressure helps explain both the magnitude of the government response and the
difficulty of capping it once it began.

Business-tax reductions and the two-front war combined to expand total demand and to propel the economic expansion. The
government was withdrawing less from the economy in taxes than
it was pumping back in expenditures. Like most economists, we
measure the expansionary impact of government fiscal policy by
the "high-employment budget deficit"—the hypothetical excess of
government expenditures over tax revenues which *would* have occurred *if* the economy had been operating at full capacity.[6] The
high-employment budget, which had been almost continuously in
surplus since the Korean War, moved into deficit in 1965 and
reached a deficit magnitude of roughly 2 percent of GNP in 1967
and 1968.[7] With the economy already airborne on the wings of
an investment boom, such budget deficits had the effect of booster
rockets.

An expansionary monetary policy completed the recipe for
growth stimulation. A relatively loose monetary rein was needed
to provide funds necessary for the government and corporate borrowing required by a go-go fiscal policy in a go-go economy.
Economists regard the growth of the real money supply *relative*
to real potential GNP as a useful indicator of the degree of expansiveness of government monetary policy. This "relative real
money supply" had contracted slightly during the years from
1948 to 1959; it grew at a pace of 1.4 percent a year from 1959
to 1966. Despite emergent signs of inflationary pressure, it continued to grow from 1966 to 1973, though more slowly, at a pace
of .3 percent a year.[8]

Economists were well aware of these expansionary pressures.
They recognized that sustained expansion can often lead to short-

ages in markets for labor and raw materials. Corporate and personal borrowing is also likely to rise sharply. Economic prudence —particularly in the age of the "new economics" and fiscal fine-tuning—counseled a recession. If the economy did not cool itself off, then the government should perform that service on behalf of the economy. Many economists insisted it was time to turn down the thermostat.

LBJ might have cooled off the economy with any of three basic instruments: an increase in taxes, a cut in expenditures, or a restriction in the growth of money and the availability of credit. He found this an extraordinarily uninviting menu of choices:

- A tax increase would surely have focused attention on the escalating war costs. Since Johnson anticipated a brief, limited, and successful war, he hoped to finesse his political problems by burying the costs of the war in the budget and disguising its impact on the economy.

- He could not easily trim the military budget, at the same time, because the costs of the war were growing rapidly. Cuts in domestic social expenditures were no more appetizing, since they were likely to spark further mobilization of black and poor voters and to galvanize further opposition to the war.

- Another constituency blocked the road to credit restriction. Cooling the economy by restricting credit would undercut those corporations whose debt positions made them vulnerable to increases in the cost of credit. The Federal Reserve Board's attempt to restrict the growth of credit in 1966 was a short-lived and much-protested flop; not surprisingly, the business community was just as effective at exercising policy vetoes as the poor and the civil rights and antiwar movements.

Straitjacketed by these political and economic obstacles to tax increases, expenditure cuts, and credit crunches, Johnson put down his menu and ordered "none of the above." The economy roared along its flight path. The recession of 1966, which most corporations eagerly anticipated and sorely needed, never happened.

With the missed recession in the dustbin, the combined effects of an investment boom, a continuing high-employment budget deficit, and an expansionary monetary policy generated an extraordinary increase in total demand. Real output had grown by

30 percent from 1961 to 1966, or three and one half times more rapidly than the adult population. The economy began to exhaust its supplies of surplus labor. The unemployment rate fell from 5.5 percent at the 1959 peak to 3.8 percent at the 1966 peak. The *average* rate of unemployment for the next seven years, through the first phase of crisis, was only 4.6 percent, considerably below the *minimum* unemployment rate of the late-1950s business cycle. The average duration of unemployment (as calculated by the U.S. Bureau of Labor Statistics) fell from 14.4 weeks in 1959 to 10.4 weeks in 1966 to an average of 9.6 weeks for the *entire* period from 1967 to 1973. Its low of 7.9 weeks in 1969 set a historical record.[9]

With unemployment low and declining, and with the last recession a fading memory, capital began to face mounting challenges on the shop floor and at the bargaining table. The whip of threatening unemployment was temporarily on the shelf, so workers were less likely to accept the continuing discipline of their supervisors. Unions were emboldened to press for higher wages. The corporate grip was slipping.

The postwar practice of "productivity bargaining," which had linked wage gains to productivity growth, was an early casualty. The rate of growth of real nonfarm private business output per hour slowed from 2.9 percent in 1959–66 to 2.1 percent in 1966–73. During the same period, the rate of increase of total worker compensation per hour, including not only wages but all benefits, rose from 4.1 percent to 6.8 percent. As a consequence, unit labor costs—the dollar cost of labor per unit of real output —increased at an annual rate of 4.5 percent from 1966 to 1973 after increasing at only 1.2 percent from 1959 to 1966.[10]

Rising unit labor costs need not squeeze profits if corporations can pass on those higher costs to consumers through equivalent price increases. As we have already seen, however, corporations were feeling pressure from other quarters. The erosion of U.S. international domination had permitted a growing penetration of U.S. domestic markets by imported foreign goods. (See Figure 4.1.) This increasingly effective foreign competition limited the extent to which corporations could afford to increase prices. Prices did rise between 1966 and 1973, by an average of 4 percent per year; but this was still not enough to offset the 4.5 percent rise in unit labor costs. Unit profits felt the pinch. And since no further tax concessions were forthcoming—the effective corporate profit-tax rate actually rose from the mid-1960s to the early 1970s[11]—the fall in unit profits contributed to the crushing post-1966 decline in the after-tax profit rate which we have already documented in Figure 4.7.

The crisis was under way.

Its onset was largely unheralded, however, by those who watch the economic wall charts. Few people recognized the turning point in 1966. Rates of profit always fluctuate, so it was hard to tell a serious downturn from a momentary blip. Business remained optimistic in the late 1960s and invested with high hopes and fulsome spirits. Mainstream economists were no more perspicacious. Though they regretted the missed recession of 1966, they nonetheless celebrated the end of the business cycle and the triumph of their fine-tuning legerdemain.

Few anticipated, in particular, that the Vietnam War boom would have such different long-run economic consequences from the World War II boom. During World War II, the high employment pressure on unit labor costs had been restrained by tight government controls on wages and, equally important, by union leadership's patriotic commitment to forgo strikes and win the "battle of production." It was one thing to win a war *against* fascism, however, and quite another to win a battle *for* the postwar corporate system.

After 1965–66, strikes escalated and the postwar labor peace began to evaporate. Unemployment was down, there were no direct controls over labor, the spirit of capital-labor cooperation was showing serious strains, and the threat to profits was becoming apparent. To those who watched the shop floor, the problems could no longer be ignored. The *Wall Street Journal* reported in 1970:

Observers of the labor-management scene . . . almost unanimously assert that the present situation is the worst within memory. . . . Morale in many operations is sagging badly, intentional work slowdowns are cropping up more frequently and absenteeism is soaring. . . . Men such as Mr. Burke at Otis [Elevator Co.] contend the problem [of declining worker productivity] is so widespread it's their major headache at the moment.[12]

The political coalition represented by the Democratic Party could not pursue the economic slowdown which many in the business community thought would restrain labor militance, since organized labor was committed to rapid growth and continued to exercise substantial leverage over the Democrats' policy direction. The advocates of contraction had to wait for a change in the political climate.

The election of 1968 seemed promising. Richard Nixon's inauguration led almost immediately to an engineered recession. Relying on discretionary spending power, the government moved quickly from fiscal expansiveness to fiscal restrictiveness. The high-employment budget-deficit stimulus—which had run at $11.4 billion in 1968—shifted to a high-employment budget-surplus drag of $5.6 billion (annual rate) in the first half of 1969.[13]

Those who needed relief spelled it unemployment, which rose sharply in late 1969 and early 1970. "Corporate executives I've checked with are cautiously optimistic," insurance executive W. Clement Stone concluded in a 1970 interview. "There is what I call a wholesome recession. . . . As for employees, with a fear of losing jobs they're really putting their heart into their work. Formerly, it was, 'What's the difference?' "[14]

But the resulting "Nixon recession" was shallow and short-lived. After little over a year of contractionary fiscal policy, Nixon shifted back to the more politically rewarding strategy of expansion. At the advice of Arthur Burns in 1960, Vice-President Nixon had vainly urged President Eisenhower to expand the economy in an effort to deprive John F. Kennedy of the unemployment issue. Now, with Burns as chairman of the board of governors of the Federal Reserve System and with Nixon graduated to the Oval Office, the Imperial Presidency was prepared to use fiscal policy for electoral ends.[15] While unemployment rose through the second half of 1971, and George McGovern geared up for a broadside on economic injustice, Nixon mounted a high-employment budget-deficit stimulus of $11.3 billion in 1971, $12.1 billion in 1972, and then a record-setting annual rate of $23.6 billion in the election quarter of 1972. Anticipating the inflationary consequences of this stimulatory package in August 1971, Nixon included a system of wage and price controls in his

"New Economic Policy," introducing such controls for the first time since the Korean War.

It worked. Unemployment had begun to fall by early autumn 1972. Wage and price controls helped prevent inflationary pressures from getting out of hand. (The price would be paid later, of course, well after the election, when the pent-up pressures burst their fragile bounds and launched a gigantic inflationary explosion.) The Democrats were robbed of their most promising domestic issue and McGovern was buried under an electoral avalanche.

There was a cost to this carefully orchestrated defeat of McGovern's populist coalition, however: the unemployment whip remained on the shelf. The economy had not yet cooled enough to salve its underlying strains. When the economy peaked a year after the election in 1973, the after-tax profit rate remained at less than two thirds of its 1966 peak. (See Figure 4.7.) Buy-now, pay-later fiscal policy had won the election, but it had hardly cured the economy's basic problems.

THE GREAT REPRESSION

The Nixon administration purchased temporary respite at the cost of deepening structural problems. Many corporate executives and government officials increasingly recognized the need to plot a longer-term strategy against continuing institutional erosion and economic decline. Singly, and through such organizations as the Business Roundtable, they launched a two-pronged microeconomic and macroeconomic counterattack.

The Workplace Counteroffensive

On the microeconomic front, many businesses turned to more aggressive shop-floor strategies. General Motors' effort to speed up the work pace at its Lordstown Vega assembly unit was an early and illustrative example.

The auto industry had been sinking fast, falling by 1971 to a postwar low in profitability. General Motors' profit margin had slipped from 10.2 percent in 1966 to only 6.8 percent in 1971.[16] The old Lordstown Chevy Impala assembly unit had recently been retooled to produce Vegas. Though highly touted in GM publicity as a new model for auto assembly plants of the future, the new Vega assembly unit had become a headache.

On paper it was a showcase that would have warmed Henry Ford's heart. Twenty-six Unimate robots had been installed to weld Vega bodies. The Product Assurance Control System (PACS) oversaw the production process with "sixteen optical scanning devices strategically located throughout the plant."[17] But despite the technical wizardry, the profit performance in Lordstown was not much better than in other operations.

In October 1971, GM turned the unit over to the General Motors Assembly Division (GMAD)—known at the time as the Marine Corps of GM divisions—in the hope of improving unit profits at the plants. Almost immediately, GMAD retooled the line to operate at a speed of 102 cars per hour, giving workers just thirty-six seconds to perform their tasks. (The old Impala line had operated at sixty cars per hour.) GM hoped to save at least $20 million a year at Lordstown on the speed-up alone.

The workers balked. Over the next five months, the UAW at Lordstown filed 5,000 grievances against the company. On the basis of her interviews with management and workers at Lordstown, Emma Rothschild concluded:

Management tough mindedness is itself a major issue in automotive discontent. Workers' grievances at Lordstown concerned not only the speeding up and intensification of jobs, but also the disciplinary character of plant management—where workers must ask, and wait to leave their job for one or two minutes; must ask, and wait for permission to get married on Saturday; must show a doctor's note if they stay home when they get sick; or a note from the funeral director when they go to their father's burial; or a garage bill if they arrive at work late because their car broke down.[18]

Absenteeism, slowdowns, and defects (which GM alleged were the work of sabotage) all mounted. The *Wall Street Journal* referred early in 1972 to the "utopian GM plant" as "paradise lost."[19]

In February 1972, workers at the Vega plants voted by a 97 percent majority to strike over working conditions. It was not a long strike, lasting only three weeks. But it seemed a bellwether. One journal termed it an "industrial Woodstock." GM's director of labor relations, George Morris, was not inclined to take it lightly: "the story of industrial life in the twentieth century will single out the Lordstown strike of 1972 as marking the explosion of youth and its rebellion against the management and union establishment."[20] By any measure, the Lordstown speed-up failed in its objectives.

Less dramatic but similar flare-ups recurred throughout U.S. industry—particularly after 1973.[21] Corporations tightened their surveillance and control of workers: the fraction of employees in nonproduction jobs mounted continuously from 1973 to 1979, growing much more rapidly than during the first phase of the crisis from 1966 to 1973; the costs of supervision increased in turn.[22] As management cut corners and increased the speed of production, accident rates soared; by 1979, the frequency of injuries resulting in workdays lost in manufacturing was *twice* as high as it had been in the early 1960s.[23] Not surprisingly, worker dissatisfaction increased substantially. One extensive study, funded by the U.S. Department of Labor, provides detailed data on measures of job satisfaction for 1969, 1973, and 1977. The decline in work satisfaction accelerated from 1973 to 1977. As the principal author of that study, Michigan sociologist Graham Staines, concluded, "The sky has finally fallen. Workers in virtually all occupational and demographic categories evidenced appreciable and unmistakable manifestations of rising discontent."[24]

Faced with rising worker discontent and the erosion of its power on the shop and office floors, business became more and more aggressive, seeking to change the rules of the game in its bargaining relationships with unions and employees. With the organizational support of associations such as the Business Roundtable, corporations mounted an antiunion drive of pre-World War I proportions. Union deauthorization cases filed before the National Labor Relations Board rose from 136 in 1966 to 213 in 1973 and 330 in 1979.[25] Corporations made increasing use of sophisticated management consultant firms specializing in union busting and forestalling union organizing drives. By the mid-1970s,

observers estimated that corporations were spending between
$100 million and $500 million on these antiunion activities. By
1979, the drive was evident everywhere. As the British magazine
The Economist concluded in a special feature on union busting in
the United States,

Managers are desperate for maximum flexibility in adopting new technology to stay ahead of the game. They are also keen to save a bit on
wages. So they would prefer to do without even the limited resistance
of unions to change. . . . Employers no longer accept unions as a
fact of life. They are fighting back—and winning.[26]

Corporations used the fearsome prospect of plant shutdowns to
goad unions into more serviceable behavior. The shift of investment and employment out of the Northeast and Midwest appears
to have accelerated in the early 1970s. Corporations continued to
shift their investment abroad: direct investment overseas increased
substantially faster than domestic investment.[27] As Barry Bluestone and Bennett Harrison conclude in their insightful book
The Deindustrialization of America, "Capital mobility itself,
whether enacted or merely threatened, was becoming a mechanism
for altering the very foundations of labor-management relations."[28]

Although the press almost entirely ignored this shift in corporate behavior, union leadership had few illusions about business
intentions. In 1978, for example, UAW president Douglas Fraser
resigned from a private and informal discussion group of leading
corporate executives and labor leaders called the Labor-
Management Group. Fraser outlined the reasons for his resignation in a letter widely circulated within the union movement:

The leaders of industry, commerce and finance in the United States
have broken and discarded the fragile, unwritten compact previously
existing during a past period of growth and progress. . . . [That
compact] survived in part because of an unspoken foundation: that
when things got bad enough for a segment of society, the business
elite "gave" a little bit—enabling government or interest groups to better conditions somewhat for that segment. . . .

But today, I am convinced there has been a shift on the part of the
business community toward confrontation, rather than cooperation.
Now, business groups are tightening their control over American society. . . . I believe leaders of the business community, with few excep-

tions, have chosen to wage a one-sided class war in this country—a war against working people, the unemployed, the poor, the minorities, the very young and the very old, and even many in the middle class of our society.[29]

An unmistakable warning signal for the union movement was the fate of the moderate Labor Law Reform Act of 1978. Labor intended it as a marginal reform in the legislation governing union organizing and elections, hoping to up the ante against companies like J. P. Stevens, the southern textile giant, which were flouting federal regulations on antiunion behavior. To the astonishment of the entire organized-labor leadership, both small and big business refused any compromise, lobbied Congress intensively, and defeated the legislation. Fraser's conclusion echoed sentiments throughout organized labor: "The fight waged by the business community against the Labor Law Reform bill stands as the most vicious, unfair attack upon the labor movement in more than 30 years. . . . Where industry once yearned for subservient unions, it now wants no unions at all." The postwar capital-labor accord was all but dead.

The Great Repression

A sharp turn in macroeconomic policy, the second prong of the business counteroffensive, dealt the accord its coup de grâce. Shortly after wage and price controls were lifted in 1973, government officials joined the antilabor brigade.

Unemployment had already begun to rise in early 1974, as another cyclical downturn was under way. Rather than pushing the countercyclical accelerator, President Ford's economic policy makers hit the brakes. A $6.5-billion high-employment budget *surplus*—combining federal with state and local government surpluses—dealt the economy a crunching blow. The OPEC price increase simultaneously withdrew an additional $2.6 billion of purchasing power from the economy.[30] The combination of the two massive drags produced the deepest recession in the postwar era. Output dropped by roughly 10 percent in the first year, and the unemployment rate rose from 4.8 percent in the last quarter of 1973 to 8.2 percent in the first quarter of 1975.

Some executives welcomed the economic jolt as potential salvation. At an important management conference in the middle of the recession, corporate leaders eagerly awaited the effects of rising unemployment. "We need a sharp recession," one said. "People need to recognize," a second added, "that a job is the most important thing they can have." A third was most hopeful: "This recession will bring about the healthy respect for economic values that the Depression did."[31]

Business had learned, however, that short-lived macroeconomic restrictiveness was not enough; the stop-and-go recession of 1969–70 had solved none of their problems. Many in the corporate and financial communities mounted pressure, therefore, for a sustained ice-water dousing of the economy to extend beyond the 1974–75 downturn. We call this the *cold-bath* treatment. The effects of this pressure show up in the record of both fiscal and monetary policy through 1979—even before Paul Volcker and the Reagan administration arrived with their replenished supplies of ice.

Restrictive fiscal policy—the deliberate generation of high levels of unemployment—became a permanent feature of the macroeconomic terrain in the late 1970s. The high-employment budget surplus, when combined with whopping state and local government surpluses and what the President's Council of Economic Advisers (CEA) calls the "oil-price drag," was contractionary in every year after 1975. If the government policy makers had wanted to pull the economy out of its doldrums, they would have run sufficiently large high-employment budget deficits to offset the effects of state and local surpluses and the oil-price drag. They did not. Our measure of overall fiscal drag (combining the above three components) averaged a sharply contractionary .4 percent of GNP over the years 1974–79, after having averaged a stimulative .5 percent *deficit* from 1967 to 1973. (The difference between the two periods may actually be underestimated, since the CEA's concept of "high employment" shifted upward from an unemployment rate of 4.5 percent in 1966 to 5.1 percent in 1979. Calculated with a 4.5 percent unemployment figure, the fiscal drag of the 1974–79 period was considerably greater.)[32] This fiscal drag increased sharply toward the end of the 1970s. The CEA, noting the large contractionary impact in their 1980 *Report,* observed: "Over the 4 quarters of the year [1979], fiscal and oil price restraint increased by $60 billion, or about 2½ percent of GNP."[33]

Monetary policy was set on a similar track after 1973. From 1966 to 1973, the ratio of the real money supply to real potential GNP had grown at .3 percent per year, reflecting relatively expansionary policies. From 1973 to 1979, this measure of monetary policy *declined* at a rate of .9 percent per year. The monetary authorities, like the teacher in a driver education training car, were applying the brakes *just in case* the naïve and inexperienced fiscal authorities missed the stop signs.

The "logic" of contraction, from the corporate viewpoint, is that deep recessions will bring business relief from wage pressures. As it was with the Vietnamese, however, so it was with U.S. workers: a short quick war could not be won. In the sharp 1975 contraction (as the President's Council of Economic Advisers later noted to its dismay), the growth of both prices and wages slowed, but prices slowed more. Hence the rate of growth of *real* wages of those who retained their jobs actually *increased.* In this respect, the 1974–75 downturn backfired.

This "perverse cycle"—as economists call it in scolding tones— appears to have resulted from a combination of heightened levels of competition due to accelerating imports, a greater coincidence of the world business cycle, and the effects of the growth of social expenditures in cushioning the depressing impact of unemployment on wages.[34] These "perverse" and counterproductive effects, from the corporate vantage point, represent yet another consequence of the institutional erosion of the postwar corporate system. U.S. corporations could no longer control their destinies through simple meat-cleaver tactics.

With no swift and decisive victory for business in sight, the macroeconomic decision makers prepared for a prolonged period of programmed economic stagnation, hoping at least that high levels of unemployment in the long run would bring labor to heel. The trench-warfare strategy involved a waiting game: douse the economy in cold water long enough, and labor will succumb. Eventually, this trench warfare began to take its toll. Real wages actually declined in the late 1970s, and the share of production-worker compensation in nonfarm-business income declined from 1973 to 1979.[35]

By encouraging the Great Repression, however, corporations were cutting off their noses to spite their faces. With idle capacity spreading as a result of restrictive monetary and fiscal policy, the incentive to build new plants and equipment vanished; corporations had enough capacity to produce what was demanded. And with utilization levels so low, the stock market recorded the immense costliness of the protracted assault on labor: the market valuation of real assets, which had remained close to their replacement cost in the early 1970s, fell to record lows at the end of the decade. (See the data on Tobin's Q in Figure 4.7.) This threw even more cold water on the incentive to build new productive capacity. If, as was the case during the 1979 *peak,* you could buy assets on the stock market for fifty-six cents that would cost you one dollar to build, why build?

This spreading domestic stagnation helps illuminate the character of foreign competition and declining U.S. trade competitiveness during the 1970s as well. Many have blamed foreign competition for nearly all of our recent economic problems, particularly declining manufacturing employment in key industries such as auto and steel. While these employment declines have been very severe, available data suggest that domestic factors have been much more important in causing the employment slowdown in the United States. A recent study by Brookings Institution economist Robert Z. Lawrence finds that, on balance, domestic demand factors account for nearly 100 percent of the changes in employment in U.S. manufacturing during the 1970s. Had the domestic U.S. economy grown more rapidly, so would have U.S. manufacturing employment. Even in such besieged industries as autos and steel, declining domestic demand accounted for a higher proportion of employment losses than rising import competition.[36] Because foreign competition seemed so visible and so ubiquitous, it was tempting to blame it for sluggish employment growth in manufacturing. The cold bath played a much more important role. (Since 1979, we suspect that import competition has played a more important role. This has been due primarily, however, to the rising relative value of the dollar, making

U.S. exports relatively more expensive for foreigners to buy. And the rising value of the dollar, in turn, has been a product of the high interest rates imposed as part of the restrictive monetary policies of the post-1979 years.)

Another consequence of the Great Repression has been that corporations began to lose either their interest in or their capacity for productive innovation. As many business observers noted, U.S. corporations began turning toward increasingly short-term financial objectives. Merger bids were flying fast and furious by 1978–79. Corporate executives were paying more attention to their quarterly reports than to their engineers' blueprints for long-term product and process innovation. The Business Week Team reported in their book on reindustrialization:

> There is a schizophrenia pervading American business today. It is a rare CEO who has not publicly expounded on the need for focusing on the future, usually in a speech castigating government or labor unions for their short-term policies. Yet . . . the corporate landscape is dotted with visible examples of the inevitable economic chaos that results from a refusal to see beyond the next quarterly earnings statement.[37]

Capital had begun to win the battle against labor, in short, but it was continuing to lose the war.

SPIRALING STAGFLATION

Continuing institutional erosion and the self-defeating corporate counteroffensive combined to produce the new and puzzling development called *stagflation*—the historically unprecedented coexistence of high unemployment and accelerating inflation. In earlier periods of capitalist crisis, stagnation and rising unemployment had been associated with declining rates of inflation and often even with absolutely falling price levels. Now, stagnation and rising unemployment were accompanied by *rising* prices; a new term was invented to draw attention to the odd economic couple.

The rising unemployment of the 1970s was both desired and

anticipated; it does not require further explanation. The puzzle
arises from the *price* side of the stagflation dyad: why should
strong inflationary pressures accompany those higher rates of
unemployment? With workers plentiful and jobs scarce, why
should the rate of price increase creep *upward* instead of *downward?*

The key to this puzzle, we think, lies in our analysis of the erosion of the postwar corporate system. We begin developing our
argument by looking at the contours of the new phenomenon of
stagflation itself. In Figure 5.1 we chart the actual inflation-to-
unemployment relationship for the United States from 1948 to
1981. Each point on the graph represents the rate of unemployment and the corresponding rate of price inflation that prevailed in
a particular year.

It is easiest to understand Figure 5.1 by following the dots
from year to year. We have not drawn a line connecting the dots
for the early postwar years from 1948 to 1953; this period dis-
plays a fairly volatile relationship between unemployment and
inflation—which can presumably be attributed to the massive
postwar reconversion from a wartime to a peacetime economy
and to the unusually disruptive economic effects of the Korean
War.[38]

The period of primary interest begins in 1954, after the Korean
War price controls were lifted. To highlight the unemployment-
inflation relationship after the early volatile years, we have drawn
a heavy solid line connecting each dot from 1954 to 1981, beginning with an arrow marking the initial year of that period.

Until 1967, as the lines sloping downward to the right suggest,
there was a fairly stable negative relationship between unemployment and inflation in the U.S. economy; if unemployment
rose, inflation slowed—and vice versa. (This is the relationship
which economists have traditionally called the Phillips Curve.)
The rate of unemployment oscillated between 3 percent and 7
percent while the rate of price inflation varied between 1 percent
and 4 percent.

Beginning around 1968, however, the picture changes dramatically. Unemployment rates increase, as we have already seen, but
inflation rates do not come down as much as the earlier relationship would have led us to expect; the line no longer slopes

Fig. 5.1
The Stagflation Spiral
annual rate of inflation plotted against annual rate of unemployment

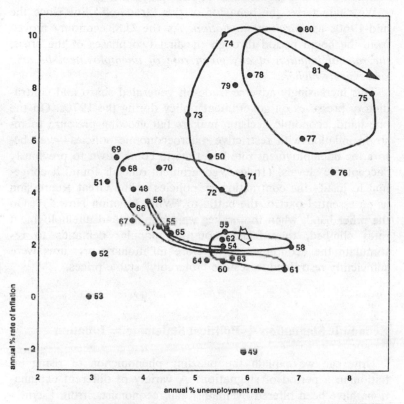

Source: inflation, % change in 4th quarter GDP implicit price deflator, NIPA, Table 7.4, unemployment, Economic Report of the President, 1982, B-29.

downward to the right. This change in the relationship seems to occur in two phases: First, in the late 1960s and early 1970s, the trade-off line veers upward and then around to the right, turning down at a level considerably higher than in the early 1960s; this constitutes a first loop. Then, in the mid-1970s, the line moves upward once again and eventually loops downward at a new and still much higher level. By the late 1970s and early 1980s, the trade-off line circles again at high levels of unemployment and inflation. This third loop appears to be at roughly the same place as the second one. In 1982 the line continued to move rightward and downward, as the Reagan administration sought to restrain inflation with ever higher rates of unemployment.

We characterize the behavior of this "trade-off" line since the mid-1960s as *spiraling stagflation*. As the U.S. economy moved from the boom period through the first two phases of the crisis, *the rate of inflation at any given rate of unemployment became successively higher*.

This increasingly adverse trade-off generated sharp and contradictory pressures on government policy during the 1970s. On the one hand, economic decision makers felt growing pressure to restrain inflation with restrictive macroeconomic policies—well before the unemployment rate had time to come down to previously "acceptable" levels. (Indeed, government officials found it congenial to justify the contractionary policies of the Great Repression as an essential part of the battle to "Whip Inflation Now.")[39] On the other hand, when the brakes were applied and unemployment rates climbed, they faced mounting popular demands to restimulate the economy—well before inflationary pressures were sufficiently restrained to restore "tolerably" stable prices.

Economic Stagnation + Political Stalemate = Inflation

How can we explain the puzzling phenomenon of rising inflation in a period of stagnation? A variety of different explanations have been offered by mainstream economists, from Keynesian to monetarist. For reasons that we detail in Appendix B, we do not find their theories persuasive.

We believe that our analysis of the postwar corporate system and its erosion points toward a more convincing analysis of stagflation. The circumstantial evidence in Figure 5.1 supports us, since the shifts in the spiraling relationship between unemployment and inflation correspond almost exactly to our dating of the phases of the crisis. But this is an insufficient argument. In order to provide a meaningful account of rising inflation at given levels of unemployment, we need to outline an alternative explanation of the determinants of inflation itself.

We think that the kernel of a useful analysis is contained in the traditional wisdom that inflation results when "too much money chases too few goods." That notion has been rejected by many economists because the traditional perspective focused almost exclusively on the "too-much-money" side of the implicit equation. But an alternative and more promising account can begin with "too few goods."

The erosion of the postwar corporate system, later amplified by capital's counteroffensive, led to slowdowns in the availability of goods. We argued in Chapter 2 that "hourly income" provides a useful measure of people's average standard of economic well-being. According to Figure 2.3, the growth of hourly income declined through successive stages of the postwar period from 2.9 percent in 1948–66 to 2 percent in 1966–73 to .6 percent in 1973–79 and to .3 percent in 1979–82.

This tendency toward "too few goods" would not have resulted in rising inflation *if* the U.S. political system had managed to induce corresponding downward adjustments in various groups' claims on hourly income. But the political system achieved nothing of the sort. At least until the late 1970s, none of the contestants had the power to reduce decisively the effective claims of any others. The deterioration of social relations after 1966 led to *escalating* conflict over the division of a more and more slowly growing economic pie. The relations of domination and subordination built into the postwar system amplified these conflicts. At the same time that the ability of the U.S. economy to satisfy real-income claims was diminishing, the competing claims pressed upon the economy by rival claimants—capitalists, workers, retirees, and so forth—were growing.

These observations suggest a more formal model of inflation.[40] A growing gap between claims and resources generates inflationary pressures *if* the political-economic environment cannot restrain competing claimants from pressing their claims in money terms—with higher prices, higher negotiated wages, and higher government benefits. If there are too few goods *and* if there is no political force which can impose limits on the amount of money with which various groups chase those goods, then inflation necessarily results.

A simple formulation summarizes the logic of this model. Two factors are necessary to produce rising inflation rates: economic stagnation and political stalemate. When stalemate does *not* exist, crisis and unemployment are likely to wring inflationary pressures out of the system. When stalemate does exist, this process cannot proceed so quickly or so automatically. Thus the equation heading this section: economic stagnation + political stalemate = inflation.

Stagflation, from this perspective, is to economic conflict what war is to geopolitical conflict. Stagflation, like war, arises when the respective actors are not able to forge a cooperative solution to their conflicts of interest *and* where neither has such unrivaled and unquestioned capacity to impose its will on the other that resistance is pointless or totally ineffective.

This economic logic is relatively straightforward. Its political implications are resonant. In the contentious U.S. political and economic climate of the 1970s, there was no possibility of a cooperative accommodation among rival claimants, no prospect of an agreement to share in the austerity implied by the slowdown in hourly income growth. Nor could the inflationary conflict be resolved by a quick and decisive victory for capital—as hard as the corporations tried. Other groups had developed sufficient power to resist major cutbacks in their economic welfare and capital's most potent weapon—unemployment—had become less effective in disciplining labor. As a result, inflationary pressures continued to grow as hourly income slowed, and the trade-off between inflation and unemployment continued to deteriorate throughout the 1970s.

It is true that the inflationary pressures generated through this process in the late 1960s and 1970s could have been restrained by a monetary policy that steadfastly refused to provide the growing supply of money needed to finance economic transactions at ever higher prices. This is the consummate cold bath, the ultimate monetarist weapon. And it was finally employed after 1979.

But during the 1970s the same pressures that generated the inflationary spiral in the first place—the insistent competing income claims of rival groups—prevented the Federal Reserve Board from clamping down on rising money incomes and prices. A persistent policy of nonaccommodation would have required a sharp and continuing contraction, precipitating even sharper long-term declines in capacity utilization and even steeper increases in unemployment than actually occurred. This would have strangled both profits and wages. During the 1970s, neither corporations nor the public were prepared to accept such a solution.

These inclinations changed after 1979. Corporations and the government shifted into overdrive, intensifying their attacks on worker and citizen power.

This intensification was signaled most clearly by the dramatic October 1979 announcement by Paul Volcker, the new chair of the Federal Reserve Board, that monetary policy would become much tighter. It was witnessed at the same time by a sharp increase in the size of the federal government's full-employment budget surplus. It also featured the beginning of remilitarization in 1978–79. Corporations poured millions into the elections of 1980, helping foster the conservative ascendancy. By 1981, business forces were launching blitzkrieg attacks throughout the political economy—gaining lucrative tax breaks from government, trimming social spending, covering the landscape with corporate propaganda in defense of the "free-enterprise system."

We will examine in Part II both the theory and the practice of conservative economics in the 1980s. Pending that appraisal, it seems obvious that business was able after 1979 to break the political stalemate of the 1970s, transforming trench warfare into blitzkrieg advances. This leads us to treat the years from 1979 to the present as a third phase of economic decline. We call it the period of "business ascendancy." We present in Figure 5.2 a capsule account of the major characteristics of the boom period and the three phases of economic decline. This periodization of economic decline provides a crucial guide to our analysis in the following chapter of the productivity slowdown.

The Strategic Options: Attack Stagnation, or Stalemate

We have argued in this chapter that spiraling stagflation resulted from the erosion of the postwar corporate system and capital's counterproductive effort to restore its predominance. The

Fig. 5.2

Phases of Postwar Boom and Decline

Phase	Economic Developments	Political Developments
Boom: 1948-1966	rising rate of profit rapid productivity growth low & stable inflation low & falling unemployment high levels of investment rising real wages	capital-labor accord Bretton Woods system U.S. international domination of 3rd World capital-citizen accord
Decline I: 1967-1973	falling rate of profit productivity slowdown accelerating inflation low, then rising unemployment high levels of investment slowing of wage growth	erosion of capital-labor accord U.S. loss in Vietnam demise of Bretton Woods OPEC emerges rise of citizen movements
Decline II: 1974-1979	low profit rates sharper productivity slowdown runaway inflation rising unemployment stagnating investment falling real wages	political stalemate Great Repression international instability
Decline III: 1980-present	low profit rates further productivity slowdown slowing of runaway inflation highest unemployment since '30s declining investment sharp decreases in real wages	business ascendancy remilitarization international debt problems

corporate offensive of the 1970s failed to revive the economy on capitalist terms because it confronted a political stalemate. As a result, the initial tendencies toward stagnation and inflation that arose in the late 1960s were exacerbated during the 1970s.

One can draw different political lessons from this analysis. Many conservatives obviously concluded that they should mobilize the political power needed to break the stalemate, mounting a much harsher offensive against every popular group that has refused to accept the burden of microeconomic and macroeconomic adjustment to stagflation. This has been the abiding political principle during the current period of "business ascendancy."

But if one rejects the conservative conclusions—either because one supports the victims of those conservative assaults or because one fears that such assaults will produce a tempest of political instability and rebellion—there is an alternative lesson. Rather than attacking stalemate by assaulting popular movements, why not attack stagnation instead? And in so doing, why not work toward an economic restructuring which helps harmonize the interests of the vast majority of U.S. workers and citizens with the requirements of economic recovery and growth?

The conventional wisdom replies insistently that this is impossible; workers and consumers must sacrifice before renewed growth is feasible. This conventional wisdom, as we have already suggested, relies on the capital-shortage analysis of economic decline. We disagree with that analysis for a variety of reasons which we have already introduced in Chapter 3. Our analysis of the rise and demise of the postwar corporate system reinforces this disagreement, for it provides the basis for a powerful alternative explanation of the main sources of economic decline. We argue that the high and rising costs of corporate power explain the slowdown of productivity growth in the U.S. economy since the mid-1960s. We turn in the next chapter to a detailed quantitative analysis which supports our view and helps confirm the power of our institutional account of stagflation. Breaking out of the stagflation stranglehold does not require suppression of popular needs and interests. Doing something about the costs of corporate power is a much more promising alternative.

6

SOLVING THE PRODUCTIVITY PUZZLE

It's dog eat dog between hourly workers and salaried employees. If management had its way, we would all be robots tomorrow. Just like that.

—Milwaukee factory worker[1]

After ten years of continuing immersion in the whole productivity analysis and debate, what comes through loud and clear is that there are some things that are common to all circumstances of high levels of performance. . . . These are matters of the heart and mind and not of hardware and capital.

—Jeffrey J. Hallett, executive of Yankelovich, Skelly and White, polling firm[2]

Stagnation has tightened its grip on the U.S. economy. As factories have closed their doors and investors have taken a nap, the casualties of the Great Repression have mounted steadily.

Most analysts agree that the productivity slowdown is central to the deteriorating performance of the U.S. economy. Slower growth in productivity has resulted in slower growth of hourly income—in what we get for the time we work. This not only explains why people have worked more and earned less since the mid-1960s. It also helps explain spiraling stagflation: it is the source of the "too few goods" which people have been chasing with "too much money."

There is little doubt that productivity growth has declined substantially over the years of economic deterioration. *Productivity* is the term used by economists and statisticians to refer to the amount of real output produced per hour of labor employed. As we have already seen in Chapter 2, U.S. private-business productivity grew at an annual rate of 3.2 percent from 1948 to 1966, then at 2.3 percent from 1966 to 1973, .8 percent from 1973 to 1979, and only .4 percent from 1979 to 1981.*

There is much greater doubt about the causes of this dramatic slowdown in productivity growth. Mainstream economists typically describe it as a "puzzle." As stagnation has continued, the economics profession has enjoyed a minor countercyclical boom; research scholars and dollars have mounted a massive search for clues to this crucial economic mystery.

By their own admission, mainstream economists have not yet solved the puzzle. William Brainard and George Perry, coeditors of the influential *Brookings Papers on Economic Activity*, summarized the state of the art in 1981:

The slowdown in productivity growth during the 1970's has added to the problems of the decade by eroding real income growth and adding to inflation. Despite numerous studies of the slowdown its causes have remained largely a mystery. In the most comprehensive study to date, Edward Denison examined seventeen alternative hypotheses and concluded that alone or in combination they could explain no more than a fraction of the slowdown.[3]

We are prepared to play Sherlock Holmes to their Dr. Watson. Our analysis of the rise and demise of the postwar corporate system provides the clues necessary to solve the productivity puzzle. We have attributed economic decline in the United States to the erosion of the institutions which had buttressed the power of capital and to the costly corporate counteroffensive aiming to restore corporate power and privilege. We show in this chapter that a

---

* As we have shown in Chapter 2, this productivity slowdown cannot be dismissed as a purely statistical artifact. But it is crucial to note here that productivity statistics do not measure what we often think of as productivity, which is something like what you get out of production for what you put into it. The standard U.S. productivity measures cannot distinguish between work efficiency and work effort. If workers should decide—or, more likely, be forced—to work twice as hard per hour, and if total output increased by 10 percent as a result, this would be labeled an "increase in productivity." It would be just as accurate to call it a decrease in the ratio of output to worker effort. The problem is not one of measurement, but one of labeling: an increase in measured "productivity" may reflect either an improvement in efficiency, a benign outcome, or a speed-up in production which cuts corners with workers' welfare and safety, a much less benign development. We would prefer a more neutral and accurate term, such as *hourly output*, but we will continue to use *productivity* because of its widespread usage.

quantitative analysis based on this institutional account provides a compelling explanation of the slowdown in productivity growth since the mid-1960s. The costs of corporate power provide the key to cracking the case.

A SOCIAL MODEL OF PRODUCTIVITY

The mainstream economists' inability to solve the productivity puzzle reflects a failure of vision, not of technique. Mainstream economists have traditionally viewed production as an obscure but well-oiled mechanical process best understood by engineers. Given existing technical knowledge, inputs such as labor and machines are translated with mechanical regularity into outputs such as cars and computers. With a meat-grinder model of the economy, all you have to do is figure out how much you put into one end and you'll know how much to expect out the other. Whatever the merits of this vision of production, it provides little help when the expected amount of output *fails* to materialize.

And this has been the problem with mainstream studies of the productivity slowdown. Applying their technical model of production, they have sought to explain variations in productivity growth—the growth of real output per hour of labor employed —in terms of such variables as (1) the capital stock available per hour of labor employed; (2) the availability of other resources, such as energy, per hour of labor employed; (3) the average age, education, or experience of the labor force, presumed to reflect the average "quality" of each hour of labor employed; (4) the rate of utilization of the available resources; and (5) the level of research and development expenditures, presumed to affect growth in the amount of output obtained per unit of all inputs into the production process. But it is precisely these variables which, as Brainard and Perry admit, "explain no more than a fraction of the slowdown."

We have never doubted that productivity would increase if there were an increase in the availability of capital goods and other inputs per hour of work, or if the available inputs were more fully utilized, or if there were improvements in skills and advances in technology. But we began our analysis of the productivity puzzle convinced that these kinds of factors get at only *part* of what determines productivity growth. We suspected that the key to the mystery lay in understanding how the people in the production process—workers, managers, and others—affect productivity independently of the mechanical or technological environment in which they work. We had been impressed by accounts of rapid increases in productivity during wartime and as a result of experimental changes in work organization. Harvard economist Harvey Leibenstein had attributed these surprising increases in productivity to "X-efficiency," thus naming the phenomenon but hardly explaining it.[4]

We therefore sought a *social model of productivity*. We wanted to understand economic actors not as cogs in a machine but as people with aspirations and inhibitions, with needs and resentments, with determined and possibly determinant reactions to inequality and hierarchy. And we sought to understand these economic actors in a particular social context, not in a vacuum; we wanted especially to understand the impact on productivity of the rise and demise of the postwar corporate system, with its specific relations of domination and subordination, of power and privilege.

Our initial problem, of course, lay in the difficulty of measuring the human and institutional dimensions of the production process; there were no available measures which could be applied to an analysis of productivity growth in the entire economy. And without such measures, we were unable to convert our hunches about productivity into propositions capable of being tested against the facts and compared with alternative explanations. This problem has plagued even those mainstream analysts who have been aware of the importance of these social factors. C. Jackson Grayson, a leading figure in business and scholarly discussions of productivity, recently admitted that "these intangibles are most often omitted from models, policies and managerial decisions, even though collectively they have a larger impact [than technical factors such as capital intensity]. As these other factors have increased in importance, their omission partly explains why our economic policies and forecasts have become increasingly inaccurate, and why our productivity slowdown has been so 'puzzling' to many."[5]

We have been able over the past two years—with notable help from other economists and labor-relations specialists—to begin surmounting this measurement problem. We have been able to focus much more clearly on three of the social determinants of productivity growth and decline typically ignored by mainstream economists. They are *work intensity, innovative pressure on business,* and *popular resistance to corporate domination.* All three reflect the values, struggles, and behavior of real people within real institutions. Through these three factors, we can see the real impact of the postwar corporate system on the productivity of the U.S. economy.

1. Corporate Control and Work Intensity

If a man works sixty minutes an hour, that's full productivity. That's how I measure it.

—Joseph Godfrey, former head, General
Motors Assembly Division (GMAD)[6]

[GMAD management] got all the technological improvements. . . . But one thing went wrong. . . . We've been telling them since we've been here: We have a say in how hard we're going to work. They didn't believe us.

—Worker at Lordstown Vega plant[7]

Mainstream economists recognize that an hour of work performed by a more skilled or experienced worker is likely to be more productive than an hour of work performed by someone less skilled or experienced. But they almost always ignore something which is transparent to workers and corporations: an hour of work can be performed with widely varying degrees of intensity as well as skill.

The intensity with which a worker does his or her work depends upon a complex array of motivational factors. A firm may be paying a worker for "an hour's labor," but it may receive vastly differing amounts of actual labor activity in return. These variations in labor intensity, therefore, could potentially explain major swings in actual output produced per hour of labor employed.

These ideas have been most actively pursued in recent writings on the labor process which build upon the Marxian tradition.[8] This literature has emphasized Marx's own crucial insight: When an employer hires a worker, the terms of that employment do not normally establish the amount of work that will actually be done. This indeterminacy of labor intensity becomes the focus of conflict and struggle between employer and employee. Harry Braverman, the late publisher of *Monthly Review* and a former craft worker, has captured this logic in his now classic book *Labor and Monopoly Capital:*

. . . what the worker sells, and what the capitalist buys, is *not* an agreed amount of labor, but the power to labor over an agreed period of time. . . . *The labor process has become the responsibility of the capitalist.* In this setting of antagonistic relations of production, the problem of realizing the "full usefulness" of the labor power he has bought becomes exacerbated by the opposing interests of those for whose purposes the labor process is carried on, and those who, on the other side, carry it on.[9]

In any modern society, whether capitalist or not, there are bound to be differences between the interests of managers and the interests of workers. But the problem is particularly acute when workers have little or no control over the production process and when they are clearly separated from management by layers of hierarchical authority and by significant differentials in income and social status. The greater the degree of class differentiation in society, in short, the greater is the potential for worker-management conflict at the workplace.

This much has been clear throughout the history of capitalist economies since at least the Industrial Revolution. Two centuries of conflict over the length of the working day, the right to organize unions, the intensity of automation, and endless other issues bear witness to the fundamental stakes involved in this continuing tug-of-war between management and labor.

But much has also changed in advanced capitalist societies. The conflicts between corporations and their employees have become much more institutionalized. On one side, workers have sought to protect their interests by formally (and informally) limiting corporate leverage over the labor process. Through union and informal work organization, they have opposed job reorganization and technological innovation when and where such changes have threatened their income, their job security, or the quality of their lives on the job.

Managers, in turn, have typically responded by establishing institutional structures of control within the firm which have aimed to overcome worker resistance and to promote ever greater effort on the job. More and more, these institutional structures have depended on a cadre of controllers who are differentiated from the actual producers in the firm. This army of supervisory personnel closely monitors worker performance so that effort can be rewarded—by promotion or pay incentives—and resistance can be penalized—by lower pay, denial of promotion, or firing.

These institutional transformations have not eliminated worker-management conflict, of course; they have simply modified its social content. Employer strategies used to be much more direct, much harsher. Some of the rough edges have been smoothed, but the problems of inducing worker effort have in many ways grown more difficult and complex. Where once there were single foremen in small factories, now there are billions spent on the salaries of supervisory personnel. And those costs are built into the prices of the goods produced. The corporate ledgers now record, in copious black ink, the critical importance of the corporate effort to control its labor force.

How much does work intensity vary? And how much has this variation affected the postwar performance of the U.S. economy?

Direct evidence would require actual measurements of the amount of effort expended by production workers in an average hour of employment. But there is no such direct evidence available; we have not been able to attach ergometers to a representative sample of U.S. workers. We must turn, instead, to indirect evidence on work intensity. If we can identify some factors which common sense tells us are most likely to affect the intensity of worker effort, we can then use evidence on trends in these factors as proxies for trends in the degree of work intensity itself.

What, then, determines the intensity with which production workers work? This will depend both on the *strength of the*

SOLVING THE PRODUCTIVITY PUZZLE

workers' own motivation to work and on the *effectiveness of management's control over their employees.*

- The more satisfaction a worker draws from his or her job, the stronger the motivation to work intensively. We would therefore expect work intensity to depend upon such elements of work satisfaction as its material reward and the quality of the working experience. We have assembled evidence in Figure 6.1

Fig. 6.1
Workers' Motivation to Work

Index	1948	1966	1973	1979
1. Real Spendable Hourly Earnings (in $1977)	$2.77	4.00	4.29	3.94
2. Work Safety (1948 = 100)	100	116	65	42
3. Job Satisfaction (% workers satisfied)	69%	71	68	59

Source: Hourly earnings, see Fig. 2.2(a); index of work safety: inverse of industrial accident rate, Michele I. Naples and David M. Gordon, "The Industrial Accident Rate: Creating a Consistent Time Series," Technical Note, Economics Institute of the Center for Democratic Alternatives, 1981; Job satisfaction, based on data reported in M.H. Cooper et al., "Early Warning Signals...," Business, Jan.-Feb. 1980

on three variables related to workers' motivation.* The *real spendable hourly earnings* of a typical production worker measures the material reward to the worker. To approximate conditions on the job, we use a measure of *work safety,* the inverse of the industrial accident rate. We glean further evidence on *job satisfaction* from the responses of workers to a question asked by the Opinion Research Corporation at different points during the postwar period; we report the percentage of hourly employees who answered the question "How do you like your job—the kind of work you do?" by saying either "Very much" or "A good deal."

- The effectiveness of management control over workers depends upon management's ability to monitor worker perfor-

* All of the evidence we present in the rest of this chapter is for the period 1948–79, spanning the boom and the first two phases of the crisis; data were not fully available for more recent years.

mance, and on the cost to the worker of being caught shirking
or otherwise resisting management control. Management's
ability to maintain control will also vary (inversely) with
workers' ability to organize resistance to that control. We have
compiled evidence in Figure 6.2 on three variables reflecting

Fig. 6.2
The Effectiveness of Management Control

Index	1948	1966	1973	1979
1. Intensity of Supervision (%)	13.7%	20.0	20.8	22.4
2. Cost of Losing Your Job (No. of weeks' pay lost)	9.8	8.6	7.4	7.0
3. Index of inequality (1948 = 100)	100	167	157	149

Source: Rate of Supervision: ratio of non-production to production employees, Employment and
Training Report of the President, 1981, C-2; cost of losing your job, see Fig. 4.5; index
of inequality, see Fig. 4.4

these aspects of management control. We measure managers'
ability to monitor workers by the *rate of supervision*—the ratio
of supervisors to production workers—in the nonagricultural
labor force. The cost to the worker of resisting management
authority will vary with the *cost of losing your job,* the variable we introduced in Chapter 4 to measure employer leverage over workers. As a proxy for an important factor limiting
workers' ability to organize resistance to management control,
we present the index of *divisions among workers* that was also
introduced in Chapter 4. This index measures the extent of
income inequalities among white male, black male, and female
workers: the greater such inequalities, the more divided and
internally disunified the labor force is likely to be.[10]
In Figures 6.1 and 6.2, a higher number along any row is conducive to greater work intensity than a lower number: either
there is greater worker motivation (Figure 6.1) or there is more
effective management control (Figure 6.2).
Looking first at the evidence on workers' motivation, each of
the variables in Figure 6.1 increased during the boom period

from 1948 to 1966, suggesting a close connection between sustained productivity growth and workers' incentives on the job. From 1966 to 1973, however, workers' real earnings continued to increase, but at a much slower rate, while our indices of work safety and overall job satisfaction both declined. From 1973 to 1979, all three variables showed significant declines, victims of the Great Repression.

The boom years also appear to have enhanced management's ability to control workers. According to Figure 6.2, both the rate of supervision and our index of divisions among workers increased significantly from 1948 to 1966, while the cost of losing one's job declined only slightly. After 1966, by contrast, the rise in the intensity of supervision slowed substantially while the cost of job loss and divisions among workers both declined significantly. We infer that management's leverage over employees diminished in the late 1960s; the lower the cost of losing one's job and the more muted the divisions among workers, other things being equal, the lower management's ability to extract additional work effort from their employees. During the second phase of the crisis, management recovered slightly: the rate of supervision increased more rapidly again and the other two variables declined somewhat more slowly than they had during the first phase. Figure 6.2 suggests on the whole that management lost substantial leverage after 1966, as compared with the boom period, and regained some (but far from all) of that lost ground during the years of the cold-bath treatment.

This evidence provides substantial statistical support for our institutional account in Chapters 4 and 5. It suggests, in particular, that the erosion of the capital-labor accord—one of the three principal buttresses of the postwar corporate system—undercut workers' motivation and management control during the first phase of the crisis.

The corporate counteroffensive after 1973 was aimed in part at restoring the earlier workplace environment. But it encountered the considerable contradictions of a full-scale assault on employees in the modern workplace. For while the corporations regained some of their ability to control workers, they further undermined workers' motivation. And the success of business in limiting wage gains had the unwanted effect of further reducing the cost to the worker of losing his or her job. Perhaps most disturbing to business, as we shall see, whatever gains were made against labor on the workplace front were paid for many times over in the sluggish product demand and underutilized industrial capacity which inevitably accompanied the engineered upsurge in unemployment. The Great Repression turned out to be a blunt instrument for promoting greater work intensity.

These indicators provide only circumstantial evidence, of course. But the general timing of the movements in our indices is at least consistent with the pattern of productivity growth and decline. Our view of workplace relations thus passes the first simple test of consistency which was flunked by so many of the proposed explanations of economic crisis reviewed in Chapter 3. Both on theoretical and on these circumstantial empirical grounds, it seems likely that changes in work intensity can help us solve the productivity puzzle. And this is exactly what our more systematic quantitative analysis—reported in the second part of this chapter —appears to confirm.

2. Competitive Pressure and Business Innovation

In today's world of increased international trade, . . . the entire economy may be penalized by poor management. . . . U.S. company executives' decisions about strategic resource allocations are therefore crucial determinants of the nation's long-term economic success.

—Ira C. Magaziner and Robert B. Reich,
Minding America's Business, 1982[11]

According to most mainstream economists, competitive pressures will unfailingly push businesses to pursue cost reducing innovations in technique and the organization of production. These pressures can hardly be denied. But there are other pressures as well. Short-run cash flows may be coveted by management on the make; longer-term investments may be overlooked by decision makers who move from firm to firm every few years. The high-risk, high-payoff project may be passed over for the sure thing by executives who correctly understand that sins of omission often go undetected or unpunished, while sins of commission may result in boardroom purges. If the big money is to be made in speculation and financial dealing rather than in breakthroughs in production, the executive may increasingly profess disinterest and reveal ignorance about the actual process of production.

Joseph Schumpeter, the Austrian finance minister and Harvard economist of the first half of this century, recognized that there are periodic waves of corporate innovation and explosive entrepreneurial energy.[12] These waves begin to roll after periods of depression, when firms must struggle to find a new basis for production and restored profitability. They crest during the long booms which follow, buoyed by the optimism and long time horizons which prosperity creates and sustains. As long as prospects seem stable and promising, firms are likely to pursue and apply longer-term innovations which improve the efficiency of their operations and, consequently, their workers' productivity.

This process is two-sided, however. Waves of innovation, Schumpeter argued, are accompanied by "gales of creative destruction." Those firms which are least able to purchase or apply the most important innovations fall victim to a Darwinian vengeance, drowned in the waves of competitive pressure. The race belongs to the strongest and the swiftest. When innovative activity spreads rapidly, the pace of the competitive race intensifies. The least productive firms die. And the average productivity of the entire economy increases simply because its least efficient units have stopped producing.

These observations suggest that productivity growth may be significantly affected by changes in the innovative activity of business—by the extent to which businesses seek to introduce new innovations and improve productive effectiveness. But it is as difficult to obtain direct measures of such business efforts as it is directly to measure work intensity. We have not been able to acquire taped records of corporate planning discussions or to chart the rate at which new ideas come clicking out of corporate research labs.

Following Schumpeter's clues about creative destruction, however, we can generate an indirect measure of the extent to which business engages in innovative activity. Since waves of innovation tend to knock out firms that cannot stand the competitive pressure, we should expect the rate at which businesses fail to be pos-itively related to the extent to which successful businesses are pursuing innovative ideas. The greater the rate of business failure, moreover, the greater the rate at which relatively high-cost firms are being displaced by relatively low-cost ones. For both these reasons, we would expect a higher *rate of business failure* to lead to greater average innovative activity and elimination of back-ward firms, and consequently to higher levels of productivity.

Figure 6.3 charts the annual rate of business failures from 1948

Fig. 6.3

Business Failures

rate of business failures per 1,000 listed enterprises

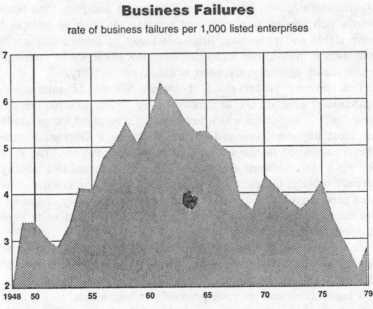

Source: Economic Report of the President, 1982, B-93

to 1979. Schumpeter's scenario appears to be fully confirmed. The rising rate of business failures from the late 1940s to the early 1960s bears graphic witness to the gales of creative destruc-tion unleashed by the postwar boom and the power and privilege enjoyed by U.S. corporations. The failure rate was at its highest in the latter part of the boom, exceeding .5 percent in every year from 1957 to 1966, and then it fell more or less steadily throughout the first two phases of the crisis. This suggests that business innovative activity declined significantly precisely during the period when productivity growth also slowed. The decline in the business failure rate after the mid-1960s is especially striking because—if anything—one would have expected increasing numbers of failures as the U.S. economy entered into a period of deepening stagflation. (Only in 1979 did the failure rate begin to rise again, as the third and deepest phase of the crisis took its toll.)

This somewhat surprising behavior of the business-failure rate helps reinforce some of the insights we drew from our institutional account of the rise and demise of the postwar corporate system. When prospects were bright and profits were booming, innovative activity appears to have increased substantially; more advanced firms raced ahead while more backward firms were pushed out of the race. As investors' evaluation of profit prospects dimmed, however (see the data on profit expectations in Figure 4.7), innovation lagged and the failure rate began to fall. This resulted in reduced pressure on corporations to adopt and apply available technical innovations, presumably contributing to the productivity slowdown. This suggests a further consequence of the Great Repression designed to quell worker resistance: it not only dampened productive investment and reduced capacity utilization, but it also moderated pressure on corporations to sustain their pace of productive innovation. Our suspicions about the effect of the failure rate on productivity growth, once again, are supported by the more systematic quantitative analysis reported below.

3. Popular Resistance to Corporate Domination

You may own the coal, but you don't own me, and I'm going to leave it in the ground.
           —Charlie King, song about 1977 mineworkers' strike[13]

The point I am trying to make is that . . . conditions are getting better, not worse . . . and that the real danger is *not* from the

free-enterprise Establishment that has made ours the most prosperous, most powerful and most charitable nation on earth. No,
the danger today resides in the Disaster Lobby—those crepe-
hangers who, for personal gain or out of sheer ignorance, are
undermining the American system and threatening the lives and
fortunes of the American people. Some people have let the
gloom-mongers scare them beyond rational response. . . .
                    —Thomas R. Shepard, Jr., former publisher of *Look*[14]

Our analysis of the rise and demise of the postwar corporate
system identified three principal elements of erosion—not only
rising capital-labor conflict but also declining international domination and spreading popular resistance to the reign of profitability. We have already considered the impact upon productivity of
deteriorating labor-management relations. Is it possible that declining international influence and rising popular rebellion could
also have affected the slowdown in productivity growth? A social
model of productivity should surely examine these dimensions as
well.

The decline in U.S. international domination after the mid-
1960s led to a deterioration of the terms on which the U.S. economy could acquire goods and services from abroad. This is most
clearly reflected in the U.S. terms of trade—the ratio of U.S. export prices to U.S. import prices—which fell dramatically from
1968 to 1979 after improving steadily since the early 1950s (see
Figure 4.3). Such a decline in the terms of trade can have a direct impact on the growth of productivity. Various imported inputs—imported oil is the most obvious example—become relatively more expensive. Businesses will try to use less of these
inputs and more of others in production. And this will mean that
the productiveness of *other* inputs—particularly of machines and
labor—is likely to be reduced in the short run. Corporations may
eventually adjust their operations to these higher import prices,
but this adjustment process is bound to take time. In the meantime, productivity growth will suffer.

Popular resistance to corporate power in the United States can
have a similar impact. Demands for greater worker safety and
health, for better consumer protection, for a pollution-free environment, for less disruption of communities, all create pressure to

use inputs in ways that do not necessarily lead to greater measured output. There are real social gains when, for example, mining companies are required to build safer mines and steel companies must install pollution-control devices. But—as the companies themselves are always quick to point out—these measures can also result in less ore mined and less steel produced per worker-hour. When citizens are successful in challenging the logic of profitability, in short, productivity growth as officially measured may begin to decline.

There is no obvious comprehensive measure of the impact of such popular rebellion. We have been able to develop one very partial measure, however, which captures some of the effects of both declining international domination and spreading popular resistance. This is an index of the *relative cost of nonagricultural crude materials,* which we calculate by dividing an index of the prices of fuels and other crude materials (excluding foodstuffs and feedstuffs) by an overall price index. This measures the costs of nature-based inputs—such as fuels, coal, other minerals, and wood products—relative to the costs of all other products in the domestic economy. This index is likely to rise *both* when the costs of imported inputs go up and when firms are obliged to deal with the social and environmental consequences of their production. It therefore captures some of the consequences for the U.S. economy of both resistance to U.S. domination abroad and resistance to the logic of profitability at home. When one or the other dimension of resistance increases, the relative cost of nonagricultural crude materials is likely to rise.

Figure 6.4 charts this index from 1948 to 1979. The substantial decline in the relative cost of nonagricultural crude materials from the late 1940s to the mid-1960s reflects the strength of the postwar corporate system during the boom years. The sharp upturn in the late 1960s and the 1970s, in contrast, reflects at least in part the growing capacity of foreigners and U.S. citizens to resist corporate domination. However imperfect this measure, it nonetheless seems likely both to reflect these two dimensions of institutional erosion *and* to provide an approximate indicator of their effects on productivity. The more rapid the increase in the relative cost of these crude inputs, the more intense the distorting

Fig. 6.4
Raw Materials Costs
ratio of nonagricultural crude materials price index to GDP price deflator

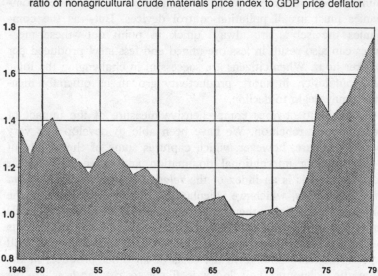

Source: U.S. Bureau of Labor Statistics disaggregated price data and NIPA Table 7.4.

effects on the efficiency of production in the United States. As
Figure 6.4 shows, indeed, these rising costs coincided with the
years when growth of measured productivity in the U.S. economy
slowed to a snail's pace.

THE COSTS-OF-CORPORATE-POWER EXPLANATION OF THE PRODUCTIVITY SLOWDOWN

We have argued that a social model of productivity can potentially provide the missing clues for solving the puzzle of declining
productivity growth. And we have also seen, in Figures 6.1
through 6.4, that our measures of some social determinants of
productivity show a strikingly consistent pattern of behavior over

the postwar period. Their movement was highly conducive to productivity growth from 1948 to 1966 and quite unfavorable thereafter.

This evidence is suggestive but not conclusive. A stronger quantitative case requires attention to three further concerns. First, we must consider the possibility that the direction of causality runs in the opposite direction from what we are inferring; that the productivity slowdown results in adverse changes in the social dimensions of production, rather than the other way around. Second, we must consider the possible effects on productivity of variables other than those on which we have focused our attention. Third, we must allow for the simultaneous impact of all relevant variables, rather than examining each of them in isolation from the others as we have done up to this point.

We address the issue of reverse causality in Appendix C, which is devoted to a technical exposition of our social model of productivity. In the remainder of this chapter we first consider other possible explanatory variables and then present our own systematic statistical analysis of the multiple determinants of productivity growth.

Other Explanatory Variables

We noted at the beginning of this chapter that mainstream economists emphasize five variables in their studies of productivity which we have thus far ignored. How much help might these variables provide in explaining the productivity slowdown?

By far the most prominent variable in conventional analyses of productivity growth is the capital intensity of production—the *capital stock per hour of labor employed*. We considered this variable in the course of our analysis of the capital-shortage theory in Chapter 3. According to the evidence presented in Figure 3.7, nonfarm private capital stock per hour actually grew more rapidly from 1966 to 1973 than it did from 1948 to 1966, providing no help in explaining the productivity slowdown during the first phase of the crisis. The growth of capital intensity did slow considerably after 1973, however, and it may well have played a significant causal role in the second phase of slowdown. We will consider this possibility more carefully in our more formal statistical analysis.

A second prominent variable in the mainstream economists' tool kit is the *availability of energy* for use in the production process. This factor we also considered in Chapter 3 in evaluating the blame-OPEC theory of the economic crisis. There we noted that any possible shortage of energy inputs could not have caused problems until 1973, when the jump in oil prices first set off efforts to reduce energy use in the United States. But after 1973 there is a more plausible case to be made that energy scarcity may have contributed to the continuing slowdown in productivity growth. Most mainstream economists themselves do not give much weight to this effect, however. Macroeconomist William Nordhaus, summarizing the results of many studies in a table of "Best Guess Sources of Productivity Decline," attributes to energy only .2 points out of a total slowdown of 2.5 percentage points in productivity growth from 1948–65 to 1973–79.[15]

The *average "quality" of labor* is notoriously difficult to measure, and mainstream economists have come up with a variety of different indicators to try to capture its movement over time. Some have used the average educational attainment of the labor force; others have worked with the age-sex composition of the labor force, relying on the dubious assumption that differences in earnings among different types of workers reflect the relevant differences in quality. Even if we take such estimates at their face value, the results show that the average educational and demographic characteristics of the U.S. labor force have not changed enough to explain much of the slowdown in U.S. productivity growth since 1966.[16]

It is recognized by all growth analysts that the *rate of utilization* of productive capacity affects the level of real output produced per hour of work. When utilization rates are below the levels for which factories and job assignments were designed, productive inputs cannot be fully or efficiently employed in the production process. Low utilization rates tend to discourage new capital formation and technological innovation, moreover, and hence to slow down the rate of growth of productivity. No less than mainstream economists, we would therefore expect low rates of capacity utilization to have an adverse effect on both the level and the rate of growth of productivity.

Once again, however, it is difficult to make a case that during the first phase of the crisis inadequate capacity utilization had anything to do with productivity problems. The economy was still growing rapidly, and the ratio of actual to potential GNP in the U.S. economy—the best overall measure of the rate of capacity utilization—was substantially higher during the period from 1966 to 1973 than it had been from 1948 to 1966; it was virtually as high in 1973 as it had been in 1966.[17] The picture then changed in the second phase of the crisis. Not only was the actual-to-potential GNP ratio significantly lower in 1979 than in 1973, but its average over the period as a whole was well below the average for either of the two preceding periods. The capacity-utilization rate is therefore a variable that we must take seriously as a possible contributor to the exacerbated productivity slowdown in the second phase of decline.

Many economists would urge us, finally, to consider the effect of *research and development* expenditures on U.S. productivity growth. According to Edward Denison, the most prominent mainstream analyst of sources of economic growth, total R&D expenditures in the United States increased rapidly (in real terms) during the boom period from 1948 to 1966 and then remained roughly at a plateau during the crisis periods thereafter; as a percentage of GNP they rose steadily until the mid-1960s and declined slowly from then on.[18] Just how the level or rate of R&D expenditures is related to growth in output per hour of work remains a very complex issue. At the very least, one would expect a considerable lag between actual expenditure and its translation into usable productivity-enhancing forms. Thus, if anything, the greatest benefits from postwar R&D expenditure in the U.S. economy should have been realized during the first phase of the crisis. And even by the second phase it seems unlikely that a constant level of R&D expenditure could be a significant source of decline in the rate of growth of hourly output. Indeed, Denison himself concluded that "there is no assurance that R&D spending contributed anything to the decline in productivity growth," and his conclusion has been reinforced by the results of several other studies of the question.[19]

Our consideration of the explanatory variables emphasized by mainstream economists has therefore added two main variables to the list we must consider more thoroughly: capital stock per hour of work, or "capital intensity," and the rate of capacity utilization. Growth of energy inputs also needs to be considered.

A Multivariate Regression Analysis

The final step in our statistical analysis of the productivity puzzle is to analyze simultaneously the effects of all the variables that we have hypothesized to have a causal impact on productivity growth. We must determine how much of the observed productivity slowdowns after 1966 can be explained by changes in work intensity, innovative pressure on business, and popular resistance to corporate domination, on the one hand, and how much can be explained by changes in capital intensity and the rate of capacity utilization, on the other.

There is a commonly used statistical technique that can shed light on this kind of problem. By means of "multivariate regression analysis" we can determine the degree to which changes in a variety of different "independent" variables—representing work intensity, capital intensity, and so on—are associated with movements in a single "dependent" variable—in this case productivity —which is hypothesized to be affected simultaneously by all the independent variables. The results of such a regression analysis permit us to compute how much of the change in productivity growth between any two periods of time is associated with—and in this sense can be accounted for—changes in each of the independent variables which we think likely to influence productivity.

We describe in Appendix C the details of our multivariate regression analysis of the determinants of U.S. productivity growth from 1948 to 1979. Here we will simply summarize our results with the help of figures that show the contribution of different factors to the two successive declines of productivity growth in the first and second phases of the crisis.

From 1948 to 1966, real output per production worker in the

nonfarm business sector of the U.S. economy rose at an average annual rate of 2.88 percent. Then from 1966 to 1973 this rate dropped to 2.19 percent per year—a decline of .69 percentage point.[20] How much of this decline can be attributed to the two principal variables stressed by mainstream economists?

Figure 6.5 provides the answer. The left-hand bar shows the extent of the productivity slowdown between the boom period and the first phase of the crisis. The next two bars show the effects

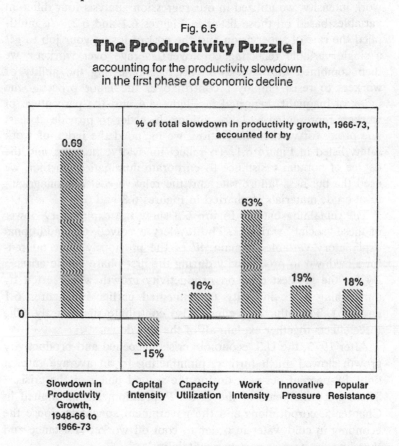

Fig. 6.5

The Productivity Puzzle I

accounting for the productivity slowdown
in the first phase of economic decline

% of total slowdown in productivity growth, 1966-73, accounted for by

0.69

63%

16%   19%   18%

−15%

| Slowdown in Productivity Growth, 1948-66 to 1966-73 | Capital Intensity | Capacity Utilization | Work Intensity | Innovative Pressure | Popular Resistance |

Source: See Appendix C; left-hand bar measured in percentage points of decline in average annual productivity growth between the two periods being compared; totals do not add to 100% due to rounding.

of changes in capital intensity and changes in capacity utilization. We note that movements in those two "technical" variables between 1966 and 1973 essentially offset each other, explaining between them only 1 percent of the .69 percentage-point decline in productivity growth. The puzzle persists. Can our social variables account for the remaining .68 percentage point of declining productivity growth?

Figure 6.5 shows that the answer is a resounding yes. To reflect work intensity, we utilized in our regression analysis four different variables based on those listed in Figures 6.1 and 6.2. We multiplied the rate of supervision and the cost of losing your job to get a single variable reflecting employer leverage over workers; we then combined this with two variables reflecting the ability of workers to resist employer control over the labor process—the index of inequality reported in Figure 4.4 and the percentage of workers represented by labor unions. In order to provide at least one proxy for worker motivation, we included the index of work safety listed in Figure 6.1. To reflect innovative pressure and the degree of popular resistance to corporate domination, further, we used the business-failure rate and the relative cost of nonagricultural crude materials as charted in Figures 6.3 and 6.4.

The remaining bars in Figure 6.5 show the explanatory power of these "social" variables. The mystery is solved. Our additional explanatory variables explain *all* of the previously unaccounted-for slowdown in productivity during the first phase of the crisis.[21] By far the greatest drag on productivity growth was exerted by diminishing work intensity (documented earlier in Figures 6.1 and 6.2). The other two effects also contribute significantly. The three effects together explain all of the slowdown.

After 1973, the U.S. economic crisis deepened and productivity growth slowed much further, plummeting to an average rate of only .88 percent per year during the second phase of the crisis.[22] These were the years of the Great Repression. As we argued in Chapter 5, corporations and the government sought to douse the economy in cold water in order to cool off worker resistance and thereby to restore corporate profitability.

Figure 6.6 summarizes the results of our multivariate analysis of the sources of slow productivity growth in 1973–79, compar-

Fig. 6.6

The Productivity Puzzle II

accounting for the productivity slowdown
in the second phase of economic decline

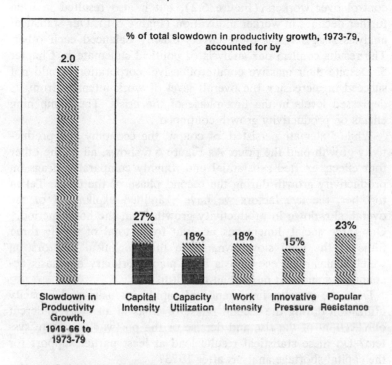

% of total slowdown in productivity growth, 1973-79,
accounted for by

2.0

27%

18%   18%

15%

23%

Slowdown in   Capital   Capacity   Work   Innovative   Popular
Productivity   Intensity   Utilization Intensity   Pressure   Resistance
Growth,
1948-66 to
1973-79

Source: See Appendix C; left-hand bar measured in percentage points of decline in
average annual productivity growth between the two periods being compared;
totals do not add to 100% due to rounding. Solid bars represent the "cold-bath"
effect.

ing it with the boom years from 1948 to 1966. Between the boom
period and the second phase of the crisis, average annual productivity growth slowed by a total of 2 percentage points—indicated
by the left-hand bar in the figure. How much of this decline can
be explained by the different variables we have considered?

Declining work intensity now accounts for 18 percent of the
drop in productivity growth; this amounts to almost exactly the
same absolute effect as in the first phase of slowdown, roughly

.4 percentage points in productivity slowdown. This reflects the contradictory impact of the Great Repression which we have already noted in our discussions of Figures 6.1 and 6.2. The cold bath did manage to reverse some of the erosion of management control over workers (Figure 6.2), but it also resulted in even further declines in worker motivation (Figure 6.1). Our statistical analysis suggests that these effects exactly balanced each other. The results confirm our analysis of political stalemate in Chapter 5. Despite their massive counteroffensive, corporations could not succeed in increasing the overall level of work intensity from its depressed levels in the first phase of the crisis. The dampening effects on productivity growth continued.

While stalemate persisted, of course, the economy and productivity growth paid the price. As Figure 6.6 shows, all of the other four effects exerted substantial and roughly comparable drags on productivity growth during the second phase of the crisis. Taken together, the five factors we have examined explain *all* of the overall slowdown in productivity growth from the boom period.* Our three social dimensions account for a total of nearly three fifths of the total slowdown, while the "technical" factors on which mainstream economists have placed primary emphasis account for somewhat more than two fifths.

Does the growing importance of capital intensity and capacity utilization during the second phase of crisis in any way undercut our account of the rise and demise of the postwar corporate system? Do these statistical results lend at least partial support for the capital-shortage analysis after 1973?

It is obvious that declining capital-intensity growth and capacity utilization had significant effects. But the story cannot stop here. We must ask *why* the growth of capital intensity and capacity utilization declined after the early 1970s. And this investigation leads us directly back to our historical narrative of the Great Repression.

The cold-bath strategy, as we have already noted, had contradictory effects. While it stalled the decline in work intensity, it also resulted in dramatically lower utilization rates and consequently diminished corporate profitability. This resulted in declin-

---

* We tested the addition of a measure of energy input growth to this model, but it did not contribute to the explanation of the slowdown.

ing investment incentives and therefore in declining growth of capital intensity. Since the political stalemate of the Great Repression lasted so long, these dampening effects on productivity growth persisted throughout the 1970s.

To support this interpretation of the sources of declining investment and utilization, we have further pursued a multivariate regression analysis of the determinants of these two variables. The logic of our complete analysis of the productivity slowdown, including the cold-bath effect, is laid out in the flow diagram of

Fig. 6.7
A Social Model of the Productivity Slowdown

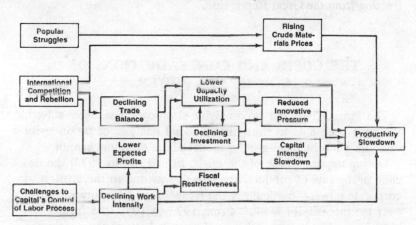

Figure 6.7. The arrows show the directions of influence highlighted by our account in Chapters 4 and 5.

Worker resistance during the first phase of the crisis, we argue, prompted increasingly restrictive fiscal policy during the second phase of decline. This fiscal drag produced lower utilization rates and sluggish investment. The arrows in Figure 6.7 pointing from declining work intensity to fiscal restrictiveness, and from there to the two other variables, capture this set of hypotheses about the Great Repression.

The additional statistical results reported in Appendix C confirm each of these hypotheses. We have been able to show that declining employer leverage over workers is associated with subsequent increases in fiscal restrictiveness. We have also found that this greater fiscal drag resulted in declining utilization and slower growth in capital intensity. We dub this rippling impact of the Great Repression the *cold-bath effect*. To show how important a role it played in the second phase of the crisis, we display its magnitude in Figure 6.6. There we have included in the bars for utilization and capital intensity our statistical estimates of the cold-bath effect, indicating its impact on declining productivity growth with solid sections on those two bars. As the sections show, the cold-bath effect accounts for more than half of the measured effects of those two variables. Corporations did not face a "capital shortage" during this period; they helped to create an economy freezing from the Great Repression.

THE COSTS AND CONTRADICTIONS OF CORPORATE POWER

The "puzzle" of the productivity slowdown has been solved. We have been able to show that a social analysis of productivity explains what the meat-grinder model of the economy cannot.

During the first phase of the crisis, from 1966 to 1973, the decline in the rate of productivity growth was due to the erosion of corporate power—particularly the weakening of corporate control over the intensity of work.[23] From 1973 to 1979, the further decline in productivity growth was the result both of the continuing erosion of the postwar corporate system and the counterproductive attempt to restore that system by means of the Great Repression. Since 1979 this corporate counterattack has been pursued with heightened political clout and with a further escalation of counterproductive effects.[24]

Our analysis points to the *costs of corporate power* as the fundamental source of the crisis in the U.S. economy. People in the United States have incurred an enormous cost as a result of our recent economic decline. Why? The economic success of the corporate system in the first two postwar decades depended upon U.S. corporate domination in its relations with U.S. workers, U.S. citizens, and the rest of the world. As resistance to that domination began to spread during the 1960s, the effectiveness of the system declined. The costs of keeping people down, which had been muted during the previous decades of relatively easy corporate domination, began to mount. By the early 1970s, the need for remedial action was obvious.

Corporate influence over public policy and priorities in the United States ruled out the possibility of a fundamental change in the system. Instead, both corporations and the government responded by seeking to restore the previous structure of corporate domination. In the case of relations with workers, they sought a cold-bath dousing of the macroeconomy. But in this and other respects, the effort to reestablish corporate domination was both very costly to the economy as a whole and incapable of achieving its objectives. History matters. The resistance that eroded the postwar corporate system could not simply be quashed by a new display of political and economic muscle. Instead, the attempt to do so compounded the problems of the economy and led to a continuing escalation of the costs of corporate power through the 1970s.

Will massive subsidies of corporate investment solve these structural problems? Could we conceivably revive our sluggish economy with little more than regressive transfers from the vast majority to the wealthy? We agree with C. Jackson Grayson of the American Productivity Center; the capital-shortage approach to solving our productivity problems misses the boat. Grayson concludes:

Any change—management, employees, unions, policies—involves a rearrangement of power, associations, skills and status. Simply more capital investment imposed on resistant individuals and systems will lead to disillusionment and continued poor results. We will not get more productivity, but political stalemates, deadwood management, featherbedding and continued adversarial labor-management government relations.[25]

But the sponsors of the postwar corporate system persist nonetheless. By the early 1980s, the costs of corporate power—the fruits of their continued counteroffensive—had become monumental. We show in the next chapter just how massive a burden they had become. Not even the original Affluent Society could afford the price.

7

MEASURING THE COSTS OF CORPORATE POWER

Whether 20 percent [of corporate revenues] for management [salaries] is wasted I wouldn't know. The chances are half of it is. Which half is the difficult problem.

—Walter B. Wriston, chairman of
Citicorp and Citibank[1]

We're told that we live in a zero-sum economy. Consumption must be trimmed, wage gains must be curbed, entitlements must be reduced—all in the service of savings and profits. We all should quit complaining and open an All Savers account.

This strategy for economic recovery flows from the structure and rules of the postwar corporate system. The zero-sum logic is flawless if higher unemployment is the *only* way to whip inflation, if centralized corporate power is the *only* means of running an economy, if top-heavy corporate bureaucracies are the *only* means of allocating resources and extracting worker effort, if we must always produce and consume *exactly* what the corporations produce and sell. These are the rules by which our economy operates, and these are the rules which brought us the current economic crisis.

We reject this zero-sum logic. We think that the costs of the postwar corporate system far outweigh its benefits. We conclude that we could increase *both* consumption *and* investment if we changed the rules of the game. Or we could cut our work time and increase leisure without trimming consumption or mortgaging the future. The key is a more democratic structure of the economy.

The zero-sum illusion is so pervasive that our conclusions may seem implausible. Where would the necessary resources come from? How can both consumption *and* investment possibly grow at the same time? How could we expand free time without tightening our belts?

We too doubted that these questions could be satisfactorily answered when we began work on this book. But our work has allayed our own doubts. The necessary resources can be found because there is massive waste pervading our economy. This waste reflects the high costs of corporate power. By making better use of our available resources, we could dramatically expand our options for economic recovery.

We present conservative estimates in this chapter of the costs of corporate power in the United States in 1980—after more than thirty years of the rise and demise of the postwar corporate system. We estimate that the U.S. economy could have produced an additional $1.2 trillion of useful output in 1980. Or that the entire population could have worked one third fewer hours and still enjoyed the same standard of living. It is the huge size of this unutilized potential—and the opportunity to use it—that makes it possible for us to move beyond the waste land.

MEASURING ECONOMIC WASTE

How do we measure the extent of waste in an advanced economy? How can we properly evaluate our claims about the size of the waste burden in the United States?

We have constructed for these purposes an *index of economic effectiveness* (IEE), a guide to the efficiency or wastefulness of any economic system. Figure 7.1 provides a key to this index. It shows both the measure by which we judge the economy's effectiveness and the critical dimensions which determine its level of performance. The factors identified in Figure 7.1 establish the guidelines for our estimation of the waste burden in the United States.

The IEE refers to *useful output per available labor hour.** It

---

* The IEE differs from the measures of economic performance which we used in Chapter 2—hourly income and productivity. The middle three terms of our IEE correspond exactly to productivity—or output per em-

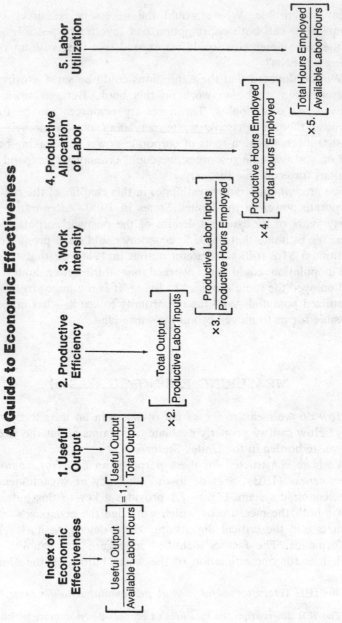

Fig. 7.1

A Guide to Economic Effectiveness

$$\text{Index of Economic Effectiveness} \left[\frac{\text{Useful Output}}{\text{Available Labor Hours}} \right] = 1.$$

1. Useful Output $\left[\dfrac{\text{Useful Output}}{\text{Total Output}} \right]$

$\times 2.$

2. Productive Efficiency $\left[\dfrac{\text{Total Output}}{\text{Productive Labor Inputs}} \right]$

$\times 3.$

3. Work Intensity $\left[\dfrac{\text{Productive Labor Inputs}}{\text{Productive Hours Employed}} \right]$

$\times 4.$

4. Productive Allocation of Labor $\left[\dfrac{\text{Productive Hours Employed}}{\text{Total Hours Employed}} \right]$

$\times 5.$

5. Labor Utilization $\left[\dfrac{\text{Total Hours Employed}}{\text{Available Labor Hours}} \right]$

measures how many useful goods and services we produce from the basic labor resources available to contribute to production. We have previously analyzed productivity, or output per em-ployed-labor hour. By focusing here on *useful* output, and not total output, we devote some attention to the *quality* of the goods and services we produce, not merely their quantities. And attention to *total available* labor time ensures that we gauge our ability to produce what we need and use with respect to *all* available labor resources, not just those of workers who have been lucky enough to find and keep a job.

Is available labor time being utilized? Are we wasting potential labor productivity? Is the economy *taut*—operating at or near its productive potential—or *slack?* As Figure 7.1 shows, there are five critical factors which influence the IEE. The higher each of these ratios, the greater the useful output per available labor hour. Since the issue of unemployment and labor utilization is most familiar, we begin on the right-hand side of the equation and move from right to left.

Labor Utilization. Obviously we waste inputs if we don't use them. Our central resource is labor. Many workers now spend their time in such vital pursuits as clipping want ads, pounding the pavements in search of work, waiting on street corners for a glimmer of economic hope, considering the calculus of a new life of crime.

We measure labor utilization by the ratio of *total hours em-ployed to available labor hours.* The higher this ratio, the more output we can potentially produce.

We should recognize, however, that there are both good ways and bad ways to increase this ratio. Providing employment oppor-tunities for the millions of workers now unemployed is clearly a desirable way to increase labor utilization. But many workers now employed would rather work *fewer* hours, not more—enjoy-ing shorter workweeks, longer vacations, and more leisure time. We do not want to endorse an increase in labor utilization

---

ployed-labor hour. We have added two factors here which do not appear in hourly income or hourly output: judgments about the usefulness of out-put and measures of available labor which is *not* utilized. We add these factors now because we aim to go beyond more familiar measures of the economy's performance in order to assess waste of both misused and unused resources.

achieved by cracking the whip, imposing compulsory overtime, inaugurating veritable work camps of enforced labor time.

We should judge our economy's performance, then, by its ability to promote increased choice in the amount of time worked. Everyone able to work should have the opportunity to make a productive contribution to the economy. Equally important, workers should have more choice about whether they would like to work more hours and consequently increase their incomes, or reduce their hours and enjoy more time for other pursuits. Our measure of waste due to a low rate of labor utilization should therefore reflect the absence of work opportunities for people ready and willing to work, not the reduced hours that some workers may voluntarily have obtained. This requires that we define and estimate "available labor hours" as the number of hours people would like to work if they had the opportunity.

Productive Allocation of Labor. We saw in Chapter 4 that U.S. corporations dramatically expanded their bureaucratic battalions after World War II. Who would argue that all of these managers and supervisors perform useful economic tasks? Who would swear upon the managerial bible that every hour of supervisory time on the job contributes to our economic welfare? Do we really need nearly 13 million managers and supervisors to keep our economy in shape?[2]

To assess the productiveness of our allocation of labor, we measure the ratio of *productive-worker hours employed to total hours employed*. If we can eliminate redundant workers without lowering other dimensions of economic effectiveness, we can allocate our labor more productively and reduce the waste burden on our economy.

Work Intensity. It's not enough simply to hire labor. Workers must be committed to their tasks and motivated to work on the job. We have already seen in Chapter 6 that an erosion of work intensity played a central role in the declining growth of productivity in the U.S. economy. This result has general implications. Workers may work more (or less) productively during any hour they spend on the job. They may toss monkey wrenches into the machines and work to rules. Or they may hum with the machines, helping figure out ways of making more effective use of their time spent on the job.

Work intensity refers to the ratio of *productive labor input to productive-worker hours employed*. How much effective worker effort do we get with each hour of work in the production process? The higher this ratio, other things being equal, the more output we will enjoy at the end of the process of production.

We must be careful with this ratio, however, for an increase in it may have *either* benign *or* destructive effects. If "work intensity" increases because of dangerous speed-up or supervisory harassment, we may get more output but workers will be much worse off than they were before—limping off the job, paying their hospital bills, watching their blood pressure rise, working more and enjoying it less. If, on the other hand, productive labor effort increases because workers feel genuinely greater commitment to their jobs, if they work more effectively without jeopardizing either their health and safety or their psychic state, then we can unambiguously endorse this source of increasing economic effectiveness.

When we evaluate the ratio of productive labor inputs to employed labor time in the U.S. economy, therefore, we shall distinguish carefully between standards for comparison which would involve reduced workers' welfare and standards which would not. We are opposed to speed-up. We are opposed to supervisory harassment. But we shall show that there are many ways of increasing worker effort which would not have such disastrous effects. On balance, we shall demonstrate, workers could produce more per hour and also enjoy it more than they currently do. As a result we could *have* more or *work* less, or both.

Productive Efficiency. We may get more (or less) total output from the resources we use, depending on the efficiency of our productive system. Do we invest wisely? Does management make effective use of the capital and labor it employs? Do our productive enterprises clank and sputter, their engines clogged with the grime and dirt of inefficient production?

Productive efficiency refers to the ratio of *total output to productive labor input*. Given an hour of productive labor time, how many goods and services do we get in return? The greater the productive efficiency and the higher this ratio in Figure 7.1, the more effectively our economy will perform.

Usefulness of Output. Is all our output useful and necessary? Or does some of it serve no one's needs? If we devote large chunks of available resources to useless output, we're wasting our time. Do we need every missile we produce? Do we enjoy higher standards of living when expensive nuclear power plants lie idle because they are unsafe and too expensive to maintain?

This dimension of economic effectiveness involves the ratio of *useful output to total output.* We could begin to eliminate economic waste if we could increase this ratio, if we stopped devoting precious time and resources to the production of useless goods and services.

Before proceeding to apply our index of economic effectiveness, we should caution that the IEE is by no means a complete measure of economic welfare. It does not measure, for example, the fear, boredom, and anomie which accompany the destruction of community life. Nor the humiliation and harassment of sexism and racism on the job. Nor the long-term environmental destruction visited upon our land, air, and water by deadly chemicals and radioactivity. Nor the waste of talent and creativity from the mindless routine of many jobs.

Those dimensions of economic waste are crucial, but we have not sought in this chapter to assess everything that is important or relevant about the effectiveness of the economy. We have sought much more modestly to establish the basis for a quantitative analysis of some of the major costs of corporate power in the U.S. economy in 1980. We are not aiming at a wholesale indictment of every aspect of the corporate system in the United States, although such an indictment is clearly imaginable. We aim instead at a guide to lifting the waste burden in the United States. Without carefully examining the costs of corporate power, one accepts the inevitability of the zero-sum illusion. By attempting to measure the current effectiveness of the U.S. economy, we can discover just how slack our economy has become. We provide some conservative estimates of the waste burden in the following sections, summing them up at the end of the chapter in Figure 7.2.*

* We provide detailed documentation of the basis for each waste calculation in Appendix D.

WHATEVER HAPPENED TO "FULL EMPLOYMENT"?

We begin our investigation with the issue of labor utilization, moving from right to left in Figure 7.1. Officially measured unemployment had risen by 1982 to more than 10 million. Some regard this as outrageous. Others sigh, practicing their staged regret, insisting that a "little" unemployment is necessary to lick inflation.

This conflict of views suggests two questions about high unemployment. The first is obvious: Why is unemployment so high in the United States? The second follows from the first: If we were willing to change some of the rules of the postwar corporate system, what kind of "full-employment" goal would be attainable?

Our answer to the first question begins with a simple observation: in capitalist economies, the business of business is profits, not full employment. The historical record confirms this general view: during the first eight decades of the twentieth century, excluding the five years of peak wartime production during World Wars I and II, the U.S. economy averaged 6.9 percent unemployment—across both good times and bad.

The era of Keynesian demand management was supposed to change all that, of course, paving the way for full employment and stable prices. Walter W. Heller, chairman of the Council of Economic Advisers under Presidents Kennedy and Johnson and one of the principal architects of a new approach to government economic policy during the 1960s, summarized in 1966 the promise of "modern economic policy":

The "new economics" can move us steadily toward the qualitative goals that lie beyond the facts and figures of affluence. . . . The term "full employment" stands as a proxy, as it were, for the fulfillment of the individual as a productive member of society, for the greater equality that grows out of giving every able-bodied worker access to a job, and for a national determination to demonstrate that a market economy, based on freedom of choice, *can* make full and productive use of its great potential.[3]

These noble promises are now tarnished. Among economic policy-makers, full employment is an idea that is no longer taken seriously. Why not?

We can sharpen our answer with a comparative focus. Public policy in many European countries has pursued "full employment" much more insistently than in the United States. We can compare the U.S. unemployment experience since 1960 with that in West Germany and Sweden—two countries with notably more aggressive public support of full employment *and* with much more rapid economic growth.[4] (Unemployment rates are available for those countries which rely on definitions comparable to those in the standard U.S. unemployment series.) Between 1961 and 1980, the average annual unemployment rate in the United States was 5.7 percent. During those same years, unemployment averaged 1.4 percent of the labor force in Germany and 1.9 percent in Sweden. Despite the slower growth of the 1970s, unemployment has averaged under 2 percent in both of these countries over the past two decades and less than one third of the average levels of unemployment in the United States. Much full employment is possible, in short, even in capitalist economies. The governing coalitions in Germany and Sweden have consistently pursued policies which aim to smooth the cyclical fluctuations of market economies, providing cushions for those who feel the sharpest jolts and reducing the inflationary pressures which full employment policies can sometimes generate.

Business in the United States has refused to consider such incursions on the unbridled reign of private profitability. Business leaders first mobilized their opposition during the post-World War II debate over the Employment Act of 1946. The original draft of the bill promised that "every American able to work and willing to work has the right to a useful and remunerative job. . . ." After the business lobby had finished in Congress, the legislation vowed that "it is the policy of the United States to foster free competitive enterprise. . . ."[5]

They have sustained their opposition throughout the postwar period. We have already seen in Chapter 5 that corporate executives had begun to yearn for a "wholesome recession" by the late 1960s. The first one didn't last long enough to curb labor, so they mobilized for the Great Repression. When that too was not sufficient, they brought us the Reagan-Volcker mini-depression.

Unemployment has persisted and risen in the United States, in short, because the postwar corporate system imposed a particular set of priorities on economic policy. Suppose we shifted priorities and played by a different set of rules. How close to "full employment" could we realistically expect to move?

We propose a full-employment target of *2 percent* as a standard for measuring wasted labor resources in the United States. This standard seems to us quite reasonable. We achieved an even lower rate of unemployment during both World War I and the last three years of World War II; this rate of full employment was achieved during World War II with average inflation rates of only 2 percent. Comparable rates of full employment were achieved during the 1950s and 1960s in many other advanced countries—as we have already noted above—with comparably low levels of inflation.

How much additional output could we generate by achieving such a full-employment target? In order to arrive at a reasonable estimate of the additional labor resources we could tap if we had operated at 2 percent unemployment in 1980, we make four simple calculations:

- We assume that all those in 1980 who were unemployed in excess of 2 percent would have been employed.
- We assume that all those officially designated "discouraged workers" who were not in the labor force but who nonetheless said they "want a job now"—people who had given up in frustration or were hobbled by personal barriers which any full-employment program could easily address—would also have been employed.
- We assume that those "involuntary part-time employees" who would prefer to work full time if they could find full-time jobs would also be able to satisfy their preferences, moving to full-time schedules.
- We also assume, finally, that many workers subjected to compulsory overtime in 1980 would have been free to determine their own hours and that some would have consequently *reduced* their working time.

Combining these four calculations, we estimate that the ratio of total employed hours to available labor hours could have been 8.9 percent higher than it actually was in 1980. An analogous calculation for 1982 (when all the relevant data are in) would show that at least 11 percent more labor hours were available for utilization. The zero-sum illusion is already fading.

WHO WORKS FOR WHOM AND WHY?

People today are willing to work hard at "good" jobs, provided they have the freedom to influence the nature of their jobs and to pursue their own lifestyles.

> —Clark Kerr, labor economist and
> former university president[6]

Continuing from right to left in Figure 7.1, we next encounter the problems of the productive allocation of labor and of work intensity. We discuss these two dimensions of economic performance together since they are intertwined. Work intensity has ebbed, we argued in Chapter 6, because of the internal contradictions of the postwar corporate system of labor management. Do we really need such top-heavy corporate bureaucracies? Aren't there better ways of dealing with declining work intensity than union busting and the Great Repression?

The Payoff to Worker Commitment

We argue that worker output per hour would be much higher in democratic enterprises than in capitalist firms. The key is worker commitment. You can give a worker a shovel and he may not use it. You can give a hotshot a computer and she may spend her time solving crossword puzzles. Labor effort varies, as we have seen in Chapter 6, and economic waste results if workers have less commitment to their jobs in the present system than in some other plausible alternative

Compare two workers. One of them works in a giant bureaucratic enterprise, surrounded by supervisors, constantly goaded to increase his or her effort in the service of corporate profits and owners' dividends. The other works in a democratic enterprise, owned or controlled by fellow employees, cooperatively managed, with year-end profits distributed equally to employees. Which worker is likely to feel more committed to productive activity on the job? Whose effort is likely to grow over the years?

We find it virtually self-evident that democratic enterprises would sustain much stronger worker commitment and effort than top-heavy bureaucracies with centralized power and supervision by command. A variety of experiences allows us to test this expectation. What happens when we compare similar enterprises which practice different systems of control? Are we correct that worker output increases in more democratic enterprises?

Researchers have studied the effects on worker productivity of systems providing greater job rotation, worker involvement in decision-making, and cooperative systems of coordination. These experiments have almost always found that workers' output per hour increases in response to greater variety in their work and increased control over their working conditions. While we should hardly find such results surprising, it is helpful to look at them a little more closely in order to assess the reasons for the observed effects. We rely for our summary on a particularly careful study of this experimental evidence conducted by three social psychologists in the mid-1970s and sponsored by the National Science Foundation[7]:

• The link between job change and productivity seems clearly to depend on worker *incentives* to change their work effort.

The key to have workers who are both satisfied and productive is *motivation,* i.e., arousing and maintaining the desire and will to work effectively—having workers who are productive not because they are coerced but because they are committed.

• These responses cannot be easily bought, induced by distributing monogrammed tie clips or suggestion boxes. Experimental results suggest that performance will improve *if*

1. The changes in job content are sufficiently non-trivial to be perceptible to the workers, typically in terms of greater self-regulation, diversity, meaningfulness, challenge, and social responsibility . . . [and]

2. the changes in job content are part of a more pervasive program of improved working policies and practices, which include also as elements adequate pay and job security, proper resources and working conditions, increased mutual influence by people at all levels, and constructive labor-management relations.

• Higher productivity is also especially likely to result from changes in the control structure of an enterprise. Better worker performance seems to flow if and when employees obtain "greater over-all influence" and "greater voice in defining work goals, methods, and compensation at both the individual and group levels. . . ."

James O'Toole, writing in *Making America Work,* agrees about the critical importance of real control:

Significantly it has been where management has withheld full responsibility from workers that the rights of ownership have had no positive effects on behavior, morale, or productivity. . . . While workers are likely to reject responsibilities without accompanying rights, they are also likely to see rights without responsibilities as no less of a sham.[8]

Many readers might reasonably be skeptical about the implications of this experimental evidence on the grounds that workers enjoyed the novelty of the experiments. By their nature, short-term experiments may not necessarily indicate longer-term effects.

There is another body of evidence which we believe carries more weight. Both at home and abroad, many worker-controlled enterprises have lasted long enough to permit actual—instead of experimental—comparisons of worker output in democratic and hierarchical workplaces.

In the United States, there are now roughly 1,000 firms that have some form of regular worker ownership and/or control. Although most of these firms are small, and therefore not fully representative of the entire U.S. economy, their experiences nonetheless are significant. The impact of worker ownership and control on worker effort has been evident. One recent review reports some comparative results:

A study done in the 1950s found that worker-owned firms averaged 20–30 percent higher productivity than conventionally owned firms. A similar study done in the 1960s found an average of 30 percent higher productivity over conventionally owned firms.[9]

There have also been significant worker-controlled experiences throughout Europe, in Yugoslavia, in Israeli kibbutzim, in Chile under the Allende regime. Here, as well, the evidence clearly supports the view that worker productivity increases substantially in democratic enterprises. A recent compilation of careful studies on this workplace effect demonstrates clearly that both in the United States and abroad, greater worker participation in and control over their workplaces uniformly results in expanding labor productivity.[10]

The Advantages of Real Workplace Democracy

There is much in our preceding discussion with which many probusiness strategists would agree. Many of the experiments we have cited, indeed, resulted from management initiatives under the careful tutelage of business-school consultants. A Business Week Team prescribing strategies for economic recovery, for instance, concludes that labor-management relations must change dramatically not only at the national and industrial levels, their first and second requirements, but also in direct administration of the production process itself:

This is where the third level of the labor-management relationship—on the factory floor assumes large importance. If rank-and-file workers can be given more responsibility and be drawn more deeply into the relationship (though not in a paternalistic way), a better understanding of the real constraints on bargaining may spread through the system. At the same time, redesigning jobs to allow greater worker participation in decision making can reduce alienation and give workers a sense of control over their work.[11]

If these probusiness strategists are so eager to involve rank-and-file workers in management decisions, why haven't corporate executives rushed to do so? What grounds might we have for assuming that workplace relations in 1980 were any less democratic than was institutionally and technologically possible?

The answer lies in a clearheaded analysis of the postwar corporate system. Large capitalist corporations pursued a particular path toward increased worker productivity in the postwar period.

They built large and relatively inflexible structures for labor management, seeking wherever possible to remove autonomy and discretion from the shop and office floor. This produced a strong and persistent rigidity in postwar corporate hierarchies *and* in their policies toward labor. Inflexibility is built into modern capitalist corporations, and nowhere has this inflexibility been more institutionalized than on questions of labor control. Top corporate management has recognized the need for greater worker motivation, to be sure, but top management has been equally determined to restore or enhance its leverage. While many called for more humane labor-management policies during the 1970s, most corporations pursued the microeconomics of the Great Repression— increasing the size of their supervisory apparatus, hiring management consultants to oust and prevent unions, threatening plant shutdowns in tough bargaining for worker concessions. Better to stay at the helm of a foundering ship than to work alongside the crew!

These perceptions echo throughout the literature on corporate experiments at workplace reorganization.[12] Substantial increases in worker productivity, as we have already seen, require nontrivial changes in job content and work structures as well as adequate pay and job security. But management has found it extremely difficult, many conclude, to make non-trivial changes in workplace organization, resulting in improved worker effort, *without also ceding significant management prerogatives.* Corporations have shown all kinds of interest in improving worker motivation, but they have shown even greater interest in preserving their centralized power and privileges. Forced to choose, one gathers, most corporations have preferred to forgo greater worker effort rather than to give up any management control.

Some recent surveys of management attitudes lend at least partial support to this skeptical view. One comprehensive survey of management attitudes in the mid-1970s revealed a clear hierarchy of executive priorities.[13] A whopping 87 percent of the managers agreed that "there would be greater productivity . . . if workers were more satisfied with their jobs." But virtually none of them were prepared to abandon traditional top-down approaches to greater worker satisfaction. Asked to rate changes which they thought would be "very important in improving productivity in your organization," 65 percent cited "better planning" and "more effective management"; only 10 percent chose "greater participation by workers in decision-making," and only 6 percent chose "more democracy in the organization." The stakes are high and the corporations know it. As one research and training executive at General Motors concluded about quality-of-work-life experiments:

What is really involved is politics, the conscious sharing of control and power. . . . [Workers participating in decisions about] rearranging the work area . . . may very well want to go on to topics of job assignment, the allocation of rewards, or even the selection of leadership.[14]

Perish the thought.

We conclude that the organization of production *could* have been much more democratic in 1980, but only if we had been able to change the rules of the game. And we further conclude that worker productivity could have been much higher than it was had there been greater workplace democracy.

Most working people seem to agree.[15] Among respondents in a 1975 survey, two thirds agreed that "people don't work as hard as they could because they aren't given enough say in decisions which affect their jobs." They were also asked the following question:

Let us suppose that the people who worked in the companies selected the management, set policies, and shared in the profits. Do you think that this arrangement would improve the economic condition of the economy, make it worse, or not make much difference?

Of those expressing an opinion, 54 percent thought this form of worker management would "improve" our economic condition and only 15 percent thought it would make conditions "worse."

We conclude that hierarchical management of production is both wasteful and unpopular. How much waste resulted in 1980 from the burdens of top-heavy management and the denial of worker involvement in production decisions?

We return to the two related factors in Figure 7.1—the productive allocation of labor and work intensity. How much higher could our IEE have been in 1980 if we had organized production more democratically? We cannot make such estimates with any great precision, but it is possible to arrive at some reasonable (and conservative) approximations. Two likely effects of democratizing the workplace may be identified: a reduction in supervisory labor and an increase in the productivity of production workers.

With more democratic workplaces, we could eliminate many unproductive supervisory jobs because some supervisory functions would no longer be necessary and because productive workers themselves would perform many of the remaining necessary functions of those managers and supervisors. We are not the only observers to suspect that there is a great deal of waste resulting from redundant managerial and supervisory personnel. Lester C. Thurow reports on widespread business views about the scale of corporate bureaucracies, reflecting that a "key to productivity improvements lies not on the factory floor, but in the office. . . . The problem is one we do not like to face. American government may be bureaucratic and inefficient, but American industry is just as bureaucratic and inefficient."[16] A study by a corporate consulting firm reached similar conclusions after case studies of management practices in sixteen major manufacturing companies: Charles K. Rourke, president of SMC Hendrick, Inc., reported in 1982 on the firm's findings:

> While many manufacturing companies would point to the rising cost of materials, high interest rates, and other problems as the cause of their current business woes, a major factor appears to be this overstaffing in the middle and upper management levels. . . . This problem is not confined to any one industry, but is a pervasive condition in U.S. business.[17]

We have chosen a conservative estimate of the waste we could eliminate through more democratic coordination of the workplace. The ratio of supervisory to nonsupervisory employees grew rapidly during the 1950s and 1960s because U.S. corporations were building new and increasingly top-heavy empires to dominate their workers and their competition. "There has been," Rourke concludes from the consulting firm study, "30 to 40 years of excessive growth." Suppose that the supervisory and managerial apparatus were no larger in 1980, in relative terms, than it had been in 1948—when this growth in the administrative bureaucracy began to accelerate. Suppose further that all of those additional supervisory personnel performed productive tasks instead. The ratio of productive-worker hours employed to total hours employed, through more efficient use of this surplus supervisory labor, would have been 6.6 percent higher than it was.

Is this measure of the waste of top-heavy bureaucracy realistic? It is difficult to make international comparisons, but it is nonetheless possible to make a consistent comparison of the relative managerial burden in four advanced economies in 1980. In the United States in 1980, "administrative and managerial personnel" constituted 10.8 percent of total nonagricultural employment. In Germany this fraction was only 3.0 percent: in Sweden, 2.4 percent; and in Japan, 4.4 percent.[18] Those three other economies were growing more rapidly than the United States by every available measure. A more productive allocation of labor surely didn't hurt.

As important as the savings to be made through the elimination of redundant supervisory jobs are the gains in the effectiveness of the production workers themselves. Suppose we had been able to achieve more democratic workplaces in 1980. How much more labor input per productive-worker hour employed—or how much greater work intensity—could we have achieved?

Available evidence on worker-managed or -controlled enterprises suggests that worker hourly output ranges from 15 to 30 percent higher in democratic workplaces, at a minimum, than in comparable bureaucratic enterprises.[19] We have chosen the bottom of this range for our estimate of the waste burden in the U.S. economy in 1980. We sacrificed a minimum of 15 percent of potential output, by this evidence, through our continued tolerance of undemocratic production systems.

We repeat that this waste estimate does not involve a call for speed-up and harassment in the workplace. Workers in more participatory workplaces are not only more productive but also much more satisfied with their jobs. We could apparently increase hourly output by at least 15 percent without pushing workers harder or exposing them to greater workplace hazards. This waste elimination would come from greater worker commitment, not speed-up. It would capitalize on all of the worker effort currently *wasted* in capitalist enterprises through working to rules, through slowdown, through plotting against the boss, through sabotage and shirking, through direct worker resistance. In hierarchical situations, worker resistance takes time and energy, diverting attention from the tasks at hand to the tasks of subversion. In democratic workplaces, this negative creativity can be translated into positive energy. If production workers controlled their own conditions of work, the returns in economic effectiveness would be enormous.

ARE COLD BATHS EFFICIENT?

Our analysis in previous chapters has already suggested that the *productive efficiency* of the U.S. economy leaves much to be desired. As with problems of labor effort, we are not the only ones to observe these problems of productive inefficiency. Indeed, management consultants and business experts have recently become some of the harshest critics of U.S. corporations. "There is now a growing consensus," journalist Steve Lohr reported in the New York *Times* in early 1981, ". . . that the performance of American management of late has been sorely lacking. . . . This indictment is heard not only from the traditional critics of business . . . but from top corporate executives as well. . . ."[20]

It sometimes appears, however, that these corporate critics are planning to solve such problems of management performance through a sort of Dale Carnegie course in positive business thinking: ". . . what is required," the Business Week Team on reindustrialization counsels, "is a willingness to bury the past and look to the future. . . . It is time for the pendulum to swing back to visionary, insightful managers who place emphasis on gut feelings and on an understanding of the total business picture."[21] James O'Toole echoes this psychological perspective in *Making America Work:* "What is unfortunate is that managers must start this reexamination where they are most uncomfortable—with introspection. They must begin by identifying their own patterns of values, beliefs, and behavior."[22]

We have nothing against management group therapy. But does it amount to an economic strategy? There have been two principal sources of sluggish productive efficiency in the United States in the 1970s, and both of them involve structural features of the postwar corporate system rather than attitudinal paralysis.

The first problem stems from the absence of any kind of long-term industrial planning; we have left such planning entirely to the corporations. If the steel companies chose to ignore necessary modernization for two decades, pity their workers. If the auto companies chose to postpone producing economical automobiles, pity their consumers. John DeLorean, former head of the Pontiac division at General Motors, recalls the thinking of GM during these critical years:

When we should have been planning switches to smaller, more fuel-efficient, lighter cars in the late 1960s, in response to a growing demand in the marketplace, GM refused because "we make more money on big cars." It mattered not that customers wanted the smaller cars, or that a national balance of payments deficit was being built. . . . Refusal to enter the small car market when the profits were better on bigger cars, despite the needs of the public and the national economy, was not an isolated case of corporate insensitivity. It was typical.[23]

The second structural problem results from corporate domination of macroeconomic priorities and the consequent pursuit of the cold-bath strategy of high unemployment and labor discipline. We have already shown in Chapter 6 that capacity utilization and investment stagnated during the 1970s as a result of the Great Repression. Corporations preferred to ice the economy rather than pursue more efficient production. Paraphrasing a U.S. general's notorious account of U.S. military strategy in the battle of Hue, South Vietnam, corporations moved to destroy the economy in order to "save" it for themselves.

These two structural sources of inefficiency combine to force a single conclusion: There has been enormous productive inefficiency in the U.S. economy because the postwar corporate system imposed profitability over planning and steady growth. Inefficiency was rampant in the late 1970s because corporate priorities prevailed. Capacity utilization and capital intensity could have promoted much greater productive efficiency in 1980 than they did, we conclude, if we had been able to change the rules.

How much difference in our IEE would such rules changes have made? We base a conservative estimate of these costs of corporate power on our analysis of productivity in Chapter 6. Setting aside the longer-term problems of industrial planning, how much damage did the Great Repression wreak? How much higher could productive efficiency have been in 1980 if we had been able to forsake the cold bath, eschewing corporate concerns for more stable growth?

We can use our quantitative estimates of the "cold-bath effect," first presented in Figure 6.6, to approximate this source of waste:

- Investment slowed after 1973. We have shown in Chapter 6 that most of the sluggish growth in capital intensity can be attributed to the effects of fiscal restrictiveness—itself an effort to curb labor resistance. If this cold-bath effect had not chilled investment, the capital stock would have been much larger in 1980 and hourly output would have been significantly higher as a result. On the basis of our estimates in Chapter 6, we conclude that the ratio of total output to productive labor inputs would have been 3.0 percent higher in 1980 if investment had not slowed from the cold-bath effects.

- Capacity utilization suffered similar refrigeration. If capacity utilization had not been pushed down by the Great Repression, hourly-output growth would also have been more rapid during the 1970s than it was. We estimate that hourly output would have been 1.7 percent higher in 1980 if the cold-bath effect had not slowed the economy and resulted in so much idle capacity.

Summing together these two results of the cold bath, we estimate that productive efficiency could have been 4.7 percent higher in 1980 than it was. Output per hour could have been that much higher as well. Escaping this wasteful legacy of the postwar corporate system would have benefited the vast majority of us through higher output or greater leisure time. And this estimate does not even include the potential gains from more effective industrial planning.

LET THEM EAT MISSILES!

People in the United States have grown more and more concerned about the social and economic costs of wasteful output. It is obvious, moving to the first right-hand term of Figure 7.1, that we could increase useful output per hour of available labor *if* we could transfer inputs from the production of some relatively useless commodities into production of more useful goods and services. Many goods and services currently produced in the United States add little or nothing to people's welfare. By eliminating this kind of waste, we could substantially increase our aggregate and individual welfare.

This is a sensitive issue. It is presumptuous for us to rank everything produced in the United States on some subjective scale of usefulness. How do we know what is healthy for children and other living things? Or enjoyable? In a democratic and egalitarian economy, these questions should be for people to decide for themselves through the market or the ballot box.

There are some cases where we think judgments can be made, however. We have chosen a few examples in this section in order to dramatize how much waste exists in our economy as a result of useless output. We have identified these examples very selectively, ignoring many other obvious examples of waste. We have used conservative methods of estimating the amount of waste in each case. We have sought simply to provide a minimum and illustrative example of the waste burden imposed by misplaced production priorities. The magnitude of this waste, even by our conservative estimates, simply underscores the need to move away from the prodigality of the postwar corporate system.

Military Waste

We are not experts on military matters. We think there is good reason to believe, however, that we could achieve our legitimate defense objectives with far less expenditure than is now devoted to them. How much fat could we trim from the rows and columns of the Pentagon budget?

There are two principal sources of military waste: the inefficiency of U.S. defense policy and the inefficiency of military production.

Defense Policy. There have been two recent and systematic efforts to reexamine the relationship between defense policy and military expenditure.

One, through the initiative of Representative Ronald Dellums (D.-Cal.), proposes a reexamination of the entire range of "national-security" objectives, which would permit substantial attenuation of our arsenal of nuclear armaments. Based on careful review of Pentagon programs and appropriations, Dellums' security advisers estimate that more modest but fully adequate defense objectives could have resulted in a saving of $54 billion in fiscal year 1983.[24]

The Boston Study Group has prepared a somewhat more conservative estimate of potential reductions in military spending. They project continued security objectives of defending not only the United States but also Western Europe, Israel, and Japan. They also propose to maintain an invulnerable nuclear deterrent. Judging from these project objectives, they have examined the 1978 defense budget in detail. They have concluded that only $73 billion out of the total defense budget of $105.2 billion was necessary in that year to meet these consolidated military objectives—allowing for a reduction of $32.2 billion in the 1978 Pentagon budget.[25]

We choose the more conservative Boston Study Group study as the basis for our estimate of the necessary level of military expenditure—not because it is clearly superior but because it is the more conservative of the two. At 1980 prices, it would imply a total 1980 defense budget of $86.3 billion.

Military Production. Few would boast about the efficiency of military contracting and defense contractors' production. In the mid-1960s, the Pentagon under Robert McNamara estimated that procurement contracts cost at least 25 percent more if they are let through noncompetitive bidding, and yet, in 1981, roughly four fifths of all procurement contracts were still being secured through noncompetitive bids. With much more direct control over the wastefulness of military production—through either competitive bidding or direct public control of expenditures—we could apparently have saved nearly $5 billion in 1980 out of the defense expenditures necessary for the Boston Study Group's established security objectives.[26]

These two calculations combine to suggest that defense spending in 1980 could have been as little as $81.9 billion without forsaking a wide range of military objectives. Actual defense spending in 1980 was $131.7 billion. We could have saved $49.8 billion, or an amount equal to 1.9 percent of actual GNP in 1980.

Energy Production

Energy policy in the United States has spawned waste on a monumental scale. We concentrate on only one dimension of the energy potlatch: the decision to pursue nuclear power in the 1950s and 1960s. (See Chapter 4 for a brief historical vignette on the origins of this policy initiative.) Corporations encouraged the development of nuclear power because of its high capital costs and potential returns on construction bonds. As was their wont, they ignored the potential inefficiencies and health hazards. When popular movements finally mobilized to block further nuclear power production and construction, we were stuck with a stockyard of white elephants—wasteful nuclear power plants, often idled, soaring costs, continual risks of radioactivity and explosion.

Suppose we had been able to block nuclear power construction during the 1960s and 1970s? Nuclear power provided only about 11 percent of total electricity in 1980. Let us assume that we had been able to meet these needs through a combination of more intense conservation efforts and through less capital-intensive coal production. We estimate very conservatively that net energy expenditures in 1980 would have been roughly $27.4 billion lower in 1980 as a result of these savings on the capital costs of nuclear power construction. On the basis of this single dimension of a pervasively wasteful energy policy in the 1960s and 1970s, we estimate that we could have transferred 1 percent of actual GNP in 1980 to other, more useful output.

Food Production

Large food corporations gained control of the food business after World War II. This oligopolistic control has pushed food processing and distribution toward more and more expensive methods of packaging and advertising. It has also substantially increased the share of food expenditures devoted to transportation costs—the price of agribusiness centralization and long-haul shipping all across the country. As a result of these developments, the costs of "marketing" foods—the difference between the prices paid by consumers and the prices paid to farmers—rose from roughly half of all consumer expenditures on food to more than two thirds. Suppose this "marketing" bill had been no higher in 1980, as a proportion of food expenditures, than it was in 1948—when more accurate data on food costs first became available. We would have saved almost 14 percent of our food bill—for a total savings of $32 billion, or 1.2 percent of the actual 1980 GNP.

Health Care

The health-care system in the United States is a disgrace. We spend more and more on "health care" but the health of people in this country lags far behind that of other industrialized countries. We spend our health dollars on sophisticated and often useless equipment, top-heavy hospital bureaucracies, high-tech medical obsessions, bloated drug prices—and rarely on the kinds of preventive health care and nutritional education which would more effectively promote good health.

We pay more for health care than any other people, yet we get remarkably little out of it. We spent roughly $1,000 per person on health care in 1980—a higher level of per capita expenditures than that in any other country. But our health record—despite all that money thrown into the health-care system—compares poorly with most other industrialized countries.

This wastefulness in the health-care sector is typical of the postwar corporate system. The costs of health care have risen but the benefits of health-care expenditures have not followed along. We pour our money into an irrational and centralized system which operates more surely to increase suppliers' profits and practitioners' incomes than to prevent disease and promote good health. It aims its services at the highest bidder, leaving the wounds of the poor to fester and spread.

How much waste is built into our inefficient health-care system? We can compare our performance with that of the thirteen countries which outperformed us on infant mortality rates in 1974—the last year for which systematic comparative health expenditure data were available for the industrialized countries. Those thirteen countries spent, on average, only two thirds as much per capita on health expenditures as the United States. Applying that expenditure rate (per capita) to the United States in 1980, we would have saved 2.3 percent of the actual GNP in 1980—for a total savings of $61.1 billion in 1980.

Crime Control

Only garrison states spend as much money on criminal quarantines as we do. (There are more prisoners per one hundred people in the United States than in any other country save South Africa and the Soviet Union.)[27] There is substantial evidence that crime-control expenditures increase in the United States when problems of unemployment and social control become most threatening.[28] Total government expenditures on the crime-control establishment—on correctional, parole, and probation officers and the judiciary—began to accelerate, indeed, around 1966—exactly when the social instability induced by economic decline first began to spread.

All governments in the United States spent approximately $30 billion in 1980 on the "crime-control" system—on courts, parole, probation, and prisons (but not including police). Let us suppose that more rational economic policies had prevailed in the United States since the mid-1960s—pursuit of full employment instead of the Great Repression, economic equality instead of profiteering, community development instead of convict incarceration. If we had spent as little—in real dollars per capita—on corrections in 1980 as we had in 1966, at the beginning of economic decline, we would have saved $12.5 billion—or .5 percent of the actual 1980 GNP.

Advertising

Advertising has come to dominate much of our lives. Kids can sing commercial jingles before they can tie their shoes. Billboards dot the landscape. Television sales pitches shape our images of what's cool and uncool, acceptable and unacceptable, chic and ugly. Our city schools are decaying, but the talent and money devoted to ads for McDonald's and Burger King alone would be enough to support several school districts.

Advertising played a critical role in the postwar system—creating demand for products which might otherwise have suffered the fate of the Edsel. (Even heavy advertising couldn't save the Edsel!) By intensifying their advertising campaigns, many large companies diverted attention away from the need for cost reductions and quality improvements. You can't fool all of the people all of the time, of course, but many corporations hoped to tally the highest possible score. Did we need every ad?

It seems reasonable to assume that we could have survived in 1980 with the level of advertising expenditures per capita which prevailed before the frantic postwar scramble for product differentiation began. Companies devoted 2 percent of the GNP in 1980 to advertising expenditures. If they had spent as little—in

real dollars per capita—as they did in 1948, we would have saved
$30.7 billion—or 1.2 percent of actual 1980 GNP.

SUMMING UP THE COSTS OF CORPORATE POWER

Gross national product in 1980 was $2.6 trillion. Much of it
was wasted. And much more could have been produced if we had
been able to change the rules of the postwar corporate system.

We have presented a series of conservative estimates of the
waste burden in the U.S. economy in 1980, relying on our index
of economic effectiveness as a guide to the sources of waste. We
compile the results of this exercise in Figure 7.2. Each of the

Fig. 7.2

How Large a Waste Burden in 1980?

Components of Waste	Estimated Total Waste		
	Amount ($billions)	% of GNP	% of useful output
1. **Labor Utilization**			
Unutilized Labor Hours	$234	8.9%	9.7%
2. **Productive Allocation of Labor**			
Surplus Supervisory Hours	174	6.6	7.2
3. **Work Intensity**			
Wasted Labor Effort	455	17.3	18.8
4. **Productive Efficiency**			
Utilization Shortfall	45	1.7	1.8
Investment Shortfall	79	3.0	3.3
5. **Useful Output**			
Excess Military Spending	50	1.9	2.1
Excess Energy Expenditure	27	1.0	1.1
Excess Food Expenditure	32	1.2	1.3
Wasted Health Care Spending	61	2.3	2.5
The Crime Control Burden	13	0.5	0.5
Excess Advertising	31	1.2	1.3
1980 Totals	**$1,201**	**45.6%**	**49.6%**

numbers in that table is based on the calculations reported in the text of this chapter and in Appendix D.* The third column in Figure 7.2 expresses all our estimates of waste as a percentage of *actual useful output* in 1980—that is, the actual GNP minus the wasted output estimated for category 5. We do this in order to measure potential useful output against that part of the actual output produced in 1980 which had some social value; this is the most relevant base for comparison.

Some of the individual sources of waste reported in Figure 7.2 seem relatively small. But they add up. According to the summary totals, useful output could have been $1.2 trillion higher in 1980 than it actually was. This means that useful output could have been 49.6 percent higher than its 1980 level.

Alternatively, suppose that we had been more interested in working fewer hours than in increasing our standards of living. The summary totals in Figure 7.2 provide a measure of potential leisure time as well. Translated from output into hours, they suggest that we could have enjoyed 1980 levels of useful consumption while working one third fewer hours in the aggregate, in order to produce that standard of living. Had the waste burden been lifted, the average workweek could have been reduced from 35 to 23 hours, with no loss of real consumption or investment.[29]

The costs of corporate power in the 1980 U.S. economy were hardly negligible. We experienced a taut economy because we played by the rules of the postwar corporate system. But those rules were themselves responsible for an enormous amount of slack. We have provided conservative estimates of the resulting waste burden. If we could lift that waste burden off our shoulders, we could promote more consumption, more investment, and more free time. Any program which ignores this massive burden is accepting the straitjacket of our current economic practices.

* For categories 1–4 we started with our estimates of percentages of 1980 GNP, and we then multiplied these percentages by the actual GNP level to obtain the corresponding dollar amounts. For category 5, we started with our estimates of the dollar amounts of waste, and we then expressed these as a percentage of the 1980 GNP.

II

The Limits of Trickle-Down Economics

We had, Reagan suggested, lost or forgotten the principles through which we had become the most productive, the most prosperous, the strongest and the most respected nation on earth. . . . [T]he lost or forgotten principle which had to be rediscovered and reanimated in this area was to promote economic growth through the encouragement of investment, enterprise, risk and the quest for wealth. In a word: capitalism.

—Norman Podhoretz, editor of
Commentary, 1982[1]

Economic decline has persisted in the United States since the mid-1960s. Do those in the driver's seat offer a way out? Will they reduce the costs of corporate power on the road to economic recovery?

It is far too soon to bury Reaganomics. Many have been writing the epitaph for supply-siders and their prayers for growth. But other right and center strategies are waiting in the wings—particularly two alternative probusiness strategies which we label *monetarist* and *corporatist*.

We argue in this section of the book that probusiness alternatives do not offer a promising approach to revival and restructuring of the U.S. economy. We base our conclusions on three kinds of arguments.

1. We turn first to the specific flaws of each of the three main probusiness contenders: supply-side economics, monetarism, and corporatism. We begin in Chapter 8 with a review of the recent supply-side follies, showing that the principal economic failures of the past two years result from the internal flaws of the supply-side program, not its incomplete application.

We then turn in Chapter 9 to a critique of the two other probusiness strategies, which will be competing more and more vigorously for popular and business support—with monetarism appealing to conservatives on the right and corporatism bidding for support among moderates and liberals in both the Republican and the Democratic parties. In both cases, we argue that these probusiness strategies could *conceivably* promote economic revival but that the economic and political costs of their success—*were they to succeed*—would be insupportable.

2. Why? The problem lies in their *common* approach to the demise of the postwar corporate system. We have argued that all three buttresses of the postwar corporate system have eroded—the capital-

labor accord, the capital-citizen accord, and U.S. international domination. Despite all their institutional differences, the probusiness strategies share some clear principles for addressing these axes of erosion:

- Investment has stagnated because of problems in production? Overcome this bottleneck by restoring profits to their position of preeminence and by redistributing resources to the wealthy. This is the principle of *profit-led growth*.
- Popular discontent has challenged the reign of profits and market prices in determining social priorities? Solve the problem by restoring private market signals to their unadulterated role as arbiters of growth priorities. This is the principle of *market-based allocation*.
- International competition and rebellion have undermined U.S. power abroad? Solve the problem in part through remilitarization. This is the principle of *arms for economic power*.

We show in Chapter 10 that each of these principles is fundamentally flawed. They represent one way of running the economy, but not the only way. Compared to some obvious alternatives, *the economics of greed is both costly and indecent*.

3. We briefly support this final conclusion in Chapter 11 by taking a longer-term historical view. We have had economic crises before. Vast institutional transformations have accompanied their resolution. Probusiness forces have dominated those processes of restructuring, and we can learn something from the results. As a consequence of the restoration of corporate power after previous crises, we argue, economic institutions have become more and more centralized, increasing the wastefulness of business bureaucracies and removing economic decision-making further and further from popular accountability.

The resolution of previous economic crises on corporate terms, in short, has led to *more* economic waste and *less* economic democracy. Must we repeat the cycle once again?

8

SUPPLY-SIDE FOLLIES

The beguiling magic of Reagan's supply-side economics promised that the Treasury would be replenished by a new era of ro-
bust industrial investment—more profits, more jobs, more federal revenue. Instead, the country got a long recession, the
highest unemployment since the early Forties, rising bankruptcy
and fear. . . .
    No politician wants to talk about it openly, but they are
driven . . . by another, even deeper, fear: if a political solution
isn't found [soon], America could be headed toward a genuine
economic collapse.
                          —William Greider, economic journalist, 1982[1]

Richard Nixon once admitted, "We are all Keynesians now." It
began to appear, by mid-1981, that Congress was affirming a similar adherence to supply-side economics. Everyone else pleaded
nolo contendere. Supply-side economics was a promise which no
one dared to refuse. But by late 1982, it was an idea whose time
had apparently come and gone.
    The supply-side promise was appealing because it offered rapid
acceleration in economic growth and a corresponding increase in
living standards for everyone. There was a simple premise: Getting the government off our backs would unleash a torrent of
hard work, entrepreneurial energy, and saving which would in
turn increase productivity and aggregate output almost immediately. Tax cuts and deregulation were the principal arrows for
slaying the big government dragon.
    Supply-side economics was good politics because it declared
everyone a potential winner. Where others promised hard times
and sacrifice, supply-siders promised a feast. If we would simply
fertilize the free market with nutritious incentives, if we would

guard vigilantly against the regulatory weeds, then who could imagine the bounty of the resulting harvest?

But was it good economics? We can judge the supply-siders' program by both the record of its application and the logic of its analysis. It fails both tests.

WHICH WAY TO DUNKIRK?

Jack Kemp and David Stockman launched the supply-side juggernaut with their notorious position paper after the November 1980 elections. They argued that economic growth offered the only possible escape from disaster, the debacle in the title of their "Dunkirk Memorandum." Did the supply-side program produce the effects they promised?

The superficial results of the supply-side experiment were hardly encouraging. Inflation did fall from an annual rate of 11.7 percent when Reagan took office to 4.5 percent in late 1982. But the costs of the Reagan program began to convince many that the cure was worse than the illness. Unemployment rose from 7.4 percent of the civilian labor force in the first quarter of 1981 to 10.7 percent in the fourth quarter of 1982, a post-Depression record. The waste gap between potential and actual gross national product (expressed as a percentage of potential GNP) soared from 3.8 percent during the quarter when Reagan took office to another post-Depression record of 9 percent in the fourth quarter of 1982. Average real spendable hourly earnings of production workers continued to fall during Reagan's first two years, dropping to a level comparable with the early 1960s.[2]

The economy, in short, was in the doldrums. Although we do not have the final figures at the time of writing, real GNP will certainly be lower in 1982 than in 1981—and most likely lower than in 1980 and 1979 as well.

This is the familiar story—the saga of economic stagnation which had led many to abandon the supply-side bandwagon almost as quickly as they had leaped aboard. But this part of the supply-side record is not really a fair test of its effectiveness. The Reagan program was a crazy quilt from the beginning, patched together from both supply-side and monetarist fabrics. Supply-side stalwarts could easily and to some degree legitimately blame the stagnation of 1981–82 on the tight monetary policies pursued by the Federal Reserve Board.

But there is a much more specific test from which it is difficult for the supply-siders to escape. This involves the sad story of investment. The key to economic resurgence, in the supply-side panacea, was an immediate recovery of business investment. Did it happen?

The supply-siders can hardly claim that this part of their program was not implemented. Congress outdid itself in 1981, tendering every possible encouragement to personal savings and business investment. "The Economic Recovery Tax Act of 1981," the 1982 *Economic Report of the President* explained, "has changed the basic character of the tax system by shifting the burden of taxation away from capital income, thereby providing substantially greater incentives for capital investment and personal savings."[3] Congressman Henry Reuss (D.-Wis.), chair of the Joint Economic Committee of the U.S. Congress, summarizes the results of a detailed committee staff study of the tax-distributive effects of the 1981 tax changes:

This study . . . shows clearly that the tax cuts presented by President Reagan and passed by Congress are tilted in favor of the top 10 percent of the income distribution, especially the top 5 percent. The cuts for the bottom 50 percent disappear, and those for the next 40 percent are nominal. The results confirm the fact that supply-side economics is indeed trickle-down economics.[4]

The most important measure of the tax changes, if we are to concentrate on investment, is their impact on the after-tax rate of return on business investment. According to the President's Council of Economic Advisers, the 1981 tax revisions changed the status of investors from net taxpayers to net tax beneficiaries. Figure 8.1 shows this change clearly. It shows how much of a *before-tax rate of return* on investment in general industrial equipment would be necessary for businesses to achieve an *after-tax net rate of return* of 4 percent. Before the 1981 tax giveaways, businesses needed an average before-tax return of 6.4 percent. After 1981, businesses would need a before-tax return, on

Fig. 8.1

Tax Breaks for Investment

before-tax rate of return necessary for
after-tax rate of 4 %

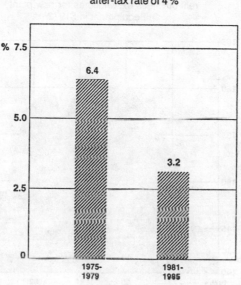

Source: Economic Report of the President, 1982, Table 5.5;
data for estimates on "general industrial equipment"

average, of only 3.2 percent. This is the same as if an average
household needed to earn only $30,000 a year *before* taxes in
order to achieve an after-tax income of $40,000. We should all get
such incentives!

Both Democrats and Republicans went along with the looting
of the Treasury, apparently because they believed that it would
spur investment. It didn't. Figure 8.2 shows that capital spending
by business was unmoved by the incentives; it *declined* by 6 percent in the year following the effective date of the tax law.

What went wrong? You can lead a horse to water but you can't
make it drink. "Company executives don't shout, 'Whoopee! Now
where can we invest this money?' the minute they get a tax cut,"
the *Wall Street Journal* quoted a machinery executive as saying
early in 1982. "They need an opportunity that promises a good
profit."[5] Confirming this self-evident proposition, a joint *Wall*

Fig. 8.2

Have 1981 Tax Breaks Revived Investment?

real business expenditures for new plant
and equipment in $1972

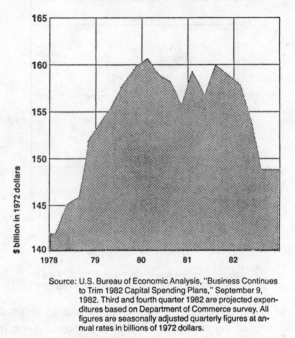

Source: U.S. Bureau of Economic Analysis, "Business Continues
to Trim 1982 Capital Spending Plans," September 9,
1982. Third and fourth quarter 1982 are projected expenditures based on Department of Commerce survey. All
figures are seasonally adjusted quarterly figures at annual rates in billions of 1972 dollars.

Street Journal–Gallup survey in January 1982 found that 58 percent of large firms expected their profit outlook to be better in
1982 than in 1981 but that virtually the same percentage (59
percent) said they had no plans to increase capital spending.[6]
Corporations had the money, but they didn't want to spend it on
investment.

We do not expect the 1982 decline to continue indefinitely; investment will eventually recover. But the upturn of the business
cycle has been long delayed. Three years of continuously rising
annual unemployment rates from 1979 to 1982 is a postwar
record, exceeded only once (from 1929 to 1933) since the official
unemployment statistics began to be calculated in 1890. The
economic signs will undoubtedly look more favorable in 1983 or

1984 than in 1982. The Reagan record may look better from the vantage point of the next business-cycle peak, whenever it comes. A fair assessment at that point would require looking at the overall performance of the economy since the previous peak in late 1979 and to compare it with other complete business cycles. The length and depth of the decline since 1979, already part of our recorded history, makes it unlikely that such a comparison will make the Reagan record look much better. Most economists agree. Harvard economic forecaster Otto Eckstein represents the center of the profession. "Like most of his colleagues," the New York *Times* reported in July 1982, "Mr. Eckstein does not expect the next rebound to match other post-recession recoveries."[7]

We share Eckstein's gloomy assessment. And so do corporations, according to the most recent survey data on investment plans available to us at the time of writing. The Department of Commerce released its annual survey of investment expectations in January 1983. It projected a level of 1983 investment equal to $144 billion (in $1972), a decline of 5.2 percent from 1982 investment levels estimated by the Department of Commerce. In some sectors—basic steel and nonferrous metals, for example—the planned investment decline exceeded 20 percent.[8] Whatever promises the supply-siders have made about the bounteous future for investment, corporations have apparently been marching to a different drummer.

It is not inconceivable, however, that a limping expansion and sustained high levels of unemployment could be accompanied by some increase in productivity growth. Our statistical analysis of the productivity slowdown and our index of economic effectiveness can be combined to assess some likely overall effects of these divergent trends.

We think it is fairest to assess the overall impact of the Reagan program by its effect on the index of economic effectiveness outlined in the previous chapter. For the purposes of this discussion, we shall even set aside the escalating waste involved in the military buildup and the recent attacks on environmental programs, limiting ourselves to a simpler measure combining the terms labeled 2 through 5 in Figure 7.1; these terms measure total output per potential labor hour. This measure of effectiveness is a combination of two distinct measures: output per hour worked and hours worked per hour of potential labor. We can therefore take account of the effects of the Reagan program on both productivity and unemployment.

The effect on unemployment is certainly negative. The ratio of hours worked to potential labor hours has fallen drastically since Reagan took office, and a return to unemployment levels of something like 6 percent seems unlikely in the near future.

But what have been the effects on output per hour worked? Here there are two opposing tendencies. On the one hand, the high levels of unutilized capacity and the low levels of productive investment will have a strong negative effect on productivity. But the high levels of business failure could boost productivity considerably if the failed firms were relatively poor performers and if the rising failure rate whips the management of the remaining firms into line. Reagan cutbacks in unemployment insurance and other social programs, similarly, may have substantially raised the costs to workers of losing their jobs. (On the other hand, if wage cuts have accompanied the social-expenditure cuts, as seems likely, the cost of job loss might not have increased much on balance and might even have been reduced. This is the case because the cost of losing your job is based on the difference between hourly earnings and levels of support if unemployed.) If the cost of job loss has increased, we might expect that workers, like managers, would be feeling the whip of economic insecurity and increasing their work intensity on the job.

Since complete data are not yet available to us for 1982 or 1983, we cannot accurately assess the relative weight of these conflicting effects on the U.S. economy. But we can use the statistical analysis of Chapter 6 to provide some illustrative numbers on the likely balance of effects. Given the lack of available data, we provide some educated guesses for 1982.[9] We assume the following values for our productivity determinants (relative to 1981 where appropriate): capital intensity, down 1 percent; the rate of capacity utilization, down 1 percent; the business-failure rate, up 3 per 1,000; and the composite index measuring the effectiveness of employer control, up 30 percent. The net effect of these illustrative changes would have been to increase the rate of productivity growth, compared to 1981, by .75 percentage points per year. Combined with an estimated decline in work hours per potential work hour of roughly 2.5 percent, this suggests that the Reagan program, overall, will have reduced output per potential work hour by roughly 1.75 percent during the year. That is hardly an auspicious start for a program aiming at revitalizing the U.S. economy.

WOULD YOU RIDE IN THIS BATHTUB?

Whenever there are great strains or changes in the economic system, it tends to generate crackpot theories, which then find their way into the legislative channels.
—David Stockman, Reagan budget director, 1981[10]

By 1983 the economic topography looked more like Dunkirk than the Promised Land. Yet the steadfast persisted in their support for supply-side economics, offering their faith and their bathtubs for escape. Jack Kemp argued in June 1982: "It is unduly shortsighted to announce the demise of supply-side economics. Despite the monetary problems we have had, we now have to go further."[11]

Should we go further? Is it possible that a pure and unadulterated supply-side program could ever work? For this, we must examine the analytical core of the supply-side doctrine and survey evidence on its principal propositions.[12]

Supply-siders suggest three main arguments:

1. Business and personal tax cuts will stimulate more work effort, higher savings, and more rapid investment.

2. Government deregulation of business will promote both investment and productive entrepreneurial energy.

3. We need not worry about the deficits or potentially inflationary consequences of large tax reductions, if that concern was holding us back, because the immediate response of productivity and output will generate more than enough additional tax revenues to cover the reductions. (This is the part of the supply-side program that builds upon the famous Laffer Curve, bequeathed to us by economist Arthur Laffer from the University of Southern California and vigorously promoted by Representative Kemp.)

The Effects of Tax Reduction

Might Reagan's tax cuts have worked wonders had other economic obstacles not interfered? We think not.

As with other arguments, we have turned first to comparative evidence. We have divided the advanced economies into two groups: those with higher rates of personal taxation than the United States—Denmark, Finland, Belgium, Germany, the Netherlands, Norway, and Sweden—and those with lower average rates—Switzerland, the United Kingdom, Australia, Austria, Canada, France, Italy, Japan, Luxembourg, and New Zealand. We can compare economic performance over the 1970s between the "high-tax" group and the "low-tax" group. It turns out that the *high* taxers (1) were on the average 22 percent richer in per capita GNP; (2) grew 10 percent faster (by the same GNP measure); and (3) enjoyed a 13 percent more rapid rate of increase in manufacturing output per hour.[13] This comparison offers little support for the proposition that high levels of personal taxation stand in the way of economic growth, sapping labor effort and blocking economic incentive.

Fig. 8.3

Labor Supply and Tax Rates

	1960-1965	1965-1970	1970-1975	1975-1980	1960-1980
Change in marginal federal tax rate on income	−2.9%	+2.3%	−0.2%	+3.6%	+2.8%
Change in labor force participation	−0.5%	+1.6%	−0.5%	+3.2%	+4.0%

Source: Tax rates are marginal federal income tax rates for one-earner married family of four, averaged over all tax brackets based on Brookings Institution data reported in the Federal Reserve Bank of San Francisco Quarterly Review, May 1981, p. 12. The labor force participation rates are from the U.S. Bureau of Labor Statistics Bulletin 2070, December 1980. 1980 rates estimated from comparable data in Economic Report of the President, 1982, B-33.

Still, the supply-siders might argue that reductions in U.S. taxes could nonetheless stimulate economic activity. What is the evidence?

The facts on labor supply are hardly supportive. The supply-side analysis would expect to find a negative relationship between tax rates on personal income and individual labor supply—since they argue that relatively higher marginal rates destroy individual incentives to earn labor income. Quite to the contrary, the historical record in the United States suggests that tax rates and labor supply—measured by the percentage of the adult population in paid employment or looking for work—have moved in the same directions, with *higher* taxes accompanying *increased* labor supplies. Figure 8.3 summarizes this record. Its results should not be surprising, given data we have already seen in Chapter 2. If taxes are higher, other things being equal, it is entirely plausible that household members will choose to work more hours in order to maintain their household spending levels.

More sophisticated statistical studies engender further skepticism about the supply-side claims. These studies suggest, on balance, that two effects roughly cancel each other: if taxes are cut, higher after-tax wages make working more hours attractive, on the one hand, and the resulting higher income makes additional work less necessary, on the other.[14] The conclusion? Tax cuts do not produce increased labor effort. If tax cuts are to spark a growth orgy, they will have to come from their effects on savings and investment.

But the evidence on taxes and savings doesn't lend support to the supply-side hopes either.

First, the tax cuts are designed to increase personal savings, but personal savings do not comprise the bulk of total savings in the economy—averaging little more than a quarter of gross business savings. Personal savings largely finance home construction, not business investment. Second, although controversy rages about the relationship between savings and personal taxation, supply-siders have found it almost impossible to produce credible estimates indicating large savings responses to tax reductions. According to the Federal Reserve Bank of New York, which conducted one careful review of the evidence, "One point seems clear: the presumption that a higher return to saving (resulting from a tax reduction) will spark a substantial increase in the amount of saving undertaken (or any increase at all) is not well founded."[15]

No help on the savings front; what about taxes and investment? There might be two positive investment responses to tax cuts. First, increased savings might expand the pool of investable funds, alleviating any capital shortage which might exist. Or, second, cuts in corporate taxes might directly encourage investment by reducing its relative cost.

The first effect is unlikely to be large because the effects of tax reductions on savings, as we have already seen, are likely to be so negligible. The second effect has been amply tested, since the government has been "spending" money on corporate tax breaks since the early 1960s. A careful study of this experience by two economists associated with the National Bureau of Economic Research, a prolific and respected font of generally probusiness analyses, concludes: "There is little evidence that a change in the investment tax credit is an effective tool for expansionary fiscal policy. . . . We are skeptical of its long-run effect on capital accumulation."[16] Joseph Pechman of the Brookings Institution, one of the most respected tax economists in the U.S., echoes this negative assessment: "In view of the tenuous nature of the evidence, there is no basis for assuming that reductions in income tax rates . . . will increase incentives and productivity growth by large amounts."[17] As eager as our politicians have been to lavish tax cuts on business, tax cuts cannot by themselves generate more rapid investment. Without such effects, all they accomplish is fatter bank accounts for the rich and cuts in needed social services.

The Effects of Deregulation

We have already examined a piece of the second supply-side proposition in Chapter 3. We argued there that it is implausible to blame our current economic problems on excessive government regulation, so it is equally implausible that deregulation will solve the problems of economic decline. Are there other positive grounds for the deregulation campaign?

Some of the conservative push for deregulation—such as relaxation of regulations on affirmative action or the reconsideration of regulations concerning sexual harassment on the job, announced in August 1981 by Vice-President Bush—probably has less to do with economic recovery than with a backlash against feminism and other progressive social movements. But the case for reduction of regulation in many areas has a much more direct economic logic, aiming to promote growth by allowing freer rein to the market and to private profitability.

Social regulation is likely, under almost any circumstances, to lower the rate of profit of the regulated company. This is the point, after all; the economic rationale for regulation is normally that the private profits of the company—say, the polluter—overstate its net social contribution. A well-conceived system of regulation would help make more sensible use of our human and natural resources than would result from the simple and unregulated pursuit of profits and would therefore promote the development of the economy's capacity to meet our needs. This is recognized in a recent U.S. Senate document on the productivity problem:

In theory . . . regulation should enhance the overall productive capacity of the economy. . . . Product safety requirements can enhance demand by granting the consumer assurance about the lack of risk inherent in some products; workplace safety rules can increase the efficiency of labor markets; environmental controls can substitute for non-existent markets for air and water.[18]

And in fact? The Senate study continues:

The chief debate has centered around the regulatory efforts of the 70s in health, safety, and environmental protection. However, the statistical data, while only suggestive, do not convict U.S. regulations of decreasing competitiveness with other nations. The U.S., for example, has less stringent air quality objectives than a number of major competitors. Nor do the figures show that regulation is the main cause of a decline in productivity growth. Compliance costs with the new regulations apparently reduced productivity growth somewhat, but these data do not reflect the other uses which the resources diverted to compliance may have had in the production of some items as clean air and water.[19]

The deregulation "logic" is a string of three confusions. It confuses the market value of something with how important or useful it is; water is precious even though its cost is low. It confuses private enterprise with productive activity in general; try cutting back on care of children because it does not produce a marketed output. And it confuses profits with an enterprise's contribution to social well-being; try selling this idea to the former inhabitants of the Love Canal area. Nobel laureate James Tobin has put the point directly, speaking to the Federal Reserve Bank of San Francisco:

. . . plant and equipment is not the only social capital. If we wish as a society to make better provision for the future, we should also be concerned with the preservation and improvement of human capital, natural resources, and public sector facilities and infrastructure, all of which are sacrificed . . . by the ideology that only private business is productive.[20]

The real logic of the deregulation campaign, this helps make clear, is not the promotion of aggregate economic growth or general social welfare but the narrow promotion of private profit. We argue in Chapter 14 that there are other ways of achieving growth than promoting profits. But business cares about its profits, not about the rest of us, and it has been running scared. Economist Frank Ackerman reaches a sensible conclusion in his recent book *Reaganomics:*

For the corporate world the risks of regulation stretch far beyond the costs that have already been imposed. There is no obvious stopping point to the regulatory process so long as dangerous pollutants, unsafe products and hazardous work practices continue to exist. A company which has not yet suffered significantly from regulation might quite reasonably fear that the social costs and benefits of its operations will in time come under public scrutiny. . . .

Reagan's deregulatory crusade aims at eliminating the abundant evidence that controls on business can be good for society. In the words of Murray Weidenbaum [former chair of Reagan's Council of Economic Advisers], "Don't just stand there, undo something."[21]

The Laffer Curve

To live up to its promise, Laffer's argument that the government deficit will *shrink* as tax rates are cut must presume that the cuts will induce a substantial expansion of labor supply, from which the increased wages and salaries will support an increase in total income-tax payments even at lower tax rates. (The effects on corporate tax revenues are virtually academic, since business has succeeded in reducing the corporate-profits tax to a marginal source of federal revenues, providing only 11 percent of total federal revenues in 1980.) If the net effect of a tax cut on labor hours is virtually zero, as the best available evidence indicates, it is not difficult to see why validation of Laffer's promise has proven so difficult.

Even assuming labor supply responses considerably higher than the available statistical estimates warrant, studies by Tobin of Yale and Don Fullerton of the National Bureau of Economic Research find that the incentive effects of a tax cut would be sufficient to maintain balanced revenue effects *only* if current tax rates were triple or quadruple their present *actual* levels. In both studies, tax payments would need to be about *five times larger* than average take-home pay before the positive Laffer effects would outweigh the direct revenue loss![22]

Investment tax credits do not rescue Laffer's promise. According to most available studies, the negative impact of investment tax credits on government revenue surplus is at least as large as their positive effect on expanded investment.[23]

The evidence is clear. One study of the Kemp-Roth tax proposals sponsored by the National Bureau of Economic Research, using estimates highly favorable to the Laffer case, concludes that "overall government revenue from the income and payroll tax will decline," not increase.[24] This results in a larger, not a shrinking, deficit. Laffer promised to recoup with the right hand what the government would give away with the left. His promise foundered on the fallacy of the basic presumptions about taxes and the economy's response which we have already reviewed. The

Laffer Curve argument, like the paper napkin on which it was allegedly drawn, is destined for the trash can.

And so is supply-side economics in general. Most economists now conclude that its propositions are implausible and that its prescriptions will prove futile. One can only conclude that the real excitement propelling supply-side economics was not the prospect of growth but the lure of personal and corporate aggrandizement. At least David Stockman was finally candid enough to admit what had become more and more obvious: "It [was] kind of hard to sell 'trickle down,' so the supply-side formula was the only way to get a tax policy that was really 'trickle down.' I mean, [our tax cut proposals were] always a Trojan horse to bring down the top [tax] rate."[25] "With supply-side economics," concludes Smith College economist Robert Buchele, "the means *are* the end."[26]

9

MONETARISTS OR CORPORATISTS TO THE RESCUE?

The standard of living of the average American has to decline. I don't think you can escape that.
—Paul Volcker, chairman, Federal
Reserve Board, 1979[1]

In the final analysis, whether America will reindustrialize depends on whether the business, labor, and political elites can get together to provide the necessary leadership. And that, in turn, depends on whether they can break out of their ideological shells to adopt a program that appears to rub, at certain seams, against the idea of a free market. Yet the great danger to the free market is in doing nothing. An enormous amount has to be done, and time is running short. America must make a start.
—Business Week team on "reindustrialization," 1982[2]

The first two years of Reaganomics have largely discredited the supply-side approach, and we have argued that more of the "real thing"—an absolutely pure and sustained application of supply-side economics—would fare no better. Keynesianism—at least in its traditional form—is no longer a political contender. What's left?

We expect that mainstream policy debate over the next several years will focus more and more closely on the two major remaining probusiness alternatives, *monetarism* and *corporatism*. Monetarism will regain its former pride of place among conservatives and free marketeers. Those who cannot stand either the costs or the risks of monetarism will lean more and more to the newer entrant in the probusiness-policy sweepstakes—a corporatist strategy which advocates selective government intervention in support of corporate interests and profits.

Who will line up on which side? The full constellation of supporters is impossible to foretell, but some of the protagonists are already predictable. The monetarist-corporatist debate is likely to pit free marketeers against planners, bankers against industrialists, and rising against declining industries and regions. While political rhetoric often veils as much as it reveals, it is even possible that the Republicans and Democrats will have chosen sides by the time of the 1984 election, with an ascendant right wing of the Republican Party leading a harsh monetarist campaign against inflation and workers' wages; and a dominant centrist coalition in the Democratic Party leading a glorious corporatist campaign for profit-led growth against unemployment and for government planning against chaos.

What matters more than the prospective lineup, however, is the inherent logic of these two probusiness strategies for economic restructuring. Each builds upon more plausible economic premises than the supply-side follies. Each is potentially capable of reviving the economy. But each strategy would impose egregious economic and political costs.

We examine first the more familiar monetarist position.

MONETARISM AND HARDBALL ECONOMICS

Monetarism is a doctrine favored by the rich for at least two centuries. Nor is its appeal misplaced. Monetarists practice flawless common sense: those who have a lot of money generally benefit by keeping money scarce. Tight money can be rough for those who do not have enough. It can also plague rapidly expanding businesses which want to borrow until their investments recoup initial outlays. In this respect, monetarism favors stability over rapid growth and "solid" money over progressive redistribution.

The revival of monetarism in the late 1960s and 1970s reflected both growing fears about the inflationary effects of Keynesian policies and the forceful advocacy of monetarist doctrine by Milton Friedman. (Keynes had written that politicians are enslaved by the ideas of some defunct economist. Friedman revived defunct ideas and has seen them sweep the political arena during his lifetime.) In the early 1980s the monetarist revival turned into a renaissance, as people became aware of the highly inflationary implications of supply-side policies. Walter Heller, former chairman of the President's Council of Economic Advisers, put the point succinctly: "Relying on huge supply-side responses to Kemp-Roth tax cuts could be tantamount to bolting the door against inflation with a boiled carrot." Heller himself is no monetarist, but many others see monetarism as the only bulwark against soaring prices.

The monetarist solution to the present economic crisis is tight money, leading to a predictable contraction of production and employment. Those who think this sounds more like the disease than the cure have not grasped the essence of the monetarist logic. The only way to control inflation—barring price controls, which are anathema not only to monetarists but to nearly all mainstream economists—is to control rising production costs. This becomes possible only if and when the balance of power is tilted from sellers, who benefit from higher prices, to buyers, who pay them. Slower growth will help shift power from sellers to buyers by contracting the total demand for goods and services. With demand slack, sellers will have to hustle to find buyers and will become less inclined to—and, importantly, less able to—raise prices. Similarly, workers will find it increasingly difficult to raise their wages. The demand slowdown must come through the slower growth of the supply of money and credit so that households, enterprises, and government will be discouraged from spending beyond their means.

The necessary—but hopefully only short-term—cost of this strategy is slow growth or even economic retrogression. With growth at a standstill and with firms operating at low levels of capacity utilization, the efficiency of production will initially stagnate or decline. The anticipated cost reductions—or, more realistically, reductions in the rate of cost increase—will come by reducing the prices of labor and other inputs or by reducing their rates of increase. Slow growth is the *necessary* instrument for achieving a supplies-in-excess-of-demand condition and thereby reducing the pressure of costs on prices.

This is all a way of saying, in economese, that monetarists believe that we suffer from a taut economy. They seek widespread unemployment and glutted input markets, shifting the balance of power toward U.S. capital and away from labor and raw-materials suppliers, in order to restore price stability. There are winners and losers in the monetarist game plan. And there are no free lunches.

But there is more to monetarism. Controlling the money and credit supply is not enough. Vigorous defense of the free market is also necessary, for tight money creates the market conditions necessary to control costs only *if* markets are allowed to work. Markets do not work, according to the monetarists, when sellers do not compete with each other or when sellers can hold off on their sales until conditions are more advantageous.

One might imagine, using this logic, that monetarists would place vigorous antitrust activity high on their list of priorities. But most monetarists do not believe that large firms interfere with the market; they assume that large size reflects efficiency. They have set their sights, instead, on labor—and particularly on the income support, unemployment insurance, and other social programs which, by their standards, undermine the "efficiency of labor markets." These programs are under attack from the monetarist camp, in plain terms, not primarily because they are expensive but primarily because they provide workers a scrap of economic security and a modicum of defense against the threat of unemployment which capital holds over labor's head.

If the expense of social programs were the main concern of the monetarists, we might expect to find them equally upset about Trident submarines and MX missiles. But there is a clear difference: while new military hardware may fill some workers' breasts with patriotic pride, it cannot be eaten; whereas some social programs, regrettably, help forestall the day when the jobless must agree to work for lower wages, or in less safe conditions, or with less job security in the future. Military hardware, for these reasons, is perfectly acceptable. Income support and unemployment insurance are not. This conclusion is not an unfortunate by-product of the monetarist program. It reflects one of its central mechanisms for restoring labor-market competition and, along with tight money, reducing costs and price pressures.

In these respects, monetarist policies clearly intend a redistribution of power and income away from labor and toward capital. This purpose, along with the free-market rhetoric, monetarists share with the supply-siders. But beyond that, the approaches are quite different. The supply-siders saw tax cuts as the direct stimulus to growth. The monetarist position is more indirect. "We know full well that Congress will spend every penny—and more —that is yielded by taxes," wrote Milton Friedman during the summer of 1981. "A cut in taxes," he continued, "will mean a cut in spending. And there is no other way to get a cut in spending."[3]

This reflects a deeper conflict between the political sources of support for the supply-side and the monetarist programs. Supply-siders attract many people of almost populist persuasion. "The political antecedents of the New Right," conservative columnist Keven Phillips notes with some exaggeration, "are more populist and Jacksonian than conservative, and its fundamental political loyalties are to anti-establishment cultural and social values, not to the free market."[4] By contrast, monetarists care about the free market, period. Where is the "popular desire," Phillips asks, "to embrace the conservative economics of Adam Smith, Andrew Mellon, [and] Milton Friedman"?[5]

The differences are nowhere greater than on the question of inflation. The supply-siders hoped to court popular support by attacking inflation through enormous and almost immediate increases in the supplies of available goods, thus *satisfying* demand pressures rather than *reducing* demand. The monetarists insist on immediate and sharp reductions in demand in order to reduce inflationary pressures. They are prepared to pursue these demand reductions regardless of the costs to ordinary people in wage reductions and unemployment.

This wrong-headed tough-mindedness earns monetarism our designation of *hardball* economics. No one ever said it would be easy, they tell us, so let's be done with the pain as quickly as we can.

The conflicts between supply-side economics and monetarism also help explain the internal contradictions of Reaganomics. Some people hoped that the President and Congress could dangle the supply-side carrot (whether boiled or fresh) of tax cuts and fiscal incentives, while the Federal Reserve System wielded the stick of monetary restraint. And while we waited for the stimulus of the supply-side incentives to take effect, we could count on rising military expenditure to maintain adequate levels of demand without increasing employment so rapidly that workers could resume the offensive.

These hopes proved largely fanciful, for they underestimated the fundamental contradictions between supply-side and monetarist economics. You cannot encourage demand and restrain it at the same time. James Tobin argued this point in his speech to the Federal Reserve Bank of San Francisco:

> The idea that money and prices can be detached and delegated to central bankers while Congress and the Executive independently take care of budget, taxes, employment, and output is the kind of fallacy that makes exam questions for freshman economics, a fallacy now elevated to Presidential doctrine. If Amtrak hitches engines at both ends of a train of cars in New Haven station—we still do have a railroad there —one engine heading west to New York, the other east to Boston, and advertises that the train is going simultaneously to both directions, most people would be skeptical. Reagan is hitching a Volcker engine at one end and a Stockman-Kemp engine to the other and telling us the economic train will carry us to Full Employment and Disinflation at the same time.[6]

Potential investors have understandably opted to sit it out until the switchman stops mixing his signals.

By the fall of 1981, it was becoming increasingly clear that the Reagan administration could not keep up its juggling act much longer. Leonard Silk, New York *Times* economic columnist, observed in early September 1981:

> Different groups of advisers are pressing various of these options upon him. But they are not consistent choices and cannot readily be compromised. Since Mr. Reagan's initial set of compromises between the supply-siders and the monetarists has failed the empirical test, he is being forced back to the drawing board. He cannot just stand there; he has to undo something.[7]

Given the independence of the Federal Reserve Board from the political system and the determination of Wall Street to keep interest rates high, the monetarist scalpel prevailed, thereby helping plunge the economy into the depths of the 1982 recession. The rate of inflation slowed notably, encouraging many of those inclined to monetarism.

But will it work? Can monetarism resolve the sources of economic decline in the United States?

We begin our response by picking up a strand of the argument introduced in Chapter 3 about conservative tendencies to scapegoat the government. The monetarist insistence on less government intervention is not a solution to stagflation. As we showed in Figure 3.4, there is a strikingly *positive* relationship between the relative size of social spending among the advanced countries and their recent productivity growth in manufacturing. There is simply no international comparative support for the idea that growth can be accelerated by *cutting* public spending for social security, income support, health, and education. There are other ways to escape from economic decline.

But most monetarists prefer hardball to softball anyway, toughing it out in the current political climate rather than pursuing the complicated political compromises which would be necessary to move in other directions. Some, building on recent strands of neoclassical economic theory, suggest that we could have our cake and eat it too. They argue that inflation reflects mostly the expectations of buyers and sellers about future price increases, not the real or actual movements in demand and supply. If we applied some very sharp jolts to the economy in the short run, they suggest, we could bring firms, workers, and customers back to their senses. If inflationary expectations could be broken immediately, prices would slow rapidly and the real value of GNP need not slow at all. They imagine something like the chiropractor's therapeutic blow, which aligns the backbone and sets the system straight with a single stroke.

So much for the imagination. After a careful study of the history of price-output adjustments in twentieth-century U.S. economic history, Northwestern economist Robert J. Gordon has concluded that price responses to negative demand shocks are sluggish and gradual. Real output is likely to decline, judging from this history, no matter how fervently we might wish otherwise. Sharp reductions in demand cannot reduce the rate of inflation, according to Gordon, without "an unemployment rate higher than we have today and a much larger budget deficit."[8] The costs of the monetarist approach cannot be ignored.

But what about the benefits? Will the effects of monetarist policies be worth the high price of sluggish demand and rising unemployment?

For these purposes, it is important to remember our analysis in Chapter 5 of the sources of inflation. Inflation in the 1970s did not result from an overheated economy. Rather, as we argued in that chapter, inflation resulted from too few goods and too much conflict: stagnation + stalemate = inflation. For the monetarist strategy to produce the benefits it claims, it would have to reverse stagnation, or break the stalemate, or both.

It is hard to see how the monetarist hardball scenario can resolve our recent problems of stagnation. Even if workers were entirely cowed by continually higher levels of unemployment, growth in hourly output would continue to stagnate because of sluggish investment, idle capacity, and limp corporate efforts to innovate. As we saw in Chapter 6, the Great Repression dampened productivity growth rather than reviving it; work intensity did not recover, while investment and innovation both stalled as utilization rates plunged.

Would an even colder bath work where the Great Repression failed? It might. But the record of the 1930s is hardly encouraging. During the first years of the Depression, when rising unemployment and the collapse of demand most closely approximated the monetarist scenario, hourly output (in real terms, controlling for prices) declined so rapidly that it was still *absolutely* lower in 1934 than it had been in 1929. After eight years of sustained "demand shock," by the business-cycle peak of 1937, hourly output growth (in real terms) was still averaging only 1.4 percent a year, 40 percent below the hourly-output growth rates of the 1920s and more than 50 percent below the pace of productivity growth during the boom years from 1948 to 1966.[9]

If the monetarist strategy will not cure stagnation, therefore, its success depends upon its ability to alter the balance of power and break the political stalemate prevailing since the mid-1960s, reducing inflation by reducing workers' and others' real claims on income. This would require reversing popular advances along all three institutional dimensions of the postwar corporate system—

involving capital's relations abroad and with U.S. workers and citizens. To work, in other words, the monetarist strategy would have to make people accept sustained reductions in their living standards, to force younger workers and women to search futilely for work, to induce the middle class to tolerate high interest rates, to impel blacks and Hispanics to bear the sharpest costs of economic dislocation, to push back the gains won by foreign suppliers like OPEC—for who knows how long?

All this is possible, of course, but ugly. And it is its ugliness which underscores its political improbability. There has been no time in U.S. economic history when sustained economic crisis and dislocation has failed to produce widespread popular discontent. Many observers of the current political scene think it extremely unlikely that the current (relative) quiescence would last for long during a sustained monetarist economic onslaught. Conservative commentator Kevin Phillips is convinced that a kind of "populism and socio-economic yeast now bubbles just below the surface of what is called Reagan conservatism, and if the current regime miscarries—in the wake of the liberal failure that preceded it—American party politics and perhaps even the American system could undergo very great change."[10] Radical social scientists Frances Fox Piven and Richard A. Cloward share a similar conviction, arguing that the Reagan administration has become "seriously vulnerable in that it has chosen to fight on many fronts. . . . And there is good reason to think protests will escalate on all sides."[11]

If sustained monetarist stagnation did prompt spreading political instability and rebellion, what would be the outcome? There are two possibilities. Either political resistance would require reasonably rapid abandonment of the monetarist strategy and pursuit of some other economic solution to the current crisis, or substantial curtailment of the democratic process would be necessary to protect the monetarist experiment from its critics and opponents. We might fairly call this the Chilean solution, since Chile has recently undergone the most rigorous experiment in monetarism. There, in order to enforce popular acceptance of huge reductions in real wages and living standards, the Pinochet regime has been forced to continue and even to tighten its political repression.

Monetarism is unlikely to solve our continuing problems of stagnation and equally unlikely to resolve the stalemates of the 1970s, in short, without seriously threatening democracy in the United States. Though a business upturn before the 1984 election seems likely, monetarism will not restore the high and secure profits so essential to long-term capitalist growth, at least for years to come, and it may cripple our political system.

The Lessons of Thatcherism

And still, hardball economics exercises a persistent fascination. Can't we somehow beat our economic problems into submission?

The recent British experience provides one final opportunity to evaluate the monetarist allure. Since its inception in May 1979, the Thatcher government in England has been pursuing a monetarist course with steadfast determination. It has attacked both inflation and persistent balance-of-payments deficits. Its strategy implied, according to the cautious country reports of the Organization for Economic Cooperation and Development (OECD), "a period of disinflation to be achieved through tight monetary and fiscal policies."[12] Although Thatcher's Britain and Reagan's United States are not entirely comparable, and although Thatcher's policies have been favored by abundant North Sea oil, the performance of the British economy since 1979 provides an unusually opportune lesson in monetarist policies and their effects.

The record is hardly auspicious.[13] Unemployment has soared, climbing from 5.1 percent in 1979 to 12.8 percent in 1982; it is still rising. Real national disposable income has continued to stagnate, with an index of industrial output in 1982 at 85 percent of its level in 1979.

Those are the anticipated "hardball" effects of the monetarist approach. What of its effects on Britain's growth prospects? Inflation has dropped—not a difficult achievement, given that it had been averaging 13.4 percent in 1979—but it was still averaging roughly 7.5 percent in the middle of 1982. Britain's export competitiveness has continued to deteriorate, although its balance of payments has improved as a result of the North Sea oil and capital flow into the country. Some monetarists point hopefully to a recent substantial increase in output per worker-hour in manufacturing, but that has resulted primarily from the massive scale of manufacturing layoffs—a very uncertain basis for future growth and recovery.

Most critically, as we might have expected from the effects of the Great Repression in the U.S. economy in the 1970s, investment has stagnated and shows little sign of recovery; real private fixed investment had fallen by 9 percent from 1979 to 1982. Demand repression does not encourage investors about future prospects, and the British case is no exception.

The choices before the Thatcher government are likely to become more and more difficult. As the July 1981 OECD report judiciously concludes,

The authorities would thus seem to face a major dilemma of how to achieve a continuing reduction of inflation and renewed expansion of activity of sufficient strength to generate a recovery in productive investment and employment. . . . The achievement of better competitiveness compatible with a rebuilding of profits and a further easing of inflationary pressures will therefore require a market reduction of wage settlements coupled with rising productivity. . . . Accordingly, it would seem desirable to consider whether the requirement of reducing pay settlements could be enhanced by achieving a closer dialogue with the social partners not only on pay but in the whole area of working practices and economic performance generally.[14]

That is diplomatic language for a familiar conclusion. Either the monetarists will have to abandon their confrontational policies, seeking real cooperation to deal with problems of endemic stagnation, or their policies will fail to restore economic growth.

The Thatcher government may be able to weather the political storms—with the help of a divided opposition—but that is not the main point. The real issue is the cost of the monetarist program. It has plunged the British economy into its worst stagnation since the Great Depression and it has shifted the burden of sacrifice almost wholly onto the vast majority of workers and citizens. Sooner or later, there is bound to be an upturn, but it is difficult to disagree with the assessment of Britain's monetarist program in a public statement signed by 364 leading English academic economists in March 1981:

There is no basis in economic theory or supporting evidence for the Government's belief that by deflating demand they will bring inflation permanently under control and thereby induce an automatic recovery in output and employment. Present policies will deepen the depression, erode the industrial base of our economy, and threaten its social and political stability.[15]

The Economist counseled its readers at the time to "Prepare for a bumpy ride through the trough."[16]

CORPORATISM: TOP-DOWN ECONOMICS

The vast center of the U.S. political spectrum is also concerned by the social and political consequences of monetarism. Felix Rohatyn, Wall Street investment banker and leading corporatist spokesman, has argued, "America cannot survive half rich, half poor; half suburb, half slum. If the country wakes up, it will not do so by way of laissez faire."[17]

Rohatyn and many others have articulated the third probusiness strategy, which we call corporatism. There are two main differences between corporatism and either supply-side or monetarist economics:

* Corporatists do not join in the conservative attack on the government. They call for a more coherent government policy to boost the rate of profit and capital formation. They recognize the necessity—even the inevitability and desirability—of substantial government involvement in the economy.
* Corporatists also eschew the free-market model of the economy's operations, to which supply-siders and monetarists are so devoted. Their model is not one of perfect competition among millions of individual households and small enterprises, but one of bargaining and consensus among the few giant corporations, large unions, and government agencies which dominate the economy. Their prophet is not Adam Smith, for

whom the invisible hand rendered general economic interdependence compatible with liberty, but Joseph Schumpeter, the twentieth-century Austro-American economist who defended advanced capitalism and liberal democracy as a dual system of economic and political competition among elites. Corporatist rhetoric speaks not of individual gain but of common good: it was Jean Jacques Rousseau, not Jeremy Bentham, whose picture decorated the 1980 declaration of a corporatist program by the editors of *Business Week*.

Business leaders have dominated the early formulations of the corporatist strategy, led by Rohatyn—the much celebrated architect of the corporatist solution to New York City's budget crises in the mid-1970s—George C. Lodge, Jr., of the Harvard Business School, and many of the thinkers in David Rockefeller's Trilateral Commission. Some liberals doubtlessly feel uncomfortable with such company, but most recent liberal proposals for economic revival, as we shall see at the beginning of Part III of our book, conform closely to the corporatist agenda.

The economic logic of the corporatist position may be easily summarized: unregulated competition among businesses, workers, and consumers gives rise to waste and needless social conflict; yet capitalism, though less atomistic and competitive than in its textbook days, is still capitalism, and profits are what makes it go. For this reason, extensive and carefully planned government involvement in the economy is necessary to rationalize production and distribution in the interests of maintaining a high level of profitability. The immediate priority is an increase in the rate of investment through transfers of income to large corporations. This requires curtailing consumption in the short run in order to permit higher levels of corporate profits and investment. In the long run, the corporatists promise, we shall realize the returns through stable and more rapid economic growth.

The political logic of corporatism is equally clear. Hoping to avoid the confrontations which monetarism portends, it seeks accommodation and consensus. It seeks the organization of private power beyond the reaches of democratic decision-making, deploying this power to raise the rate of profit and investment. Harvard historian Charles Maier describes the political dimensions of this approach in his study of the origins of corporatism in Europe during the 1920s:

> . . . the new institutional arrangements and distributions of power . . . that I have chosen to call corporatist . . . involved the displacement of power from elected representatives or a career bureaucracy to the major organized forces of European society and economy, sometimes bargaining directly among themselves, sometimes exerting influence through a weakened parliament, and occasionally seeking advantages through new executive authority. In each case corporatism meant the growth of private power and the twilight of sovereignty.[18]

There are a variety of possible approaches to achieving the corporatist agenda, and we will undoubtedly witness considerable debate about some of its details. Whatever the variations on this theme, however, corporatism as we understand it has three general distinguishing characteristics: support for corporate profits, centralized state guidance of the economy wherever and whenever necessary, and restricted popular access to economic decision-making.

Since centralized state power is hardly a popular program in the United States, corporatists typically underplay this aspect of their strategy, minimizing their advocacy of central planning or federal control. But the logic of the corporatist program points in this direction nonetheless, as even the most delicate recent formulations begin to reveal.

Perhaps the best-articulated corporatist blueprint was the June 1980 special issue of *Business Week,* expanded into a 1982 book entitled *The Reindustrialization of America.* The Business Week Team defines the problems of the U.S. economy as those of deindustrialization, which they argue has been both cause and effect of declining U.S. international competitiveness. Their outline of an "effective reindustrialization policy":

- It will require an emphasis on investment over consumption, and on investment towards the production of capital goods over quality of life improvements.
- It will require a massive investment in human capital to shift people off welfare and into jobs.
- It will require indicative planning involving government participation.[19]

is fair to say, too, that to the extent that these new attitudes, especially their extreme manifestations, focus attention and resources on how the economic pie is divided, they divert attention and resources away from how to make the pie bigger. Says Reginald H. Jones, chairman of General Electric, Co., "We have become so concerned with problems of redistributing wealth that we've forgotten all about creation of wealth."

A New Accord with the Rest of the World?

There is a third pact hidden between the corporatist lines. Corporatists are firm believers in U.S. dominion in the world economy. But they are also terrified of extremist nuclear policies which would engulf most of the rest of the world in radioactive debris. They have understood the madness of fighting in the Third World in order to open up and preserve markets.

What is required, in their eyes, is an implicit social contract with the rest of the world which would promote three corporatist objectives on the world scale: (1) They want more trade and they therefore want the U.S. government to engage in aggressive export promotion; this is a kind of corporatist neomercantilism, 1980s style. (2) They want a stronger set of international financial institutions which can renegotiate and stabilize world debt. (3) They also want the most favorable possible conditions for U.S. overseas investment, promoting rapid mobility of capital and political immunity to overseas political convulsions.

The corporatists' program for a new international accord is probably their most slippery project. Underlying it is a threat of remilitarization—the *arms-for-economic-power* principle to which we return in Chapter 10.

The Complexities of the Corporatist Agenda

Obviously, these are complicated accords to strike. Will the corporatist strategy work? Can it achieve economic revival and rapid growth?

The corporatists have a better shot at stable recovery than either the supply-siders or the monetarists. But the internal complexities of the corporatist program pose grave obstacles to its effectiveness. And were they somehow to overcome these obstacles, we believe that the resulting regime would be profoundly undemocratic.

It is easiest to review the difficulties facing corporatism by considering two dimensions of the corporatist program, one vertical —involving the relationships between the largest corporations and everyone else—and one horizontal—involving the relationships among the corporations themselves, as altered by indicative planning and collectivized private investment.

Top-Down Economics and Democracy. The corporatist program depends on its ability to convince the people to *agree* to sacrifice consumption. This is a neat trick. If people are to make significant sacrifices, either they should make decisions about the scope and objectives served by those sacrifices, involving a dramatic extension of economic democracy, or they will have to suffer a significant reduction in their economic and political power. The corporatists do not want the former, and they are smart enough to recognize the likely necessity of the latter. An erosion of democracy could easily result.

Many liberals will fervently hope to escape from such stringent trade-offs. Many recall the success of the New Deal–Fair Deal coalition in the 1930s and 1940s. Won't we be able to ally with corporatists to replicate something like that combination of stable growth and democracy?

Such easy compromises can potentially work when both sides can clearly gain from the economic strategy. If the dominant problem facing the economy is inadequate aggregate demand, for example, as it was during the immediate postwar period, increases in public social expenditure and rapidly rising wages are the most effective methods for stimulating economic growth. The vast majority benefits, and therefore will support the accord; corporations benefit too, and therefore will remain committed to the compromise.

But corporatists are convinced that inadequate aggregate demand is *not* the basic problem plaguing the U.S. economy. They are convinced that corporate power has eroded, and that popular demands have squeezed corporate profits. They are therefore prepared to insist that the imperatives of profits, growth, and restored international competitiveness require a regressive redistribution—out of workers' and consumers' pockets and into the corporate coffers. And they are also convinced—with a clarity which we shall soon perceive—that the postwar extension of democratic and social rights went too far. Therefore they call not only for redistribution of income and wealth but for a restoration and consolidation of corporate power. This is not the only way out of the crisis, as we shall argue in our discussion of a democratic alternative, *but it appears to be the only terms on which corporatists will participate in a renewed social contract.*

A preview of this kind of corporatist determination can be seen in the experience of New York City in the mid-1970s. This was the first major corporatist experiment in the United States and it considerably emboldened the corporatist prophets. (It also catapulted Rohatyn to their front ranks.)

New York City had been experiencing a debt crisis—an early casualty of spreading economic decline. Leading bankers David Rockefeller and Walter Wriston (of Chase Manhattan and Citicorp, respectively) called for tight controls on city expenditures. Rohatyn engineered those controls, securing a new Emergency Financial Control Board (EFCB), which would "in essence assume the function of the city's budget bureau and controller." It would be a "mechanism of state control of city expenditures of the most drastic kind." The bankers called the shots, effectively vetoing any budget proposals which they felt were unwarranted. In order to roll over the debt, the bankers had to sell bonds. "Every few weeks another bond issue had to be sold," Rohatyn recounts. "Each required concessions."[24]

The concessions were stark. As Rohatyn later reminded Congress,

New York City was kept out of bankruptcy by a wage freeze, a 20% reduction in [municipal] manpower, shifts in pension costs, a tuition charge at the City University, transit fare increases, and savage cost control coupled with a variety of state tax cuts, and inflation-driven tax increases; but it was the lower income families that got hurt.[25]

Few liked the concessions, Rohatyn admitted; "this result is unfair, but it is to some degree inevitable, and its consequences must be faced."

There was, in effect, a minor coup d'état in New York City—with bankers usurping the basic decision-making powers of elected officials and, in the end, the electorate.

We are not the only ones to draw corporatist lessons from the New York City experiment. The bankers extracted concessions through their financial leverage: no concessions, no loans. And they can extract such concessions in the future, they feel confident, by applying that leverage more widely. As Rohatyn explained in a 1976 speech,

I can't tell you how convinced I am that many of our problems stem from structural weaknesses in our political system. But I believe the trigger for political change could be new economic activity. . . . We will have an entity which could say to [some state] Governors, "We have $2 billion to invest which we might make [available to you]. But first we need to make the following changes in the tax structure or changes are needed in union work rules. . . ." Because of the possibility of economic activity, the Governors will accept political change. . . . That's the way we got reforms in New York City's government.[26]

In less polite company, this would be called blackmail. The corporatists are banking on the possibility that they can exercise such blackmail on a national scale, much as the International Monetary Fund has done on a world scale. Rohatyn concludes:

The influence that the private members of MAC [the Municipal Assistance Corporation] and EFCB exerted was on the political process itself. . . . The direction and philosophy of a large unit of government was fundamentally and permanently changed as a result of the involvement, some would say intrusion, of the private sector in government. In my judgment, this is a principle that is applicable to a vast array of national problems for reasons not too dissimilar to the New York City experience. . . . The United States today in many ways is similar to New York City in 1975.[27]

Managing Capital. The corporatist agenda becomes no less complex when we turn to its second critical task: managing the *horizontal* relations among capital, particularly the allocation of investment funds.

Consider the "major objectives" of *Business Week*'s proposed "new industrial policy": "to provide support for high technology industries; to facilitate adjustment to a world of high priced energy; and to foster the adjustment of some of the nation's basic industries to a new wave of international competition." The heading of this section in the *Business Week* issue is "Industries to push—or to prune." But the editors have not yet come up with a clear and logical set of criteria for pushing or pruning.

The problem with relying on profitability as a primary choice criterion, in this context, is that future profits are so unpredictable and current profits reflect the current situation which the corporatists are out to change. And if, with the clearheaded detachment and foresight induced by the twenty-seventh-floor view from the McGraw-Hill Building in New York, the *Business Week* editors cannot come up with coherent choices among industries, one wonders how much better our pork-barrel Congress and lobby-infested executive branch will be able to perform. "A potential problem with this approach [to managing capital]," *Business Week* concedes, "is that it could become . . . 'lemon socialism'—the government rescuing the losers, and nothing would be done to promote potential winners."

The specter of lemon socialism haunts the corporate planners not because our system is too democratic, but because it is not nearly democratic enough. The basic problem, in other words, lies in the narrowness of the interest groups which would be represented in the corporatist investment program.

On the one hand, a small and powerful interest group, such as the owners of the oil industry, doctors, or the major real-estate speculators, can further their objectives by promoting policies which give them a larger share of the pie, even if those policies simultaneously shrink the pie as a whole. The profits of the major military contractors, for example, will increase enormously from the current military buildup—even though the net effect on the total income of the United States is likely to be negative.

On the other hand, broad interest groups cannot so easily reap profits from such narrowly self-interested approaches to capital management. The larger the interest group, in other words, the less effective will be the robbing-Peter-to-pay-Paul strategy. If almost everyone is a Paul and nobody is a Peter, then robbing

Peter won't make much sense *unless* it helps the economy work better rather than worse. The economic interests of the vast majority of U.S. workers, or of the bottom 80 percent of the income distribution, are served *not* by pork-barrel policies which confer special privileges and retard the rate of economic growth, but rather by rational economic policies for expanding the productive system's overall capacity to meet all of our needs. Pork-barrel politics succeeds, in effect, only by limiting the number feeding at the trough.

The horizontal strategy for intercapitalist cooperation thus confronts a fundamental political problem. A system of economic planning in a capitalist economy committed to the priority of profitability is extremely vulnerable to narrow-interest-group strategies unless the dominant force in the planning system is the organized and overwhelming majority of the people, who will be uninterested in beggar-thy-neighbor policies not because they are so unselfish but because they are so many.

Without such majoritarian control, corporatist planning can only work if it is controlled by a kind of corporatist "philosopher king." (Remember the Nixon administration's "price czar" and the Carter administration's "energy czar"?) Or the corporatists could invent a modern-day equivalent to the traditional English House of Lords, an arena in which major capitalists can thrash out their differences, decide where to cut their losses, come to common agreements, and wield sweeping economic power. Or they could extend the powers of the Federal Reserve Board, which presently serves as an insulated and relatively effective public representative of the private banking community.

What About the Japanese "Miracle"?

Or, perhaps, they could seek to emulate the corporatist system in Japan, a notion that has been spreading like the common cold among corporatist protagonists. Hasn't corporatism worked in Japan? Can't we apply its lessons in the United States?

There is little question that Japan represents a highly successful model by corporatist standards. The government participates actively in the planning-and-allocation process, particularly through the Finance Ministry and the Ministry of International Trade and Industry (MITI). Large corporations both dominate the core of the private sector and cooperate closely with each other and the government. Labor-management systems in the core of the economy are much more cooperative than in the United States, with substantial employment security for many workers. And, of course, the Japanese have placed central emphasis on maintaining a high rate of capital formation, ensuring that sufficient resources continue to flow into investment and innovation.

As if all that weren't enough to captivate the corporatists, the system works without substantial "democratic" interference from the political system. The Japanese system functions through elitist decision-making, with both corporate and government bureaucrats rising to the top of their respective hierarchies and, once they arrive, exercising extraordinary decision-making leverage. As Ezra Vogel, a leading Japan scholar in the United States and a prominent analyst of the Japanese "miracle," explains:

The politicians make many important political decisions, but compared to the American government the top politicians have little leverage over the bureaucracy. . . . The key decisions in the ministry are made by the permanent bureaucrats rather than by the politicians of the Diet and the cabinet.

Not only is the central bureaucracy much more powerful than in the American system, but other parts of the government, like the judiciary and local government, are much weaker. The top cabinet officials have considerable power, but the Diet is relatively weak compared to the American Congress, and most of the legislation is in fact drafted by bureaucrats rather than by Diet members.[28]

Shuichi Kato, another Japan scholar, echoes Vogel's conclusions:

Since the end of the Occupation the ruling elites have so strengthened their position that a democratic transfer of power to an opposition party has become virtually inconceivable. The triumvirate of Liberal Democratic Party (LDP), business, and government bureaucracy *is* the system under which the country is managed; even in the unlikely event that an opposition party or coalition gained a parliamentary majority and formed a cabinet, it would still not have gained the full power to rule and would soon be shown to be helpless. . . . So, year after year, the governing managerial elites pass power back and forth among themselves, all the time increasing and centralizing their control over people's lives. . . .[29]

But there are several important reasons for doubting that the Japanese economic model is as easily importable as a Toyota. Corporatists will have to use their own wits, not some foreign model, to overcome the complexities of their program for restructuring the U.S. economy.

First, relatively few Japanese workers share in the employment security and nonconflictual management systems which help secure rapid hourly output growth in the largest Japanese firms. Less than a quarter of the Japanese work force is employed by the large firms (employing more than five hundred). A considerably larger number work in firms with fewer than thirty employees. Wages in the small companies are less than three fifths of those in the larger group, while bonuses and cash handouts in the smaller firms are only about half. Henry Scott-Stokes reports in the New York *Times:*

. . . in Japan, far more than in the West, bonuses and fringe benefits, and especially job security and union protection, produce entirely different environments in the two tiers. The big companies find this "dual structure" profitable. It provides a cheap, flexible pool of unorganized workers at their subcontractors for which the "mother" company is not legally responsible.[30]

Women workers, in particular, cushion the shocks of economic adjustment in the Japanese system by moving in and out of different industries, and in and out of the labor force, as employment expands and contracts. Kathleen Molony, an East Asia specialist, has concluded:

. . . the success of the system depends to a considerable degree on the peculiarly Japanese belief that it is acceptable, and even necessary, to "sacrifice" a large segment of the working population so that a select few may enjoy the benefits of the permanent employment system. And the brunt of the sacrifice is borne by women, who make up nearly 40 percent of the labor force.[31]

The lessons of the postwar period in the United States should make it clear that such a two-tier labor market will work here only at great cost. This segmented labor market was one of the foundations of postwar prosperity. But those excluded from the fruits of rapid growth—primarily minority workers and women—were increasingly unwilling to accept their subordinate status and increasingly able to impose costs on those who sought to defend the old ways. It is unimaginable—at least to us, if not to the Moral Majority—that the United States can permanently turn back the clock on its halting but continuing progress toward greater racial and sexual equality. The U.S. economy will have to find some other way, in the end, to provide decent and stable employment for *all* of its participants. The Japanese model would represent a clear step backward for the United States, which the strength of egalitarian pressures in our country would make extremely costly, if not simply impossible.

Second, the lack of meaningful democratic participation in economic decisions in Japan makes its corporatist model unlikely in the U.S. context—not to say highly undesirable. "Democratic politics is . . . ineffectual" in Japan, writes Harvard policy analyst Robert B. Reich; there are occasional protests, "but they have little effect on the daily process of politics and economic administration in Japan." Those who aspire to some kind of transplanted Japanese model in the U.S., Reich concludes, have "a common ancestry in Herbert Hoover's dream of an associationist state" which would not provide "for direct review by, or accountability to, the people in the factories, towns, or regions that will be affected."[32]

Hoover's dream has not yet been realized in the United States and we seriously doubt that it can be. Democratic forces are much too strong in this country, we presume, and "associationist" bonds much too weak. We find it particularly unlikely that large majorities of the U.S. labor force and citizenry will support corporatist policies which so starkly demand transfers of wealth and power from so many into the hands of so few. Those who are affected by economic growth and transition, as Reich concludes, "must be included in the process of industrial policy making itself. Anything less, and they will resist—and will have a right to resist."

This expectation is reinforced by an examination of the sources of Japanese cooperation with its own corporatist system. Chalmers Johnson, a Japan scholar at the University of California, cautions about attributing this cooperation to Asian "temperament."

For one thing, it was the history of poverty and war in Japan that established and legitimized Japan's priorities among the people in the first place. The famous Japanese consensus, that is, the broad popular support and a willingness to work hard for economic development that have characterized the Japanese during the 1950's and 1960's, is not so much a cultural trait as a matter of hard experience and of the mobilization of a large majority of the population to support economic goals. The willingness of the Japanese to subordinate the desires of the individual to those of the group is markedly weakening as generations come on the scene who have no experience of poverty, war, and occupation. To date Japan has not faced the egalitarian problems of other states for the simple reason that all Japanese were made equally poor by the war and postwar inflation and because, for all practical purposes, it bans immigration into its social system.[33]

It seems difficult to imagine that a homegrown corporatist model in the United States could reproduce this particular set of historical circumstances.

There is a third reason for doubting the usefulness of the Japanese model. It involves international politics and the structure of the world economy. The Japanese economy was spared the costs of military buildup during the postwar period. It prospered within the center of what Japanese political scientist Yoshikazu Sakamoto has called the "doughnut-shaped" structure of postwar imperialism, protected within a ring comprising both U.S. military power in the Pacific and neighboring military dictatorships in South Korea and Taiwan. According to Jon Halliday, author of *A Political History of Japanese Capitalism,* "the huge armies of the United States, Korea and Nationalist China made it possible for Japan to remain relatively demilitarized."[34]

This freedom from the burdens of militarization nurtured the rate of productive capital formation and technological change in Japan. And yet the doughnut-shaped structure of postwar imperialism also meant that it could operate within a stable world economy in which trade was expanding relatively rapidly and reliable currency transactions greased the growth of international exchange.

It is virtually inconceivable that such fortuitous historical opportunities will be available to the United States in the future. For the corporatists—no less than for others committed to free trade —the horns of the contemporary dilemma are inescapable. Either push for restored U.S. power in a U.S.-centered world economy, and a large military drain on capital formation and productive technological innovation, or cope with the problems of pursuing a free-trade strategy in an unstructured, polycentric, unpredictable, and unstable international economy. One horn of the free trader's dilemma promises orderly economic decline under the shadow of global conflagration; the other offers the chaotic gyrations of laissez-faire economics on a global scale.

Ezra Vogel is nonetheless hopeful: "Now that postindustrial America, too, requires higher levels of cooperation and more central leadership oriented to a modern economic order, there is no reason why Americans could not borrow and adapt Japanese models which, with a different tradition, it could not have originally created."[35] We would hope, on the basis of our analysis in Chapters 4 through 6, that the costs of relatively "more central leadership" in the U.S. economy would now be relatively clear. The postwar corporate system rested on a highly centralized, hierarchical, and bureaucratic structure of private power. The corporatists would have us maintain and almost certainly strengthen that private corporate center—with all of the contradictions which such a system poses in the United States. Even if they are able to pull it off, the costs of such a corporatist future for most people will be even higher, we fear, than the costs of the postwar system have been. And we think that most people have grown tired of paying the price.

IS THIS A CHOICE?

As the economy continues to deteriorate, as the supply-side promise continues to fade, we think that pressure will build over the next several years for a choice between monetarism and corporatism. We think that the current structure of politics in the United States makes one or another variant of corporatism the likely victor over the long haul—even though monetarists might enjoy a brief heyday of hardball economics. We suspect that the strength of popular resistance to monetarist deflation will make the odds on an eventual corporatist triumph look more and more favorable over time.

We can hardly feel sanguine about such a prospect. We have argued in this chapter that the costs of corporatism are likely to be very high, generating serious threats to our basic democratic rights and processes. These risks do not flow from the venality or elitism of individual corporatist protagonists, but from a more basic characteristic of the corporatist program. It, like both the supply-side and the monetarist strategies, embodies certain fundamental principles of the probusiness approach to restructuring the U.S. economy. These principles, we argue in the next chapter, are the ultimate source of the danger to our economic and political lives.

10

THE WORLD ACCORDING TO BUSINESS

The only sure results [of the current conservative policies] . . . are redistributions of income, wealth, and power—from government to private enterprises, from workers to capitalists, and from poor to rich. A revolution is in process all right, social and political more than economic. A capsule symbol is the nearly universal enthusiasm in Washington to rid the federal tax system of all semblance of taxation of intergenerational transfers of wealth.

> —James Tobin, Nobel Prize Laureate in economics[1]

The majority of Americans now believe that government serves the interests of big business rather than of all the people, that birth and connections matter more than effort and ability in getting ahead.

> —Kenneth Keniston, Yale social psychologist[2]

The problem with supply-side economics is that it has tried to ignore some basic economic rules. There is almost no economic evidence, as we saw in Chapter 8, to support any of its key propositions—but supply-siders have hoped against hope that everyone might be surprised, even including themselves.

The problem with monetarists and corporatists, quite to the contrary, is that they adhere too insistently to the rules—the rules of the world according to business. If we play by their rules, as we argued in Chapter 9, we are likely to bear enormous costs. In order to explore the possibility of escaping those costs, we must be very clear about the logic of the rules about which they remain so adamant.

All three probusiness strategies share a commitment to the restoration of corporate power in the domestic and world economies. This requires some kind of reconstitution of corporate power along all three axes of domination in the postwar corporate system—involving corporate control over production, the domestic reign of profitability, and U.S. domination in the international economy. The world according to business converges on three basic principles for promoting this restoration of business rule. These are the principles, as we have already seen at the beginning of Part II, of *profit-led growth, market-based allocation,* and *arms for economic power.* We believe that each of these three principles is based on flawed economic analysis. If these are the rules of the world according to business, we can do better.

THE PRINCIPLE OF PROFIT-LED GROWTH

We are told that we must restore profits to their uncontested reign and that we must replenish corporate coffers in order to stimulate investment. This insistent demand reflects an abiding and largely unchallenged macroeconomic principle—that the level and priorities of corporate profitability should determine the pace and direction of economic growth.

This principle of profit-led growth involves two kinds of arguments, one focusing on the *funds effect* and the other focusing on the *incentive effect.*

The funds effect reflects familiar propositions. If corporations have more profits, then their investments will increase and productivity will grow more rapidly; hence income should be redistributed from wages to profits. If the wealthy have more money, further, their savings will increase. These more ample savings, in turn, will drive down interest rates—through the greater supply of investable funds—and increase investment.

These propositions are conceivable, but neither logic nor the factual record speaks clearly in their favor.

First, it may be the case that higher levels of savings will help lower interest rates—although the monetary policy of the Federal Reserve Board has a much more direct effect. But will lower interest rates stimulate investment? Study after study of investment has found that the overall rate of growth of the economy, not the relative availability of investable funds, has the primary influence over the pace of investment.[3] If there is no promise of expanded demand, corporations will not invest—no matter how much more money you throw at them or how low real interest rates have fallen. If the costs of investment were so important, then the prodigal tax breaks for investment granted by Congress in 1981 would have restored the pace of investment. As we have already seen in Figure 8.2, they didn't.

Second, there is an equally serious problem with the argument that redistribution will increase profits. Suppose that consumption is heavily taxed to finance tax breaks for corporate profits and that wage concessions help bolster corporate profits through the collective bargaining process. This will certainly increase the *share* of profits in aggregate income. But what happens to the *level* of aggregate income itself? Consumption will fall, reducing the level of effective aggregate demand. Income will fall *unless* an increase in investment or net exports compensates for the decline in consumption. It is extremely unlikely that investment will increase while consumption is falling—because, as we have just argued, the level of aggregate demand is the most important determinant of total investment. It is no more likely that net exports will increase enough to offset declining consumption, since the rest of the world needs dollars to buy our exports but the dollars spent on U.S. imports will have fallen as a result of the fall of consumption in the United States.

The gap in aggregate demand could be filled, of course, by an increase in government purchases of goods and services. The prime potential areas for such an increase are social programs and military activities. More social spending is clearly anathema to the probusiness strategists, since it violates their principle of market-based allocation. Increased military spending, on the other hand, is potentially attractive to them, since it supports their principle of arms for economic power. To concentrate demand-boosting government expenditure on the military sector of the U.S. economy, however, is likely to cause serious economic dislocations. A rapid buildup of military-supplying industries would cause shortages of key materials and skilled personnel, and it would compound the wastefulness already embedded in the military-industrial complex.

On balance, then, a redistribution from wages to profits is a hazardous strategy for promoting investment. Without increases in final demand, the necessary increases in investment are unlikely. Profits may flourish, but investment may stagnate. "One can spend money on men and materials only at a given rate," according to Ben Heineman, chairman of Northwest Industries. "Beyond that it becomes foolish."[4] And while they wait, they speculate.

These are not new or novel observations. They have been self-evident to both economists and to workers since the Great Depression. Keynes himself emphasized the crucial importance of aggregate demand in determining levels of investment. And unions have equally emphasized the relationship. It is reported that Henry Ford once taunted Walter Reuther, pointing to some new automated equipment: "Walter," he asked, "how are you going to get those new machines to pay UAW dues?" "Henry," Reuther replied, "how are you going to get them to buy cars?"

Probusiness advocates would also stress the incentive effect of promoting higher profits. They argue that workers will supply more effort if they are not able to live on easy street; relatively lower wages, in other words, will encourage greater labor supply. They also argue that a more disciplined (and compliant) labor force would be more likely to exert greater work effort. And they argue continually that higher profit rates would stimulate technical innovation and cost reductions.

These propositions are dubious as well. Workers may be driven into submission, exerting greater effort through fear and hunger, but we have also emphasized in Chapter 6 that worker motivation is likely to depend on positive inducements as well as negative incentives—on the carrot as well as the stick. (For all of the intimidating effects of the Great Repression in the 1970s, as we have seen in Chapter 6, levels of work intensity were not restored in the 1973–79 period.) Higher levels of corporate profitability may stoke the entrepreneurial fires, similarly, but how will those technical innovations be applied if there is little investment to support them (as a result of dampened aggregate demand), or if there are fewer competent personnel to implement them (as a result of starved public support for education and training)?

These problems besetting the profit-led model of growth are not the result of managerial ineffectiveness or entrepreneurial torpor. They flow from the fundamentally contradictory nature of growth in an economy driven by private profitability.

We can look at the dual role of the wage in capitalist economies for one example of these contradictions. From the point of view of both capitalists and the aggregate economy, it would be better if wages were both *lower* and *higher* at exactly the same time! Each capitalist would like to pay his workers the minimum wage and have all other capitalists pay fifty dollars an hour. This being impossible, there is what economists sometimes call a "knife-edge" problem: a balance must be struck in the economy as a whole between reduction of costs, including wages, and support of the total demand for goods and services.

The same holds true for worker incentives. If capitalists push down wages, they may be able to take advantage of a chastened labor force. But if wages fall, the costs to the worker of job loss also fall—and workers may have less to lose from work resistance or from simply taking it easy on the job.

Even for capitalists, and certainly for the rest of us, there can be such a thing as too *high* a profit rate. High profits and low wages are not a guarantee of rapid economic growth—although, as James Tobin points out in the head quote to this chapter, their combination will certainly guarantee a regressive redistribution of income. What matters much more than the current profit rate, in determining both profits and growth, is the general institutional climate. The postwar corporate system worked for a while because it achieved a widespread political moderation of the problems which would otherwise have deterred corporate investment. Once those conditions for both profits and growth eroded, growth could not be guaranteed no matter how much money we fed into the corporate coffers.

We have witnessed this truth before. The unbridled and successful assault on labor and the pursuit of high profits in the 1920s, it is worth remembering, was remarkably lucrative for corporations and the wealthy, but it was a prelude, not to stable expansion, but to social dislocation, rampant fears of economic collapse, sluggish investment, and eventually the Depression. Can we learn the lesson only through further painful repetition?

THE PRINCIPLE OF MARKET-BASED ALLOCATION

The probusiness strategies insist not only that we enhance profits but also that we honor the market. They urge us to follow the principle of market-based allocation, relying on market price signals to light the path to economic recovery.

This principle builds on a single major argument. Prices are taken to be an accurate reflection of scarcities, measuring at once the real costs of goods and services and the capacity of goods to meet people's needs. If oil becomes more scarce, its price will go up. If pocket calculators become more plentiful, their price will go down. Were we to ignore these market indicators of relative scarcity, we would ignore some basic information—inexpensively obtained—about the opportunity costs of producing and consuming different kinds of goods and services.

This argument reinforces the maxims of profit-led growth. Since market prices are taken as accurate measures of resource scarcities, firm revenues per unit of output are treated as an accurate index of that firm's contribution to social welfare. If we as consumers didn't value a firm's products so highly, then they as producers would not be able to earn such a hefty net return. The higher the profits, the more the firm will be encouraged to produce what we value so highly. As long as we can rely on market prices as reliable indicators, we can trust in the meaning of profits as well. The chief executive officer and chair of Texas Instruments recently enshrined this view of the inner logic of his firm: "Texas Instruments exists to create, make and market useful products and services to satisfy the needs of our customers throughout the world. Our ability to meet those demands is determined by our innovative skills and measured by our profit."[5]

We do not doubt for a moment that market prices can provide useful information. But the probusiness strategists insist that we should rely almost exclusively on market signals (whether domestic or worldwide) as our beacons for economic growth. The principle of market-based allocation founders on the shoals of this claim about the *sufficiency* of market prices.

Economists have long recognized that business profits overstate a firm's net contribution to social needs when the business does not pay for its full costs of operation—as when it freely pollutes a river with its wastes or slowly kills its workers with deadly chemicals on the job. The dead fish in the river and the workers' hospital bills don't show up on the firm's books, but their costs are real nonetheless. Milton Friedman calls these "spillover effects"; they are also called "external diseconomies."

In the presence of these spillover effects, profits become an imperfect guide to economic decision-making. The result is an "overproduction" of external diseconomies. Unless firms are forced to pay the full costs of their pollution and environmental devastation, through one mechanism or another, market price tags will not reflect the true measure of the social value of the goods and services to which they are attached.

Market exchanges work best in those cases where what we want and need can be bought and sold. People can buy cloth instead of making it, for example, concentrating their own labor on wheat or corn or whatever is most remunerative. Market exchanges can handle, moreover, potentially sharp conflicts among its participants; you might hate your grocer's guts, but money takes no sides and bears no grudges. You can buy or sell as you like or take your business elsewhere.

But our economic lives involve many needs and desires which money cannot satisfy. Some examples: We care deeply about a safe and clean natural environment, but it is neither bought nor sold. We care more and more about our development as people, but most of our learning and growing does not and cannot be transacted on the market.

Information provides a particularly interesting example. Consider the plight of the record and tape industry. They now engage in costly legal and technological efforts to prevent low-cost copying of music and the written word. Why? Because making the goods available at the cost of their reproduction—their real scarcity prices—would virtually eliminate the profits of the original producer, no matter how rational it might be for society as a whole. (And thus the recent suits against stores which rent records to allow home taping, or the absurd efforts of airports to prevent more than one person watching pay TVs.)

Issues of geographic location provide an even more important example—particularly in the context of recent political debates. If firms are the only units making decisions about production and location, they will choose their locations solely on the basis of their input costs and market access. Because there is no market in "community life" or "neighborhood ties," people's continuing historic concerns about the quality of their lives in their communities is not reflected in the prices to which firms respond. Corporations have found it expedient to move to the Sun Belt and overseas, imposing many of the costs of the move on the affected communities. Our aggregate net social welfare may well decline as a result. The market cannot determine whether lower product costs make up for the destruction of local communities, the psychic costs of relocation, or the sense of personal rootlessness which results.

Just as the probusiness advocates link their first two principles of profit-led growth and market-based allocation, so do we combine our doubts about these two economic axioms. Market prices cannot measure all of the costs and benefits of everything we consume or value. They have become, indeed, an increasingly imperfect guide to our economic and social welfare. This means, in turn, that profit-led growth will not point toward or reflect all of our most important economic objectives—and that its targets will diverge more and more from what we care about and seek. The profits and prices which brought us Love Canal are hardly reliable guides to economic restructuring.

THE PRINCIPLE OF ARMS FOR ECONOMIC POWER

The third probusiness principle calls for remilitarization. The sources of this drive for higher arms spending are complex, but the economic arguments advanced to justify it are much more straightforward. The logic of the arms-for-economic-power principle builds on three main arguments:

- Mobilized military spending creates productive technological spin-offs, marshaling research and development for the entire society. We can have our military security and enjoy more rapid growth at the same time. This is the *more*-guns-and-*better*-butter argument.

- Remilitarization will restore U.S. economic power, according to its proponents, reversing some of the slippage which has afflicted the United States since the early 1960s.

- As long as we're at it, we should also recognize that people need jobs and that military spending will help generate both employment and effective demand.

The arguments supporting this remilitarization principle are particularly dubious.

The first argument about productivity and technological spin-offs represents only one side of the productivity balance sheet, and not the decisive one. It is true, indeed, that some innovations fostered through defense spending are transferable to the civilian economy. But military spending also saps our aggregate productive capacity. The labor and resources devoted to military production are wasted unless the resulting military equipment is put to some socially valued use. The more of our resources we devote to military spending, the less are available for other uses of more immediate value. Military spending may conceivably improve the quality of our butter—although we doubt this alluring argument —but it certainly reduces the quantity available. Moreover, if we are really suffering from inadequate technological progress (though the evidence we cited in Chapter 6 suggests that this has not been a very significant factor in the productivity slowdown), surely it would make more sense to promote R&D in the civilian sector—where it can have a direct payoff—than to hope for an indirect spinoff from R&D oriented toward military projects.

The second argument in favor of remilitarization seems equally problematic. The arms advocates worry about our terms of trade, and particularly about access to resources such as imported oil. But the lessons of the postwar period, and especially those of the Vietnam War, should certainly have taught us that neither millions of soldiers nor billions of dollars spent on weapons can secure international domination or prevent its erosion. If the hundreds of billions spent on defense in the postwar period could not sustain U.S. dominion, given the overwhelming initial advantages enjoyed by the U.S. armed forces immediately after World War II, how could we possibly presume that remilitarization will now *restore* what we have already lost? And if it did, what would be the cost in lives (and perhaps liberties) lost?

The jobs argument is no more compelling. We need jobs created by wasteful spending *only* if there are no other ways to create jobs. But if we can imagine alternative uses of public funds —for schools and hospitals and roads and child-care centers— who would argue that missiles and bombs *always* make a greater contribution to economic and social welfare?

FORCED CHOICES?

Probusiness proponents normally play a final trump card at this stage of the argument. Our probusiness principles aren't flawless, they might be willing to admit, but *there is no other way*. We must build profits, follow the market, and remilitarize, they argue, or condemn ourselves to stagnation and decline.

There are two reasonable tests of this final argument.

The first involves the kind of intercountry comparisons we have made throughout the first part of this book. Other countries have not applied the probusiness principles with anything like the militancy and persistence which we are witnessing in the United States:

- Other countries have achieved far more rapid productivity growth and higher rates of capital formation at the same time that they have achieved much more equal distributions of wealth and income. The total share of wealth controlled by the wealthiest 2 percent of households in the United States has been roughly 25 percent higher than in West Germany, for example, while the rate of capital formation has been 25 percent lower.[6]
- Other countries have grown far more rapidly than the United

States despite much lower levels of corporate profitability. As Figure 10.1 indicates, the average after-tax rate of profit in the United States was higher during the 1970s than in Japan, France, and the United Kingdom, the only advanced countries for which fully comparable data on after-tax profit rates were available. Despite those higher average profit rates, however, U.S. manufacturing productivity growth and aggregate investment levels lagged considerably behind those of the other three countries. The U.S. growth in per capita gross domestic product also fell far short of per capita GDP growth in France and Japan, managing to nose out Great Britain by a hair.

• We have already seen in Figure 4.2 that there was an almost exact inverse relationship over the 1960s between the relative levels of military spending in major advanced countries and their fortunes in world markets. The greater the portion of economic resources devoted to military spending, according to those data, the greater the loss in world-trade shares over the same period. Similarly, according to U.S. Bureau of Labor Statistics data, levels of manufacturing productivity growth in those advanced capitalist countries with low levels of military spending considerably outstripped the lagging manufacturing productivity growth of the United States, the United Kingdom, and other big military spenders.[7]

Fig. 10.1

The Profit Rate and Economic Growth, 1970-1979

	Average net rate of return[a] to fixed capital	Average ratio of gross capital formation to GDP[b]	Average annual rate of growth	
			output per hour in manufacturing[c]	per capita gross domestic product[b]
U.S.	8.7%	17.3	2.5	2.0
Japan	7.0	33.1	7.0	3.6
France	5.5	23.1	4.6	3.1
United Kingdom	3.5	19.0	2.8	1.8

[a]After tax for non-financial enterprises. For U.S. and Japan, from P.J. Hill, unpublished OECD study; for France and U.K., from J. Mairesse and M. King, unpublished study, Paris.
[b]OECD, National Accounts, Vol. I, 1982.
[c]U.S. Bureau of Labor Statistics, Dec. 1981 (unpublished tables).

But a second test remains necessary. The probusiness advocates can always argue, after all, that other countries are very different from the United States and that foreign experiences are not transferable to ours. Probusiness strategists insist that their principles are the *only* ones which can effectively guide economic restructuring in the United States.

This argument fares no better than the first. We present in Part III of this book a twenty-four-point democratic alternative to the probusiness strategies for economic recovery. There *is* a choice. We do not have to accept the inevitability of the costs of corporate power. The world according to business has led us into economic decline. We should think twice about the perilous escape route which they recommend.

11

PROFITS BEFORE DEMOCRACY?

As the business of the country has learned the secret of combination, it is gradually subverting the power of the politician and rendering him subservient to its purposes.

—*Bankers' Magazine,* 1901[1]

America has embarked on a career of imperialism, both in world affairs and in every other aspect of her life. . . . The path of empire takes its way, and in modern times . . . the scepter passes to the United States.

—Management consultant, 1941[2]

. . . if the economics of the "invisible hand" and "reprivatization" fails to deliver a buoyant economy, pressure will mount to create state economic mechanisms and political processes that will work, that can manage the task of allocating economic resources, sacrifices, and reward . . . If the New Deal of 1933 to 1936 could be accused of . . . a corporate state dictatorship . . . , the political economics I have sketched here would better merit the term.

—Kevin Phillips, conservative columnist, 1982[3]

We do not need a crystal ball to assay our political and economic prospects; the muse of history offers some historical parallels. This is not our first economic crisis; it is our third since the Civil War. The first lasted from the late 1880s through the 1890s. The second encompassed the 1930s. Each rocked the foundations of the economy just as the recent crisis has shaken our own economic base.

In each of these two earlier crises, moreover, basic changes in economic and political institutions proved necessary before a return to prosperity was possible. The paths to this economic restructuring were tangled with thickets of competing political interests. It took years to clear the way for a decisive political resolution.

These earlier experiences with economic restructuring underscore our fears about the future consequences of a probusiness strategy for economic recovery in the United States. The capitalist economy survived its earlier crises, but the resolution of each crisis witnessed an intense struggle between democracy and profitability as competing first principles for U.S. society. And while the survival of capitalism did not see the demise of democratic forms of government, the control of the economy became much more centralized and unaccountable. The private and public costs of concentrated economic power mounted. Democratic movements themselves advanced, winning direct election of U.S. senators, extension of suffrage, and other important gains, but more and more of our economic resources were devoted to containment of popular influence and protection of private wealth. The waste of centralized corporate power increased in turn.

We take the time to review some of these historical lessons because we seek to avoid yet another saga of wasteful private power and yet further encroachment by authoritarian prerogative. Trickle-down economics would love to involve us in the fanciful details of its future balance sheets. But where in those balance sheets is the entry for democracy?

THE POLITICS OF ROLLER-COASTER ECONOMICS

Living in the United States draws our gaze to the future, not the past. There is much to forget: the economy has often failed. The pendulum has swung historically between growth and crisis, compromise and rebellion, stability and chaos. These pendular swings have forged a continuing saga of public conflict and encroaching private power.

We shall turn to the historical record of economic boom and bust in a moment. But it seems useful first to retrieve some of the historical flesh and blood of these swings between growth and crisis. We introduce this historical excursion with a series of textbook cameos, beginning in the middle of the nineteenth century.

The montage starts with the entrepreneurial heroes of early U.S. capitalism: Samuel Morse with his telegraph, Cyrus McCormick with his reaper, Thomas Alva Edison with his light bulbs, and Andrew Carnegie with his new and improved steel ovens. The arteries of economic growth spread quickly across the country—commemorated by the classic photo of the "golden spike," with smiling managers and coolie labor blessing the final transcontinental railroad connection.

Expansion gives way to venality and discontent. In Washington, D.C., Civil War hero Ulysses S. Grant now plays host to the charlatans of industry, watching benignly as the captains of capitalism divide up public bounty from the Age of Enterprise. And there are the long winters of unemployment and poverty in the 1880s and 1890s—recorded compassionately by Jacob Riis and etched more dramatically with portraits of bearded and wild-eyed anarchists ostensibly provoking crowds to insurrection during the famous Haymarket massacre of 1886.

Soon enough, corporate leaders race to escape from the eddy of competition and rebellion. They bend every effort to eliminate cutthroat competition, vainly constructing "pools" and "trusts" before J. P. Morgan and his friends finally buy up nearly everything in sight. They counter William Jennings Bryan's Cross of Gold with their own favorite political mouthpiece, William McKinley, propped up by support from Mark Hanna and his plutocratic allies. William Randolph Hearst helps organize diversionary actions, inciting the masses with lust for foreign conquest, while Teddy Roosevelt consummates their passions with his charge up San Juan Hill.

These efforts pay off. By the time the dust of World War I has cleared, we see the long lines of Model T Fords, the swirling flappers and the hidden speakeasy delights, the speculative booms in Florida real estate and the ostentatious luxury of the Great Gatsbys. Main Street ascends in U.S. cultural life and Herbert Hoover seems the perfect and righteous repository of Republican (and therefore American) virtue.

That was, as Frederick Allen observed, only yesterday. The Depression follows hard upon the Wall Street suicides of 1929. The postwar system emerges fitfully through the 1940s, bearing the dappled markings of New Deals and Fair Deals, hot wars and cold wars, union loyalists and traitors, Progressives and Dixiecrats, isolationists and internationalists, McCarthy and MacArthur, the Missouri haberdasher and the comforting general from Abilene.

And then, once again, buoyant prosperity. And now, once again, stagnation and crisis.

The Timing and Magnitude of Crisis

This montage suggests a historical rhythm:

• The first wave of entrepreneurial expansion lasted through the 1870s. Prosperity surrendered to instability sometime during the 1880s. By the early 1890s, economic crisis had arrived.

• Prosperity returned around 1900. The economy picked up steam through World War I, racing during the 1920s. The faster it sped, the harder it crashed; the 1930s were *all* Depression.

• Perked up initially by World War II, the economy launched its postwar expansion by the late 1940s. After booming through the mid-1960s, as we have already seen, it began to sputter and then sink into crisis again. We're still sinking.

The threads connecting these cycles of expansion and decline are political and macroeconomic. Economists continue to debate both the theory and the evidence of long economic swings—or "Kondratieffs," as they are often called, after the Russian statistician who first highlighted this historical pattern. We cannot even enter, much less resolve, these analytic debates in this book.[4] We extract a single, simple conclusion: after long periods of growth, the U.S. economy has experienced crises in the 1890s, the 1930s, and the recent period.

Figure 11.1 provides some partial evidence of this pattern of boom and bust in the U.S. macroeconomy. Where the data per-

Fig. 11.1

**Boom and Crisis
in the U.S. Economy, 1873-1981**

	I		II		III		Averages	
	Boom 1873-1892	Crisis 1892-1899	Boom 1899-1929	Crisis 1929-1937	Boom 1948-1973	Crisis 1973-1981	Boom	Crisis
Average Unemployment Rates	n.a.	11.8	4.9	18.3	4.8	6.9	4.8	12.3
Average annual growth in gross domestic nonfarm product	6.6	2.9	3.7	−0.5	3.9	2.2	4.7	1.5
Average annual growth in gross domestic private fixed nonresidential investment	8.0	1.3	2.4	−0.3	4.0	2.0	3.5	1.0

Source: Historical Statistics of the United States and U.S. Department of Commerce, Long Term Economic Growth. The dates for the crisis periods refer to the late years of accelerating decline; although we argue in Chs. 2-6 that economic decline began in 1966-73, the 1973-81 period is more comparable to the earlier periods of "late crisis."

mit, we compare the years of expansion and of crisis during the three long swings in U.S. capitalism since the middle of the nineteenth century. The onset of each crisis—the late 1880s, the late 1920s, and the late 1960s—are included as the end of the boom rather than the first years of the crisis, for the major macroeconomic indicators (growth of output and investment), as we have seen in Chapters 4–6, generally decline only after the crisis is well under way. Each of the indicators in the table reveals the notable differences in economic vitality between the years of expansion and crisis.

- Accurate unemployment data are not available annually before the 1880s, but unemployment rates for the subsequent periods clearly alternate. Across the three long swings, unemployment during the periods of crisis has averaged two and a half times its levels during the booms.
- Aggregate output and gross investment also reflect the pendular swings. Growth rates slowed most dramatically during the 1930s, but they also slowed during the 1890s and the 1970s. Both rates averaged three times higher during the long booms than during the crises. By either measure, it seems evident that the economy sagged during these years of crisis.

If this is our third period of economic crisis, then, it is pertinent to examine the process by which the economy escaped from the earlier two crises and reestablished the basis for growth and expansion. We provide a condensed outline here in order to highlight the political dynamics of economic restructuring.

The 1890s and the Big-Business Coalition

Entrepreneurial expansion after the Civil War began to fizzle for three related reasons.

First, the frontiers of the market did not extend forever. Once the national rail network was completed, transportation costs plummeted and price competition became more and more intense. With thousands and thousands of small enterprises pushing and tugging for a share of the new, larger national trade, there were no available mechanisms for blunting the razor's edge of capitalist competition. Andrew Carnegie aptly summarized the corporate view in 1889:

Manufacturers have balanced their books year after year only to find their capital reduced at each successive balance. . . . It is in soil thus prepared that anything promising relief is gladly welcomed. The manufacturers are in the position of patients that have tried in vain every doctor of the regular school for years, and are now liable to become the victim of any quack that appears. Combinations, syndicates, trusts —they are willing to try anything.[5]

Second, firms had not yet succeeded in gaining effective control of either production or their workers. As prices fell, they naturally tried to reduce labor costs and increase productivity in order to protect their profits. They pulled at the levers, but neither wage-cutting nor speed-up had enough effect. As a result, while prices continued to fall, unit labor costs rose, tightening the vise on firm profits.[6]

Third, agriculture had expanded rapidly along with the rest of the economy. Farmers had borrowed heavily to finance this expansion, plunging deeply into debt. As farm prices fell along with the general deflation, the incomes with which farmers could repay their debts slackened. Fixed debt obligations weighed more and more heavily upon declining money incomes. Farm prosperity soured, and the contribution of agriculture to the aggregate growth of the economy began to diminish.

These contradictions had combined by the late 1880s to produce both spreading economic crisis and increasingly frequent political eruptions. Popular reaction against business power was spreading on two horizons.

Farm protest focused on prices and credit. Farmers began to see bankers' faces behind every crop and a debt notice in every mail delivery. By the early 1890s, the National Farmers Alliance had hundreds of thousands of members. Its newspapers and magazines reached several million. Its chapters focused on some basic agrarian populist demands: easy money, increasingly linked to the demand for silver-backed currency; public control of the banks; and public ownership and control of the railroads and telegraph lines. Alliance members in the South, at least through the early 1890s, struggled to counter Dixie racism and establish political bonds among black and white farmers.[7]

On the urban front, working-class protest was episodic but nonetheless threatening. The Knights of Labor collapsed after the left-baiting which followed the Haymarket massacre in 1886. But local movements were beginning to escalate protest by 1890. Dockworkers organized a massive strike in New Orleans. Miners continued to rise against their working conditions in both the northern and the southern coal fields. In 1892, armed steelworkers fought a pitched battle against the Carnegie lockout at Homestead, Pennsylvania.

The election of 1892 was a watershed. The People's Party had formed officially in 1890. Although dominated by farming interests, the 1892 convention clearly signaled its intention to forge a close alliance between agrarian and urban working-class interests. The convention preamble advertised these political intentions in ringing language:

The urban workmen are denied the right of organization for self-protection; imported pauperized labor beats down their wages; a hireling standing army . . . [is] established to shoot them down. . . . The fruits of the toil of millions are boldly stolen to build up colossal fortunes. . . . From the same prolific womb of governmental injustice we breed two classes—paupers and millionaires.[8]

To capitalists, the most threatening aspect of the emergent populism was its commitment to take democracy seriously. As

Grant McConnell observes in his classic book *The Decline of Agrarian Democracy,*

> Yet, in 1892 . . . the farmer's movement was something more than a challenge to industrialism. There were economic demands, the class demands of agrarianism, to be sure. . . . But, equally, farmers demanded a graduated income tax, restraints on monopoly, education, the direct election of senators, the Australian ballot, the initiative, and the referendum. These were not narrow class demands. They were honest and genuine attempts to ensure the operations of democracy, to make certain that *no* group was excluded from sharing in the political process. . . .
>
> Even more important, the Alliance gave birth to a genuine political party. This implied that the agrarians were prepared to accept the responsibility of building a majority, even if that majority included other than farmers. It implied a willingness to seek political solutions of a general character. This was the ultimate promise of agrarian democracy. . . .[9]

This promise seemed to be blossoming. In 1892, James Weaver, the People's Party candidate for president, won more than a million votes, nearly 9 percent of the total popular vote. The populists also took eight congressional seats, three governorships, and innumerable county offices.

The economy crashed in 1893, with unemployment climbing quickly to 18.4 percent in 1894, and protest seemed to spread even more rapidly. The Pullman strike captured national attention, building toward a dramatic confrontation between Eugene Debs' American Railway Union and federal troops; roughly fourteen thousand police, militia and troops were called upon to crush the strike, with hundreds arrested and at least thirty killed. Troops later routed Coxey's Army of unemployed marchers in Washington, D.C.

The emergent protest movement suddenly seemed momentous. As McConnell concludes: "Its onslaught shook to their foundations the structures of organizations and political alignment which had been long in building. Even more, it seemed to threaten the destruction of all the economic winnings of a capitalism so far everywhere victorious. For here was the fury of common men. . . .[10]

Business interests rallied as if in a fire emergency. They concluded that agrarian and urban industrial interests must be split.[11] After two decades of inconsequential and essentially issue-free debate between the Democrats and the Republicans, the contest between the political parties suddenly became a matter of life and death for northern industrialists. Beginning with the congressional elections of 1894, the wealthy mobilized their support behind the Republican Party, pouring millions into their campaigns. They concentrated on building an electoral alliance with industrial wage earners, seeking to forestall their potential coalition with populist farmers in the West. The Republicans promised tariffs, protecting industrial employment, and stable currencies, protecting the purchasing power of urban wages. When the Democrats won populist support behind the silver-currency candidacy of Bryan in 1896, the Republicans stepped up the pace. They outspent the Democrats by five to one, doubling the money they had poured into the 1892 campaign.[12] Mark Hanna and his monied circle virtually controlled the party and its campaign strategy, issuing directives to the compliant McKinley.

The strategy worked. While the Democrats carried the states where the People's Party had scored most substantially in 1892, McKinley won the election on the strength of his margins in the industrial states—New York, Pennsylvania, Ohio, and Illinois. The populists lost, soon to disappear from the political arena, and a new and powerful electoral coalition guided by big business had triumphed. The election returns of 1894 and 1896, as historian Samuel Hays concludes, produced "one of the greatest bloodless political realignments that this country has ever experienced."[13]

Big business moved quickly to consolidate its new political strength. The merger movement between 1898 and 1903 produced giant new industrial consolidations, accounting for as much as one third of total industrial assets in the United States.[14] Business groups began to promote foreign adventures; Teddy Roosevelt echoed their hopes when he wrote to a friend in 1897, "I should welcome almost any war, for I think this country needs one."[15] The Spanish-American War provided them (and TR) exactly the opportunity they sought. The new industrial giants also increased their leverage over workers, pitting Poles against Germans, Italians against Irish, waging protracted battles against the IWW, the Socialist Party, and industrial union-organizing campaigns, perfecting what many called the "drive system" of labor management. They also planned for some government regulation to curb the excesses of continuing combination.

In building this new institutional strength, big business continued to fight two brush fires. One involved the resistance of small business, organized primarily through the National Association of Manufacturers. The other involved the socialist and revolutionary legatees of the earlier populist tradition. While big business fought a crafty battle, it sometimes relied on pure brute strength. It organized private militias to beat back unions, calling in federal troops whenever needed. It helped orchestrate the political purges during and after World War I, when thousands of radicals were jailed or deported as part of the "Red Scare." And it resisted to the end such popular reforms as the direct election of the U.S. Senate, hoping to keep its hands on as many political controls as possible.

At the same time, big business also found it necessary to respond to and eventually to court an important new political force: middle-class reform movements and their progressivism. These reformers helped ensure that big business would not engage in entirely unrestrained pursuit of profits, curbing some corporate excesses, such as child-labor abuse, and requiring some corporate attention to public opinion. Once Woodrow Wilson was finally able to shape a relatively successful integration of reform ambitions and corporate goals after 1913, the big-business coalition was complete. During and after World War I, more and more middle-class voters felt comfortable supporting the new reign of profits.

In the end, the big-business coalition reshaped the U.S. economy. Four main institutional transformations promoted economic recovery. Business had itself helped resolve the anarchy of competition through merger and consolidation. It had gained additional leverage over workers through mechanization and the added strength which its more sophisticated and aggressive strategies helped provide. Through its new imperial adventures and favorable tariff policies, it had both won political and economic breathing space and begun to develop access to new markets for agricultural and industrial products. And it had helped to shape some carefully modulated government reforms coordinating the centralization and extension of its private domain.

These transformations emerged through political struggle. The populist challenge had initially spurred big business to organize and operate as a class. After the turn of the century, as the secretary of the principal big-business association, the National Civic Federation, observed, "our enemies are the Socialists among the labor people and the anarchists among the capitalists."[16] By winning both these battles, the big-business coalition secured a new basis for capitalist growth. The Roaring Twenties were its reward.

The 1930s and the Growth Coalition

The Depression of the 1930s provides a more recent and more familiar example of the politics of economic restructuring.

The Depression had itself resulted from a complex combination of three important contradictions in the turn-of-the-century foundations for capitalist growth. First, imperialist rivalries among all the advanced powers led to continuing international instability which World War I failed to resolve; the 1920s therefore featured sharp swings in world prices and trading relations, contributing to the vulnerability which the crash of the 1930s so bitterly exposed. Second, the very power of the big-business coalition led, during the 1920s, to a regressive distribution of income and wealth; this eventually led to slackening demand for consumption goods and an increased susceptibility of the economy to swings in the always volatile demand for investment goods.[17] Third, this surplus savings fed increasingly bullish financial speculation—whose unregulated bubble eventually burst in the 1929 crash.

As at the turn of the century, there were both a small-business backlash and a popular rebellion.

Small-business forces were inclined to ride out the crisis, hoping that the free market would quickly resolve the system's imbalances. Herbert Hoover's inaction during the first three years of the Depression reflected this faithful pursuit of the competition-as-usual response. Initial business opposition to political reforms such as the Wagner Act, legalizing unions and collective bargaining, equally reflected this knee-jerk preference for cure by the acid bath of the market.

Popular forces galvanized in the early 1930s. Tenant organizations and unemployed councils grew increasingly effective in 1931–32. The union movement spread like a prairie fire after 1935. Socialist and communist presidential candidates gained a combined total of a million votes in the 1932 election and, as before, third-party candidates won congressional and local elections. Much more significantly, the discontented were taking it to the streets, expressing their frustration not only with the economy but with the political mechanisms through which they were supposed to communicate their dissatisfaction.

Large corporations soon recognized that business as usual was suicidal. However well the turn-of-the-century institutions had worked for a time, they were now clearly falling apart. There was strong and continuing business opposition to the New Deal, as might be expected, but growing numbers of business leaders recognized, as they had in the 1890s, the need for urgent action. One New Dealer recalled the growing receptiveness of corporate leaders to government reforms:

The fact that people acted as they did, in violation of law and order, was itself a revolutionary act. . . . The industrialists who had some understanding recognized this right away. [Roosevelt] could not have done what he did without the support of important elements of the wealthy class. They did not sabotage the [New Deal] programs. Just the opposite.[18]

In moving toward coordinated action, the most forward-looking corporate leaders pursued three principal strategies:
- They accepted the need for even greater government regulation of excessive competition, supporting and helping chart the National Industrial Recovery Administration (NIRA), using it to help strengthen their monopoly leverage.
- They also began planning for dramatic extension of U.S. power overseas, aiming to overcome the slack demand for

corporate products which had underlain the 1930s crunch. "The future of capitalism depends," as one government adviser concluded, "on increased foreign purchasing of our exports."[19]

• They also appreciated, however reluctantly, the need for compromise with the liberal and popular insurgencies against economic insecurity. Roosevelt aired some of their motivation midway through the New Deal effort: "The true conservative seeks to protect the system of private property and free enterprise," he concluded, "by correcting such injustices and inequalities as arise from it."[20] It was a proper measure of the strength of popular discontent that such widespread New Deal reforms proved necessary in order to "protect" that system.

But New Deal reforms were not enough. Business forces were unable to break the political stalemates which had emerged by the late 1930s. On one side, small-business forces had enough control over the conservative wing of the Republican Party to prevent the party from embracing the New Deal program. On the other side, popular discontent continued into and after World War II, exploding in strike waves immediately after the war.

Hot and cold war finally helped finish what the New Deal had begun. Wartime business strengthened large corporate control over its own markets and industrial wealth. The war itself produced a world economy in 1946 in which the United States accounted for half of all industrial output.[21] And postwar anticommunism provided the final weapon in the battle against radicals and insurgents, fostering the purges of "reds" from unions and popular movements, helping cement the bonds between large business and an increasingly cooperative organized-labor movement.

It was a powerful one-two punch. Government spending and international power fostered rapid economic growth, while anticommunism sealed an accord that further domestic conflict would be limited to the distribution of its rewards. Through that dynamic, a new political coalition, which political scientist Alan Wolfe calls the "growth coalition," was born. It was led by large corporations and included much of organized labor. Wolfe concludes that:

This coalition advocated an overall expansion of the economy through macroeconomic policies made acceptable to the monopoly sector of the economy. . . . Based upon the rapid expansion of the economy, it developed a foreign policy that combined a reorganization of the world under American economic hegemony with military power to ensure American influence. . . . The tasks established by the growth coalition were herculean, but anything seemed possible in an expanding economy. America had never before seen anything like this coalition, and it may never see anything like it again.[22]

Once again, large corporations had managed to resolve the crisis through a process which eventually restored and enhanced their economic power. Substantial institutional restructuring took place, resulting in the postwar corporate system we described in Chapter 4. This system now seems to have been inevitable only because of the narrowness of retrospective vision. The postwar corporate system emerged not from the inevitability of history but from the dialectics of choice and compulsion, conflict and struggle, attack and counterresponse. And it ultimately decayed because of mounting foreign and domestic resistance to the costs of private power it embodied.

FROM PAST TO PRESENT AND FUTURE

We have not taken these brief excursions to present a complete history of crisis resolution. We have a much more modest objective. We want to use this historical background both to highlight the antidemocratic consequences of probusiness victories in the past and to ponder their likely consequences in the future.

In each of the two previous crises, the wealthiest and most powerful business interests clearly contended with two alternative currents of political response. One, the more historically conservative, reflected small business interests and acted to protect the operations of the "free market." The other, reflecting sundry and shifting popular impulses, sought democratic control over the economy, hoping in often unspecified ways to shift economic priorities from profitability to popular needs.

In each case, as we have seen, large corporations triumphed against both tendencies, but the character of their triumph was somewhat different in the two successive episodes of institutional restructuring. In the first period after the turn of the century, they so successfully restored their economic and political power—particularly following their final victories against both unions and radicals after World War I—that they reigned virtually unchecked during the 1920s. After the second period of restructuring, in contrast, the postwar corporate system involved a much more complex balance of forces—with significant concessions to organized labor and substantial improvements in income security. Democratic forces had much greater effect on the second institutional transformation, in this respect, than they had on the first.

This suggests a political dynamic which is central to our concern about probusiness strategies in the current crisis. When corporate profitability and power dominate a period of restructuring, the thrust of institutional innovation intensifies the continuing conflict between economic recovery and democracy. The costs of private power rise, as we saw in Chapters 4 through 6, because corporations must marshal more of the resources under their command *against* popular power. Insisting on profits before democracy, they expand the institutional mechanisms devoted to their own self-protection. Waste results from their fears of democratic control.

Yet democracy has not atrophied through the successive episodes of economic restructuring. Quite to the contrary, people have been able to extend their political power as they have needed more and more effective instruments for the fight against private power and privilege. But the corporate defense of profits before democracy has produced a substantial increase in the centralization of private economic power in the United States.

We document our conclusion with data on the two principal tendencies underlying this trend.

Figure 11.2 presents the most obvious result of centralized private power, showing the portion of total industrial assets controlled by the largest one hundred industrial corporations. Comparable data on industrial concentration are not readily available

254 THE LIMITS OF TRICKLE-DOWN ECONOMICS

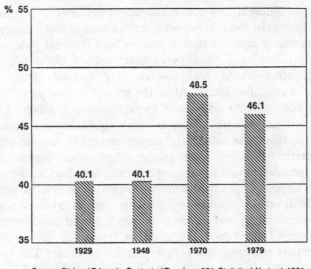

Fig. 11.2
Rising Corporate Concentration
largest 100 industrial corporations' share of industrial assets

Source: Richard Edwards, Contested Terrain, p. 221; Statistical Abstract, 1981,
p. 541; 1929 figure is linear interpolation of figures for 1925 and 1931;
1948 figure is adjusted to take account of slight difference in two different series.

before the 1920s, but the evidence on the last 50 years suggests a significant pattern: centralized corporate control over basic industrial capital moved a notch higher during the most recent boom, but remained constant or declined during periods of crisis.

Figure 11.3 tracks the rising institutional costs of administering this corporate empire. The bars measure supervisory workers' share of total employment. (Data are available only for manufacturing before World War II.) Here too, the pattern is significant. Big business substantially expanded its administrative apparatus during the periods of economic restructuring—from the bottom of the crisis through the years of expansion—in order to extend and consolidate its restored power. The growth of the bureaucratic apparatus has been much more rapid from the trough to the peak of the last two long swings than from the peaks into the years of crisis.

The centralization of unaccountable private power has resulted both from the victory of large corporations in the political struggles over restructuring and from their efforts to consolidate their strength against challengers to the corporate regime. More centralized asset control strengthened their hand against small business, while the burgeoning bureaucratic apparatus increased their leverage over workers and consumers. The result has been growing economic waste—a continuing rise in the costs of corporate power, of which we have already provided some conservative estimates in Chapter 7.

Could It Get Worse Still?

Prevailing probusiness strategies for resolving the current crisis seem destined to reinforce these earlier tendencies toward centralized and unaccountable power. We have argued in the previous

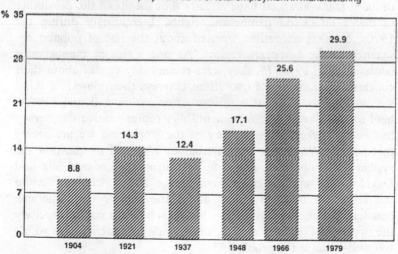

Fig. 11.3
Growing Corporate Bureaucracy
nonproduction employment as % of total employment in manufacturing

Source: Historical Statistics of the United States, Series P4-5; Employment and Training Report of the President, 1981, p. 212

chapter that these strategies share three basic principles: profit-led growth, market-based allocation, and arms for economic power. The first of these principles involves a transfer of resources to the wealthiest and largest corporations. The second extends the dominion and reduces the accountability of corporate decisions—by insisting on the primacy of profitability in economic life. The third strengthens the hand of corporate interests against those abroad while sacrificing the needs of the poor in the United States for the sake of military spending.

It is clear to us that democracy will suffer if any of the probusiness strategies is pursued. Either people will cower before the reassertion of corporate interests, paving the way for rapid centralization of private power and the erosion of popular rights, or popular forces will mobilize, insisting on the importance of their own needs and interests. If this latter tendency is strong, but does not succeed in displacing a probusiness strategy, then corporations will be likely to waste even more of our economic resources to curtail popular power—building up their bureaucratic empires and extending their influence over the government. And they may move directly to curb democratic rights and privileges.

We fear for democracy in particular because there is clear evidence that corporations have already thought about the possibility of direct attack on democratic rights. Increasingly during the 1970s, business executives worried about the rise of popular resistance to the corporate regime. At one series of management conferences in 1974–75, they were remarkably candid about their concerns. A sampling of quotations conveys their views: "I think we are long overdue for a serious examination and major overhaul of our system of government." "A representative democracy has never worked in the history of the world and we are seeing that here." "We are in serious trouble. We need to question the system itself: one man, one vote."[23] Journalists Leonard Silk and David Vogel reported on the conference and concluded: "while the critics of business worry about the atrophy of American democracy, the concern in the nation's boardrooms is precisely the opposite. For an executive, democracy in America is working too well—that is the problem."[24]

Some task-force reports for the Trilateral Commission—an association of corporate executives with a sprinkling of representatives from the academy and organized labor—have expressed similar doubts about democracy. The postwar corporate system had served business so well, they observed, because of the close political connections between Wall Street and Washington. After the mid-1960s, as these reports noted at length, popular rebellions spread—undercutting the "governability" of the system. One task-force report reached a stark conclusion:

Al Smith once remarked that the "only cure for the evils of democracy is more democracy." Our analysis suggests that applying that cure at the present time could well be adding fuel to the flames. Instead, some of the problems of governance in the United States stem from an excess of democracy. . . . Needed, instead, is a greater degree of moderation of democracy.[25]

Martin Feldstein, appointed chair of the President's Council of Economic Advisers in 1982, raises similar concerns about the compatibility of democracy and the kinds of regressive redistribution upon which the probusiness strategies insist:

There is, of course, the risk that the democratic political process . . . may not be able to look far enough into the future to adopt appropriate policies. . . . An inability to look ahead and to postpone gratification makes it impossible to develop policies to encourage saving. And a demand for instant solutions to difficult problems causes excessive attempts to use government intervention without a proper regard for its adverse long run consequences. In economic policy, as in so many other areas, myopia is the enemy of reform.[26]

Mark Shepherd, Jr., chief executive officer of Texas Instruments, also worries about the capacity of the electorate to deal with the complex problems of economic restructuring: ". . . knowledge concerning the free enterprise system and the many key issues to be resolved is at such a level that the public is simply not equipped to make the difficult choices." It may prove necessary to insulate government officials from the rigors of democratic politics, Shepherd concludes, by lengthening the terms of congressmen and the President in order to "diminish the demands of reelection campaigning on the time of public servants."[27]

There is yet another reason to fear for democracy if probusiness strategies prevail during the coming years. Probusiness programs would enhance the power of the largest multinational corporations. These megacorporations consider the entire world their backyard; they will locate their next assembly plant or develop new sources of components in light of what they perceive as the long-term economic and political developments in each of over a hundred countries. Their global reach provides them with more leverage against the popular will than the large national corporations struggling for restored profits and power during the Depression. Then, as corporations continually discovered, popular coalitions could impose some progressive reforms on large corporations *through their access to the national government and domestic political power*. Now, increasingly, large corporations use their international mobility and global scale as bargaining chips in their poker game with popular forces. This international leverage has already played a critical role in corporate demands for wage concessions from workers and tax concessions from the government. If we don't oblige them, they can more and more credibly threaten, off they'll go—and where they'll locate, nobody knows.

Democracy thus may hang even more critically in the balance than it did in the 1890s and 1930s. The globalization of capital may represent a much more fundamental threat to popular political power than either the mergers at the turn of the century or the ferocious anticommunism after World War II. Well aware of their enhanced bargaining power, corporations show every sign of using it to the hilt.

These observations are not original with us. In a little-known essay published in the *Yale Review* in 1933, John Maynard Keynes warned about the political risks of policies which elevate "free" international trade above popular needs and sovereignty. The more we subject ourselves to the discipline of the world market, Keynes argued, the less leverage we maintain over our own economic destinies. There is a fundamental economic trade-off, Keynes concluded, between zealous promotion of "free trade" and the sovereignty of a people to experiment in search of their own solutions to an economic crisis. We can have the rule of the world invisible hand, or the rule of the visible domestic citizenry —but not both.

[Capitalism] is not a success. It is not intelligent, it is not beautiful, it is not just, it is not virtuous—and it doesn't deliver the goods. In short, we dislike it, and we are beginning to despise it. But when we wonder what to put in its place, we are extremely perplexed. . . .

We each have our own fancy. Not believing that we are saved already, we each should like to have a try at working out our own salvation. We do not wish, therefore, to be at the mercy of world forces working out, or trying to work out, some uniform equilibrium according to the ideal principles, if they can be called such, of *laissez-faire* capitalism. . . . We wish—for the time at least . . . to be our own masters, and to be as free as we can make ourselves from the interferences of the outside world. . . .

It is my central contention that . . . we all need to be as free as possible of interference from economic changes elsewhere, in order to make our own favorite experiments toward the ideal social republic of the future. . . . We shall discover it as we move along, and we shall have to mould our material in accordance with our experience.[28]

We think that Keynes was right. Probusiness programs for economic recovery would result in less control over our own destinies.

We do not regard the probusiness approach as invincible. Its economic flaws are all too apparent. And our reading of past periods of crisis resolution reveals a resiliency of democracy—sustaining the ability of ordinary people effectively to impose real limits on capital. Capital has won in the past not from omnipotence, but on the basis of its ability to define alternatives, and to pose continued economic stagnation as the price of deepening democracy. But like so many other "trade-offs," the democracy vs. recovery apposition is a fiction.

We turn now to an alternative program which can provide both economic recovery *and* more democracy.

III

An Economic Bill of Rights

My pa was a mill hand and a self-educated man. He brought me up to believe in the American system. I believe in the words of Jefferson and Tom Paine: the American Dream that people have a right to say what they wanta say, do what they wanta do, and fashion a world into something that can be great for everyone.

—Ed Sadlowski, steelworkers' union local official[1]

The U.S. economy can be driven by greed and fear. Or it can be propelled by commitment and cooperation. We think the latter makes more sense.

We propose a democratic program for restructuring the U.S. economy. It has two fundamental advantages over probusiness alternatives: It would more effectively promote economic recovery than supply-side, monetarist, or corporatist programs. And it would consistently foster economic and political democracy. These advantages seem to us overwhelming.

Probusiness advocates will surely disagree—on two grounds. First, they reject any approaches to economic recovery that do not pay proper respect to the priority of profitability. Second, they pit the objectives of recovery and democracy against each other, presupposing a conflict between economic growth and deepening commitment to democracy. We disagree. We argue that a democratic program has both economic *and* political promise. A more democratic and egalitarian economy has economic promise because people want it, and it costs less to put people in charge than it does to keep them down. It holds political promise, as well, because it builds on the democratic strengths of our political system rather than suppressing them.

These claims will seem novel to readers grown accustomed to the limited menu of economic-policy options in mainstream discussion. But it should not be surprising that new ideas emerge during periods of economic crisis.

The Great Depression of the 1930s, for example, gave rise to an entirely new way of looking at the economy—one which both offered a convincing account of the causes of the Great Depression and provided the analytical basis for postwar innovations in economic policy. Keynesian economics gradually gained intellectual and political sway because it both made sense of what had gone wrong and helped provide the basis for a politically successful economic program grounded in consistent economic principles. The most important of these principles, in the end, were the Keynesian commitment to more rapid economic growth and a more equal distribution of income.

Those were the 1930s. The present economic crisis bears little resemblance to the Great Depression. But the demands of the current situation are parallel. Any program for economic revival which ignores or misunderstands the sources of the present crisis, first of all, will fail to gain long-run acceptance—precisely because it will fail to establish the basis for long-run recovery. The second requirement is equally important: the long-run potential of any economic program will depend critically on its ability to help cement a political coalition capable of translating economic blueprints into new institutions, new laws, and new ways of organizing the economy.

We offer a program which we think meets these two requirements. Because both its logic and its content are so unconventional, we first provide an introduction to its underlying principles. These principles clearly differentiate our Economic Bill of Rights, as we have called it, from probusiness competitors, and these principles also hold the key to our program's economic and political promise.

REVIVING THE SLACK ECONOMY

The economic analysis underlying our program could be given various names; we have chosen to label it *democratic economics*—an analysis which pays central attention to the power and motivation of the vast majority of people who make our economy tick.

The normative principles of democratic economics reflect popular concerns. Most successful struggles in the United States have flowed from a deep and continuing concern for six popular priorities: democracy, security, equality, community, efficiency, and liberty. As democratic economists, we support these traditional priorities. We think that people should control their own lives democratically. We think that an economy should provide as much freedom from insecurity as possible. We think that economic and social institutions should promote as much equality among workers and citizens as they possibly can. We think that traditional values of sharing and community in families, neighborhoods, workplaces, and churches should be affirmed and strengthened. We think that our economy should make the best possible use of our available resources. And we think that an economic system should enhance individual and group opportunities for self-definition and self-expression.

Democratic economics also suggests that these popular priorities make good economic sense. Our reading of U.S. history convinces us that programs which undermine these shared values must bear the substantial economic costs of going against the popular grain—the costs of supervision and police and troops and the price of purchasing people's acquiescence. There is a clear economic corollary: policies which *support* these popular priorities are likely to reap the benefits of releasing our productive energies and harnessing them to meet human needs. A program based on democratic economic principles, in this sense, will work well because it supports rather than controls the people who produce the goods and services we need.

Mainstream economists may take exception to this introductory set of premises. They portray almost every kind of economic choice as a "trade-off"—the cost of more of one thing is always less of something else. The whopper of economic trade-offs, according to the late liberal economist Arthur Okun, chairman of the Council of Economic Advisers under Lyndon Johnson, is "the pervasive trade-off . . . between equality and efficiency." Okun's book *Equity vs. Efficiency* argues that societies must continually confront choices offering somewhat more equality at the expense of efficiency—or vice versa. He further argues that these choices create inescapable tensions between the efficiency imperatives of capitalism and the egalitarian principles of democracy. "We can't have our cake of market efficiency," he argues, "and share it equally."[2] We are, however, "free to choose."

We agree that issues of economic efficiency are important. People should not need to labor wastefully or sacrifice potential free time doing unnecessary or unproductive work. And the economy must deliver the goods. If it doesn't produce decent goods and services at costs which everyone can afford, ordinary people pay the price of those economic failures. And that makes it very difficult to build popular support for economic programs generating inefficiency and waste.

But we disagree with the analysis underlying the conventional wisdom. We think that mainstream economists are fundamentally wrong about the trade-offs between efficiency and democracy. More democracy does not have to mean more inefficiency and waste.

Ours is *not* the traditional Keynesian critique of waste inherent in laissez-faire economies. Keynesians focused on demand-side waste, identifying the unnecessarily low levels of output and employment which can result when the free market operates entirely on its own and when, as a result, demand for goods and services is much lower than it might be without such market failures. This analysis played a central and salutary role in postwar economic policy. We have not come to bury Keynesianism, since its basic critique remains resonant, but we have not come to acclaim it either.

The problem with the inherited Keynesian wisdom is not that aggregate demand shortfalls never happen or never matter. They often happen. And they do matter. But demand-side expansion is never enough. A viable Keynesian program for economic growth must involve a "supply-side" program as well—whether tacitly or explicitly—turning attention to the effect of production and distribution systems on the supply of goods and services. This supply-side orientation may accept and promote private production and profits in a market setting, as did John F. Kennedy's probusiness tax cuts and many other government policies in the postwar corporate system in the United States. It may include oppressive controls on labor to contain the powerful potential of full employment, as in Hitler's Germany. It may seek changes in private-sector approaches to production and distribution, advocating selective or wholesale democratic planning, as we shall advocate in our program. In any case, some kind of supply-side analysis must be part of any strategy which relies on the expansion of aggregate demand.

What matters, then, is not simply one's position on demand stimulus or contraction. What matters as well is one's approach to the supply of goods and services. What separates us from both probusiness and traditional Keynesian programs, indeed, is our understanding of the *slack economy* and what to do about it.

We argue that the rules of the contemporary U.S. political economy create enormous waste. They foster both demand-side waste—*unused* labor and industrial capacity—*and* supply-side waste—*misused* resources. The rules of the game creating such waste are the rules of capitalism—the principle that profits should be the final arbiter of the worth of a person or a product.

If one accepts these rules as binding, one must accept the permanence of supply-side waste. But why must these rules govern? If we can change them in sensible directions, we can create the promise and possibility of regenerating our slack economy.

Our principal differences with the probusiness alternatives thus emerge:

- The supply-siders have failed not because they did not recognize that the U.S. economy is slack, but because they did not understand the basic sources of the slack in the economy. Nowhere did they demonstrate that big government was a major source of waste. They ignored available economic evidence that tax cuts and deregulation would have little impact on economic growth. They failed to establish that the productivity slowdown could be attributed to increased taxes or overzealous regulators. Their program was an ideological pipe dream masquerading as economic analysis. The U.S. economy failed to revive, in the end, because supply-siders failed to understand the nature of the waste that plagued it.

• Monetarists and corporatists miss their target because they believe that the U.S. economy is not fundamentally slack but taut —that we must honor the zero-sum trade-offs between consumption and investment. They constrain their position by insisting on the current rules of the game, opposing those who would reject their trickle-down economics with the threat that capital would otherwise go on strike. We believe that changing the rules of the game would dissolve the zero-sum illusion, making it possible to restructure the economy on much less regressive terms.

If our capitalist economy were in fact more efficient than any other possible alternative, in short, we might indeed be forced to choose between efficiency and democracy. But democratic economics suggests that there are more efficient economic alternatives. If one plays by the capitalist rules, one accepts their consequences. If we play by more democratic rules, we can structure our own range of economic possibilities. Monetarists and corporatists argue that we must accept the probusiness emphasis on profits before democracy. Democratic economics argues that this is not a necessity but an imposition.

Is there a *liberal* alternative to the probusiness programs for economic restructuring?

There is a spreading grassroots populist liberalism which is beginning to point toward some very different kinds of programmatic initiatives—focusing on pension-fund investment and environmental safeguards, on occupational health-and-safety and plant-closing legislation.

The problem is that these popular initiatives have been neither promoted nor reflected in the policy positions of the leadership of the Democratic Party.

Some have clung to the Keynesian faith, believing that expanding aggregate demand would achieve full employment and somehow solve our current problems. We think that this is a mistake. We advocate full employment, but we also believe that a progressive economic program must address not just demand-side problems but *all* the waste currently plaguing the U.S. economy. A traditional Keynesian program falls silent on too many important issues.

Other liberals—rallying under the "neoliberal" label—have essentially accepted the probusiness analysis. We have looked at the economic programs of "neoliberal" figures such as Gary Hart, Paul Tsongas, Bill Bradley, and Daniel Patrick Moynihan. The liberal political and social outlook of these neoliberals provides welcome relief from the prevailing conservative consensus. But on economic policy matters, all share at least two of the three flawed probusiness principles—and appear at least implicitly to accept the third.[3]

• Neoliberals insist on the priority of subsidizing investment, moving resources from consumption and wages into the pools of corporate liquid capital. Gary Hart: "If we are to set a course for sustained economic growth, . . . we must continually expand America's productive capital base. . . . The centerpiece of a policy to expand our capital base . . . must . . . promote saving and investment." Bill Bradley: "America needs a fairer tax policy that encourages more productivity and more savings and investment." Paul Tsongas: "The solution is to increase the financial attractiveness of investment. For Democrats, this can be hard to accept, since we have traditionally viewed investing as a rich man's endeavor; and we have always been hard-pressed to sympathize with the need to provide business with greater advantages. Yet that is what must happen."

• They have also failed to challenge the corporate premise of the priority of profitability. Where in the neoliberal catechism does one find doubts that what's good for General Motors is good for the country? The private sector will continue doing its thing, and far be it from the rest of us to call this "thing" into question. Gary Hart: "Most of the action will likely take place in the private sector. The principal role of the government is to provide a generally supportive context. . . ." Paul Tsongas: "The future of America lies inside the heads of its talented people. . . . The nation needs [the] counsel [of the leaders of America's private sector], for the simple reason that they know better, and can bring America into an unprecedented appreciation of just what resource allocation is all about. . . ."

• What about arms for economic power? Neoliberals favor a verifiable nuclear freeze, but they also refused to oppose the post-1979 arms buildup. Felix Rohatyn has led the way, acknowledging that military waste undoubtedly exists but finally demurring: "whether that means you should spend more in different ways, I can't answer." Gary Hart has helped lead the campaign against military waste, but toward what end? He has urged U.S. investment in small, fast, light, and expendable ships, concentrating on the development of a quick-strike capacity, for example, presumably aiming at more flexible military leverage in Third World countries. Paul Tsongas:

There are those who argue for what is termed "sufficiency." The rationale is that our capacity to destroy the Soviets is adequate to safeguard against any overt attack. That part of the argument is correct. However, the advantage of superiority to the Soviets is political as much as military. And we live in a time when other nations are guided by coldly calculated perceptions of relative ascendancy. . . . What we need . . . is intelligent decision making on quality. In my view, the items should include (in order of priority) first, conventional weapons parity; second, a mobile, lean, small vessel-based capability; third, the Cruise missile; fourth, an effective penetration bomber such as the Stealth; fifth, the upgrading with Trident of our sea-leg portion of the nuclear triad; and sixth, the paced development of the MX missile. . . .

This leadership orientation was recently reflected with particular clarity in a major economic policy statement issued by the House Democratic Caucus in September 1982, the principal Democratic leadership pronouncement before the November elections. The report began with a clarion call to increased investment, swallowing the "capital-shortage" explanation of our current problems without a moment's demurral: "To create a favorable climate for investment we need, in the 1980s, to control federal spending, to revise our tax laws, and amend the regulations governing financial institutions." A challenge to the priority of profitability? "We must develop, within the framework of our free-enterprise system, an economic strategy of our own to identify opportunities for growth. . . ." Arms for economic power? Not a word about cutting military spending as a principal source of potential revenues for social programs.

We do not think that these three probusiness principles form a sound basis for any economic recovery program, for reasons we have already argued in Part II of this book. This suggests that there are real and distinct choices we must make about economic strategy—between the principles of probusiness programs, whatever their stripe, and the principles of democratic economics. Either one accepts the inevitability of the waste burden in the U.S. economy or one moves to change the rules which have created that waste.

Democratic economics points precisely toward the possibility of such changes in the rules. It provides three alternative principles to contrast with the basic probusiness approach. Each of these principles points toward the kind of economic restructuring policies which a democratic alternative should pursue.

- Probusiness strategies insist on profit-led growth. Democratic economics stresses instead the necessity and advantages of *wage-led growth*. By rewarding the vast majority instead of suppressing it, wage-led growth policies can stimulate aggregate employment *and* investment, promoting more rapid growth both through the demand-side effects of full employment and the supply-side effects of greater worker motivation and innovative pressure.

- Probusiness strategies insist on market-based allocation. Democratic economics counters with the principle of *needs-based allocation*, the proposition that an economy will most directly and democratically serve its members if there is at least some substantial direct planning to identify and meet people's needs for current consumption and personal development. We show in Chapter 14 that a democratic planning system can provide much more certain fulfillment of basic needs than the market's flickering and wayward signals.

- Probusiness strategies insist on arms for economic power. Democratic economics pursues *cooperation for economic security*—on both the domestic and the international planes. It stresses the importance of cooperation not merely for moral reasons but equally because of the waste and insecurity which efforts at economic domination have historically produced. Domestic and international cooperation promises one of the surest steps toward reduction of the massive waste burden afflicting the U.S. economy.

These principles may sound vague in the abstract. We present in the next four chapters an Economic Bill of Rights which builds on our three democratic economic principles. It is neither vague nor abstract. We list its principal proposals in Figure III.1. Because democratic economics places such strong emphasis on the sources of waste in the current U.S. economy, we have organized our Economic Bill of Rights to address the four main sources of waste which we identified in our effort to measure the costs of corporate power in Chapter 7. Each of the four chapters which follow corresponds to one of these principal sources of waste. We justify the scope of our program in part by its attention to each of the four main sources of waste in the U.S. economy.

Our twenty-four points are tangible and concrete; wherever we formulate a specific policy proposal in the text, we have flagged it with an arrow (▶) to help readers keep track of the specific planks in our program. We have tried throughout to formulate the language of

Fig. III.1

An Economic Bill of Rights

I. Right to Economic Security and Equity
1. Right to a Decent Job
2. Solidarity Wages, Comparable Pay,
    and Equal Employment Opportunity
3. Public Childcare and Community Service Centers
4. A Shorter Standard Work Week
    and Flexible Work Hours
5. Flexible Price Controls

II. Right to a Democratic Workplace
6. Public Commitment to Democratic Trade Unions
7. Workers' Right to Know and to Decide
8. Democratic Production Incentives
9. Promoting Community Enterprises

III. Right to Chart Our Economic Futures
10. Planning to Meet Human Needs
11. Democratizing Investment
12. Democratic Control of Money
13. Promoting Community Life
14. Environmental Democracy
15. Democratizing Foreign Trade

IV. Right to a Better Way of Life
16. Reduced Military Spending
17. Conservation and Safe Energy
18. Good Food
19. A National Health Policy
20. Lifetime Learning and Cultural Opportunities
21. Payment for Home Child Care
    in Single-Parent Households
22. Community Corrections
    and Reduced Crime Control Spending
23. Community Needs Information
    and Reduced Advertising Expenditures
24. Equitable Taxation
    and Public Allocation of Resources

our proposals in terms which respect and which could be translated into the existing constitutional and legislative structure of politics in the United States. This is a program for the 1980s, not the twenty-first century.

And yet many will wonder if this program is practical. Could it happen? Will people respond?

Our program could be implemented soon if an overwhelming majority of the population demanded it; it does not depend on changes which would require decades to implement; it involves changes which could technically be introduced within a short period of time.

It would, moreover, take advantage of traditions and skills which many in the United States already command. Our program proposes many concrete institutional instruments of local democracy. The public school system in the United States provides an interesting and promising *existing* example of the flexibility and capacity of such systems. Local public school boards make a wide variety of important institutional decisions, functioning as a kind of local planning board. They seek to weigh and balance the sometimes conflicting interests of parents, teachers, and students. These school boards work, in general, as effective examples of local democracy. We think that the local institutions proposed in the Economic Bill of Rights could work at least as well.

At least as important, *our Economic Bill of Rights would pay for itself*. Probusiness proponents have pounded the fear of government intervention into our heads, haranguing us continually about government deficits and government waste. They will undoubtedly level such charges against our proposals for a democratic alternative. We have prepared ourselves for those charges. We present in Appendix E a detailed two-year projection of the probable government revenues and expenditures if our Economic Bill of Rights were inaugurated in 1984. The conclusions of that exercise are both surprising and dramatic. We show that private consumption could increase under our program— despite simultaneously large increases in investment. We show that the personal-income-tax rate would be reduced under our program rather than increased, despite substantial increases in both government planning and government expenditures. We show, further, that government spending as a share of GNP would actually decline under the Economic Bill of Rights, despite substantial additional government programs, because of the rapid economic growth the program would generate.

These promises may sound like a democratic version of the Laffer Curve—pious and vacant promises that the economy can have its cake and eat it too. The difference between our claims and Laffer's, however, is quite basic. We have grounded our projections in careful analysis; our appendixes provide detailed documentation of the basis of our estimates. We offer substantially more reliable foundations than the back of a paper napkin.

And here the contrast becomes most ironic: In the first two years of the Reagan administration, the increase in government expenditure amounted to nearly 40 percent of additional national product. In the first two years of the Economic Bill of Rights, according to our estimates in Appendix E, the government would control only 25 percent of additional national product. Why is the free marketeer's government budget so much more expensive, in relative terms, than the budget of our Economic Bill of Rights? The Reagan program has been forced to bear the costs of corporate waste resulting from recession and military spending. Even in its first two years, our program would begin to lift those costs. Even the government reaps the harvest.

The critical issue is therefore political, not technical. Our program can work and pay for itself. But will people respond? Does our Economic Bill of Rights offer the possibility of a viable long-term alternative to trickle-down economics? Can it provide the basis for popular mobilization and an alternative direction for economic restructuring?

We think that it does. We believe that a program based on democratic economic principles can and will command popular support. We save for the final chapter of the book a more detailed discussion of the political possibilities of moving toward a democratic economy. Here we conclude simply that concrete programmatic alternatives can be politically popular—as long as they counter the wasteful principles of probusiness alternatives. The first test of a democratic program is that it provide clear and consistent alternatives to the priorities of profitability. This is a test that our program has been designed to pass.

Our Economic Bill of Rights has many roots. It builds on and overlaps with several other recent program discussions, reflecting widespread grass-roots concern with possible alternatives to trickle-down economics.[4] It also takes advantage of recent program ideas and experience in many other countries, particularly in Northern and Western Europe.

But it is much more than a shopping list. We have added a number of original proposals where we have found that existing programmatic discussion has fallen short of the full requirements of a democratic economic agenda. We have also paid special attention to the implications of our account of the causes of the current economic crisis in the United States, relying heavily on our analysis of the sources of the waste burden currently shackling conventional approaches to economic recovery. And we have placed particular emphasis on the problems of and requirements for building a coalition among the wide variety of persistently fragmented progressive groups in the United States. What good is a democratic economic program, indeed, if it does not help unite the full variety of popular movements which can engage the vast majority of workers and citizens in the U.S. economy?

These are ambitious objectives. The probusiness forces have mobilized their propaganda machines. A democratic alternative cannot easily compete with the conventional views. But the tests for our program are simple and self-evident. Does it make sense? Will it promote economic recovery without compounding the waste which currently afflicts us? Does it promote democracy rather than constrict it? By any of these standards, in the end, does it provide a democratic alternative to the economic waste land?

12

THE RIGHT TO ECONOMIC SECURITY
AND EQUITY

*I don't think our system is all bad. . . . What I object to is,
there's no planning. I don't care how much money it takes. They
should put every guy that wants to work, to work.*
—Retired policeman and former marine[1]

"Full employment" in our economy was once defined as under 4
percent of the labor force. Then closer to 5 percent. And now
inching up toward 6. Futurist Herman Kahn is preparing us for
even further redefinition, arguing in his recent book *The Coming
Boom* that "a 6–7 percent rate of unemployment will come to be
recognized as acceptable and that it will be relatively easy to hit
this target."[2] Like hitting the side of a barn.

Each of these percentage-point redefinitions requires that we
"accept" the unemployment of over 1 million additional workers
as tolerable, as standard operating procedure for an advanced
economy. Economists who condone this callousness point to their
concern about inflation. They argue that unemployment should be
high enough to prevent the rate of inflation from increasing. "Full
employment" is defined as whatever level of joblessness this
requires, whether it means 4 million or 12 million out of work.
The jobless are the sacrificial lambs. Stable prices are the Holy
Grail. And private-market determination of employment and
prices is the Holy Bible.

We reject this view. Direct intervention to promote the right to
a job, to promote employment security and equity, is the first requirement of any democratic alternative. This requires, in turn,
achieving real full employment at decent wages; removing discrimination and other barriers to economic security faced by par-

ticular groups; and coping with the inflationary pressures which any full-employment policy would inevitably engender. The five points of our program presented in this chapter address each of these problems directly.

Is real full employment possible? We have argued in Chapter 7 that there is a vast waste land of unutilized resources available to support the movement toward a full-employment economy. We must simply plan to make effective use of those resources. One critical distinction will help us clarify the kind of planning and thinking required. This is the distinction between *job security* and *employment security*. The former is a defensive demand in a hostile economic environment. The latter is a precondition for a democratic alternative.

Job security as a demand asserts an employee's right to retain his or her particular job throughout the twists and turns of both the specific enterprise involved and the whole economy. If successful, the job-security demand imposes considerable economic rigidity—making it relatively difficult to change staffing relationships within enterprises or to shift investment and output from one enterprise or industry to another. It also creates a natural suspicion of technological change, since automation may obliterate the particular job which provides a worker's ticket to regular employment.

But the demand for job security has also been a natural worker response in an unstable market economy. If no provisions are made for economic adjustment in uncertain times, if no guarantees of alternative employment are available when layoffs spread, workers have little choice but to dig in their heels and guard their individual enclaves from economic attack.

Employment security shifts the focus from a particular job to employment in general. The demand for employment security affirms every worker's right to be employed with decent wages *at some job or another*—but not necessarily always at the same job. It has obvious advantages over the job-security demand: it can foster greater flexibility within the enterprise, helping to moderate worker suspicion of efforts to increase productive efficiency. It can provide for workers' employment even when interfirm and interindustry shifts require changes in the job composition of the economy. And it can help reduce mutual suspicion among workers—the continuing fear, in an unregulated market regime, that everyone else is out to get one's own job.

We believe that *community security* along with *employment security* is a sensible economic demand. Community security would promise that shifts in output and technology should not dictate the continued uprooting of people from neighborhoods, communities, and families as workers are forced to hustle after jobs. A reasonable approach to full employment should not encourage our current levels of unnecessary costly and involuntary geographical mobility of labor. Nor should a sensible economic policy seek to promote full employment in ways that will undermine our communities, families, and neighborhoods. We have aimed in formulating our proposals for full employment to capture the spirit and advantages of this understanding of employment security. Far from imposing further rigidities on the economy, the sustained pursuit of real full employment, defined in this way, can free up and make productive use of presently and continually wasted resources.

Point 1: Right to a Decent Job

The original language of the Employment Act of 1946 proposed that every American have the right to a job. We begin our Bill of Economic Rights by proposing that the U.S. economy finally fulfill that goal.

Such a commitment is clearly possible. Sweden is the advanced capitalist country with the most active program of public employment in support of full employment. When the sharp worldwide recession of 1974 first began to ripple through the Swedish economy, for example, the government responded quickly and dramatically with countercyclical, publicly guaranteed employment. Its policies were so effective that the absolute number of unemployed actually fell during the recession, dropping by one sixth from 1974 to 1975. The unemployment rate, as measured by U.S. procedures, dropped from 2.5 percent in 1973, before the recession began, to 1.6 percent in 1975 and 1976. (By contrast, the

U.S. unemployment rate climbed from 4.9 percent in 1973 to 8.5 percent in 1975.)[3]

Some simple specifics can make this proposal concrete:

► The federal government should establish a permanent goal of a "full-employment unemployment rate." We suggest that this target be 2 percent of the labor force. (See Chapter 7 for a justification of this target.)

► Whenever the actual unemployment rate exceeded 2 percent in a local area, the federal government should make funds available to local governments to finance guaranteed public employment for anyone who needs and is able to work.

► Local governments would organize the provision and administration of this public employment, directing public workers toward projects recommended by community planning boards. (Point 11 outlines the structure and purview of these boards.) Project supervision would be the responsibility of relevant local government agencies, if particular projects fit under their auspices, or of a separate municipal public-enterprise division, if projects involved special departures from the regular responsibilities of local governments.

► In order to guarantee that these jobs provided the basis for a minimally adequate standard of living, the wages in these guaranteed public jobs would pay no lower than a minimum pegged to the U.S. Bureau of Labor Statistics' "lower budget standard" for a family of three—which would be equivalent to roughly $6.50 an hour for full-time year-round work in 1980.[4] (Prevailing union wages would apply to those public jobs created within covered municipal bargaining units.)

This demand for employment security through public employment is only a minimum precondition, as part of a broader program, for employment security and decent wages for everyone. But many economists, needless to say, have had serious reservations about public employment. We turn now to the most important of their objections.

What about the inflationary impact of such a full-employment program? We respond to this problem with a system of flexible price controls in Point 5.

What kind of work would these public employees perform?

There are scores of needs for goods and services in the United States which are currently frustrated or inadequately filled and which would be well suited for provision through guaranteed public-employment projects. Public workers could provide child-care services, neighborhood street security, paramedical help in community health centers, park maintenance support, shelters for battered women, or household assistance for the elderly. They could work as teachers' aides in schools or as apprentices on infrastructural projects improving roads, sewers, or public buildings. Some of these services would be provided fairly regularly— as with public child care (Point 3) or community health centers (Point 19). Others could be provided periodically, absorbing extra workers during periods of private-sector recession; this could be true of public employment on infrastructural renewal projects (Point 13), where the intensity of work could vary with the size of the public employment work force. The same holds true for public employees working on crash conservation programs (Point 17). We outline mechanisms for determining public-employment priorities in Point 10.

What about the alleged inefficiency of public enterprises? Won't government spending for public employment result in gross inefficiencies, wasting our tax dollars in a quagmire of red tape and idle government bureaucrats?

There will certainly be waste and red tape, but, as we have seen, this is no monopoly of the public sector. And the gains to be made by putting people to work will far outweigh the bureaucratic cost. Indeed, these costs may be quite minimal. When local public agencies have had a chance to serve useful economic functions in the United States—an unusual occurrence, given our historic bias toward the private sector—their economic track record has been superb.

We can compare, for example, the cost performances of private and public utility companies.[5] During the postwar period, roughly one quarter of electrical power in the United States has been generated by publicly owned utilities or rural electrical cooperatives. Throughout that period, public utilities supplied electricity at roughly one third less per kilowatt-hour delivered than private utilities. These cost efficiencies extended throughout the production and administrative structure. In 1979, for instance, generation and transmission costs in the public utilities were 17 percent lower (per unit of output) than in their private counterparts, while general administrative costs were 31 percent lower (per kilowatt-hour delivered). Public red tape is often much less burdensome than the private variety.

Point 2: Solidarity Wages, Comparable Pay, and Equal Employment Opportunity

We waste an enormous amount of economic resources because we do not make full use of the skills and talents of all U.S. workers. Some, particularly women and minority workers, suffer systematic misuse and underutilization because of the historic impact of discrimination by race and sex. Pay differences between men and women also reinforce unequal power relations in the home; as long as men's wages exceed women's, for example, it is economically sensible for families to divide up tasks so that men work for wages while women do most of the housework, preserving traditional patterns of sex-typing and segregation.

When people are not allowed to develop and make full use of their potential productive contributions, moreover, the economy suffers as well as the individuals afflicted. When artificial divisions and historic inequalities create conflicts and tensions among the populace, we all suffer too. We therefore place the highest possible priority on rapid movement toward greater equality—precisely because of the clear conjuncture of individual and social benefits which would result.

The logic of our proposals is unusual, however, as it is based on a common sense but novel analysis of the relationship between low wages, low productivity, and income inequality.

Our basic point is very simple: The problem in the U.S. economy today is not low-productivity *workers* but low-productivity *jobs*.[6] Low-productivity jobs exist (and proliferate) because low-wage workers are abundant and make low-productivity jobs profitable for employers. The solution is to shift workers from low-productivity to high-productivity jobs. This can be accomplished by eliminating the availability of low-wage labor. How?

Millions of workers in the United States work with primitive equipment, outmoded procedures, and poorly designed products —as in many garment and shoe factories. Millions more work in much more modern enterprises—such as fast-food places or nursing homes—where prices must remain relatively low because their outputs are minimally valued on the market; these enterprises cannot afford to pay decent wages because the productivity of the work, as measured by the market, is so low. In either case, the source of the low wages does not lie with the workers but in *structural* barriers to higher-productivity jobs—either because these firms do not modernize or because of the low market value of their output.

These firms nonetheless stay in business. The reason: labor-market competition, high unemployment, and historic patterns of discrimination keep wages for many workers at minimal levels— far below the potential productivity of the workers holding those jobs. Given such low wages, firms can continue to survive—taking advantage of artificially inexpensive labor in their pursuit of artificially easy profits. Such low-wage employment may evidently persist in large or small industry and in young or old firms; McDonald's, one of the largest employers of low-wage labor, is both young and very large.

In order to break out of this vicious circle of low wages and low productivity, one must attack on two fronts. First, one must develop mechanisms to make funds for modernizing investment available—either in currently low-productivity sectors, where substantial improvement is possible or in currently high productivity sectors. Second, one must intervene in the labor market in order to raise the floor on workers' wages; without such intervention, one simply allows the historical forces which have generated labor-market competition and discrimination to subsidize the continuing existence of unproductive and inefficient enterprises. Our economy has too many problems—particularly the survival problems of those earning low wages—to tolerate this kind of subsidy of unproductive backwardness.

We detail our proposals below. Their result would be a shift of workers from low- to high-productivity jobs and an intensified pressure to raise productivity in low-productivity jobs. Where these pressures might make some necessary services too costly or scarce—as with care for the elderly—then direct subsidy of the services affected would be warranted.

We illustrate the impact of our proposals with a highly simplified example.[7] Suppose that an economy consists of just two sectors. In one, which we call electronics, workers use modern equipment and firms apply effective methods for organizing production. World market demand for the product is expanding. In the other sector, which we call textiles, employees work in antiquated mills and face stiff competition from imports.

Our strategy is twofold: to force modernization of textiles and to induce a shift from textiles to electronics. Let us suppose that one hundred employees work in each sector. Suppose further that the average value of output per worker-hour in electronics is thirty dollars, three times the level in textiles. Because the work force is equally divided between the two sectors, hourly output for the entire economy is halfway between the two, or twenty dollars.

A high-wage strategy will drive some of the least productive textile firms out of business. Their former workers will be guaranteed a job, if necessary, in public employment (by virtue of Point 1). Most, of course, will seek employment in the high-wage electronics sector. Assume that, over a ten-year period, the electronics sector came to employ 150 workers and the textile sector shrank to fifty. Assume, for the sake of simplicity of argument, that the value of output per worker-hour remained the same in the two sectors (although textile productivity would surely rise under the wage pressure). Then average productivity for the whole economy would have risen to $25 per worker-hour simply as a result of the shift of workers from the one to the other sector. This sectoral shift alone—even without assuming any increases in productivity within the two sectors—would result in an average annual rate of productivity growth of 2.2 percent. The productivity dividends from such induced sectoral shifts can be enormous.

The increase in productivity isn't entirely free, of course, since the new employees in the electronics sector must be equipped with much more machinery and other production equipment than they were using in textiles. The principal cost of the shift of labor from one sector to the other, therefore, will be the difference between how much it would have cost to replace worn-out machinery in textiles and how much the new machinery in electronics will cost. If the average value of all production equipment per worker in electronics is $30,000 and that in textiles is $15,000, the total cost of moving one worker from one sector to the other is $15,000, and the cost of moving the entire fifty workers is $750,000.

But the output of our model economy as a whole will be $2 million larger as a result of the shift *in one year alone*. (This results from 200 workers working 2,000 hours a year, producing $25 of total output per hour instead of $20.) The capital costs of the employment shift will therefore be more than twice repaid by the productivity gains *in a single year alone*. The productivity gains, in contrast, are permanent.

But can textile workers perform electronics work? We are certain they can. The training time for most jobs in the U.S. economy is measured in days, not in months. There is historical precedent, moreover, for the kind of shift we propose. During the Second World War, military production was spurred by an influx to the labor force of millions of women whose only work had been in the home, and whose prior experience with machinery was with home appliances. Productivity grew rapidly during the war years, despite these problems of inexperience.

Economists accept the logic of this kind of sectoral-shift argument when it is applied to earlier stages of economic development. Commerce Department economist Edward Denison has shown, for example, that a major source of productivity growth in the United States and Europe in the twentieth century was the shift of employment out of low-productivity sectors, particularly agriculture, into sectors with much higher and more rapidly growing hourly output, particularly manufacturing.[8] The critical mechanism propelling the shift, indeed, was high wages in manufacturing. Moreover, Cambridge University historian H. J. Habakkuk attributes the nineteenth-century international superiority of U.S. technology to the pressure of high wages.[9]

Since that period, however, U.S. economic policy has allowed wages to be determined by the inefficiency of backward firms, giving in to the fervent pleas of businesses for relief from wage pressure. Our priorities should finally be reversed. Instead of pegging wages to the requirements of inefficient firms, we should begin to use wage policy to create pressure on inefficient firms. We should peg productivity to decent wages, in short, and push enterprises to make the investments and innovations necessary to increase average hourly output to levels which would support these decent wages.

We deal with the problems of investment and modernization in several subsequent proposals (see Point 11 in particular). We deal here with the tasks of direct labor market intervention. Such intervention requires three sets of proposals: a solidarity wage policy, equal pay for comparable worth, and equal employment opportunity. We introduce each in turn.

Solidarity Wages. This concept is relatively unfamiliar in the United States but widely discussed in Northern Europe and a long-standing practice in Sweden. "Solidarity wage" policies aim to raise the wages of low-wage workers more rapidly than those of higher-wage workers, promoting income equality and generating wage pressure on backward firms. They are called *solidarity* wage policies because their proponents argue—and we agree—that they serve the interests of all workers, not just those of low-wage workers. They do so by helping increase the level of effective demand in the macroeconomy, by spurring rapid growth and investment, and by reducing divisions within the work force, increasing workers' bargaining strength. Above all, they help promote more rapid productivity growth through rising wage pressure, a clear benefit to all.

The Swedes have pursued such policies and reaped their benefits most directly. The Swedish labor unions helped pioneer solidarity wage policies in the early 1950s. An early union document supporting these policies stated the objective clearly: "From the point of view of general solidarity, priority should obviously be given to those who, despite recent large increases, are still too far below the average, while highly-paid groups should not be given priority on account of a lower rate of increase. . . ."[10] The success of these policies in Sweden has been evident. One study concluded that the spread of wages between higher- and lower-paid workers in Swedish trade unions, representing nearly 80 percent of all Swedish employees, "declined by almost a half in fifteen years" between 1959 and 1974.[11] This narrowing of the wage gap helped promote rapid growth of productivity; as we have already seen in Chapter 3, productivity growth in Sweden between 1960 and 1979 was twice that in the United States.[12]

Trade unions in the United States represent a much smaller portion of the labor force than in Sweden, of course, so that solidarity wage policy in the United States will require two instruments, not just one:

► Workers and unions should pursue solidarity wage bargaining in firms and industries—and, where possible, between industries—seeking constantly to increase the lowest wage rates more rapidly than higher wage rates.

► In order to promote rapid increases in the lowest wages prevailing throughout the economy, the government should raise the minimum wage substantially, pegging it as close as possible to the minimum guaranteed wage in public employment (see Point 1). It should also index the minimum wage so that it grows at a faster rate than inflation. This proposal, modeled after the Italian national escalator clause, would help narrow the wage gap in jobs not covered by collective bargaining and would help sustain real wage pressure on all firms, whether unionized or not.

It may appear, because of the tradition of debate about the minimum wage in the United States, that our proposals are aimed vindictively at small enterprises as a class of firms. Those who have followed the lead of E. F. Schumacher, believing that small is beautiful, may be especially concerned. But this is neither our purpose nor the necessary consequence of solidarity wage policies and rising minimum wages.

About the dimensions of beauty we remain agnostic. What we do believe, for reasons that we have already stressed, is that *backward* is ugly and *low wages* are indecent. There is plentiful evidence that relatively small firms can achieve much higher productivity than larger firms; examples abound, for instance, in the rapidly innovating high-technology sectors. There are also giant firms which pay very low wages; McDonald's is probably the best example. The combined effect of solidarity wage policies and rising minimum wages should, indeed, both increase the competitive advantages of smaller and more productive firms and reduce the margin within which firms like McDonald's or J. P. Stevens can make their millions by relying on racism, sexism, and discrimination against the old and the young to keep wages low. Our intention, with this proposal, is to promote more rapid productivity growth and greater equality, not to promote larger enterprises. We devote special attention to the need for supporting and assisting small businesses in our proposals for promoting community enterprises (Point 9) and democratizing investment (Point 11).

Equal Pay for Comparable Worth. Solidarity wage policies are most effective at equalizing wages among firms and industries, not within firms. And they do not directly attack the effects of historic and continuing discrimination.

The links are essential. If firms can manage to pay women, minorities, the old, and the young lower wages on a continuing basis—because of the relatively weak bargaining position of women and minority workers—they will continue to have an escape hatch from pressure toward rising productivity. And there can be no effective solidarity, of course, if women and minority workers remain a kind of underclass throughout the economy.

A major barrier to wage equality by race and sex, many proponents of affirmative action have concluded, comes not from unequal pay for the *same* work but from unequal pay for work in jobs of *similar* responsibility, training, and skill requirements. This has led increasingly to a focus on proposals for equal pay in jobs of comparable worth. A research commission established by the National Academy of Sciences recently completed a careful review of the problem of wage discrimination and inequality by race and sex, for example, and reached two conclusions critical for this discussion.[13]

First, they concluded that wage discrimination persists:

Our economy is structured so that some jobs will inevitably pay less than others. . . . However, . . . it is also true in many instances that jobs held mainly by women and minorities pay less at least in part *because* they are held mainly by women and minorities. . . . The evidence is not complete or conclusive, but [various considerations] . . . strongly suggest that wage discrimination is widespread.

Second, they concluded that pressure toward equal pay for comparable worth can play an important role in reducing wage discrimination.

Although no universal standard of job worth exists, job evaluation plans do provide standards and measures of job worth that are used to estimate the relative worth of jobs within many firms. . . . In our judgment job evaluation plans provide measures of job worth that, under certain circumstances, may be used to discover and reduce wage discrimination for persons covered by a given plan. . . . By making the criteria of compensation explicit and by applying the criteria consistently, it is probable that pay differentials resulting from traditional stereotypes regarding the value of "women's work" or work customarily done by minorities will be reduced.

We share these conclusions. Job-evaluation plans, aiming to facilitate equal pay for comparable worth, cannot be instituted overnight. But several specific steps are clearly warranted.

► Both unions and the government should press ahead with efforts to establish standards for evaluating the comparability of the worth of different jobs, widely disseminating their findings and suggestions about alternative job-evaluation plans.

► Unions should themselves bargain vigorously for equal pay for comparable worth wherever possible and relevant.

► Individual workers or groups of workers should also be able to petition the government in protest against unequal pay for comparable work. If, by prevailing government standards, employers are not providing equal pay for comparable worth, the government should pursue steps aimed at reducing pay inequalities among job categories which mirror its recent efforts to reduce discrimination against individual workers.

Although much work remains to be done to develop the instruments of job evaluation to determine comparable worth, we cannot overemphasize the importance of this set of proposals. They are essential to the battle against discrimination and inequality— a central concern of any truly democratic alternative to pro-business economics. And they represent a necessary complement to solidarity wage policies themselves. As the Swedish labor unions recognized in their original argument for solidarity wages, their wage policies also required that "one must aim at some sort of equal pay for equal work principle. Work of a similar nature should, to the greatest possible extent, cost the same for all employers."[14] If not, pressure for higher productivity growth is undercut.

Some trade unionists in the United States agree. Public employees in San Jose, California struck in 1981, for example, in support of demands for equal pay for comparable work. They argued that women were continuing to suffer systematic discrimination as a result of lower wages in jobs traditionally held by women. The strike settlement provided for significant wage adjustments in female-dominated job categories which had traditionally been underpaid and undervalued. The strikers were not just women; nearly 60 percent of the strikers were men. "There was a lack of division," reports Bill Callahan, the local union business agent, "a feeling of solidarity and support from men because of the fairness of it." The strikers had to compromise in the final settlement, but Callahan reports nonetheless that "the strike was a success. . . . It was an historic strike for dignity, equality and pay equity. . . . People will begin to be paid what they're worth."[15]

The Supreme Court has joined in this recognition, ruling in 1981 that unequal pay for jobs of comparable worth was discriminatory. Its majority decision, although decided on relatively narrow grounds, nonetheless stressed the inadequacy of the traditional legal strictures that women could charge discrimination only if and when they were paid less money in the same specific job classification as men. "A 'broad approach' to the definition of equal employment opportunity is essential to overcoming and undoing the effect of discrimination," the majority decision argued. Without such an inclusive approach, it argued, "a woman who is discriminatorily underpaid could obtain no relief—no matter how egregious the discrimination might be—unless her employer also employed a man in an equal job in the same establishment, at a higher rate of pay."[16]

Equal Employment Opportunity. Discrimination in hiring and promotion will nonetheless remain. It is therefore necessary to intensify public and union efforts against direct discrimination by race and sex. Since efforts at affirmative action have suffered setbacks recently, we see the need to make four general comments about the importance and possibility of intensified support for equal employment opportunity.

First, racial and sexual barriers to economic opportunity show little sign of weakening without sustained public pressure. The median income of black households rose only one quarter as rapidly in the 1970s as that of white households. Female-headed household incomes actually *declined* in real terms during the 1970s.[17]

Second, equal employment opportunity is in the interests of *all* who work for a living—not simply those of women and minority workers suffering the most severe effects of discrimination. Recent research by economist Michael Reich, of the University of California at Berkeley, reported in *Racial Inequality: A Political Economic Analysis,* has affirmed this conclusion.[18] Reich studied the relationship between racial discrimination and income inequality *among* whites. It is commonly believed that white workers benefit from large earnings differentials between whites and blacks. Reich found exactly the opposite. He discovered that the share of income going to white workers is lower in areas where racial disparities are the most accentuated. His findings suggest that the wealthy reap the gains from discrimination—and that white workers lose—as a result of the greater divisions among workers that are caused by severe racial discrimination. As unions have discovered through painful bargaining experience, the most divided work forces are the weakest at pushing their claims against those of their employers.

Third, the joint pursuit of employment security and equal employment opportunity need not set worker against worker. Many whites and men have worried about the divisive effects of strong support for affirmative action, holding back because of uncertainty about their own job prospects. These are the fears and hesitations of an economy *which has averaged over 6 percent unemployment during the twentieth century.* It is always difficult to work toward the "general interest" when one's own economic security seems so fragile. We propose vigorous support for affirmative action *in the context of our equally firm demands for full employment.* As long as *both* men and women and *both* whites and minorities are secure in their jobs, as long as employment security is affirmed, as long as the economy is growing, the pursuit of affirmative action need not evoke the rancor and mutual suspicion which it has recently encountered. We recognize that residues of historic prejudice remain and will not disappear overnight. We argue simply that our Economic Bill of Rights, with its strong commitment to full employment, would be likely to *reduce structural barriers to affirmative action,* not to exacerbate them.

Fourth, affirmative-action and other antidiscrimination programs can and have had effect. After the Equal Employment Opportunity Commission (EEOC) was first installed in the mid-1960s, it dissipated its early energies soliciting and pursuing individual complaints. Like other similar agencies, it eventually realized that corporations and institutions such as universities are the appropriate locus for affirmative-action pressure. It pushed forward on charges of "systemic" discrimination—against widespread practice of institutionwide discrimination by race and by sex. It was able finally to win some substantial victories with corporate giants such as AT&T and General Electric.[19] These companies eventually paid millions of dollars in back settlements and substantially upgraded women and minority workers. Strong affirmative-action programs appear to have been one of the principal sources of improvement for women and minority workers during the late 1960s and 1970s.[20]

We therefore include two proposals for equal employment opportunity:

► The federal government should affirm its commitment to equal employment opportunity and substantially increase funding to the EEOC. State and local governments should similarly increase their support for their own agencies empowered to investigate and redress discriminatory practice.

► Equal employment opportunity programs should particularly stress efforts to discover and redress systemic discrimination, pushing large institutions to promote greater equality among their employees and, if necessary, instituting legal suits for affirmative action toward equality by race and sex.

We should note, in concluding the full range of proposals in Point 2, that we do not underestimate the difficult transitional problems which these policies would encounter. We must deal with the legacy of decades of backward firms and centuries of discrimination. Were these proposals to be advanced singly, in isolation, they would meet stiff opposition from those caught in the transition. But we suggest them as part of a substantial program for full employment and democratic planning, outlining a wide range of instruments and cushions with which to smooth the transition. The choice to undertake a systematic assault on low wages and inequality is not a minor one, but it is a choice we must make if we are ever to escape from the economic backwaters and divisions which currently slow our movement toward an effective and decent economy.

Point 3: Public Child Care and Community Service Centers

One of the principal barriers to full utilization of available labor in the United States is the lack of child care and family-support services. Many single mothers are convinced that their own full-time care is best for their children; they are forced to eke out a living on inadequate and humiliating welfare payments. Many women (and growing numbers of men) would like to work outside the home but find it nearly impossible either to find or to afford child care for their children. As more and more women have both chosen to work outside the home and found themselves solely supporting their children, in particular, the problem of child care and family support has grown acute.

The magnitude of these problems seems clear enough. In 1980, there were 1.2 million adults who "wanted a job now" but were not looking for work as a result of "home responsibilities." Another 920,000 women, either married or widowed, divorced or separated, were working part time "involuntarily"; they wanted full-time jobs instead.[21] It seems safe to assume that most of both of these groups were frustrated in large part because of their parenting responsibilities and the lack of available child care.

By 1980, according to the most recent figures available from the census, 23.4 percent of all children aged seventeen or under were living with only one parent (or another adult). Of the 8.4 million families headed by women, 5.9 million contained at least one child seventeen or under; this represented a 72 percent increase over 1970 in the number of families headed by women with children. And these women can hardly count on stable or luxury support from the children's fathers: of all the women raising children alone, only 35 percent receive any payments from the children's fathers at all.[22]

We argue, in short, that public child care is both economically sensible and deserves urgent political priority. We address the issue of public support for child rearing at home in Point 21. Public provision of child care makes sense because it represents a key to much fuller utilization of available labor—and fuller utilization of labor is a key to eliminating waste in our economy. It also deserves urgent support because more and more families have no other recourse if the adults want and need to work; because women suffer a special burden as a result of the historic presumption that they must shoulder the primary responsibility for child care even while they are more and more likely to pursue paid employment; and because many children themselves have no other way of securing decent care, security, and opportunity for healthy recreation.

► Local governments should therefore directly provide or subsidize the costs of child care for children enrolled in child-care programs. The balance between direct provision and public subsidy would be determined by individual local governments.

► The federal government should distribute a "child-care allowance" subsidy, pegged at roughly half of average local child-care costs per child enrolled, for each child publicly or privately enrolled in child care within each local jurisdiction. This subsidy would partly offset local child-care costs.

We shall not take time here to review the recent debates about the appeal of the Moral Majority to traditional family values and bonds. We pursue a much simpler and more direct line of argument: as family patterns change, the broader society needs to help provide a wider range of options to those who are moving from one set of household arrangements to another, to those who need a margin of adjustment to explore new opportunities and horizons.

It is not a question of choosing or endorsing one form of family relation or living arrangement over another. We do not think that care outside the home is necessarily better or worse for children; we *do* think that single mothers or fathers who care for their children full time should be adequately supported (see Point 21) and that those who choose some amount of child care should have high-quality, affordable options available. It is simply and most importantly a question of providing people with more choice over possible living arrangements.

Changes in household arrangements have been going on for centuries; a single economic program neither can nor should provide complete responses to such deep-seated and complex trends. Through public support for child care *and* through public support of other family functions, however, we can at least ease pressures on households and help relieve special burdens on women. Through that support, we believe, we can help foster new and much more fruitful relations between parents and among parents and children. That seems to us to be a challenge worthy of any democratic alternative.

► Local governments and communities should therefore situate child-care facilities, whenever possible, within more broadly provisioned community service centers. These centers would be publicly funded and would provide, in addition to child care, community health care and health education, consumer buying information, transportation services for the aged and the mobility-impaired, job counseling and training, and family counseling services.

Point 4: A Shorter Standard Workweek and Flexible Work Hours

Some of us are overworked. Others cannot find work. Some have little time for family, recreation, education, church, or politics. Others have too much time on their hands. This imbalance does not make sense, creating anxieties, promoting tensions between the fully employed and the underemployed, and forsaking opportunities to develop rewarding community and family lives. There is a relatively simple solution: share the work and share the free time.

Full employment has been difficult to attain in the postwar United States, at least in part because productivity gains have not been shared among all workers—both employed and unemployed. If some workers continue working the same number of hours over a long period of time while productivity grows, this reduces the growth of *employment* which output growth might otherwise ensure.

Equally important, attempts by families to take joint responsibility for child care often founder on the lack of available part-time work or on the lack of pension and health-insurance coverage for part-time work. And when it is either thirty-five hours of work or nothing, the generally higher income opportunities of the father make the Dad-at-work, Mom-at-home option too attractive to pass up.

We see no reason why the increased productive capacities of our economy should be used solely to consume ever more goods, using up natural resources and making free time a dream that only comes true in the nightmare of unemployment. It seems imperative, therefore, to ensure more flexibility in working hours—both to support the full-employment objective and to provide all working people with more choice about their work and leisure time.

This emphasis on flexible work hours seems unusual only because we have such short memories. Between the Civil War and World War II, a shorter workweek was a continuing and fundamental demand of working people. From 1909 to 1947, the average workweek in manufacturing declined from 51 hours a week to 40. Since then, reductions in working hours have been scant. (Average hours in manufacturing remained virtually constant, while average hours for the total private economy declined from 40 in 1945 to 35.6 in 1979. This latter decline largely reflected rising proportions of part-time workers outside manufacturing; it did not directly represent a reduction in average hours for full-time workers. Indeed, what economists call the full employment workweek, after falling by nearly 30 percent from 1901 to 1948, did not decline at all from 1948 to 1977.[23])

This plateau of weekly hours is not some technical consequence of industrialized societies, a function of complex manpower needs and work scheduling problems. For while the decline in the length of the workweek essentially stopped in the United States, the average workweek continued to shorten in Europe and Japan. By standard reporting procedures, for example, average weekly hours declined by only 1.7 percent in the United States between 1950 and 1981, while average weekly hours over the same thirty years were falling by 28.8 percent in Sweden, 27.1 percent in Germany, and 20.7 percent in the Netherlands—all countries which simultaneously grew much more rapidly than the United States in these postwar decades. After having been longer than working hours in the U.S., hours in these countries are now lower than ours—in some cases considerably lower, as in Sweden, where the average weekly hours fell to below 30 hours in 1981.[24]

A significant reduction in the workweek and an increase in regular vacations is thus a far from utopian objective. Suppose, to take a very modest objective, that the rate of productivity growth were merely restored to our 1948–66 average of 2.9 percent annually. Over the next generation (thirty-three years) the workweek could be cut from five to four days, with proportional reductions for those now working longer or shorter hours, *at the same time that living standards*—measured by output of goods and services per capita (corrected for inflation)—*would double*. If, instead of doubling output per capita, a 50 percent increase was thought sufficient, a reduction from five to three days of work a week would be possible.[25]

► The Fair Labor Standards Act should therefore be amended to provide for regular five-year reductions in the "standard workweek." (The legislative definition of the "standard workweek" does not limit employees to a certain number of hours per week but merely requires that employers pay overtime beyond that standard level.) The first reduction would take place five years after the amendment; that and each subsequent reduction would be indexed to take account of increases in hourly output per person in the interim.

This revision would help create downward pressure on average weekly hours, but it might also push some employers to try to concentrate overtime among even fewer employees. In order to permit greater employee choice, we therefore recommend two other steps to promote both full employment and more flexible work-time adjustments.

► The Fair Labor Standards Act should also be amended to prohibit compulsory overtime. (According to survey data from the

University of Michigan, roughly half of all overtime is now at the employer's discretion—what is called "involuntary overtime."[26])

► Workers and unions should also seek to negotiate work-sharing agreements, providing that all reduction and expansion in company employment are more equally shared among production and nonsupervisory employees. (This would provide, for example, that a 10 percent reduction in labor demand in a particular firm would result in approximately 10 percent fewer hours for all workers rather than the complete layoff of 10 percent of the employees and no reductions for the rest.)

Taken together, these two demands would help promote greater equality in working time—sharing the fruits of growth among all employees—and would help involve employees more directly in one of the most important decisions we face: the length of time we spend on the job.

Older workers are often expelled from the workplace when they reach mandatory retirement age. As a result, we deprive our economy of their productive capacities and in many cases consign older people to lonely lives at home, cut off from friends and co-workers. We should end this unnecessary waste and humiliation.

► Congress should enact legislation making mandatory retirement illegal.

Point 5: Flexible Price Controls

The principal causes of inflation, we have argued in Chapter 5, are the slowdown in the rate of growth of productivity and the escalation of social conflicts over the distribution of the economic pie. As the stimulus of our program took effect and the economy began to revive, making goods and services more plentiful, inflationary pressures would be reduced. In the meantime, however, the stimulus provided by the full range of proposals outlined in this chapter would have fueled inflationary pressures. We therefore propose a system of flexible price controls with several novel features.

Before turning to the details of our proposals, however, we

must first deal with the deep-rooted skepticism about the idea of price controls of any sort. Virtually all mainstream economists fervently object to such controls on grounds of basic economic principle, and their endorsement of business opposition to price controls has prevented serious discussion of alternative approaches to price stability for many years.

Mainstream economists begin their objections with a strong belief in the effectiveness of the market system of prices. We think that their support for market pricing systems has become increasingly archaic. They assure us that the "free market" will promote price stability through competition, but large corporations have developed remarkable immunity to this competitive vaccine. They argue that market prices reflect an equilibrium between the forces of supply and demand, but the forces of crisis, industrial transition, and outside price shocks have made *dis*equilibrium and rapid volatility in prices the rule, and stable equilibrium the textbook exception. The "market" seems incapable of producing the adjustments its protagonists promise. As Brookings economist Barry Bosworth, former staff director of the Council on Wage and Price Stability, concludes:

If the economy were an aggregation of competitive auction-type markets such as the one that now exists for wheat, a relatively small reduction in demand and employment would be enough to have a quite substantial impact on both price and wage decisions. In a perfectly competitive economy individuals are supposed to be restrained in their wage and price demands by fears that they will lose jobs or sales. In modern industrial economies, however, markets are much more complex than wheat markets. The process works very unevenly; inflation persists even in the face of substantial unemployment.[27]

Still, most mainstream economists argue that a system of price controls or a similar system of "incomes policies," of the kind adopted in some European countries, cannot work. But the historical record of price controls suggests a different conclusion. During World War II, a period of very rapid growth and massive government deficits in the U.S. economy, price controls limited the rate of inflation to 2 percent a year from 1943 to 1945, the years in which the controls were most actively implemented. Since 1940 there have been only six years in which the rate of unemployment fell and the rate of inflation fell: four of these years —1943, 1944, 1952, and 1972—came during the operation of price controls. (One of the keys to price stability under price controls during World War II, we should note, was that productivity growth increased rapidly, helping limit a buildup of inflationary pressures. This serves as yet another reminder that programs for price stability cannot be evaluated outside of the context of an entire program for economic restructuring.)

Many economists also suggest, finally, that price controls are self-defeating because inflation will resume once "temporary" controls are lifted. Since we propose a *permanent* program of government price stabilization, this objection is irrelevant to our endorsement of flexible price controls.

But won't price controls, especially permanent controls, involve lots of red tape? We share this concern. We therefore support proposals for *flexible* price controls grounded in tax disincentives rather than administrative regulation. Administrative controls involve the government in a determination of actual and justifiable enterprise costs and a stipulation of the permissible prices markup over costs. Under a tax-incentive system, in contrast, the government simply collects data on unit prices and establishes tax disincentives to unit-price increases above a target level of price stability. This does not involve comprehensive government determination of "warranted" costs and it involves little more bureaucracy than the current (and, by all admissions, efficient) system of sales and excise taxation. It would be up to workers, managers, and owners in enterprises to determine whether they wanted to pay the tax penalties for price increases over the target levels or whether they would prefer to try to reduce their costs in order to expand profit margins *under* the implicit ceilings established by the tax-penalty threshold.

These arguments in favor of a tax-based system are attractive. They have led some economists toward advocacy of what is most commonly called the tax-based incomes policy (TIP) approach to price stability. While we share their preference for the greater administrative flexibility of tax-based rather than administrative approaches, our proposed system of flexible price controls departs from other TIP proposals in several important respects. We present the details of our points here and then comment on the principal differences with other TIP proposals in the following paragraphs.

► A federal Office of Price Information would collect quarterly data on each *corporation's* unit prices. (Only corporations would be covered, not proprietorships or partnerships, thereby exempting nearly 90 percent of all business enterprises in the United States, but including 85 percent of all sales. The pricing power of corporations is what requires most attention, not that of much smaller enterprises, and a limitation of coverage to corporations would help contain the administrative load.)

► If a firm's unit prices had increased at an annual rate of more than 2 percent in the previous quarter, the price agency would automatically assess a supplementary "price-stability excise tax" equal to 50 percent of the "excess price increase." These supplementary excise taxes would be collected on a quarterly basis through the Internal Revenue Service corporate taxation division.

► Tax revenues from the "price-stability excise tax" would accumulate in a special "price-stability investment fund." These funds would be allocated for cost subsidy and investment subsidy in industries whose average profit margins were squeezed by cost increases *outside* of their respective industries. (The funds would be allocated through the instruments for investment allocation which we outline in Chapter 14.)

► The Office of Price Information would review basic unit costs in the largest fifty firms in each three-digit industry, such as automobiles and basic steel, every four years (on a rotating basis) to check for large swings in relative costs among industries. If warranted by this review, the unit-price trend line for a given industry could be revised to accommodate shifts in unit costs.

Two particular features of this program for flexible price controls deserve further commentary:

First, we differ substantially with most TIP proponents on the treatment of wages. They typically argue that rising wages constitute the principal source of inflation and therefore hinge their price-stabilization proposals on their ability to dampen wage increases.

We reject wage controls because we disagree with both the analysis and the policy priorities underlying demands for control of wage and salary costs. As we have argued in Chapter 5, inflation is due primarily to the stagnation of productivity growth. The key to reducing inflation, by this analysis, is to revive the rate of growth of productivity, not to reduce the rate of growth of wages. How, then, can we raise the growth of productivity?

We have argued that declining work intensity represents a key source of the productivity slowdown and that policies aimed at restoring a rapid growth of productivity must increase worker commitment. If wages are controlled, then workers will have little incentive, other things equal, to increase their effort; they may be inclined, indeed, to reduce their effort. If wages are free of controls, in contrast, workers may be increasingly attracted to enterprise initiatives which would increase their productivity and create a dividend which could, at the least, be shared in the form of rising compensation. With wages controlled, a priori, one eliminates this possibility. With wages unconstrained, one at least keeps open the possibility of providing rewards for those workers who help promote cost reductions and productivity gains. Economists who insist on wage controls are the same who have failed to solve the productivity puzzle by ignoring the problem of work intensity.

We acknowledge the risk, with this approach, that workers would adopt an "I'm all right, Jack" attitude toward wage bargaining and push for wage increases substantially greater than either productivity increases or price increases, effectively squeezing enterprise profits. We address this problem directly through incentives to workers to improve productivity and share responsibility for enterprise profitability; see Chapter 13 and particularly Point 8.

Second, no other program for price stabilization, particularly including TIP proposals, has tied the funds generated by "price-stability excise tax" payments to the potential frictions and bottlenecks which price controls, however flexible, might create. This is a critical feature of our proposals, outlined above, and deserves careful attention.

Many have leveled a sharp charge against programs aimed at direct price controls: suppose that some outside price shocks, such as the OPEC price increases, push up the domestic costs of production. If one does not allow these costs to be passed on, one artificially squeezes profits and encourages disinvestment in those industries. Bottlenecks will develop.

The problem, on the other side, is that direct cost pass-alongs of such shocks simply perpetuate a prior inflationary spiral. Our proposal for a price-stability investment fund attacks this dilemma directly. If cost increases outside of firms' control force them to increase prices, despite the tax penalties, then the revenues raised from this tax should be allocated directly to alleviate the cost pressures which have forced their costly price increases.

Consider the OPEC price hikes in 1973. The proceeds went into the coffers of the oil companies. They were spent in ways designed to maintain higher (not lower) prices of oil—lobbying for price deregulation, for example. As the prices of gas and other oil derivatives rose, other industries, auto in particular, were hit with staggering reductions in profits which prevented needed retooling for energy conservation. By contrast, the price-stability investment fund would have been used in the years immediately following those staggering shocks to reduce the blow to enterprise costs and to promote reduced vulnerability to energy-cost increases. Funds would have been targeted among industries, for example, in proportion to their share of costs devoted to energy consumption, and these industry funds would then have been targeted among enterprises on the basis of proposed investment projects which would reduce the share of energy expenditures in the firm's total bill for purchases of input supplies and equipment. Additional funds, further, would have been allocated to alternative sources of energy and conservation.

This approach seems to us to make perfect sense. If price increases prove necessary, then the tax revenues from those price increases should in general be used to subsidize those firms which are making the most concerted efforts to minimize the impact of those rising costs. The carrot of cost-and-investment subsidies, administered to those enterprises which are making the most intensive efforts to reduce the rate of increase in their costs, would therefore complement the stick of tax disincentives.

Our proposal for periodic four-year review of unit-cost trends, finally, helps ensure against longer-term distortions in relative price structures among industries. It avoids the bureaucratic rigidity of fully administered price controls, while it helps protect against some of the unaccommodated shifts in relative cost structures about which opponents of price controls continually wring their hands.

This system of flexible price controls would not be easily established. No basic change in our economic system can be implemented without significant costs of adjustment, learning, and retooling. Price controls, in this respect, are no exception.

But consider the alternatives. Monetarist generals would invoke the human-wave strategy in the war against inflation. They would force us to fight inflation with years of stagnation, wasting the potential labor of millions of unemployed workers and forsaking hundreds of billions of dollars of lost output. The crushing effects of this strategy on productivity growth would likely lead to an acceleration of long-run inflationary pressures. Corporatists are more closemouthed, but it is virtually certain that a corporatist program would involve some kind of wage-and-price controls or incomes policy. The difference from our approach is that the corporatists would place very strong emphasis on the need to curb wage growth—in the interests of regressive redistribution—and would insist on the need to protect profits. (This was the case with the Nixon price controls in 1971–73; the deputy director of the Cost of Living Council later admitted that they were "reluctant to control profits at a time when . . . they were already at a relatively low level."[28]) The effects would most likely be to retard productivity growth further. One way or another, the probusiness strategies would force the jobless or the wage-earning population to bear the costs of counterproductive assaults against inflation.

Inflation is too serious a problem either to ignore or to leave to the vagaries of the market or the elitist priorities of corporate managers. A democratic economic approach to flexible price controls, as we have sketched it here, seems to us to have four strong merits: (1) It takes the problem seriously. (2) It would encourage decentralized decisions about the economic adjustments to inflation. (3) It provides the vast majority of people the opportunity to adjust to restrained price growth in ways which serve both their own and society's interests. (4) It would provide flexible mechanisms for responding to external sources of cost increase. Granted, our program could give rise to some price rigidity and some official bungling as part of the bargain. But it is a good bargain nonetheless, for it promises to slay the inflation dragon and liberate economic policy to put 10 million people back to work and bring dying communities back to life.

This final discussion points as well to the core of the argument for our approach to economic security and equity. We have been told for decades that people cannot work because full employment would cause inflation. We have been warned for years about the inefficiencies of employment security and greater equality. We have been blocked in our efforts to improve the flexibility of our working hours because those at the top insist on retaining control over such decisions.

These are the rules which brought us the current economic crisis. These are the rules which have generated the more than $1 trillion of waste we identified in Chapter 7. A democratic economic program is based upon the reduction in waste made possible by changing the rules, by putting people at the wheel instead of stuffing them in the trunk. The necessary first step is to provide more employment security and a more equitable distribution of economic rewards.

THE RIGHT TO A DEMOCRATIC WORKPLACE

When we own land and we're working it for ourselves, we're gonna save everything that we can. We're not about to waste anything or lose anything. . . . There were no fights about who's doing more work, who's getting paid more money. When you sit down with a group of people and discuss how you're gonna do things, things will work out fine.

—Member of family farming cooperative[1]

The Bill of Rights should not be checked at the factory gate.

Many will support greater workplace democracy on moral grounds. Others may recognize that heightened worker commitment will be necessary if we are to move toward full employment. In the past, as we have shown in detail in Chapters 4 through 6, the fear of losing one's job has been the principal whip with which capitalist corporations have extracted greater worker effort from their employees. If we succeed in moving toward real employment security and equity, this whip will be lifted from the managerial grasp. As long as work remains little more rewarding than a painful necessity, the elimination of unemployment and the spread of economic security will lead to rapid declines in work intensity. Greater worker commitment is therefore a necessary complement to real full employment.

Unless, of course, one wanted to trade in the whip of unemployment for some other spur. Nazi Germany pursued this tack, replacing the threat of unemployment with the police state. When workers didn't respond, they faced the work camps. Hitler found one key to full employment capitalism.

This sobering reminder, however remote from the United

States, points to a fork in the road. There are two different ways of increasing the ratio of productive labor inputs to total hours employed—as we have identified the problem of work intensity in Chapter 7. In the workplace no less than in society at large, one approach relies on the stick of harsher discipline and stepped-up bureaucratic supervision. The other approach involves the carrot of worker cooperation in production and participation in decision-making. We have grown so accustomed to work life organized by the former regime that we have overlooked the latter possibility. When we think about increased work intensity, we automatically anticipate speed-up. But what about all the worker effort that is *displaced,* under hierarchical production, into resistance and self-protection? With workplace democracy, this negative effort could be translated into positive effort. Both worker output and worker satisfaction could increase simultaneously.

The need for workplace democracy is heightened by the dynamics of the current crisis. Corporations have demanded wage concessions from their workers. Many employees might choose to grant such concessions if they thought this would help restore industry competitiveness in world markets. But how can they be certain that management will take appropriate steps to effect improved competitiveness? Direct worker involvement in enterprise decisions is the best guarantee. When the economic health of an enterprise and an economy are at stake, it is only reasonable that those whose work commitment is critical be able to ensure that their short-term sacrifices afford modernizing investment and innovation rather than union-busting, worker surveillance, real-estate speculation, or Persian rugs.

Can greater workplace democracy work? Will more democratic workplace relations lead to more productive enterprises?

Greed and fear are necessary methods of motivation if people enjoy neither security nor direct identification with the results of their economic activities. Provided with both security and democratic participation, people are more than capable of commitment and cooperation. Despite the current fascination with the *numero-uno* ethic, we have all had experiences in our families, clubs, teams, or friendships in which we and others have motivated ourselves and cooperated freely to achieve mutually desired outcomes. Motivation by commitment and cooperation, in the proper context, is clearly possible. Nor are these motives limited to small-scale, face-to-face encounters. Witness the surge of commitment and cooperation which is evoked by natural disasters in distant parts of the globe, or the dedication and often almost unlimited willingness to make sacrifices which is elicited by a just cause—whether a political campaign or a charity. Cooperation and commitment can generate effort—if people care about the cause.

Motivation by commitment and cooperation is also preferable to motivation by greed and fear on purely economic grounds, for it costs less: fewer armies of supervisors, producing nothing but grudging effort; fewer costly episodes of unemployment, leading potentially to higher crime and social unrest; fewer prisons for containing the "unmotivated." With cooperation and commitment, one substitutes the honest effort and creativity of unalienated labor for the reluctant performance of those who are cowed and fitfully subdued.

But cooperation and commitment does not result from simple prayer or limited corporate efforts to invite occasional worker suggestions. Worker commitment can only replace fear, as we have already seen in Chapter 7, if workers have *real* influence over workplace relations and decisions. Production workers in the United States do not now have such influence and control. Fundamental changes in the rules of production will be necessary. While such changes cannot happen overnight, there are concrete and tangible steps on which we could begin immediately.

Point 6: Public Commitment to Democratic Labor Unions

One of the most economically counterproductive features of the U.S. economy is its built-in institutional bias against labor unions. Unions are treated to private scorn and public indifference. A necessary and inescapable condition for an effective and democratic recovery is that this bias be reversed.

The first reason, in the U.S. context, seems the most counterintuitive. We are used to hearing that labor unions impede productivity—that union workers shirk and goldbrick, working to rules, defying the boss, engaging in what Frederick Taylor once called "systematic soldiering." Recent research has confounded this view, suggesting that labor unions promote more rapid productivity growth. Harvard economists Richard Freeman and James Medoff conclude that productivity in unionized establishments, other things equal, is probably 10 percent higher than in nonunionized shops.[2] This output gain is undoubtedly a product of two effects—one on enterprise productive efficiency and the other on worker commitment. As Medoff explains in an interview with *Fortune* magazine,

When a union comes into a competitive industry and gets increased compensation for the employees, as unions typically do, then everything has to be working to bring about higher productivity or the establishment will go out of business. You'll find efforts on the part of management because it wants to stay in business. You'll find efforts on the part of unions because they want to keep their new members. And you'll find efforts on the part of workers because they want to keep their jobs.[3]

European experience is certainly consistent with these observations. Many of the economies with the most rapid post–World War II growth are those with the highest union representation and the strongest trade-union movements—certainly including Sweden, Germany, Austria, Denmark, and the Netherlands. Especially when the trade union movement is positively and constructively involved in the growth effort, worker productivity seems to flourish.

The second reason for supporting unions builds upon the first. It is conceivable, of course, that work intensity could be restored by decimating unions and beating workers into submission. But the results of the Great Repression of the 1970s suggest that this approach is unstable and ultimately ineffective—even when viewed through purely economic lenses. And its political implications are nothing short of disastrous, leading toward a kind of South Korean exit from economic crisis, toward an economic recovery based on a crusade against workers' rights. It is a productivity drive which smacks of fascism. Support of unions seems much more promising and attractive.

If unions are so great, the skeptic responds, why doesn't everyone join one? There are several reasons for the decline in the unionized share of the U.S. labor force over the past twenty-five years.

There is no lack of workers who would like to join. Of those who do not now belong to a labor union, according to a 1977 survey, one third said that they would like to become members.[4] And this is surely an underestimate of the potential base of support for unions: more than 90 percent of employees think that they should have at least "a good deal of say" about wages, working conditions, and health and safety on the job. If there were more public and community support for unionism, and if workers felt that unions gave them a say, the percentage favoring union membership would undoubtedly be higher.

So why are unions losing ground?

First, it is extremely difficult for workers to achieve union representation in the United States. The Taft-Hartley law outlaws secondary boycotting, which means that relatively strong unions cannot help workers in weak bargaining situations gain greater leverage against their employers. (If secondary boycotting were legal, for example, southern textile workers would have had a much easier time overcoming the recalcitrant opposition of companies such as J. P. Stevens.) It is also illegal for unions to engage in organizing activities during work time; companies can suit themselves, distributing memos to employees warning against the effects of unions or calling meetings for similar purposes, while union organizers can operate only during breaks and off-work hours. Even organized unions are largely prohibited from relating to their workers during work time. Of all manufacturing workers covered by major collective-bargaining contracts, for example, more than 70 percent are covered by contracts with restrictions on the posting or distribution of union literature.[5]

A second problem is more recent: corporations have recently stepped up their antiunion activities, hiring management consultants to resist union drives and oust their current unions. A special feature of *The Economist* magazine concluded in 1979, "Union busting has become big business [in the United States]. A new breed of management consultancy is roaming the American labour scene these days, specialising in creating the 'union-free environment'. . . . Industry as a whole could be spending over

$100 million a year on such fees."[6] Given the relative advantages which corporations enjoy under the laws governing labor relations, this intensive corporate drive has borne fruit.

The third problem flows from the effects of the Great Repression of the 1970s. In periods of high unemployment, employees are naturally fearful that support for a union organization drive will lead to loss of their jobs—and the huge delays involved in petitioning the National Labor Relations Board against "unfair labor practices" are scant comfort for those who take the plunge in spite of the risk of dismissal. New "union-busting" techniques have simply perfected methods of playing upon these fears, finding ways of constantly reminding workers about the threats to their jobs. One control inspector at an electrical plant observed:

I'll give it to the company: they're great with the public relations bit. They put out 2, 3 bulletins a week, and they're always telling [the workers] . . . that if they don't work harder, if they don't stop taking off-days off . . . and so forth, that they're gonna have to take the plant and move it to Singapore. . . . They've scared people with it. This company, like a lot of companies, runs the thing by fear.[7]

Our proposals for full employment would provide some measure of relief for the third of these problems. But the first two problems would remain. The current structure of both corporations and the public law provides corporations with big advantages over labor unions. And, if one can properly interpret the straws in the wind these days, many corporations are leaning toward even more vigorous attacks against the basic rights of unions to exist. An article in *Fortune* magazine in July 1982 revealed a growing temptation on the part of many corporations to throw down the gauntlet and challenge unions to a final duel:

The ultimate question—do we really want to encourage collective bargaining—could begin to look more interesting in the years ahead. Right now, any notions about changing the basic statutes, and depriving the unions of the monopoly powers they have enjoyed for the past 45 years, have to be thought of as somewhat utopian. But the momentum behind the [recent wave of wage] givebacks may be signaling some larger changes down the road a bit. Those who believe that the giveback phenomenon is transitory . . . may be in for some surprises. . . . In the [present] circumstances, [many industries] can no longer opt for business as usual in dealing with organized labor's monopolists.[8]

We have little doubt that many corporations will be inclined, over the coming decade, to push their campaign against union power to the limit. This would be a disaster for the U.S. economy, we conclude, precisely because it would eliminate both productivity pressure on corporations and essential protection for working people. As with so many current economic controversies, the emergent debate about unions dissolves into a much more fundamental debate about the probusiness path to economic recovery. The *Fortune* article admits unions "might increase productivity on average" but says their ultimate sin is that unionism "lowers the return to capital in the long run." They conclude that "such discouragements to investment lower incomes overall."

This is true only if one believes that the *only* route to more rapid growth is via higher profits. We have already argued in Chapter 10 that this is far from the case. There are other paths to rapid economic growth which involve lower private-sector profits and which undoubtedly serve the general welfare much more directly and immediately. More widespread trade unionism, we think, is one absolutely necessary condition for such alternatives to the economics of greed.

We therefore argue that a democratic alternative must *actively* promote trade unionism in the United States. We argue that unions are a "public good," contributing to higher productivity growth and a more democratic economy. This suggests that the public as a whole has a strong vested interest in promoting trade unionism. This would require, in our judgment, public aid to help labor unions overcome the political and financial disadvantages they face in their organizing efforts.

► Congress should repeal the Taft-Hartley Act of 1947 and pass the Labor Law Reform Act of 1978, moving quickly to ease the process of union organization and to protect workers from employer harassment.

► The federal government should also establish a Union Organizing Campaign Fund—providing taxpayers the opportunity to check off up to two dollars of their personal income taxes, designating that money as a contribution to support union organizing expenses. The money would be administered by the AFL–CIO and could be used only for help in organizing workers into trade unions through the established democratic process.

The first demand follows directly from our conclusion that unions currently face substantial obstacles in their unionizing efforts and that legislative action can help clear the road of at least some of those impediments. The Taft-Hartley Act is the source of many of those obstacles—originally pushed through a compliant Congress by probusiness lobbyists in the wake of post-war strike waves in 1946; it includes a proscription against secondary boycotting and an authorization of state right-to-work laws, the biggest obstacle to union organizing in the South. The Labor Law Reform Act of 1978, solidly supported by the entire organized labor movement, sought to address many of the loopholes in the current National Labor Relations procedures, particularly those which make it possible for corporations to delay union election proceedings with virtual impunity.

The second demand symbolically reflects our argument that union-organizing deserves public support as part of a program for a democratic economy. It would make use of the mechanism which now supports federal election campaigns; we would argue that effective labor unions are as important to our political economy as well-financed elections. It would provide enough funds, potentially, so that working people could counter the huge financial advantages which giant corporations currently enjoy. And the procedure would be entirely voluntary, so that labor unions and their supporters would need to persuade the public that union-organizing warranted their contributions. If they fail, no harm done —other than a missed opportunity. If they succeed, then the public would have a convenient and reliable mechanism for manifesting their commitment to a more democratic economy.

A central problem remains. Many doubt the democratic effectiveness of union representation—worrying about union bureaucracy and corruption, about entrenched union officials and impoverished rights of opposition. While this charge is often exaggerated, fueled by the small-business campaign for "right-to-work" legislation, we think that the issue of union democracy itself is absolutely crucial. The first step toward greater union democracy should be fully democratic procedures within trade unions. Some major labor unions, such as the United Steelworkers of America, do not provide for rank-and-file ratification of negotiated contracts. This insulates the leadership from their ultimate constituency and therefore discourages democratic participation. Universal voting rights within unions would go a long way toward improving their performance.

► Workers should organize internally for the most democratic union structures and procedures possible.

► Congress should pass an amendment to the Landrum-Griffin Act requiring rank-and-file membership ratification of all union contracts.

While this latter provision involves an otherwise unwelcome government stipulation of union practices, we think that unions face a kind of *quid pro quo* compromise. Unions expect and need public support in their battles against corporations. The public (and union members) can reasonably ask in return that unions provide certain basic democratic rights internally. It would be painfully ironic if unions joined in the demand for democratic workplaces and resisted the drive for democratic unions.

Point 7: Workers' Right to Know and to Decide

Wider union representation is only a first step toward workplace democracy. Workers also need to become directly involved in planning and decision-making about production. And for that to happen, needless to say, they need to be *able* to participate. Calls for greater worker commitment without guaranteeing workers' right to know and to decide are like invitations to a poker game in which the dealer holds all the chips.

The first problem is workers' lack of information about corporate finances. Workers cannot be expected to bargain intelligently about production and investment decisions unless they have access to full financial information about the state of the corporation and the economy. Public corporations are currently required to provide only the most general information for public consumption—through the reporting procedures of the Securities and Exchange Commission. Privately held corporations are not required to make any information legally accessible to their workers or the public. A recent House Democratic Caucus position paper issued an appeal to management and labor, arguing that "when American industry is not competitive, they both suffer, and their suffering can only be reduced if they work together to increase our competitiveness."[9] How can workers be expected to cooperate when they know little or nothing about the extent of "suffering" and the potential for cost reduction? The need for widely shared financial information and corporate management data is basic.

And yet remarkably little discussion or acknowledgment of this basic need occurs in public circles. In 1980, three progressive groups—the Public Citizens Congress Watch, the Council on Economic Priorities, and the Building and Construction Trades Department of the AFL–CIO—jointly proposed a "Corporate Democracy Act." It included detailed legislative proposals for corporate disclosure. The legislative language is straightforward and the bureaucratic requirements no more imposing than current tax reporting or informational requirements of the Securities and Exchange Commission. But the proposal was greeted in Congress by the sound of one hand clapping. This neglect is egregious; it is time for U.S. workers and citizens to be able, at last, to acquire the information necessary to make informed judgments about the best solutions to their critical economic problems.

► Congress should pass a Corporate Disclosure Act, mandating full disclosure of detailed firm information on finances, taxes, stock ownership, employment, environmental impact, and health-and-safety conditions. This information would be freely available to the public. Those corporations who refused to disclose covered information would be subject to fines and withdrawal of government contracts—and, upon repeated violations, withdrawal of their right to conduct business in the United States.

The second problem involves workers' legal rights to participate in bargaining over issues of production. Unorganized workers now have no rights to participate in discussions of anything related to their work. Even unionized workers, surprisingly, have virtually no voice in decisions about production or investment. Most major collective-bargaining contracts in the United States include what is commonly called a "management-rights"

clause, a managerial invention of the late 1940s. These clauses
reserve to management the sole prerogative to decide virtually everything of significance within the firm. We quote from this clause
in the current contract between General Motors and the United
Auto Workers:

The right to hire; promote; discharge or discipline for cause; and to
maintain discipline and efficiency of employees, is the sole responsibility of the Corporation. . . . In addition, the products to be manu-
factured, the location of plants, the schedules of production, the
methods, processes and the means of manufacturing are solely and exclusively the responsibility of the Corporation.

Little wonder that problems of worker commitment are endemic,
that workers feel such little involvement in production and so little motivation to increase their effort.

In Sweden, in sharp contrast, such clauses are now effectively
illegal. The 1976 Act on the Joint Regulation of Working Life
abolishes "management-rights" clauses and sanctions "the opportunity to bargain on work organization and personnel policy."
According to Rudolph Meidner, prominent Swedish advocate of
workplace democracy and one of the principal architects of this
recent legislation, this new act "means that the legal position of
the employee has been strengthened, with a view to making it
possible for him or her to exercise some real influence over conditions at the place of work."[10]

The justification for this legislative approach to bargaining
should be clear. Many in the United States have expressed hope
that U.S. workers might join in a new "social contract," bending
every effort to help restore U.S. competitiveness in the world
economy. How can workers be expected to commit themselves to
such efforts if they are not even legally entitled to participate in,
much less influence, any of the important decisions affecting their
productiveness? Corrective legislation seems to us to be the most
obvious and elementary precondition for restoring workers' commitment to aggregate economic performance.

▶ Congress should amend the National Labor Relations Act to
include a "Bargaining Rights" clause which would sanction and
legally protect workers' bargaining over job design, investment,
and all other issues concerning the organization of production.

Point 8: Democratic Production Incentives

We cannot blithely assume that workers will automatically pursue greater involvement in production decisions simply because they acquire the right to know and decide. We propose here two mechanisms that would stimulate greater workplace democracy. Though novel, each stands within our reach and each would contribute enormously, we think, to a democratic revival of the U.S. economy.

Cooperative Work Agreements. The first issue involves potential mechanisms for worker involvement. We have argued that productivity will increase if (1) workers participate more actively in production decisions and (2) the tasks of coordination are transferred from redundant, top-heavy supervisory cadres to production-worker groups themselves. This requires the transfer of significant decision-making and coordinative responsibility to production-worker organizations.

There are some clear precedents for movement in these directions in several European countries.

In Sweden, both Saab and Volvo have pioneered cooperative work organization in automobile production, moving toward cooperative work teams as primary production units. They based their restructuring on the potential advantages of what several research institutes have called "autonomous work groups." These groups make decisions about their internal organization and work assignments. The assumption, to quote one recent review of the literature promoting this concept, is that "most employees can relate better to a small and identifiable member group than to a large, impersonal organization."[11] Both Saab and Volvo reported significant increases in labor productivity after they instituted cooperative-work-team organization.

Italian corporations have been less forthcoming, so Italian workers in the steel, chemical, and auto industries have helped pioneer employee bargaining over investment planning and production decisions. After the wave of strikes in Italy crested in the late 1960s, many workers recognized that they were angry at least partly because they were so limited in the range of issues over which they could bargain. They formed workers' councils in the factories which, as one study of the experience reports, "accepted no limitation on which topics could be brought up in negotiations." Fiat workers exchanged a slowdown in the reduction of working hours for company acceptance of a specific plan to increase investment in the impoverished regions of Southern Italy. Chemical workers bargained for tighter pollution control. In many instances, workers were able to raise new issues and win new demands. "The significance of the councils," the case study concludes, "has not been just in the fact that they now confront the employer on an unlimited range of issues, but in that they now *define the issues*."[12]

▶ Workers and unions should form "worker production committees" to propose and implement plans for greater worker involvement in production decisions. These committees should seek "cooperative work agreements," as separately negotiated contracts with management, to transfer significant portions of decision-making and supervisory responsibility from corporate ranks back into the collective-bargaining unit.

The rationale for this approach to a mechanism promoting worker participation seems clear for the United States. We cannot assume, for reasons which we have outlined in Chapter 7, that U.S. corporations will themselves take significant initiatives toward greater worker responsibility for decision-making—particularly since we propose wholesale dismantling of the wasteful bureaucratic apparatus. Workers and unions will therefore need to take full responsibility for movement in these directions. "Cooperative work agreements," negotiated by democratically elected worker production committees, would seem to provide a good mechanism for such initiatives. The more that workers succeed in negotiating transfer of responsibility from their bosses to themselves, we argue, the more cooperation and initiative workers will exercise in the production process.

Profit Sharing and Collective Worker Funds. Many corporatists have grown fond of employee profit-sharing schemes. Felix Rohatyn suggests, for example, that a good way "to attain productivity and involvement is to have a larger part of compensation paid out of profit-sharing."[13] They have pushed for ESOPs (employee stock-ownership plans) as part of their effort to turn individual workers into individual capitalists.

We think that these plans put workers at a sharp disadvantage. Corporations have huge cadres of economists, lawyers, and accountants advising them on sound and self-serving investments. Individual employees cannot possibly match this expertise—and are therefore likely to rely on management decisions about investment and profitability. This would doubly confound the objectives of a democratic program for economic recovery. First, it would leave unchecked the kinds of corporate decisions which have led to massive waste in the U.S. economy. Second, it would in no way substantially alter the balance of power between mammoth corporate bureaucracies and isolated individual employees. Real worker influence over the organization of production requires real and collective employee influence on investment.

We therefore support the Swedish Labor Organization and Social Democratic Party in their innovative approach to collective profit sharing. In a historic agreement in 1982, these two organizations jointly endorsed what had long been known in Sweden as the Meidner Plan for Economic Democracy, named after its principal author in the Swedish labor movement. The Meidner Plan calls for a share of profits to be distributed to collectively owned "wage-owner funds." As profits are paid into these funds, they acquire corresponding new equity shares in the corporation. This form of profits distribution leads to increased worker ownership in individual enterprises, enhancing individual motivation through the dividends potentially payable on a per capita basis to individual employees. Even more important, endowment of a *collective* worker fund encourages individual employees to participate in a democratic and cooperative process for determining the allocation of new equity capital.

Profit sharing through collective worker funds provides the best possible opportunity, we think, for a meaningful allocation of enterprise profits and capital to useful longer-term projects. Rudolph Meidner, author of the Swedish proposals for employee investment funds, argued their importance in a 1978 book:

Irrespective of who owns it, the total stock of capital forms the foundation of our economic and social progress. It is nothing less than a gross illusion to give the individual partner (the employee) the opportunity to dispose as he sees fit over "his" or "her" share. It is of doubtful value to the individual, and obviously harmful in the long run not only to the employees as a group but to the whole community.[14]

It is interesting to note, finally, that Swedish employees have expressed a clear-cut preference for collective use of these funds rather than individual dividends paid out on a per capita basis. A 1975 survey, Meidner reports, found that "94 per cent of the total wished to see the income used in some collective manner." The four leading preferred uses: education in economics, safety at work, further investment in firm shares, and support for weaker and more backward firms.[15]

We therefore propose a variant of the Meidner Plan for the United States:

► Workers and unions should promote *collective profit-sharing agreements*. Through these agreements, a portion of net corporate (after-tax) retained earnings—the Swedes have proposed 20 percent—is set aside for firm employees. The company issues new equity shares in the corporation equal to the value of this profit distribution; ownership of these new equity shares is vested in the enterprise's *employee investment fund*. Both dividends and voting rights in the enterprise would be allocated on a per capita basis, with the employee investment fund making its own decisions about the allocation of employee dividends to individual employees or to enterprise investments.

► Federal legislation would be necessary to provide support for these collective profit-sharing agreements. Just as recent legislation has proved necessary to regulate the operation of union pension funds and corporate pension payments, statutes would be necessary to govern the valuation of shares issued to employee investment funds and the allocation of voting rights to stocks of different kinds.

These proposals cannot easily be separated from and evaluated independently of the rest of our Bill of Economic Rights. Full-employment policies would help strengthen worker bargaining power. Public commitment to democratic trade unions would help spread access to such agreements. Proposals for a systematic and democratic approach to union pension fund investments—outlined in Point 11—would help coordinate capital allocation through employee pension funds with our proposed employee investment funds.

As part of this broader program, nonetheless, our collective profit-sharing proposals seem to us both essential and innovative. They are necessary to help structure the process through which workers, even in companies dominated by outside ownership interests, could begin to move toward much greater involvement in decision-making. The innovativeness of the proposals flow precisely from their attention to the incentives which might encourage both workers and unions to take the problems of work intensity and productivity much more seriously and involve themselves much more actively in steps toward greater workplace democracy. None of this process will come easily. But movement toward a more productive and democratic economy is likely to reward every effort in that direction.

Point 9: Promoting Community Enterprises

The previous three demands aim to encourage workplace democracy in an economy dominated by large bureaucratic enterprises preoccupied with private profitability. In order to support the progress which these demands might achieve in the private sector, it is important to begin developing alternative vehicles for spurring and stimulating a dynamic economy. While we cannot erase the irrationality of profit-seeking enterprises overnight, we can begin to move toward more direct and sensible enterprise-development policy even in the short run.

We therefore propose a new policy emphasis on development of "community enterprises." A "community enterprise" is any registered corporation in which decision-making power is held by a board elected by all production workers, or by all members of the surrounding community, or by some combination of both.

We think that such democratically controlled enterprises would warrant public support for two important reasons. First, we assume that they would be relatively small; a wide variety of recent evidence suggests that small enterprises generate more technical innovations than larger firms.[16] Second, we think that only with such community enterprises can we begin to forge a core of firms in the economy which will place higher priority on social needs than on private profit. The weight of democratic decision-making in these enterprises, combined with public investment incentives, will push them in directions which profit-seeking firms neither prefer nor tolerate. Given the divergence between the objectives of profit-seeking firms and the values of workers and citizens, it is imperative for a program for a democratic economy to develop and support a sector in which social priorities receive top priority.

But why bother? Won't we just be pouring money down a black hole, wasting resources on a wish and a prayer?

We think that an economic strategy of promoting community enterprises holds promise. Their decision-making accountability would help guard against the top-heavy inefficiencies of large corporations. Because there would be no necessary limit on the number of community enterprises which might choose to produce specific goods and services, a system of community enterprises would help to avoid the problems of concentrated economic power in large private corporations or centralized government bureaucracies. And community enterprises would be capable of coming closer, in many cases, to serving popular needs than small for-profit enterprises.

In order to realize this promise, two dimensions of a prospective community-enterprise development strategy seem essential. First, community enterprises need to be able to gain access to adequate funding. Second, a system of rewards and incentives must effectively combine the advantages of democratic control with the stimulus which market signals help provide. Our proposals seek to combine these two necessary elements.

▶ Workers and citizens should establish "community enterprises" with democratic decision-making structures—either by buying out existing enterprises or by launching new ones.

▶ Government planners, union pension funds, employee investment funds, and community investment boards (see Point 11 for their definition and mandate) should explicitly subsidize established community enterprises by providing them with subsidized loans—making investment funds available, for example, with interest charges below the established rates for traditional commercial enterprises.

The policy of loan subsidies would manifest explicit public priority for community-enterprise development over promotion of more traditional capitalist enterprises. The advantages of direct democratic participation in economic decision-making warrant this explicit priority in investment policy.

At the same time, community enterprises would have to "compete" through the market, finding customers for their products. Highly inefficient community enterprises would suffer continuing losses which no amount of loan subsidy could overcome. Community enterprises producing poor products would be unable to attract customers.

Two questions remain—about instability and growth potential.

Potential problems of instability might prevail—since the policy of interest rate subsidies would hardly be sufficient to cure the difficulties of finding and keeping customers in the market. This is where the potential marriage between democratic enterprises and democratic investment boards becomes crucial. We save discussion of the possible terms of this marriage for Chapter 14.

The issue of growth potential is difficult to handle conclusively, of course, since there has been relatively little experience with community enterprises in the United States or other advanced countries. But there are recent developments which encourage us to believe that community enterprises could flourish and grow.

Haltingly, with sputters and starts, a significant community development movement has emerged in the United States in spite of the lack of public support. There are probably more than five hundred community development corporations operating in the United States.[17] Some have grown very rapidly through their strong roots in local communities, including the East Los Angeles Community Union—with an asset base of more than $20 million, over a hundred direct employees and fourteen subsidiaries—and the Delta Foundation in Mississippi—a vehicle for channeling both public and private funds into ongoing enterprises which had something like twenty-four companies in its portfolio in 1982. A recent survey provided only a partial list of the activities of these community enterprises:

housing renovation; operating supermarkets and food co-ops; making attic fans, tents, electrical goods, toys, and goose down comforters; owning and leasing buildings; operating beauty shops; running lumber yards; raising various crops, animals, and fish; owning banks and retail outlets; running hotels and lodges; and building solar panels. The list goes on and on.[18]

It is impossible to assess the efficiency performance of these scattered enterprises, but participants in the community-enterprise movement are hopeful and enthusiastic. Roughly seventy-five organizations—including a wide variety of unions, minority groups, and community development corporations—sponsored a major conference on new enterprise development in 1981, reviewing alternative mechanisms for launching, financing, organizing, and sustaining community enterprises. The introduction to the conference report both summarized the movement represented there and captured some of the spirit of its participants:

During the last fifteen years, thousands of community-based, local enterprise development institutions have grown quietly but persistently in precisely those poor communities most in need of job generation and economic development. Though often removed from economic, social and political support, the record of community development corporations, cooperatives, tribal enterprises, public-private joint ventures and the like is promising. They represent a rapidly developing institutional infrastructure for enterprise development which has proven to be particularly effective in matching jobs to those most in need of them and development to depressed communities. With access to mainstream government support and linkages to new industries, it is reasonable to suspect that the number of such institutions will multiply even as their capacity matures.[19]

Corporatists echo some of the ideas in our proposals in this chapter—intoning, for example, about worker commitment and "quality circles" for improving employee productivity. There is a clear difference between their approach and ours, however, and we conclude by underlining the distinction.

Corporatists are interested in preserving their profits and their power. They recognize that worker commitment is key to workplace productivity, but they must constantly walk a delicate line between the kinds of substantive extensions of worker control which would most enhance worker commitment and the bottom-line protection of managerial autonomy upon which they depend. This leads to a continual effort to substitute the *form* of worker involvement for the *substance* of worker power.

Democratic economics insists on the centrality of real employee involvement *and* real worker influence. For a democratic program, the form matters much less than the substance. Will employees exercise direct and continuing influence over the actual content of decisions about production and investment? Or will their participation simply legitimize the decisions which corporations would otherwise prefer to make?

These distinctions are not always easy to make in concrete situations. But their effects cumulate. A democratic program will constantly promote *independent* centers of employee influence and decision-making power. A corporatist program will undermine with one hand what it has bestowed with the other. We have outlined some concrete proposals in this chapter for beginning the journey toward democratic and productive work relations. Corporatist alternatives will lead us on a detour. There is no substitute for the real thing.

14

THE RIGHT TO SHAPE OUR ECONOMIC FUTURES

The city neighborhoods can be self-reliant. You can have a neighborhood that can get together and rebuild. . . . We're gonna have to start talking about big changes. . . . What [people] want here is a community. . . . I don't think it has to have a label. It's just the way a lot of Americans have worked together, cooperatively.

—Community organizer in West Virginia[1]

One of the most crippling problems in the U.S. economy is our failure to make sensible use of our productive resources. We have bountiful productive capacity. But we squander it through misplaced allocative priorities and through our costly homage to the private and powerful interests which dominate the economy.

A major source of these problems is our abiding reliance on profitability as the guiding principle determining what will be produced, how, where, and when. The familiar justification for this reign of profitability is that profits measure the producer's contribution to human needs.

We think this proposition is flawed and its programmatic consequences misguided. We propose five steps toward a more rational and reliable system of economic allocation.

1. Because market prices of goods and services do not measure their contribution to meeting social needs, we propose a social-needs inventory and a democratic planning administration to supplement market allocations.

2. Because profit-motivated investments are frequently wasteful, ineffective, and unjust. we propose the expansion of com-

munity-based investments and other means to control democratically the expansion of our productive capacity.

3. Because bankers do not represent the public interest in steering monetary policy, we propose a system of democratic control over the Federal Reserve System and the financial sector.

4. Because the profit motive and the undertow of markets tends to erode communities and neighborhoods, we propose steps to allow more community initiative in industrial location decisions and infrastructural development.

5. Because the pursuit of profit is wreaking havoc with our natural environment, imposing painful costs and bitter trade-offs on families and communities, we propose a more democratic approach to necessary and difficult choices about decisions affecting the environment.

We are proposing, in short, to rely much less on markets and to make much greater use of a planning system to promote a democratic economy. The choice is clear. Do we continue to base our economic priorities, choices, and directions on whatever the profit motive dictates? Or do we open up many more opportunities for direct public choice among potential economic alternatives?

The former method of economic allocation relies on the "invisible hand," presuming that self-interest will somehow promote the general welfare. The latter method encourages more straightforward (if difficult) approaches to the determination of the general public preferences: to a much greater extent, let the public decide directly rather than through the indirect and distorted signals which market prices and private profitability convey. Alone among the advanced economies, U.S. corporations have succeeded in elevating the economics of greed to uncontested primacy. "The American fixation upon private market solutions to public problems," economist Robert Lekachman writes, "is an aberration even in other capitalist societies."[2]

Many will pale at the thought of dethroning profits as the final arbiter of economic allocation. Discussions of economic planning have traditionally been cast as a choice between free enterprise and centralized government.

But we think that the terms of this choice are misrepresented—and dangerously so. We think that market systems encourage a host of private bureaucratic mechanisms of economic allocation, that market exchange invites Big Brother to play a major role in private garb. A third system of economic allocation—involving democratic planning—is necessary to escape both from the limitations of the market and the unaccountable power of Big Brother. Why?

When markets are unsuitable for allocating the costs and benefits of an economic exchange or production process, some kind of nonmarket system is called for.[3] The typical capitalist response is to set up a private bureaucratic system, one over which those with economic power can maintain control. Bureaucratic systems are likely to flourish, in short, whenever there are sharp conflicts of interest among economic groups and where the goods and services being exchanged are not easily appropriated by one or another party to market exchanges. If private interests want to control the exchange of information, for example, they must create bureaucracies rather than relying on the market.

This dynamic is floating us on its tide. The specter of 1984 is now haunting many capitalist economies precisely because of this emerging market-bureaucracy symbiosis. We propose a way out— a democratic alternative which seeks simultaneously to limit the cost of inappropriate reliance on the market and to reduce our dependence on bureaucratic instruments by moderating the conflicts which planning decisions are likely to provoke.

One objection to nonmarket systems is that they *necessarily* involve an elite at the keyboard—telling everyone else what is good for them. This objection, we believe, can be overcome by the kinds of democratic planning mechanisms which we propose in this chapter.

The second objection requires more serious attention. Because prices measure both scarcity and need, we are told, markets allow decentralized decisions which do not require centralized concentrations of information. When these issues were hotly debated a generation ago, nonmarket advocates had to concede that the information burdens of a nonmarket system were awesome. (Justifiable, perhaps, but still awesome.) We cannot completely dismiss this concern, but we find it encouraging that information-processing costs have fallen drastically with the rise of modern computational systems. For the first time in human history, we think, information technology now allows the diffusion of current information previously retained only by experts. The technology is as compatible with decentralized communication as the telephone system.

We conclude, that the balance of advantage favors much greater use of democratic planning mechanisms. They can make up for market failures, on the one hand, and prevent bureaucratic stasis, on the other. It is time to take advantage of these possibilities.

Point 10: Planning to Meet Human Needs

Profits are supposed to provide the best possible guide for resource allocation, according to the mainstream economic faith, because people register their preferences in the form of "dollar votes" for particular products. But, as we have already seen in Chapter 10, this guide is often misleading.

Many in the United States would probably agree. They feel that they cannot find what they want or need on the market. Some are beginning to doubt that natural scarcity is the culprit: Housing is far too expensive for most households, while the market in vacation homes booms. Health care is often either unavailable or exorbitant, while billions are squandered on high-tech care for those who can pay the going rate. Mass-transit systems continue to deteriorate in many areas; solar power and conservation systems remain underdeveloped; we continue to pay large portions of our food budgets for packaging, additives, and advertising costs. Equally important, many are coming to recognize that profits are to be made not only by producing needed goods and services but also by cutting corners on workers' health and safety or by shifting the costs of poisonous-waste disposal onto the often unknowing public.

The first requirement for a system of democratic planning instruments is therefore a method for assessing public needs. As obvious as this imperative might seem, we currently have no systematic and regular sources of information about public needs and wants. The federal Bureau of Labor Statistics was originally intended to provide information about household needs and to promote concern for inadequacies in household standards of living. But the history of developing affluence in the United States after World War II resulted in diminishing attention to this function and increasing neglect of such BLS investigations. We now have a government Survey of Consumer Expenditures only once a decade. Even that survey provides remarkably little information about what people need as opposed to what they spend.

It would be relatively inexpensive to restore to public priorities a focused concern for people's basic needs for new and different goods and services. We propose a simple set of instruments:

▶ The Current Population Survey, which presently surveys a .1 percent sample of U.S. households, would annually include a supplement on major household needs, emphasizing the goods and services which households are not currently able to acquire in sufficient quantity or quality on the market. This annual survey would be supplemented by continuing public hearings aimed at identifying some of the qualitative consumption needs which households feel are least adequately met through their current purchases in the market.

▶ These two sources of information would provide the basis for an annual *needs inventory* prepared by the U.S. Bureau of the Census. This review would summarize the most urgent social needs and rank those needs by kind and intensity of popular expression.

▶ A Public Planning Administration, working with this needs inventory, would produce an annual *Report on Requirements for Balanced Production*. Relying on already widely-used input-output techniques, this report would estimate the annual production targets in goods-producing industries—steel and energy, computers and the like—as well as services—schools and restaurant meals, for example—which would be necessary to realize the major priorities established by the needs inventory.

▶ These production targets would be compared to recent trends in production output in the sectors involved. Where current output (or its growth) was falling far below production needs, the Public Planning Administration would provide investment subsidies to private firms, unions, community investment boards, and

328 AN ECONOMIC BILL OF RIGHTS

other democratically controlled investment institutions in order to
encourage investment in sectors whose increased output seemed
of the highest public priority.

What would such a needs inventory show? We cannot perfectly
anticipate the results of such surveys, of course, but some results
seem fairly likely. We can imagine that large numbers of people
would express demand for more publicly subsidized child-care facilities; community-based preventive-health-care centers; instal-
lation of insulation and solar heating equipment; technical and
marketing services for food producers' and consumers' cooperatives; construction of low-cost housing; more teachers and aides
to permit reduction of school class size; and extended fire and
police protection. If we are way off target with this list, it simply
helps dramatize the need for more systematic information than
three economists can surmise.

Our proposal for what is often called *indicative planning* seems
novel only because the U.S. economy has been so *un*planned
since World War II. The basic principles of this kind of targeted
or indicative planning have been extensively used in many advanced capitalist countries in the postwar era. Some examples:

• In Japan, the Ministry of International Trade and Industry
  (MITI) targets priority industries for public financial assistance and incentives.
• In Germany, the centralized banking system plays a similar
  role, establishing investment priorities and channeling capital
  to those sectors which seem most deserving of support. "The
  essence of the German system," as one observer reported to
  Business Week, "is that there are few surprises."[4]
• In France, throughout the decades from the early 1950s, the
  government has developed a general economic plan through
  the National Planning Commission (le Commissariat du Plan).
  Within the framework established by the general guidelines of
  this plan, specific contracts are negotiated with corporations
  which, if they cooperate, may receive tax incentives, subsidized loans, and other official aid in return.[5] For all the other
  differences between the new Socialist administration under
  President François Mitterand and the earlier Gaullist regimes,

the Socialists are continuing these general planning techniques and extending them in their first term in power.

None of these models is worthy of transplantation without adaptation, in our view, because none pays sufficient attention to popular needs and none involves sufficiently democratic decision-making structures. The mechanisms proposed in this chapter seek to remedy some of their deficiencies. While untried, we think that our proposed needs inventory and Public Planning Administration will make sense to many who are dissatisfied with recent economic miscreations. Our ideas are shared by a group of liberal executives and academics, including former U.A.W. head Leonard Woodcock and the Nobel-prize winning economist Wassily Leontief, who suggested in their 1975 initiative for national economic planning:

It should be clear that the planning office would not set specific goals for General Motors, General Electric, General Foods, or any other individual firm. But it would indicate the number of cars, the number of generators and the quantity of frozen foods we are likely to require in, say, five years, and it would try to induce the relevant industries to act accordingly.[6]

Until we adopt such planning instruments, we will have little control over our future economic trajectories. "America now has an industrial policy," as M.I.T. economist Lester Thurow puts it. "It just happens to be an industrial policy to shoot ourselves in the economic foot."[7]

Point 11: Democratizing Investment

We cannot produce more of what we need unless we can *invest* in its production. Private capital may not find it profitable to invest in producing what is most needed. Or it may fear the long-term logic of a democratic economic program and prefer to build its next factory where the political climate is more favorable.

Controlling the Sources Investment. Many progressives have traveled this far along the odyssey of alternative economic logic but have then thrown up their hands in despair. One cannot afford to disturb the goose that lays the golden egg. Large corporations have all the capital. Alternative economic policies will wither from investment malnourishment. Where will the investment come from?

Investment means expanding the stock of productive equipment —buildings, machinery, and whatever else is needed—in order to increase our capacity to produce more, or more cheaply, in the future. Investment is possible when an economy consumes less than it produces or acquires additional capital through foreign exchange. Investment does not require private profits; it simply requires production in excess of current consumption and control of the resulting surplus by those who will devote it to increasing the nation's productive capacity.

Profits *may* be the major way that investment is financed, but they *need* not be. The profit rate in Norway during the 1970s, for example, was lower than in any of the dozen or so countries for which we have data. Yet Norway invested a share of gross national product almost twice that of the United States and ranked second among the advanced nations in investment, narrowly outpaced by Japan. The Norwegian secret: public investment. Part of its surplus was controlled by the government—through taxation—and then used to invest in socially necessary projects which were not profitable or safe enough to attract private investment.[8]

But taxation and public investment by the government is far from the only potential source of financially increased productive capacity in socially necessary areas. Personal savings provide another source. And personal savings and assets are substantial; we have simply failed to use them for socially-determined purposes.

What instruments could be used to make intelligent use of households' own savings? And what methods could be deployed to channel those savings in more productive directions?

There are three important steps which can provide mechanisms for democratic involvement in investment:

► Labor unions should establish democratically elected pension-fund investment boards to determine investments from both private and public union investment funds.

► All banks and insurance companies should be publicly controlled, operating within statewide banking and insurance systems. This public control would ensure popular accountability of the investment uses of all personal savings maintained in time deposits and insurance reserves.

► Local governments should establish democratically elected community investment boards to determine investments from personal savings deposits and insurance reserves. Each community investment board would be able to decide about the allocation of savings from households in their respective geographic jurisdictions.

These proposals—particularly our call for public control of banks and insurance companies—may strike some readers as too unusual and too radical. But they flow naturally from the rest of our analysis and the rest of our program. And, it seems to us, they make perfect sense.

The first argument on behalf of these proposals is their clear necessity as a basis for a democratic investment program. It would be pointless to call for popular control over investment priorities if people could not gain access to the principal sources of personal savings available for investment. Many workers and unions have recently recognized the critical importance of more direct control over the allocation of union pension funds. The argument for direct control over savings and insurance assets is perfectly parallel: both kinds of funds represent deferrals from present household consumption for the purposes of future household consumption and security. It seems clear, once one thinks about such a parallel, that popular and accountable bodies should determine priorities for the allocation of personal savings.

The main difference between pension funds and personal savings is where they come from. Pension-fund contributions are negotiated by workers and unions at the workplace, while savings and insurance deposits are allocated by individual households in communities. It therefore makes the most sense, we think, for unions to establish democratically elected pension-fund investment boards and for local communities, through their municipal governments, to establish democratically selected community investment boards. (There are elected community planning boards in New York City each of which currently represents about 100,000 residents and which already make decisions, however advisory, of the sort which community investment boards would make.) Public acquisition of and control over banks and insurance companies is simply a necessary condition for community investment boards to be able to marshal the funds for which they are responsible.

Many will wonder about compensation for the owners of banks and insurance companies. We agree with the French government of François Mitterand, which provided 100 percent compensation for the value of the equity ownership of the banks it nationalized in late 1981.[9] But we do not think it advisable to make full immediate payment for purchase. We would recommend instead that the government issue to previous owners long-term (say, fifteen-year) bonds in the public banks and insurance industries. This system would have two obvious advantages: it would spread payment over a longer-term amortization period, reducing the short-term financial barriers to public acquisition, and it would also provide previous owners a stake in the financial health and viability of the public banks, helping reduce the likelihood of "capital strikes" and "capital flight" from the United States after acquisition.

We can imagine two residual objections to these demands for democratizing the instruments of personal savings.

Some may worry, in the first instance, whether ordinary citizens can decide about complicated issues involving investment of large funds. Corporatists certainly have their doubts. But many unions and consumer cooperatives have already demonstrated that their elected representatives can make intelligent decisions and can draw sensibly upon technical advice. In Kansas, for example, the Public Employees Retirement Fund has begun to channel some of its money into local projects initiated by nonprofit development corporations. Returns on these investments have been high enough so that at least sixteen other state funds have begun to follow the Kansas fund's lead.[10]

The State of California now has an even more elaborate structure of public institutions guiding public union pension fund investments, including a Pension Investment Unit, an Employee Advisory Council, and a Council of Pension Trustees and Managers. These agencies have been able to manage funds whose total assets have reached roughly $50 billion, earn a market rate of return on their assets, and begin to pursue some articulated social goals for their investments all at the same time.[11]

Much work would nonetheless need to be done in order to train investment-board trustees and to develop sophistication about investment priorities. "Even where [popular representatives] are already represented on trustee boards," Lawrence Litvak observes in his book *Pension Funds and Economic Renewal,* "they often do not have the preparation or information necessary for playing an active role in investment decision-making and must too often defer to experts on the board or staff."[12]

Such training would not be difficult to provide, however. We vest our currently elected public representatives with vast responsibilities for the intelligent allocation of billions of dollars of tax revenues. There is no reason that we cannot further entrust our own representatives with the responsibility for decisions about the allocation of investment funds as well. It is a choice between unaccountable investment decisions, with their decisive importance for future economic trajectories, and accountable investment decisions, with some focused training to enable publicly selected representatives to establish popular investment priorities. The training requirements seem like a minor price to pay for the possibility of an authentic democratic alternative to the economics of greed.

Some may also object that publicly controlled banks and insurance companies would not provide either efficient service or safe management of personal savings.

Here, the objections are purely reflexive. One can compare the Social Security system with insurance companies to assess relative efficiency. The Social Security system, by and large, is administered fairly and efficiently. Administrative expenses fluctuate at less than 3 percent of total social-insurance expenditures.[13] By contrast, private insurance companies are enormously wasteful. In his best seller on the insurance companies called *The Invisible Bankers,* Andrew Tobias has documented widespread inefficiency, discriminatory practices, and gross waste in the private insurance companies.[14] "There are ways to improve the [insurance] system radically," Tobias concludes. "But this is not an industry, by and large, that seeks radical improvement."[15] Respondents in a recent

survey were asked to rank thirty-two different industries for relia-
bility. The insurance industry finished twenty-ninth—comparing favorably only with the oil, chemical, and tobacco industries.[16] When we have spoken to groups about the possibility of
public control of the insurance industry, many have applauded
loudly with enthusiasm. It is difficult to find *anyone* who does not
feel that he or she has been rooked by a private insurance company at some time or another.

One U.S. example clearly dramatizes this point. The Wisconsin
State Life Insurance Fund is a self-supporting state-owned business founded in 1911. Jeremy Rifkin and Randy Barber summarize the facts of the Wisconsin fund's comparative performance:

. . . this insurance company provides Wisconsin residents with the
least expensive life-insurance costs in the United States. While an ordinary ten-year private insurance policy might cost somewhere around
$3.50 per $1,000 of coverage, a comparable Wisconsin Fund policy
costs only 15¢ per $1,000. This incredible difference is partially a re-
sult of the fact that the Wisconsin Fund has such a small overhead
compared to private insurance companies. Because it has no advertising costs and no sales commissions to pay out, its administrative expenses are virtually zero compared to industrial giants like Pruden-
tial.[17]

There is equally good reason, we think, for preferring publicly
controlled banks. There is probably not as much waste in the private banking industry as in the insurance industry since the insurance companies, as Tobias suggests, have been able to remain
more "invisible." But public banks in both the United States and
Europe have excellent records both for efficiency and for respon-
siveness to public needs. The state-owned Bank of North Dakota,
for example, has a long record of efficiency and public service.
According to Rozanne Enerson, author of a history of the bank,

It created the nation's first secondary market for federally insured student loans, and the state's first secondary market for FHA/VA residential mortgages. It manages the state's Municipal Bond Bank, which
purchases and packages the securities of the political subdivisions of
the state. It provides beginning farmers a 2 percent interest rate dis-
count for the first five years of their loans. It trades on the federal
funds market. It has also established a Bank of North Dakota prime
rate, reflecting the cost of money to the Bank, usually one-half to one

percent lower than the national prime. In addition, it has returned over $100 million of its earnings to the state's general fund.[18]

Public control over the banks seems to us a necessary condition for democratizing investment; it can only tailor the financial sector more and more closely to actual popular needs.

Controlling the Allocation of Investment. If these are the mechanisms for democratizing investment, what methods would these democratic instruments use for distributing investment funds among various potential capital needs? The challenge for a democratic alternative is twofold. How do we identify "socially profitable" investments? And how do we provide a set of incentives to encourage investment in these activities which both maximizes democratic participation in investment decisions and minimizes inefficient administration of investment planning? The set of demands we outline here, in the overall context of the Economic Bill of Rights, provide promising answers.

► Democratic investment boards should establish investment priorities which combine attention to investment return and social need. In order both to ensure accountability to borrowers and to promote investment priorities directly, union pension-fund boards and community investment boards should negotiate planning agreements through which negotiated enterprise objectives are rewarded with subsidized investment funds.

The idea of such planning agreements has been developed by British planner and member of Parliament Stuart Holland, and the British Labor Party has embodied it in specific legislative proposals.[19] Planning agreements, following Holland's suggestions, would be negotiated between corporations and the respective investment boards for five or ten years. On the enterprise side, the firm would project detailed plans for output, consumption of inputs, and unit costs. On the investment-board side, the funds would invite unions and community groups to comment on the combined impact of the assembled corporate plans. After a process of negotiation, the planning agreement would embody both the firm plans for which the subsidized investment was being provided and the criteria by which the investment boards would continue to provide funds or withdraw them.

The planning-agreement format provides a convenient mechanism through which both community enterprises—see Point

9—and private corporations could bid for investment board funds and subsidies. Private corporate eligibility for investment support would help provide an additional standard by which the cost effectiveness of community enterprises could be judged. As long as community enterprises were able to gain access to start-up resources and managerial skills, the relative success in the planning-agreement competition between community enterprises and private corporations would provide a fair measure of their comparative advantages.

Summarizing the effect of the last three sets of proposals, we note that we are proposing three levels of subsidies to help guide investments in a democratic economy. At one level, reflecting the priorities culled from the annual needs inventory, the Public Planning Administration would make subsidies available to private firms, local, union, and community investment boards to encourage the development and growth of industries whose goods and services are most urgently needed. At a second level, investment boards would provide subsidies to community enterprises generically—reflecting the general social priority *and* return which we have argued would redound to increasingly democratic control over production and distribution. Third, we propose subsidies through planning agreements, by which investment boards would seek to secure specific enterprise agreement to stipulated union and community goals such as product development, provision of child-care facilities for employees, or guaranteed production levels over a relatively long planning horizon. It is certainly possible, within this three-tiered structure of investment subsidies, that a single community enterprise could receive all three levels of subsidies for particular investment projects: (1) by producing goods and services targeted in the report on requirements for balanced production; (2) by satisfying the criteria which identify community enterprises; and (3) by agreeing to specific projects embodied in a particular planning agreement.

With this recapitulation, it is also possible to compare our approach to investment planning with more conventional corporatist discussions of "sunrise" and "sunset" industries. Liberal economists such as Lester Thurow worry with good reason that investment subsidies doled out in response to current political and profit imperatives would amount to a kind of lemon socialism, propping up politically entrenched but dying industries while future growth prospects remain in the shadows. Many corporatists have therefore proposed policies which would concentrate investment subsidies in industries with either the most rapid recent growth histories or the most glittering balance sheets.

We propose, by contrast, a system that would work from direct assessment of popular needs, not through indirect and unreliable measures like market growth and private profitability. The needs inventory would identify key sectors which deserve public encouragement and support, industries in which it would serve the general welfare to encourage rapid productivity growth and continuing cost reductions. We would also place explicit social priority on encouragement of democratic enterprises—because they will help provide the means for lifting the waste burden in our economy. We would place our trust in union and community investment boards to choose among enterprises—because of both their cost performance and their commitment to social goals identified by those investment boards—in ways which would most directly advance the general social well-being. And we have confidence that workers with guaranteed jobs in a growing economy would be far less likely to obstruct necessary phase-outs of obsolete industries or processes and far more likely to welcome favorable opportunities in other lines of work.

Would these criteria mean that savers would earn a lower rate of return on their savings than they do under current private-sector arrangements? It is difficult to say. Admirers of the free market argue that the current pattern of investments captures the highest possible return and that investment boards concerned about "social investing" will necessarily pursue investments earning a lower rate of return. But even the highest return in a stagnant and wasteful economy may be far below the returns to social investors in a growing, technologically dynamic economy which makes full use of its productive assets.

Democratic decisions about investment priorities would help realize these public benefits. And our three-tiered system of public subsidy of democratically targeted investments would guarantee that individual savers were not penalized for the sake of these socially necessary projects. Democratizing investment can work.

Point 12: Democratic Control of Money

Money is to economic exchange what language is to verbal communication. It is sometimes easy to mistake the medium for the message. Money, after all, is not what we live on, any more than language is what we say. But just as language shapes what we say and how we relate to one another, so money has a major impact on how we exchange our goods, how we labor, and how the economy evolves.

Money and the policies regulating it therefore have a fundamentally collective nature. Money is so important to the whole society that it is both undemocratic and economically senseless to leave its control in the hands of a tiny financial aristocracy— which often profit from policies that inflict monumental costs on others. This reminder has been etched deeply in recent economic events, since elite banker control over monetary policy and our financial institutions has played a central role in obstructing recent efforts to revive capitalist economies. We see no reason to allow the persistence of this threat to popular economic sovereignty. We advocate democratic control of the money supply in the United States.

▶ A Federal Reserve Board would continue to regulate the rate of expansion of the economy's money supply. Its board of governors would be elected by the House of Representatives—our most representative national body—to four-year terms coinciding with the presidential term of office.

Democratic control of the money supply has been a long-standing popular demand, dating back to agrarian protests in the nineteenth century and the bank controversies of Andrew Jackson's day. Knowing that borrowers generally outnumber lenders, bankers and the wealthy have always opposed those demands, hoping to protect "tight money" and high interest rates from the "easy money" policies and lower interest rates generally preferred by the majority of the electorate.

What matters for the health of the economy, however, is not simply the profitability of lending money. What matters much more centrally, instead, is the manner in which monetary policy can help finance necessary investments. We assume that a democratically elected board of governors of the Fed, in the context of our proposals for democratizing investment, would be sensitive to the need to maintain some positive rate of interest in order to attract and reward personal savings and to ration the use of savings for investment projects. We also assume that, in the context of full employment and solidarity wage policies, most households would be able to improve their standards of living to a point where they would feel comfortable about setting aside some of their current earnings for the purpose of future consumption—and thus would be likely to generate a stream of savings even at low interest rates. Harvard economist Stephen Marglin has argued that households' income levels are a much more important determinant of savings than the level of the real interest rate on savings deposits.[20] Only the wealthy have the luxury of tailoring their current consumption and savings decisions to the marginal variation in interest rates on deferred consumption.

How would interest rates themselves be determined under our proposed restructuring? We would suggest reliance on a market-based system for determining the particular interest rates which individual banks would charge. It is likely that there would be ebbs and flows to the demand for and supply of loanable funds. It seems to us both pointless and ultimately inflexible to impose stringent regulation of the specific interest rates which local and state banks could offer and charge. States could establish ceilings on interest rates if they chose. And the democratically elected Fed could adjust the rate of growth of the money supply if interest-rate pressures were pushing against state-regulated ceilings. Beyond those potential instruments for protection against possible interest-rate gouging by local banks—even publicly controlled ones—we assume that state banking commissions would be in the best position to weigh public needs for stable and low interest on loans against the need to attract additional loanable funds for future investment projects.

Democratic control of the Fed is the final cornerstone of a system that would prevent private financial interests from interfering with the public agenda for economic revitalization.

Point 13: Promoting Community Life

One of the principal advantages of community enterprises, as economic journalist Neal Peirce has concluded, "is that they have roots in the community." But community enterprises alone are not capable of some of the steps necessary to promote strong and vibrant community life. Communities face two critical problems which require broader attention through democratic planning.

The first problem involves community vulnerability to plant shutdowns and capital mobility. By threatening to close their doors in a particular community, firms can exercise a kind of blackmail over other community policies or worker demands. Plant closings and rapid geographical shifts in production lead to a highly mobile work force which passes through communities so rapidly that local roots cannot take hold. We place fundamental priority on stable communities of neighbors who know one another and can work together for community development. We place equally high priority on legislation to halt the forced march of workers in search of jobs and to undercut the power of corporate blackmail threats.

It is absolutely critical that we reverse locational priorities in the U.S. economy. Capital now moves and people must follow. We think that capital and infrastructural location should correspond to and strengthen desired patterns of community life. We think that lower costs of community disruption will more than outweigh the increased costs of transporting goods and producing goods by a less mobile work force. There are important reasons, moreover, for concluding that goods should move more and people should move less.

Defenders of unimpeded mobility for firms assert that economic efficiency requires it. But their argument presumes that the owners of firms which move pay all the costs—direct and indirect —of the movements which they mandate. But in a world of cities and states competing for jobs with business-tax favors and subsidized services for industry, this could not be further from the truth. Our major objective is to force those who profit from plant relocations to pay the full costs of their wanderlust.

► The federal government should pursue several legislative steps to block capital flight from individual communities and to reduce its impact. It should enact plant-closing legislation. It should institute full taxation of corporate profits on overseas investments. It should eliminate blanket federal insurance of overseas investments whereby U.S. taxpayers foot the bill for U.S. corporate losses.

We are the only advanced country, to our knowledge, without some kind of prior-notification provisions regulating plant closings. "America is the easiest place in the world," Lester Thurow observes, "to fire workers."[21] In West Germany, for example, Martin Carnoy and Derek Shearer report that

any relocation or transfer of work must be approved by the government and submitted to a works council elected by employees. If they do not agree to the proposed shifts, binding mediation occurs. No plant may close without a permit from the state exchange, which can reject the proposed action when substantial unemployment exists in the areas affected.[22]

A "plant-closing" movement has been spreading rapidly in the United States, pushing for state versions of the kind of federal plant-closing legislation we advocate here. Many have adopted the model of some legislative proposals developed in 1977 by the Ohio Public Interest Campaign. Their draft bill involves three principles: advance notification, income maintenance, and job replacement. These principles are advanced through six specific provisions:

- prior notification of major cutbacks and total shutdowns;
- discharge or severance payments for all workers, whether or not they are unionized;
- continuation of health-insurance coverage for some period following the layoff, paid for by the company;
- increased rights of transfer to other plants or stores in the company's system (if any);
- lump-sum payment to the local municipality, to help finance economic redevelopment; and
- preparation by joint company-union-government committees of

economic impact statements, to facilitate the redevelopment effort.[23]

Such legislation can work. Recent research on a Maine plant-closing notification statute, on the books since 1972, has shown that notification has greatly reduced the amount of joblessness suffered by communities as a result of plant closings.[24]

There is a parallel need for new legislation on overseas investments. Multinational corporations have largely determined federal tax policy in this area, and it has created a substantial incentive to overseas capital flight. Barry Bluestone and Bennett Harrison have concluded in their recent study of capital flight, *The Deindustrialization of America,*

it is not the case that the preferential tax and tariff treatment of foreign investment *caused* U.S. corporate managers to shift their capital abroad. Rather, these public policies *reinforced* corporate decisions that were based on more important factors: markets, labor costs, and political security. But this is not a trivial point. It implies that managers who invested abroad were rewarded with windfall profits from the IRS.[25]

As a result of the wide array of tax breaks on foreign earnings, Bluestone and Harrison report, U.S. corporations in 1972 paid an effective tax rate to the U.S. government of only 5 percent on overseas profits. We favor wholesale elimination of tax and insurance subsidies of foreign investment.

The second critical problem affecting communities in the United States is infrastructural deterioration. Water and sewage-disposal systems are decaying in many communities; transportation networks are almost beyond repair; electricity networks are increasingly at risk in many areas.

This deterioration has not been inadvertent. Few recognize how much infrastructural development is now being left to private corporations. Current and future development of satellite communications technology is almost entirely in the hands of private corporations. Transportation planning has tended increasingly to defer to individual private interests, reflecting the growing private role in alternative freight and haulage systems; this has fostered further decay in the nation's rail network and, at least in some areas, highway and transshipment facilities. Even access to clean

water and green spaces is now gained more and more exclusively
by the affluent in suburban communities. Private benign neglect
has reinforced the uneven development of individual communities, creating new divisions, heightening old conflicts, and posing
additional obstacles to the revitalization of local community life.

▶ State and local governments, with appropriate borrowing support from the federal government where necessary, should promote and guide a rapid renewal of community infrastructure—
particularly including the physical infrastructure necessary for
efficient systems of transportation, communications, electricity,
energy conservation, and sewage and water treatment. These
infrastructural investments should be focused on where people
live today, not where the corporations would like to expand employment tomorrow.

There is an interesting European example of the importance of
such infrastructural support. In many regions in Northern Italy,
local community and public government support has helped foster extremely rapid enterprise growth. M.I.T. social scientists
Michael Piore and Charles Sabel describe the economic core of
the "new wave" of economic growth in Italy:

The center . . . is a vast network of very small enterprises through
the villages and small cities of central and Northeast Italy, in and
around Bologna, Florence, Ancona and Venice. . . . These little
shops range across the entire spectrum of the modern industrial structure, from shoes, ceramics, textiles and garments on one side, to motor
cycles, agricultural equipment, automotive parts, and machine tools on
the other. The firms perform an enormous variety of the operations
associated with mass production. . . . The average size of the units
varies from industry to industry, but it is generally extremely
small. . . .[26]

This network of small firms appears to be growing very rapidly.
These regions are now among the most rapidly growing in
Europe, and living standards have been increasing substantially in
that area of Italy. Although there are many features of this Italian
model which make it unique, several of its characteristics carry
important lessons for the U.S. debate about revitalization: (1)
The union and artisan tradition in Italy has helped integrate
workers into the process of production in these small firms, pro-

viding strong foundations for their rapid increases in hourly output. (2) The small firms have been able to achieve substantial and continuing technical innovation at least partly because they also cooperate with each other, pooling information and technical advice; this parallels many of the efforts of fledgling community development corporations in the United States to pool resources and share market information. (3) They are able to take advantage of and build upon modern educational, transportation and other infrastructural support because the local governments, almost all of them controlled by coalitions of socialists and communists, have placed high priority on supporting enterprise development. This infrastructural support has helped provide some of the stability and strong foundations which the private sector, by itself, has been unable to afford in the United States.

The Italian example builds, in short, on what Piore and Sabel call "a mixture of entrepreneurship and cooperation." It is this mixture which our demands for community development would hope to promote. Strong communities are crucial for our ability to recognize and honor each other's needs—as well as for our personal security, individual safety, and the vibrancy of our democracy. We must not allow either capital flight or infrastructural deterioration to erode these basic foundations for a democratic alternative.

Point 14: Environmental Democracy

Modern societies have encountered yet another problem with which democratic planning systems must contend—the proliferating environmental hazards from nuclear and chemical waste, from the deadly materials which are spewed and scattered around us. Some of these problems, for instance the disposal of long-lived nuclear waste, pose almost insurmountable challenges to any decision-making structure. As a first step toward ensuring the integrity of community life and its balance with nature, it is imperative that we establish an Environmental Bill of Rights to guide the trajectory of future economic growth.

►The U.S. Congress should pass a no-pollution-without-representation act. This legislation would establish the absolute right of local communities, through referenda, town meetings, or elected municipal governments, to bar the disposal or transshipment of hazardous or environmentally destructive material and to reject the location of nuclear power plants. These local rights should not be abrogated even in the fabled interests of "national security."

► The U.S. Congress should also pass a community right-to-know law requiring businesses operating in a locality or transshipping goods to make available full information on the chemical and other relevant properties of potentially hazardous substances which they use or transport.

Many communities have already exercised these rights for themselves: Fishing towns in Maine have voted to reject the oil-spill dangers of a petroleum port, and Vermont town meetings have rejected uranium-mining contracts. In Massachusetts environmental health and safety activists have organized in favor of a community right-to-know act, and such a bill was passed by the Massachusetts electorate in November 1982. Others have placed before the voters a nuclear democracy act similar to our no-pollution-without-representation act.

Some may object that such policies would stand in the way of necessary energy development. We cannot agree. We present in Chapter 15 a set of policies for conservation and safe energy which would rapidly free us from reliance on unsafe energy sources, such as nuclear power. Until then, our concern in this chapter on democratic planning seems to us more fundamental.

We recognize, of course, that obstacles to coordinated long-range choices will arise if each unit in society insists on having undesirable activities located in someone else's backyard. Our no-pollution-without-representation act does not preclude cities and towns from making collective choices jointly, with compensation being paid where no locality would otherwise welcome a socially needed project. Nor does it preclude private corporations or community enterprises from providing such compensation. It simply states that whatever arrangements are made must meet with community approval.

Communities must be free, in short, to choose to place absolute priority on their own lives and those of their children and descendants. Recent policies in the United States leave companies free to dispose first and face potential opposition and civil suit later, as residents of the Love Canal have so tragically discovered. The burden of adjustment should be reversed. Communities should be free to ban hazardous threats to their environments; let private companies pay to win a fully informed citizenry away from such blanket refusal. If corporations cry about constraints on future growth, let them put their money on the table. Evaluation of the *full* social costs of alternative environmental policies must come first. And local communities must conduct those evaluations themselves. Nothing less will do in a democratic alternative.

Local autonomy is no substitute, at the same time, for nation-wide environmental and safety standards. Without such national standards, municipalities can easily find themselves repeating the recent vicious cycle of competition among cities and towns, each bidding for new sources of employment and tax revenues, offering to lower their environmental standards for the sake of employment expansion. Both nationwide standards and environmental democracy are necessary.

Point 15: Democratizing Foreign Trade

Economic recovery in the United States will not take place in a global vacuum. Foreign-trade policies are central for any comprehensive approach to economic restructuring.

Three principal approaches to foreign trade have dominated recent economic policy debates: *protectionism,* the *big stick,* and *export promotion.* Our approach differs strikingly from each of these major emphases.

We are not opposed to short-term recourse to tariffs for adjustment purposes; indeed, we are persuaded that many protariff, antifree-trade arguments make sense as grounds for temporary tariff protection to ease necessary adjustment processes, as with the job-content legislation currently advanced by the United Auto Workers. We oppose tariffs as a long-term solution, however. Unemployment and declining job opportunities in manufacturing have much less to do with imports than with restrictive domestic economic policy. Partly for this reason, tariffs are a very costly way to achieve employment security. Tariffs are divisive, moreover, pitting the interests of workers in import-threatened sectors against those in exporting sectors and sacrificing the interests of consumers who benefit from low-cost imports to those of workers whose products compete with import bargains.

Some probusiness advocates oppose tariffs and endorse the big-stick approach to foreign trade, arguing that U.S. power and rapid economic growth depend on a reassertion of our political and military might in world markets. Irving Kristol, acknowledged guru of the neoconservative movement, has probably expressed this approach most directly, writing in the *Wall Street Journal* in 1979:

The 1980s will see a disintegrating international order in which economic growth is going to be extraordinarily difficult to achieve. . . . It will therefore have to be an overriding goal of American foreign policy to help shape this world. . . . If the 1970s were dominated by considerations of domestic economic policy, the 1980s are going to be dominated by considerations of foreign and military policy. . . . A whole new set of priorities will have to be established, as we come to grips with the fact that the American economy does not exist in isolation from world politics. . . . What will be relevant is an American foreign policy in which power, and the readiness to use it boldly, will play a far more central role than has ever before been the case in our history. . . . Our economic growth will henceforth be as dependent on our foreign policy as on our economic policy. . . . Today it is military rearmament that is the first priority, economic as well as political. And if there are going to have to be massive increases in military spending, then we shall have to put up with . . . many sacrifices, but so long as the goal is visibly there, the sacrifices are tolerable. If the goal is not there, our situation will gradually deteriorate until we end up divided among ourselves and destroying our institutions in a frenzy of recriminations.[27]

As Kristol affirms, the big-stick argument applies most directly to the issue of resource access, particularly access to oil: "The Middle East is the most obvious source of trouble. . . . Oil at $50–$75 a barrel is not too far down the road, and chaos in that region might well result in no oil being available at any price. All this would seem to suggest the likelihood of some American military involvement in the Middle East to protect our interests, both economic and strategic."

We disagree with this approach to foreign trade on two central grounds. First, as we have already suggested in Chapter 10, we doubt its feasibility; we do not think that political power or military might can guarantee international economic domination. Second, and much more important, we fundamentally disagree on moral grounds. We do not think that people in the United States have a right to place our interests *ahead* of others' needs and interests around the world. However trite, "Might does not make right" is a reasonable guide to foreign policy in a democratic society committed to humane and egalitarian values. We think, moreover, that an increasingly democratic process in the United States will lead to increasing disavowal of the big stick in foreign policy —simply because we believe that a vast majority of people in the United States are not committed to U.S. domination of people in other countries. Normative values and political practice will converge, we think, under a truly democratic regime in the future.

We are no more inclined to agree with the export-promotion approach of many corporatists. The Business Week Team insists, for example, that "creating a new trade priority" is one of "four cornerstones" of a national economic policy. In sections with such stirring titles as "Export or Die," the Business Week Team outlines a variety of measures which would promote free trade and the competitiveness of U.S. exports in world markets. They provide a vigorous justification of that approach:

What this implies . . . is an understanding of the crucial importance of the global market for U.S. industrial expansion . . . policymakers and lawmakers must grasp the fundamental correlation between the nation's strength as a trader in an increasingly interdependent world economy, its domestic prosperity, and the augmented political influence that a competitive economy will enable the United States to exert around the world. Recognizing this, legislators and policy formulators must make a strong commitment to create a framework of laws and regulations that will encourage export industries, and beyond that must supply the direct government support that is indispensable if U.S. producers are to compete on equal terms against foreign rivals that are backed to the hilt by their governments.[28]

We disagree with this emphasis on export promotion for two main reasons.

First, we do not believe that world market prices should form the basis for economic planning and economic policy. The limitations of world market signals are even more striking than those of prices set on domestic markets. They do not reflect all of the social costs of production. Most likely they have not been set in competitive markets. They may reflect the lower costs of labor in countries with authoritarian regimes where workers have few rights. Do we really want to "compete" with goods produced under totalitarian regimes, to pick an extreme example, and accept the domestic cost pressures imposed by some other country's policies of virtual enslavement? Do we seek to raise our standard of living by buying the cheap fruits of labor's bondage elsewhere in the world?

Second, we oppose reliance on foreign trade policy to try to rectify our domestic economic problems. We have the greatest chance of shaping our future economic lives if we gain as much domestic control over our economic destiny as possible. The corporatists would encourage us to skew our domestic priorities toward the tasks of competing in the world market. Unbridled free-trade and export promotion, as Keynes warned us, reduces democratic control over our domestic economic lives. One of our most important policy priorities, as the postwar experience ought to remind us, is to reduce our vulnerability to international developments beyond our control, not to increase it.

If we reject protectionism, the big stick, and export promotion, what's left?

The issues are complex. We do not hold a magic telegram with complete instructions. But we do think that there are important guidelines toward which a democratic alternative can point.

First, we favor trade if and when it seems useful or necessary. There are international differences in resource endowments, cultural traditions, and technical specializations. We see no point in withdrawing from the world economy or eschewing the potential gains which foreign trade might provide. The basic issue, then, is not *how much* trade there will be but *in what way* the patterns of international specialization and exchange are to be determined.

The second guideline is relatively limited and noncontroversial.

We should reduce our vulnerability to foreign-trade shocks. Some external supplies are especially prone to disruption or instability in either their quantities or their prices; foreign raw materials are obvious examples. There is substantial room, with long-term democratic planning, to reduce our vulnerability to external shocks through expanded domestic production of those supplies and through careful policies establishing buffer stocks and domestic price controls. We could free ourselves from most of our dependence on foreign oil supplies, for example, through aggressive domestic development of alternative energy supplies and crash conservation programs (see Point 17).

► The U.S. government should promote domestic production of supplies which are especially vulnerable to volatile swings in their foreign quantities or prices. It should also plan, through domestic pricing policies and accumulation of buffer stocks, to reduce the domestic impact of such foreign shocks.

Third and most important, *we should face the difficult trade-offs in foreign policy posed by the potential conflict between economic interest and political morality.* We can afford to give priority to economic interest in domestic planning decisions because we expect to shape the domestic environment in a democratic way. We do not have such an opportunity to shape the international environment. We cannot guarantee, as a result, that the prices at which we evaluate foreign goods embody the kinds of democratic production conditions which we seek domestically. Our foreign economic policy should therefore condition our trade planning with clear and direct evaluations of the morality of production conditions and domestic politics in the countries with which we might eventually trade.

This suggests the use of *democratic trading agreements.*

► The U.S. government should pursue, as much as possible, mutual trade agreements with other countries—coordinated with targeted planning for domestic production—in which we combine our economic interests with our political concern for democratic and human rights. If we seek foreign trade, we should introduce an evaluation of the kinds of conditions—democratic or oppressive—which prevail abroad into our consideration of the available costs and prices of international goods and services.

What would this mean in practice? If goods were available from two countries with different kinds of political climates, we should import them from those countries with more democratic regimes—even if the labor costs were higher. This would involve a trade-off: we would need to rely on the democratic mechanisms built into and guiding our economic planning instruments to determine the proper balance to strike between these economic and political factors. The costs of such trade-offs, as we show in Appendix E, are likely to be quite small.

In general, our comments at the beginning of this chapter about different systems of resource allocation apply to foreign trade as well as to the domestic economy. The "market"—which translates as "free trade" on the international plane—does not guarantee either efficiency or freedom. Multinational corporations exercise enormous leverage over world markets, and we can hardly count on their support for or promotion of popular needs and interests. That leaves us with democratic systems for resource allocation—difficult enough at the local level, even more difficult on a world scale. We cannot presume to support democratic values, not only for ourselves but for others around the globe, unless we are prepared to accept the ultimate international logic of democratic politics. And this requires political negotiation of mutual trade agreements, not pursuit of "free" trade.

We cannot precisely or perfectly chart the future international trajectories of economic democracy. But we are convinced that movement in this direction, not the promotion of U.S. exports, is necessary for a democratic alternative in the United States. And we can reasonably hope that millions around the globe will join in exploring the paths to a safer and more democratic world.

15

THE RIGHT TO A BETTER WAY OF LIFE

A corporation is a business structure whose sole reason for existence is the earning of profits by manufacturing products for as little as possible and selling them for as much as possible. It does not matter whether the product does good or evil; what counts is that it be consumed—in ever-increasing quantities. Since everything the corporation does has, as its ultimate goal, the creation of profit, it offers its workers no deep personal satisfactions, no feeling of contributing anything worthwhile to society, no true meaning to their activities. Go to work for a corporation and you are, through good salaries and fringe benefits, installed as a faceless link in the lengthening chain—completing the circle by becoming one more consumer of all that junk. And, like all circles, the whole structure signifies nothing.

> —Jacques Maisonrouge, IBM executive,
> characterizing the critics' view of
> the large corporation[1]

Our proposals in the previous three chapters have focused on the economy as a whole. In this chapter, by contrast, we address particular sectors of the economy and focus on specific issues of production and distribution. Our aim, throughout, is to suggest some concrete steps for directing our economy toward more useful output and reducing its pervasive waste.

We do not pretend that our set of proposals provides a comprehensive sector-by-sector guide to more sensible goods and services in the U.S. economy; such a guide is far beyond our capacities and would require a book of its own. We hope to accomplish three more modest objectives.

First, we aim to illustrate the concrete and tangible ways in which the waste we identified and estimated in Chapter 7 could be eliminated. We have premised our democratic alternative on the reduction of wasted resources; some of this waste elimination requires the production of more useful goods and services than we currently produce. We provide some proposals for transforming each of the six sources of wasted output identified in Chapter 7 into much more useful goods and services.

Second, we aim to clarify the need for democratic control in the production of different kinds of goods and services. There are certain kinds of products for which government control is useful and necessary. These tend to be products in which one or both of two conditions prevail. Either economies of scale and information are so vast that a single government producer makes economic sense or a product is so vital and so vulnerable to manipulation for narrow private ends that government control is necessary to protect the larger society against private manipulation of the centrality of that product.

There are many kinds of products in which public control is neither warranted nor advisable. We present several examples of these in this chapter in order to underscore the difference between the two kinds of products and to emphasize that an Economic Bill of Rights need not wallow in the dogmatism of the left or the right which insists that government control of production is either *always* good or *always* bad.

Our third objective is the most difficult and the most important. We hope to use our examples in this chapter to illustrate the possibility of a new model of consumption in a democratic economy aiming at needs-based allocation. This new model of consumption depends on a critical distinction between two very different economic concepts: *market price* and *social need*.

A good or service has a *market price* in a market economy as long as someone is willing to plunk down cash on the barrelhead. This provides a commodity an identity and an economic role.

Social need expresses the value or usefulness which something serves in directly enhancing our well-being. Consumers will not be willing to pay for a good unless it fills (or is thought to fill) some social need. For this reason market price depends on social need.

How are they different? The distinction is illustrated classically by Adam Smith's celebrated paradox of the high price of diamonds compared to water: water is very useful but commands a low price; diamonds have little intrinsic value but command a very high price. Corporations typically insist that profits measure a producing company's contribution to social welfare because the market price of its products measures that product's contribution to general social welfare. But as the diamond/water paradox suggests, there may be cases in which market price is a poor proxy for usefulness.

- Some highly useful things have no market price at all; clean air and water are important examples. Information and general knowledge are also very useful, but their price is often very low because they are so inexpensive to reproduce.
- Some things both have a market price and fill a social need, but are valued primarily for establishing individual position in the social pecking order. Their consumption makes one person better off primarily by making someone else feel worse off. We call this *invidious* consumption. If one $20,000 car makes ten people feel dissatisfied with their $7,000 cars, the $20,000 price tag does not properly measure the contribution of the car to total social welfare.
- Some products may have use value only to those in control of an economy—and not to the rest of us—because they provide the means for maintaining undemocratic control. In-plant cameras and other equipment for the surveillance of workers, or the "services" of union-busting consultants are examples. Were it possible to run the economy some other way, eliminating the centralized and authoritarian power of those in the driver's seat, these goods and services would lose their use value.
- Some products may have social need because they are the only goods and services available for satisfying certain basic needs, not because they are valued for their own sakes. If public transportation is inadequate, we have to buy cars. If public parks are run-down, unsafe, and scarce, a backyard lawn has a much higher value than it would with more adequate outdoor recreation facilities available. If it were possible to change the rules of the game, permitting alternative ways of satisfying people's needs, then the social value of

many goods and services would be very different from how they appear now.

• Goods may have a relatively low social value, similarly, because they are not generally available and the taste for those goods has consequently failed to develop. How many more opera lovers would there be if easy access to the opera were not limited to that part of the population living in large urban centers which can afford high-priced tickets?

This concern for projecting the possibility of a new kind of consumption helps explain some of our choices about inclusion and exclusion in this chapter. We are concerned to illustrate the distinction between consumption for the purposes of *getting* commodities and social status and consumption for the purposes of filling social needs and fostering personal development. We have included a discussion of education and advertising, for example, in order to illustrate the different kinds of social needs which learning and information can fulfill. We have excluded proposals for better housing and transportation not because we think that housing and transportation are adequate in the United States— both necessities are far too expensive and far too irrationally provided—but simply because others have already provided useful suggestions for those sectors.[2]

Point 16: Reduced Military Spending

The military budget is a lode, a rich repository of resources which could have beneficial social use. The defense budget for fiscal year 1983 is $176 billion, the equivalent of $2,000 for every household in the United States. Mining this treasure requires both clarity about defense objectives and control over military production.

Much military spending, we have already noted in Chapter 7, is not necessary to meet conventional defense objectives. Some of it is aimed at controlling Third World countries—motivated by a neo-imperialist impulse to restore U.S. international domination and protect multinational interests in those areas of the world. We think that there is very little popular support for such objectives, particularly given the experience of the Vietnam War. We also believe that such policies are autocratic and counterproductive. We think that they should stop. The Boston Study Group estimates, as we report in Chapter 7, that nearly one third of 1978 defense spending could have been eliminated if such programs were pruned from the defense budget.

► The U.S. government should eliminate military expenditures on any items or programs which have as their direct or implicit objective interference with or control over the lives of people in any other country.

We also believe that military production is enormously wasteful. Even David Stockman, conservative whiz kid in the Reagan administration, admits that there must be at least "ten, twenty, maybe thirty billion dollars" of waste in military production by private companies.[3] James Fallows provides ample illustrations of such waste in his recent book *National Defense*.[4] Many now recognize that most of this waste results from the cozy and incestuous character of relationships among private defense contractors and the Pentagon and the continuing sway which private military firms have been able to hold over Congress.

It is absolutely imperative that the public directly control expenditure on defense objectives. We find it unconscionable that private profit imperatives could drag us into such a swamp of inflated contracts, cost overruns, useless technology, and escalating danger to life itself.

Our proposed solution is neither a panacea nor a guarantee of wasteless military production. But we think that the profit motive must be eliminated from the defense industry. We therefore call, simply, for direct public control and management of all military production.

► In order to reduce waste in military spending, all military production should be publicly controlled, under the direct jurisdiction of the federal government. Profits should not be paid on direct military production.

Few people suggest that profits should be earned on public police or fire protection, on community health services, or on the school system. Imagine inviting Boeing to administer your neighborhood school. The logic of public control over military production is just as clear.

Point 17: Conservation and Safe Energy

The list of structural defects in our energy system is nearly end-less. We are too dependent on external oil supplies. We waste en-ergy resources prodigiously. We neglect obvious conservation measures. We cede initiative and control to a cartel of energy gi-ants who are interested in creating energy bottlenecks, not in breaking them. And we eschew the kind of strategic planning and public control which might have prevented or moderated the sharp price increases and long gas lines of 1973–74 and 1979.

Many in the United States, fortunately, have begun to realize the prodigality of energy policy in recent years. Asked to rate al-ternative energy policies in a 1980 Gallup poll, for example, the public preferred conservation and solar energy over all other alter-natives.[5] The environmentalist movement continues to grow, and there is much more widespread understanding and recognition of the requirements of sensible directions in energy policy.

We think that a democratic alternative energy policy should rely on three principal foundations:

Conservation. Energy conservation is like preventive health care. Successful conservation can permanently reduce demand for scarce resources just as successful promotion of good health can permanently reduce demand for health-care services. We could save energy resources rather than squandering them. Harvard Business School analysts Robert Stobaugh and Daniel Yergin, au-thors of the careful study called *Energy Future,* conclude that "if the United States were to make a serious commitment to conser-vation, it might well consume 30 to 40 percent less energy than it now does, and still enjoy the same or an even higher standard of living."[6]

Mark Green, consumer advocate and author of *Winning Back America,* has summarized the principal dimensions of an inten-sive commitment to energy conservation; such a policy would

• continue, and then make stricter, the fuel efficiency standards for au-tomobiles;

• continue, rather than phase out, federal subsidies for energy-efficient mass transit;
• impose energy efficiency standards for appliances, which should have readable labels describing the energy costs of running them;
• provide businesses with investment tax credits and accelerated depreciation of up to 40 percent of energy-related capital improvements;
• give tax credits of up to 50 percent of the costs of retrofitting homes and commercial buildings (which consume 37 percent of all energy);
• push ahead to draft standardized building codes (required by the Energy Conservation and Production Act of 1976) so that new structures can reduce energy use at little cost.[7]

All of these steps are essential. They would free up many of the resources that we now divert to the production and distribution of energy. They simply require a rational and planned approach to the allocation of economic resources.

Safe Energy. There are two problems with our recent reliance on energy sources such as oil, natural gas, coal, and nuclear power. One involves the fact that the consumption of nonrenewable resources permanently depletes the stock of available energy supplies. The second is that some of these supplies, primarily nuclear power, involve intrinsically hazardous production materials and techniques. This suggests a double imperative for moving toward safer and renewable energy supplies.

The energy giants, nuclear-reactor vendors, and the Defense Department have long maintained that such energy sources are impractical. Despite their near-monopoly on the relevant information and research capabilities, evidence has continued to mount which refutes their claims. A wide variety of technologies now exist or are technically feasible which could facilitate rapid expansion of production from safe and renewable energy sources. The 1978 *Report of the President's Council on Environmental Quality* concluded that "it is now possible to speak realistically of the United States becoming a solar society. . . . [A] goal of providing significantly more than one-half our energy from solar sources by the year 2020 should be achievable if our commitment to that goal and to conservation is strong."[8] The problem is not the technical barriers to safe energy; the problem, as the President's Council continued, is the "economic and institutional barriers" to its promotion.

▶ We propose the closing of all nuclear power plants over the next five years, with a vigilant enforcement of safety standards over the intervening period. The output now produced by these plants (about 10 percent of all electricity) can be made up through use of the substantial excess capacity in conventional forms of electricity generation and through conservation.

▶ Federal funds for research on conservation and renewable energy sources—solar, hydro, wind, and geothermal—should be quadrupled in real terms over the next 10 years. This expenditure would bring to safe energy research—in the development of photovoltaic cells, for example—the benefits of the kind of massive research impetus squandered on nuclear energy during the 1950s, 1960s, and 1970s.

Public Energy Control. The folly of free-market policies in energy, as more and more people have realized, is that the energy sector is an outstanding case of market failure, combining monopolized markets with important spillover effects and resource-depletion problems ill suited for market calculations. The real impetus behind deregulation is not the prospect of a more efficient energy sector but the lure of gigantic windfall profits for the energy companies, and the extraordinary leverage over our political system which these huge surpluses confer upon private energy interests.

These excesses have led some to suggest the creation of a single public Energy Corporation of America to compete with the private energy giants, providing a kind of public yardstick by which to measure private companies' performance. We think that this proposal would improve upon the current situation. We prefer, however, full and direct public control of energy production and distribution.

There are two principal arguments pointing toward full public control.

The first flows from purely economic logic. Because of the scale of investment involved and the time horizon over which energy research and development must be planned, the energy sector is a classic industrial example of the applicability of the arguments for public control on account of economies of scale and investment time horizons. Lower average cost curves for large scales of production enable a small number of enterprises to dominate all others; firms that get a head start can potentially and continually underprice their competitors. In energy as much as or more than in any other sector, economies of scale are likely to lead to a single or a few private corporations dominating the market and realizing extraordinary monopoly power. Economists have long recognized the case for public production or regulation in these cases in order to protect against abuses of private monopoly power.

Similarly for the problem of time horizon and risk. Because energy investments are so problematic and take so many years to amortize, private investors are typically hesitant to undertake commitment to many projects without public guarantees or direct public subsidy of the capital required. Thus the call for public construction of dams and bridges, turnpikes and highways. Once the public is asked to assume the risks of an investment project, as with the energy corporations' recent calls for synthetic-fuel development, then it makes perfect sense for the public to control and allocate the stream of benefits which result. Otherwise it becomes a free ride for the corporations involved.

The second argument for full public control is based on the particular character of energy production. Because many energy sources are not renewable, they can easily be monopolized; the opportunities for private windfall profits are vast. (This explains the economic power of many of the OPEC nations.) Energy is also absolutely vital to economic production and survival—just as some military spending is vital for national security and money is vital for the circulation of commodities. If we are to gain greater control over its economic destiny through a democratic alternative, therefore, it is imperative that it fully control those elements of the political economy which are most essential, particularly where the alternative to public control is concentrated control in private hands. We add energy to the list of sectors—already including the financial sector, infrastructural provision, and military production—which warrant full public control.

We do not propose, however, the creation of a single federal energy company. We favor, instead, an umbrella of centralized public regulation under which state and local governments would promote decentralized enterprises aiming at conservation and safe energy production. We specifically favor:

► Control of energy prices through our system of flexible price controls;

► A National Energy Investment Administration which would

supervise research on energy technology, plan long-term development of energy resources and production technique, and supervise allocation of a National Energy Investment Fund. Revenues for this investment fund would come from a federal excise tax on all energy consumed.

► A National Public Energy Corporation which would extract and refine into crude supplies all nonrenewable energy sources. It would also be the single authorized importer of foreign energy supplies. Energy prices would be subject to the system of flexible price controls.

► State Energy Administrations which would coordinate local, publicly controlled energy production and distribution for final consumption, emphasizing the development of decentralized conservation and safe energy production. When and where necessary, the State Energy Administrations would purchase nonrenewable energy supplies from the National Public Energy Corporation.

This proposed structure seems to us to promise both centralized coordination and decentralized initiative. Would it promote efficiency in the public sector? The energy giants are hardly paragons of efficiency themselves. Recent experience both with the Tennessee Valley Administration in the United States and with public energy production in Europe, as in Italy's Ente Nazionale Idrobarburi (ENI), suggest that public energy agencies can be efficient and competitive.[9] Most dramatically, as we have already noted in Chapter 12, public utilities have provided electricity in the United States during the postwar period at roughly one third lower cost (per kilowatt-hour delivered) than privately owned utilities. The energy giants are skilled at advertising their virtues, but they are much less skilled at producing safe and inexpensive products.

Point 18: Good Food

We have already noted that we waste substantial resources in food production in the United States. Some important grass-roots movements, both rural and urban, have begun to mobilize against this waste, pushing for the kinds of changes in food policy which would promote less expensive and better-quality food.

As with energy, there is more and more information available on both the wastefulness of current food production and distribution and the variety of possible alternatives to our present system. We think that food policy in a democratic alternative should focus on four principal programmatic directions.

Democratic Land Reform. We make poor use of available land in the United States. At least 10 percent of tillable and fertile agricultural land lies unused.[10] Many poor communities, particularly in the South and in the Appalachian region, find that their access to potentially fertile agricultural land has been blocked by centralized private ownership of land—held largely by a loose combination of energy interests and railroads.[11]

Worse, the ownership of land in the United States is remarkably unequal: 3 percent of households owned 90 percent of all privately owned land in the United States in the late 1970s, significantly more concentrated ownership than any other asset except possibly municipal bonds and trust funds.[12]

► State governments should establish public land banks. When agricultural land comes available on the market, they should use their powers of eminent domain to claim the land at reasonable prices and then turn over the land on a low-rent lease/purchase basis to family farms and community enterprises engaged in agricultural production. This would not ensure more land available for agricultural production, but it would at least protect farmers from the speculative spirals affecting agricultural land prices.

Agricultural Efficiency. Family farms have been fighting a losing battle against agribusiness—not because large farms are more technically efficient than small farms but because banks, public agencies, and food-processing companies have all combined to favor agribusiness development. There is wide evidence on the comparable efficiency of small and large farms. The source of "market failure" in the case of family farms is not technical inefficiency, but the problems of fluctuating interest rates, financial discrimination against smaller agricultural enterprises, and the preferences of large food-processing companies and grain distributors for dealing with fewer suppliers.[13]

Several states have recently moved to begin reversing this institutional bias against family farms, enacting legislation which limits the influence of corporate farming and exploring technical and financial assistance to smaller farms. Farm and consumer groups have also combined in 1978 to help draft the Family Farm Development Act, introduced in Congress by Representative Richard Nolan (D.-Minn.); the bill mandates a significant shift in Department of Agriculture policies toward support of family farms through technical research, extension-service adaptations, and tax changes to discourage tax-loss farming. In Canada, both Manitoba and Saskatchewan have passed laws which place strict limits on the amount of agricultural land that can be owned by nonfarm corporations, aiming to reduce tax-loss farming and land speculation.

All these initiatives aim at a common goal: reduction of the distortions introduced into U.S. agricultural production from agribusiness power and centralized production. Clear public support of family farms, according to all the available evidence, would encourage more decentralized agricultural production, more closely directed toward domestic food needs, without reductions in agricultural productivity.[14]

▶ Both Congress and individual states should pass Family Farm Development Acts encouraging technical development compatible with smaller farms, limits on outside ownership of agricultural land, tax provisions reducing the advantages of tax-loss farming and tax-shelter landownership, and subsidized loans available to family farms.

Decentralized Food Processing. Food-processing corporations have spent more and more on packaging, advertising, and transportation since World War II. (This has resulted primarily from their efforts to increase profits through product differentiation.) Local communities could dramatically enhance the quality and cost effectiveness of food processing in the United States by promoting local community enterprises in the food-processing sector. Public support, through community investment boards, could be tied (through planning agreements) to the equivalent of generic drug packaging—the simplest possible packaging without any effort at brand recognition or product gimmicks. Public subsidies could help launch such enterprises; planning agreements could ensure the quality of the food produced; and community information centers (see Point 23) could help create markets for less expensively packaged food.

► Community investment boards should place special emphasis on promoting food processing community-enterprises, aiming at the lowest cost and most effective decentralized food packaging and distribution.

Rural-Urban Marketing. In many regions around the country, especially in the West and New England, rural and urban groups have begun to establish independent marketing networks designed to bring rural food into the cities without greasing the palms of the major food chains and distributors. This has led to a growing movement supporting farmers' markets, buying clubs, and consumer cooperatives.

► State and local governments should establish food marketing boards which co-ordinate, subsidize, and otherwise promote decentralized and low-cost distribution mechanisms linking small farmers and community enterprises with consumers and consumer cooperatives.

Many city consumers have already experienced the benefits of an informal process which has established such links. Voluntary organizations, and in some cases public consumer agencies, have helped establish "green markets" at which local farmers set up shop one or two days a week, helping establish much more direct and much less expensive direct consumer access to fresh fruits and produce.

If we are to move beyond the waste land, the least we can do is ensure good food for the journey.

Point 19: A National Health Policy

We can deal with issues of waste and useful output in health care much more briefly than in many other program demands—for some obvious reasons.

First, we think that public recognition of the failures of the U.S. health-care system is spreading very rapidly: in a New York *Times* poll in 1982, for example, roughly 54 percent of those responding said they would prefer comprehensive national health insurance run by the government.[15]

Second, European countries have achieved much better public

health at lower costs, clearly manifesting the advantages of national health insurance and more rational health-care policies.

Third, model legislation is already available which reflects careful consideration by a wide variety of progressive health-care analysts and which, in our view, warrants wholesale incorporation into our proposals.

Representative Ronald Dellums (D.-Cal.) introduced the Health Service Act to Congress in the mid-1970s. We quote at length from a description of the bill's intentions and provisions, prepared by Marilyn Elrod, an assistant to Congressman Dellums responsible for health-care issues:

The act would establish a publicly controlled and operated health service which would employ health workers who would directly serve the public. Comprehensive, high-quality health care would become the right of everyone with no restrictions on eligibility or benefits. All services would be provided on a no-fee-for-service basis by salaried health workers, stressing the maintenance of good health and the prevention of illness.

The health service would be run by democratically elected representatives of local communities who would plan health delivery systems, hire health workers, and assume overall responsibility for community health services. The community health boards would elect representatives to district boards, whose responsibility it would be to oversee general hospitals and the health team schools. These boards would elect representatives to the regional boards, which would oversee specialized care facilities. Members of the national board would be chosen by the regional boards, and would be responsible for carrying out overall planning, budgeting, and establishing guidelines for the provision of health service. . . .

The health service would assume control of the education of the health workers and would operate schools. It would assure that health workers are properly distributed throughout the country, especially in areas which are critically in need of better health service. . . .

Quality control would be addressed by providing for continuing review and assessment of the competence of health care providers, with oversight by representatives of those who use the health services as well as by those who provide them.[16]

As Congressman Dellums explained in introducing the legislation, "health care is not a consumer good whose availability and quality can be allowed to depend on income."[17]

Two conclusions seem to us virtually self-evident. (1) The medical profession, particularly doctors and hospital administrators, will continue to press vigorously against such public health-care provision. (2) The quality and cost effectiveness of health care in the United States would improve dramatically through a coherent national health policy.

This amounts to a clear choice between the general public interest and a particular (if vigorous and affluent) lobby. It is time that the hundreds of millions who pay the costs and bear the suffering of our irrational and ineffective health-care system ended the reign of the medical oligarchy, the drug companies, the high-tech medical-hardware providers and others who profit from our poor health. This is surely a prime case for democracy before profits.

Point 20: Lifetime Learning and Cultural Opportunities

If we seek a decent economy, we should place high priority—among many other objectives—on dramatically improved opportunities for popular education, culture, recreation, and just plain free time. This leads us to demands for both lifetime learning and enhancement of free-time opportunities.

Education. Learning is a public good. It is rapidly becoming a private preserve for the affluent. A program for democratic recovery must include provisions for long-term investment in people. These opportunities must be available for everyone.

We are particularly concerned about the need for expanded public support of public education because we waste so tragically our potential human talent and creativity in the United States. Many do not study hard because they assume that they will be unable to afford to go to college—and without a college education, their schooling will afford them little economic benefit. Many do not continue their educations because they must work to support themselves—and cannot afford either the loss of work income or the tuition costs that further education would involve.

We argue that higher education is a process which everyone should be able to enjoy and whose fruits redound to society as a whole. A better-educated citizenry is a more informed and ultimately more intelligent citizenry. A better-educated work force is also more capable of participating in and helping manage a democratic economy. Dramatically expanded participation in higher education seems to us to be yet another necessary precondition for a democratic economy. Elite and expensive education reflects and reinforces an elite and unequal society. Universal and democratic education is essential for popular participation in shaping our society.

► State governments should finance, with federal aid where necessary, sufficient expansion of higher education to permit free undergraduate education to all who seek it. State banks should continue to provide low-interest loans to all who seek and are accepted for graduate education.

► Unions and workers should demand paid release time through union contracts, allowing for up to two hundred hours per year of fully compensated time off from work for attendance at degree-granting courses within institutions providing high school equivalency or higher education.

Why paid release time? Many need to work while they study. And many older workers have not had the opportunity in the past to take advantage of higher education. It seems to us essential that companies begin permitting their employees, without loss of income, to attend courses during working hours. In the long run, the gains in productivity from a better-educated work force, particularly in the context of the proposals for workplace democracy outlined in Chapter 13, will help recoup some of the lost work time resulting from this provision.

Better Free Time. This demand may seem slightly out of place to many readers. When people debate economic restructuring, they usually focus on machines and investment. Where do museums and parks enter the calculus?

We argue that explicit public promotion of better free time has fundamental economic importance for three important reasons:

First, the economy itself will benefit if people feel that it is providing not only improved standards of living for individual households but also an opportunity to share in improved quality of consumption with the leisure time it makes available.

Second, this program suggestion, like our proposals for public child care and community service centers, will help moderate the shocks of recent transformations in the family. Family lives have been shaken, but many hesitate to venture outside of the family structure at least partly because they worry about the absence of free-time opportunities outside of the family. Social commitment to improved free time should help ease the tensions of internally turbulent family life.

We argue, finally, that we must reverse past trends, that we must clearly and directly improve the quality of life instead of acquiescing in its deterioration through the accumulation of material goods governed by the relentless pursuit of private profits. The combination of proposals outlined in our program would help support this reversal because they would help, to a large degree, in limiting the devastation which unfettered profit-seeking has wrought.

► Governments at all levels should preserve and extend the land available for public recreational purposes, including both parks in cities and scenic and wilderness areas in the countryside.

► State and local governments should engage in a massive physical program of construction and renovation of libraries and museums, creating a decentralized network of community cultural centers providing access to the most modern technology of information-sharing and retrieval.

► Unions, community organizations, and local governments should join in promoting expanded educational and cultural programs to widen the range of resources and activities available for free-time use, including expanded public access to cable television, local artistic exhibits and popular celebrations, and organized participation sports.

There are some precedents in other countries for such concern with the quality of free time. Following the leadership of its principal trade-union affiliate, for example, the French Socialist Party has moved to promote programs aimed at improved free time as a high political priority under the Mitterand government.

Much more important, this set of demands also fits well with the recent priorities of many movements in the United States. Many groups have mobilized to improve the quality of our environment, to preserve and extend our cultural and educational resources. Many have fought, much more broadly, to preserve or recapture a sense of community in what often seems like a cold and heartless ocean of economic competition.

But popular mobilization for public support of improved free time directly confronts an opposing tendency of growing importance in the United States. Private corporations have come to dominate many of the traditional free-time outlets, for instance public television and spectator sports. There has been a sharp cutback in public and nonprofit grants leaving cultural institutions more dependent on corporate philanthropy and leading to rising corporate influence over the cultural activities supported in the United States. The likely effect of increasing corporate domination of culture is increasing homogenization, as mass-market mentality and profit priorities reject cultural diversity on cost-effectiveness grounds.

Economists have long argued that parks are "public goods" and should therefore be provided for and controlled by the public. Culture and the heritage affecting people's free time is equally a public good. To enhance the free-time opportunities available to all of us we must provide a democratic alternative to the culture as well as the economics of greed.

Point 21: Payment for Home Child Care in Single-Parent Households

Our distorted valuation of labor is nowhere more glaring than in our underpayment of people who produce and reproduce the rest of us. With the few exceptions, those who care for children, who attend to their health needs, who teach in grade school and secondary school are vastly underpaid when compared to people with similar training and responsibility.

The most underpaid are those who receive no pay at all: the parents, largely mothers, who perform the socially essential tasks of child-rearing on a full-time basis and who, for this reason, are unable to gain paid employment. Even under the most favorable circumstances, public support for a single mother with two pre-school children at home now leaves the family unable to make even the most minimal provisions, living at well below the officially designated poverty line. The result is an almost impossible struggle to provide adequately for necessary child-rearing tasks and an almost overwhelming imperative to stay in an income-earning couple (or get into one) no matter how difficult or destructive the relationship. Such single parents perform some of our most socially valuable labor and we reward them with material poverty and a sharply constricted range of options.

► We propose direct and adequate payment for single parents working at home and for families in which no adult is capable of working. For households with two or more children, we propose a payment of our minimum public-employment wage (roughly $6.50 in 1983 dollars) for the equivalent of full-time work when no adult in the household is working; this would amount to a full-time year-round income of roughly $12,000. The payment for a parent of one child (or eligible family with no employed worker) would be roughly four fifths of this level.

This is not a welfare program; this is payment for highly skilled, demanding, and socially valued work. We do not call for expanded general public assistance or income maintenance. We call for full employment and flexible work hours, instead, and we think that those who are capable of working should make a valuable social contribution. If our full-employment program were implemented, therefore, we would provide public assistance to single adults who were not parents only in cases of disability.

With this proposal for payment for home child care, we simply recognize that single parents may prefer to care for their children at home and that child care is an absolutely vital form of employment. With this proposal, single parents would at least have a choice between working at home with their children and working in the "paid labor force." The availability of that kind of choice is vital both for a democratic economy and for women's ability to chart their own life choices.

Point 22: Community Corrections and Reduced Crime-Control Spending

Substantial portions of national output are wasted as a result of crime-control expenditures. We expect that crime will itself decline as the economy moves toward employment security and equality. Even for those continuing to commit crimes, however, there are methods of "correction" which would waste far less money than the present system.

That system is neither effective nor economical. The evidence is overwhelming that, for most offenses, imprisonment does not provide either deterrence or rehabilitation.[18] And prisons cost vast sums—as much as $30,000 per year per cell to maintain and $70,000 to $100,000 to construct a single new maximum-security cell.[19]

Small wonder that community alternatives are taking hold all around the country. In Boston the Earn-It program substitutes restitution for incarceration for young property offenders. In traditionally oriented Indiana, several cities are participating in a mediation system which brings victims and perpetrators together to reconcile their differences and agree on proper compensation for property lost in burglaries. These programs not only avoid the social and economic costs of prison but also strengthen a community's ability to deal with its own problems. The Community Board Project in San Francisco uses neighborhood dispute resolution to address community conflicts *before* they turn into thefts or assaults; the aim is for all residents, whether potential offenders or not, to sense the possibility of richer and better-integrated social lives. Given our emphasis on the importance of strengthening community ties, we place special importance on this constructive approach to criminal justice. Sociologist Robert Woodson, one of the principal proponents of neighborhood action against crime, suggests:

We cannot look to any large institution, in or out of government, to design for us a formula for survival. Such institutional resources, where they exist, must be brought down to join hands with people in the neighborhoods in an atmosphere of parity. There is much that can be learned from those who are directly experiencing the crime problem. Just as the body marshals its antibodies to confront its own disease, the neighborhoods possess their own resources for life.[20]

▶ Community enterprises and justice-system officials should work together to develop third-party custody arrangements where offenders can make restitution for their crimes and be responsible both to their victims and to their own communities, contributing to local economies and to their own capacity for productive work.

► Local governments, in coordination with community-enterprise correctional programs, should seek the most rapid possible reductions in jail and prison populations, mandating to community programs all but violent offenders. Corrections costs would be immediately reduced without decreasing public safety.

There are no magic models for these programs. And it is clear that one cannot eliminate the need for prisons and jails entirely. But we could make substantial progress toward the recognition that isolating offenders does not eradicate the problems they pose for society. Our Economic Bill of Rights would strengthen social bonds in communities and would, therefore, enhance local ability to apply meaningful sanctions *within,* rather than outside, those communities. And the savings on correctional expenses which deincarceration would help provide could be used to finance more productive programs which would, in turn, help to prevent crime.

The crime problem is severe. And the issues of crime control are urgent. But large-scale imprisonment is no solution. Community control over sanctions may be.

Point 23: Community-Needs Information and Reduced Advertising Expenditures

We spend too much money on advertising. We need relatively little of the "information" it provides. Nonprofit organizations such as *Consumer Reports* serve more useful functions than most advertising information. Advertising not only wastes money, it also pollutes the environment through billboards and insistent commercials over the air.

► Community service centers (see Point 3) should include community information centers providing full information about marketing and entertainment, publishing community information bulletins and providing consumer purchasing counselling.

► A special state excise tax would be placed on the purchase of advertising space in any available commercial medium. These revenues would be used to finance the community information programs.

These proposals are consistent with the democratic and decentralized thrust of our Program for a Democratic Economy. Local communities are best equipped—much more than exalted executives on Madison Avenue—to marshal local information about local prices, local quality, and local needs and tastes. Community information centers seem to us to provide a perfect mechanism through which such information could be provided. A national Consumer Products Agency could make testing information on standardized products available on a national scale so that each community information center would not need to duplicate such efforts.

The excise tax on advertising would treat advertising like liquor and tobacco, goods which we do not prohibit but whose social costs we may wish to include within their prices. Such a tax could be most easily administered on the side of the advertising medium, such as newspapers or television—and not on the ad purchaser; the tax would simply be added to the sales taxes they already charge. This advertising tax, perhaps equivalent to 50 percent of the purchase price—could be collected along with sales taxes and would help discourage advertising at its roots. In so far as corporations chose to continue placing their ads, advertising excise tax revenues would help finance the services of community information centers. If corporations cannot bear to go without their illuminating messages to the consuming public, let them pay for the privilege.*

Point 24: Equitable Taxation and Public Allocation of Resources

Any program for democratic recovery must include a set of provisions for tax reform. We need to ensure that we would be

* We recognize that such policies would affect the media currently providing radio, newspaper, and magazine information. We think the impact of reduced dependence on advertising would undoubtedly warrant the fiscal adjustments required, but we understand that this would also require substantial reconsideration of public policy on communications and the media.

able to finance the substantial public programs we stipulate in the rest of our proposals, and we need to overcome the irrationalities and inequities of the present system.

The essence of our difference from other reform proposals is fairly simple: we think that most progressive tax reforms have tried to accomplish too much with the tax system and too little with other, more direct democratic mechanisms of economic reform. Tax instruments are inherently blunt as tools for a decent economy: they rely on indirect effects, they take time to induce desired responses; and their highly technical nature makes them a difficult arena in which to mobilize a democratic consensus and prevent predation by private-interest lobbies. We have concentrated in our Economic Bill of Rights on proposals for a wide variety of direct instruments for popular influence and control over basic economic decision-making. In the context of this broader program, therefore, we can avoid dependence on tax reform to pursue objectives which our proposals allow us to achieve through much more direct means.

This permits a much simpler, more manageable, and more effective set of tax-reform proposals than are common in most other progressive discussions. Our chief objective here is to simplify and improve the distribution of the tax burden, not to guide the reallocation of resources in productive enterprises. The most important principle in framing truly progressive tax proposals, we think, is to transfer income away from those individuals who receive the greatest income from wealth—because they have done least to earn this income and can most afford to give some of it up—and to shift claims on resources toward collective democratic auspices for decisions about its investment and expenditure. Collective allocation of a larger share of individual income from wealth, in the end, will better promote a democratic economy than individual allocative decisions by the wealthy individuals who receive it.

In order to underscore the breadth and simplicity of our reform proposals, we first present an outline of the full set of our proposals and then review that outline with a discussion of the rationale for each of the major substantive proposals.

► We propose an integration of all current local, state, and federal income, property, payroll, and business taxes into a single comprehensive federal income tax. This tax would:

a. Provide a standard exemption (in 1983 dollars) of $5,000 per household member;

b. Eliminate all deductions against income-tax liability (except state and local taxes);

c. Tax the first $50,000 of wage and salary income at a standard (constant) tax rate, with a supplementary rate of 1.25 that base rate against wage and salary income above $50,000; and

d. Tax income from asset ownership at a rate equal to 2.0 times the base tax rate on income from wage and salary sources.

► State and local government would be free to add taxes on and beyond this comprehensive federal income tax; tax payments to state and local governments would be deductible against income taxable under the comprehensive federal income tax. At the same time, the federal government would make substantial block grants to state and local governments, on a per capita basis (with a supplementary adjustment to equalize revenue capacity between poorer and richer states), in order to compensate fully for the substitution of the comprehensive federal income tax for the current complex of local and state income, property, and business taxes.

Comprehensive Income Taxation. The current system has two general faults to which this general proposal is addressed. First, many of its constituent taxes, particularly including property taxes, sales taxes, and payroll (primarily Social Security) taxes, are "regressive," imposing high tax rates on less affluent families. Second, the fragmentation of the tax system, with jigsaw-puzzle pieces of the tax system scattered among local, state, and federal jurisdictions, exposes local and state governments to the dynamic of tax competition: corporations can force local jurisdictions to bid against each other for tax benefits and subsidies, reducing local tax bases to the lowest possible common denominator. A comprehensive income-tax system would reduce both of these problems.

Thus we join with many others in proposing a dramatic simplification of the personal-income-tax system. Under the current regime, lobbyists can achieve deductions for almost any of their favorite projects. The result has been that the wealthy reap a harvest of tax privileges—all hidden under the veil of nominally progressive income-tax rates. This results in the "tax-expenditure industry"—a legion of lobbyists and lawyers whose business it becomes to secure special tax favors for their clients and wreak administrative havoc on the Internal Revenue Service. Congressman Byron Dorgan (D.-N. Dak.) observes about the present system, "you've got a system where almost every secretary, clerk, fireman, or policeman in the city of New York is paying more income tax on an effective percentage basis than Exxon is. . . . The reason we continue to allow it to exist is that the people in whose interest it is pay a lot of money to keep it there."[21]

A reformed system with comprehensive income taxation and *no* deductions (other than state and local taxes) would simplify the tax collection business and virtually eliminate the "tax expenditure industry" with a stroke.

Watch Out for Flat Tax Fever! As public abhorrence at the tax-expenditure industry has spread, many have begun to jump on the "flat-tax" bandwagon. The wealthy have promoted tax deductions. And now they are concerned to channel the "flat-tax movement" to their own advantage—eliminating progressive income-tax rates and special taxes on certain kinds of wealth-based income, such as capital gains. While we favor *simplification* of the tax system through a comprehensive federal income tax, we are hardly in favor of joining forces with the wealthiest beneficiaries of the current system.

It is essential to maintain some progressivity in income-tax rates. This involves basic principles of equity—premised on the notion that those with more income can afford to provide greater support, at the margin, of public programs. We therefore propose a higher tax rate on wage and salary income above $50,000.

Much more important, we advocate a surtax on income from wealth. (Those of moderate income who rent a room or two would pay no supplementary wealth tax since their income from property would be protected by the high standard exemption under our proposed system.) Wealth is socially determined, in large part, and its benefits should be subject to higher rates of marginal taxation than income from labor expended. This would permit increasingly democratic decisions about the allocation of income from wealth.

These two provisions, though still simple to administer, would eliminate the fearful concerns that many progressives have already voiced at various proposals for "flat taxation." Earned-income rates would be progressive and there would be higher taxation on income from wealth.

We should note, finally, that our proposals do involve the elimination of the corporate-profits tax as a separate source of income-tax revenue. There are three reasons for transcending the reflexive suspicion of such a proposal which many progressive tax reformers might display. First, there has been, indeed, a double taxation of dividend income under the present system—first in the form of corporate-profits taxation and then again as dividend-income taxation; this seems unwarranted, for it arbitrarily discriminates against one particular form of wealth-based income. Second, our objective is not to tax income at its source but to tax income at the location of its final individual recipient. Corporate profits, by themselves, do not necessarily benefit their owners; it is only after the receipt of those profits in either managerial salaries, ownership dividends, or capital gains that the wealthy tangibly benefit from high corporate profits.

Finally, and certainly most important, we favor the elimination of the corporate profits tax *only in the context* of the full range of proposals embodied in our Economic Bill of Rights. These proposals would help ensure that there was full and democratic bargaining within the corporation over the disposition of corporate-retained earnings. Without such a program, we would agree, elimination of the corporate-profits tax would leave large corporations even freer than at present to dispose of that portion of total social income however they choose. With such a program, however, it is important to leave workers and managers free to debate and struggle over the social uses to which they would allocate any net surplus which an enterprise might earn. We would rather let a community enterprise dispose of its own surplus earnings than the federal government. If they decided to pay out those surplus earnings in the form of high individual dividends, then those dividends would be taxed (at a relatively high rate) as capital income under the comprehensive federal income tax system.

Fiscal Federalism. We favor a comprehensive approach to fiscal federalism. The federal government should be the principal source of tax-revenue collection, we argue, in order to avoid competition among localities and in order to even out tax-base potential. Block grants from the federal government to state and local governments, at the same time, would help finance the large number of public programs which our proposals would locate at the state and local levels. This form of fiscal federalism would avoid the risk of widening disparities in fiscal capacity among regions, on the one hand, and permit substantial decentralization of administrative responsibilities, on the other.

The combined effect of our tax proposals and our program taken as a whole would almost certainly be to lower the total tax bite taken out of the incomes of the vast majority of U.S. families. As we demonstrate in Appendix E, our proposals for stimulating the economy and cutting the military budget will both reduce needed social expenditures in major areas and increase private incomes more than enough to offset proposed increases in public expenditure. A further reduction in tax burden for the typical family may be anticipated by the slight up-bracket shift in the tax burden which would result from implementation of our proposals.

This has been a long list of suggestions. It would be even longer if we had dared to venture a comprehensive catalog of proposals to promote more useful goods and services throughout the U.S. economy. However long the list, our basic point is simple enough. An Economic Bill of Rights can do more than promote employment security and stable growth. It can also have direct and dramatic effect on the kinds of goods and services we consume—their usefulness, their quality, and their costs. The connections between the requirements for democratic recovery and the actual social needs it fulfills helps dramatize both the possibility and the urgency of a democratic alternative.

16

TOWARD A DEMOCRATIC ECONOMY

Down in the country, we used to have to ring the bell if there was trouble or we'd ring it for dinner. You used to pull this rope. Sometime, especially if it was cold, you'd keep pullin' and keep pullin' the bell. You'd think you'd never hear a sound. Maybe by the time your hands got raw almost, you'd hear a little tinklin' of the bell. That's just the way I visualize the community. We all keep pullin' at the rope and our hands are gettin' raw, but you do hear a little tinklin'. It does give you some hope that after a while the bell is gonna ring. We gotta do it, we must do it. We have no other choice. As my father said, "If you're the only one doin' it, the only one left in the world to do it, you must do it." We gotta keep pullin'. And I believe the bell will ring.

—Retired community organizer in Chicago[1]

If there's ever gonna be change in America, it's gonna be cause every community in America's ready for it and—boom! There's gonna be a big tidal wave, and it's just gonna crash down on Washington, and the people are finally gonna be heard.

—Community organizer[2]

Our Economic Bill of Rights cannot be separated from the analysis on which it rests. We have argued that symptoms of economic decline in the United States reflect a real structural crisis—a crisis resulting from the erosion of the postwar corporate system and its relations of domination. Some kind of restructuring of the U.S. economy is necessary before real and lasting economic recovery can begin.

We now face two distinct paths toward restructuring. *Probusiness* programs share three basic principles: profit-led growth, market-based allocation, and arms for economic power. At their best, these principles force the majority who can least afford it to finance and sustain future economic recovery. At their worst, and most likely, these probusiness strategies will dramatically increase the costs of corporate power in the U.S. economy and pose serious threats to our political democracy.

Many readers will find these criticisms plausible. Some will have directly experienced the recent costs of corporate efforts to restore their power—through unemployment, falling wages, supervisory harassment, safety hazards on and off the job, or the insecurity of soaring prices and interest rates. But most have hesitated in recent years to express and act upon their frustration and anger. "Have they an alternative?" President Reagan asked of his critics.

The answer is yes. We have outlined a detailed *democratic alternative* to trickle-down economics. For all its twenty-four points and detailed proposals, our Economic Bill of Rights is based on a simple set of underlying strategies:

- A program for economic recovery must make use of *all* our resources and *all* our economic potential. With a clear commitment to *economic security and equity,* we can make the economy work for all of us. Without such a commitment, we fight with each other over the crumbs.

- Work commitment is a serious problem. Our approach is to lay down the whip of unemployment, to find more productive work for the armies of supervisors, and to provide workers with a real and lasting stake in their performance and output by moving quickly toward fundamentally *democratic and productive work relations.* A democratic alternative offers workers a real opportunity to determine their economic fate.

- We cannot pursue full employment or workplace democracy without being able to control the resources we need. Private profitability is not a safe or reasonable guide to a healthy and decent economic recovery. Effective mechanisms are required for *democratic planning in a democratic economy*—mechanisms for determining our needs and investing to meet them.

- We must be able to gain control over what we consume as well as how we produce it. This requires that we ensure our *right to a better way of life*—beating swords into good food and a safe environment, creating rich and supportive opportunities for free time, supporting our communities instead of tearing them apart. Sector by sector, industry by industry, there are specific and practical steps we can take to improve the usefulness of available goods and services. We do not need more guns. We do not even necessarily need more butter. We need living conditions and social relationships more supportive of our growth as people. Our proposals for more useful goods and services can begin to realize those ambitions.

These four key principles—economic security and equity, democratic and productive work relations, democratic planning, and the right to a better way of life—are clearly attractive. Equally important is that our Economic Bill of Rights *holds together as a whole*. It is internally consistent in that its proposals are mutually reinforcing and, as we show in Appendix E, the program as a whole can pay for itself. It aims to mobilize and unify progressive groups not by aggregating the particular demands of each group, but by proposing a new approach to economic revitalization which by serving our common interests would heighten our sense of unity.

LOOKING AHEAD

The economic payoff to our program is what makes it possible, not what makes it desirable. The reason why we need a democratic economy has more to do with the quality of life than with the calculus of taxes and expenditures. The easiest way to dramatize the need for a democratic economy and to illustrate the differences among economic alternatives is to give each the benefit of the doubt and project its programs forward. Suppose the monetarist or corporatist or democratic strategy took hold. What would the economy look like in 1990 in each case? How would we experience the fruits of these different plans for economic restructuring? While such projections cannot possibly pretend complete accuracy or anticipate all possible developments, this exercise can at least clarify and help concretize the choices we face.

The *monetarist* program is the least comprehensive, so there is the least to project. Between 1983 and 1990, there would be a long period of continued deflation and high unemployment while we waited for the cold bath to take final effect. Not even the monetarists are willing to predict how long it will take, but the Thatcher program had been in place for more than three years by the end of 1982, and it had succeeded in doing little more than flattening the British economy. While we wait—until 1986 or 1987 or beyond—unemployment would continue to be the lot of between 20 and 30 million people a year (nearly 25 million were unemployed at some point during 1982). It is highly likely, under monetarist auspices, that we would build more prisons to contain those who can least tolerate the consequences of continued stagflation; even if we simply project recent (1979–81) rates of increase in incarceration, without assuming any further acceleration as a consequence of sustained monetarist ice water, there would be more than 750,000 people in prisons and jails in the United States in 1990, a 50 percent increase over the present population. Similar projections suggest that there would be roughly 3.5 million under correctional jurisdiction—including prisons, probation, and parole—the equivalent of the total size of the army at the peak of the Vietnam War.[3]

Under the monetarist program, there would undoubtedly be more cuts in social programs—leaving millions in 1990 without any kind of public support. Women and minorities would be especially hard hit by these cuts. The feminization of poverty would accelerate. The decay of schools and parks and the eclipse of public life would usher in the era of the shopping mall as our most vibrant social and cultural institution. Withering public support for the arts, and for any but the most applied research, would increasingly reduce both beauty and wisdom to marketable commodities.

Although the monetarists claim to support small business, large corporations would be much more likely to weather a continued monetarist deflation than small firms; it is therefore likely that large corporations would have even greater economic power in 1990 than today, with virtually no government restraints on how they spend their money or what they do with their power.

Perhaps the most pertinent projection is the most speculative: A monetarist United States in 1990 would be tough and acrimonious, threaded with hardship and divisions, girding for outbreaks of social protest, mean-spirited in public policy and tough-handed in treating (and confining) those who protest. Foreign policy, we can assume, would be no less "firm." Ours would be a bitter, distrustful society, full of contention and selfishness. Monetarists promise a reign of creative individualism. We project a world of grief, strife and shame.

What would a *corporatist* United States look and feel like in 1990?

The (roughly) two hundred largest corporations would have enormous power—probably controlling something like 70–75 percent of total industrial assets.[4] A cozy circle of national "leadership"—from corporations, those unions included in the new social contract, and the ruling political elites—would tightly control economic decisions and economic debate. More than 20 percent of all employees would probably occupy managerial and supervisory positions, with more than a quarter of national income devoted to their salaries. Probably only about one sixth of the work force would be unionized.[5]

A national investment agency—the child of the Reconstruction Finance Corporation—would play a central role in determining which industries received the most public support. Those decisions would themselves be based on an analysis of the world market, not of domestic needs. Trade would probably have increased to nearly one fifth of total national product, exposing us even more to the vagaries of world trade patterns and world prices beyond our control. There might be a fairly decent program of income maintenance to support those who could not find stable employment at adequate wages, but there would probably be relatively few other public programs to provide for social needs. Between now and 1990 family and neighborhood ties would be sundered as people continually moved around in search of work during a period of transition and restructuring. We would know far less about the people around us—both on and off the job—and far more about the daily television fare.

Much of our lives would bear the imprint of the top-down approach of corporatism. Most of us would work in large bureaucracies with elaborate rules and standards. Leaders would make decisions for us, filling the air with somber appeals for our support in the "national interest" of a "forward-looking America."

The corporatist program would inaugurate the era of Big Brother in a pin-striped suit.

Is it possible to make parallel kinds of projections about a *democratic economy* in 1990?

Economic life would be more decentralized than now, organized more around community institutions. There would be more concentration on the production of basic goods and services, responding to local community needs—both because there would be a much more equal distribution of income and because private profitability would play a much smaller role in investment allocation. Both private and community enterprises would be turning, for example, toward safe and inexpensive food packaging, small-scale computer production for home and business needs, decent and much more varied housing, development of new kinds of equipment for tapping renewable energy sources, and a wide variety of goods and services for entertainment and recreation. Public funds would provide more services for child care and the elderly, for recreational facilities, for community health care and preventive health training, for lifelong education and skills training, and for serving people's transport needs in more flexible ways.

Much more important, we think, people would be actively involved in a much wider variety of institutions affecting economic decisions—in work teams implementing cooperative work agreements, in union investment boards allocating both pension funds and collective profit shares, in the boards of community enterprises and community investment agencies, in hearings on consumption needs, and in a wide variety of public agencies aimed at determining priorities for public programs. Many more economic decisions would be made at the local and community level, with active—and, we assume, lively—political debate about their directions. Communities would begin to acquire much more focused definition in people's lives—both because they constituted much more of a locus of economic activities and because there would be much less economic pressure to move around from place to place.

The average workweek would have fallen considerably; correspondingly, a boom may be anticipated in sports, cooking, dieting, block parties, local politics, and the pursuit of self-understanding. Complaints would be heard that reduced work hours have been offset by more meetings. Flexible work-time options would have opened new opportunities for the sharing of child-rearing tasks and for making more productive use of the creative energies of older people.

Perhaps most important, a democratic economic program would have begun to transform the waste in our present economy into useful goods and services. Substantial progress would have been made toward the full-employment goal of 2 percent, making the right to a job at decent pay a reality. An adequate program of child care and payment for single-parent home child care would have begun to broaden options facing parents. People would be able, in short, to move beyond nagging worries about where the next paycheck is coming from and to pay more attention to improving the quality of their lives. A democratic economy could be on track, by 1990, because all of us would be contributing to its direction.

THE POLITICS OF A DEMOCRATIC ALTERNATIVE

We imagine that this portrait of a democratic economy, however schematic, will look attractive to many readers. But is it a serious possibility? Could we actually achieve such a dramatic shift in the direction of our economy between now and 1990?

We would be quite unrealistic if we *promised* such a prospect. Too many people believe that it is necessary to tighten our belts, and corporations have too much power in this country, for us to be wildly optimistic about the prospects for our Economic Bill of Rights.

We want to emphasize, instead, that popular mobilization around a democratic alternative like ours is *essential* to improve the prospects for any kind of progressive change and any kind of progressive movement in the United States. We base this conclusion on our evaluation of both the possibilities for real progressive change and the problems which such a mobilization would face.

We think there are realistic possibilities for widespread mobilization around our Economic Bill of Rights for three important reasons.

First, we think that there is already widespread popular support for many of the specific proposals included in our program. Consider the following poll results:[6]

- As many as two thirds of respondents have consistently favored price controls if they would help curb inflation.
- Two thirds responding to a 1975 poll said they would prefer to work in an "employee-controlled company" while only 20 percent preferred an "investor-controlled" company. In a 1976 survey, half of workers answered yes when asked whether it was a good idea for corporations in America to become more like what they are in Europe, in offering workers more involvement in corporate governance. In 1979, 74 percent answered yes. More than half have said that they would "definitely" or "probably" support a presidential candidate who "advocated employee ownership and self-management."
- Almost twice as many in a 1982 poll said there was "too much" defense spending as said there was "too little."

These results are not really surprising, but they get little attention because such questions are so rarely asked.

There is comparable evidence to suggest that people are ready for a change.[7]

- In 1966, 26 percent of U.S. adults felt that "people running the country don't care what happens to people like me." By 1977, that figure had soared to 60 percent.
- In the early 1960s, 28 percent agreed that "government is run for the benefit of a few big interests." By the late 1970s, the percentage had climbed to 65 percent.
- In a 1975 poll, 41 percent agreed that there should be a "major adjustment" in the economy, and only 17 percent thought that we should "keep it as it is." (We do not think they got the adjustment they were looking for.)

Second, our analysis of the waste burden casts new light on the latent potential of the U.S. economy. If there were not so much waste, we would face some very tough zero-sum choices about who sacrifices for whom in a program of economic restructuring. But we have argued in detail in Chapter 7 that there was more than a trillion dollars of waste in the U.S. economy in 1980—almost half of useful output in that year. The opportunity to transform that waste into useful output or increased free time provides plenty of margin with which we could chart new directions and institute new programs. Probusiness strategists argue the need for regressive redistribution. We argue the possibility of moving beyond the waste land.

Third, we think that clear discussion of and mobilization around a *comprehensive* democratic economic program could help solve some critical problems which have recently hampered progressive movements in the United States. One problem has been our hesitation and uncertainty; some have doubted the feasibility of a democratic alternative, while others have assumed that it would be too costly. Our program lifts the burden of defensiveness under which proponents of progressive change have had to labor in recent times. Progressive political activists have continually run up against the charge that their proposals would be costly to the economy in terms of economic efficiency or growth. We have shown that there need not be such a discouraging trade-off; building a more humane society is part and parcel of the process of revitalizing the economy.

Another problem has been our fragmentation, bred in part by the persistent and nagging fear that what one group gains will come at another group's expense. We do not pretend that such suspicions will disappear overnight. But we do think that mobilization for a comprehensive democratic economic program such as the one we have elaborated here will provide the most favorable possible opportunity for beginning to overcome some of those divisions and mutual recriminations. Simply knowing that there is a democratic alternative to regressive redistribution, in the first instance, makes an enormous difference. Much more important, the possibility of real job security through active full-employment policies helps remove the occasion for much of the fragmentation and mutual suspicion. Given employment security, for example, union members could recognize that job opportunities for everyone can help sustain rapid growth and do not pose a threat to their own employment. Given a more securely protected natural environment, correspondingly, environmentalists will be less likely to see the insistent demands of lower-income people for jobs and for a higher material standard of living as a drain on limited natural resources and as a threat to ecological balance.

The more that an economic program recognizes the needs of

disparate groups as *interdependent,* in short, the greater the likelihood of building a strong economic movement among a broad majority of workers and citizens. The key is rather like the solution to the famous prisoner's dilemma: if everyone acts individually, then each individual's gain comes at someone else's expense and rational behavior leads to a suboptimal outcome. If people perceive, in contrast, that common efforts can make everyone better off, then it is possible to cooperate in attaining the best solution for all.

If this is the promise, there are also clearly problems in pursuing something like our Economic Bill of Rights.

One is that corporate opposition will accelerate with every flicker of interest in taking democracy seriously. Corporations will warn grimly about chaos and inefficiency, about disruption and short-sightedness, about the primacy of profitability in any program for restructuring. They will blackmail us by threatening to move their businesses. They will warn of capital flight overseas. Financial speculation may spread ripples of destabilizing effects. Capital may even consider, as mobilization around a democratic alternative mounts, moving politically to curtail popular rights and abridge democratic freedoms. While we are disinclined to warn of such a political Armageddon, we think it is equally foolish to ignore the lessons of history and the evidence of recent corporate concerns: corporations value profits more than democracy, and it is certainly possible that they will move to curtail the latter before they will agree to reduced priority for the former.

The best defense of democracy is more democracy. By revitalizing local, state, and federal government functions as well as promoting the proliferation of community organization and the expansion of union membership, we think our program would be an essential part of a viable strategy for turning back corporate encroachments on democratic rights.

The defense against capital strike (noninvestment) and capital flight is more complicated. Both capital strike and capital flight, if not countered, result in short-run declines in employment and long-run declines in productive capacity. But they can be countered. The runaway shop does not itself move to greener pastures; what moves is the management and the money. But neither management nor money produces output: machines and labor do. The plant and equipment as well as the work force which knows how to use it generally stay put. Our program would greatly facilitate workers assuming ownership and democratic control of plants threatened by closedowns. Our public-investment programs at local and federal levels could compensate for shortfalls in private investment, while our subsidies to selected private investments would discourage capital strike in strategic economic sectors. The increased unemployment stemming from short-run declines in the demand for goods and services resulting from an investment strike can be countered by familiar short-run fiscal and monetary policy, as well as by the expansion of public employment.

The disruptive effects of a capital strike could be tempered; but a massive refusal to invest would most likely promote a serious economic and political crisis, the resolution of which might require a considerable expansion of the public sector of the economy. Whether capitalists would willingly provoke such a crisis depends of course on their estimate of the chances that the democratic economic program could thereby be discredited. We think the vast majority of the people of the United States would be at least as likely to blame the capitalists and press for further democratization of investment.

Another problem likely to confront a democratic economic restructuring is that the bases for division among different popular groups are deeply rooted and will not evaporate as soon as we mobilize around a common economic agenda. Sexism is real, creating a vast legacy of suspicion and conflict among men and women. Racism is real, posing huge barriers to cooperation among whites, blacks, Hispanics, Asians, Native Americans, and other minorities. Ageism, a less familiar source of problems, is also real, fostering sharp and increasing divisions among the young, the old, and those in between.

Moderating these problems will take time and commitment. Our economic proposals do not address all of their roots. We do not offer an exhaustive social program in this book. We have focused on but one problem—the poor performance of the U.S. economy—and have presented concrete and comprehensive proposals for a democratic approach to solving those problems. Our program, in this sense, is not exhaustive but essential. It does not deal with all our needs, but it provides a basis for dealing successfully with one of the most important. Mobilization around a democratic economic alternative, we think, can provide the most favorable possible position from which to deal with the rest of our problems.

Many will hesitate, wondering if less sweeping programs could do the job. We wish it were the case. We do not enjoy confrontation for its own sake. We do not relish such sweeping challenges to the established economic powers. We, like many others, are pushed in these directions quite simply because the imperatives of the probusiness strategies leave so little room for compromise. They want more wealth and more power. Their strategies for serving those ends require that the rest of us sacrifice our welfare and our rights to augment theirs. The probusiness strategies insist that we act out the zero-sum illusion. They call for subordinating other economic interests to their own bottom line. Their bottom line, as we have seen throughout the book, does not pay much attention to the needs or concerns of the great majority of us.

The economics of greed has reigned long enough. Large corporations dominated the postwar era and we are now paying the price. It is time to assert our own priorities, to propel the economy in a more rational and democratic direction. We could succumb once again to the costs of corporate power—moved either by the spirit of compromise or by a sense of political weakness—but these costs will simply recur and undoubtedly rise if we do. It is time instead for a *real* change in the way we run our economy.

We are committed to traditional popular values of democracy, equality, community, security, efficiency, and liberty. We refuse to believe that these values must be abandoned or compromised in the search for economic revitalization. Our analysis of the possibility of moving beyond the waste land convinces us that a successful and effective program for economic recovery can advance these traditional popular values, not suppress them. Popular groups can build a decent society without undercutting its economic viability. Democracy is not a cost but an essential ingredient of economic recovery.

APPENDIX A

The Relevance of Hourly Income

Economists generally measure the average level of well-being in a society by its real per capita GNP—the gross national product divided by total population and expressed in terms of the (constant) prices of a particular year, so that year-to-year changes reflect changes in real output rather than just changes in prices.

It is well known that there are serious shortcomings to the use of real GNP as a measure of total well-being. For example, this measure does not take into account many factors affecting our standard of living because these factors are not readily quantifiable in dollar terms. Excluded are such important considerations as the amount of free time available to people, the quality of community life and working conditions, the condition of the physical environment, and the degree of people's personal security. Moreover, GNP does include many goods and services that make no significant positive contribution to our standard of living—notably military weapons. Indeed, the true benefits of many goods and services—their "use values," in Marxian terms—are poorly reflected by the prices—or "exchange values"—at which they are measured in the national accounting system.

Dividing real GNP by total population to measure average well-being is also subject to serious reservations. Real per capita GNP tells us how much real GNP is available on average for each person in the society, but it takes no account of the amount of time or effort that went into production of the output. The same level of real per capita GNP might be achieved—under different circumstances—by people working an average forty-hour week or an average thirty-hour week. Surely a society would be better off in the latter case, for then people would have much more time to engage in other pursuits such as child care, education, recreation, or home improvement. And even if a given level of per capita GNP were produced by the same number of hours of work, the amount of effort required by the work could vary widely depending on the nature and pace of the average job.

An ideal measure of average well-being would meet these short-comings of real GNP per capita first by reevaluating the numerator—real GNP—in terms of the use value of the goods and services produced, also taking into account any changes in the social and physical environment that affect the quality of life. Second, the denominator—population—would be revised to take account of the sacrifice of time and effort actually involved in producing the (broadly defined) output of the society.

Such a task of reevaluation was well beyond the scope of our project.[1] But to avoid some of the most serious biases in the conventional measure, we made three adjustments in real per capita GNP to arrive at our preferred concept of "hourly income."

First, we subtracted from GNP that portion accounted for by the "capital-consumption allowance" to obtain what economists call the "net national product" (NNP). The logic of this correction is that the output corresponding to the capital-consumption allowance does not add to society's welfare. It serves instead to maintain at its previous level the society's stock of physical structures and equipment, by making up for deterioration through wear and tear during the year. NNP measures the amount of output available for consumption (private and public) and net investment (net additions to the society's stock of structures and equipment).

Second, we used a different price index from the conventional one to adjust for the effects of price inflation and thus to express NNP in real terms. The conventional "implicit price deflator" for NNP reflects changes in the prices of the components of output produced in the economy. But to measure the value of the output from the point of view of those who use the corresponding income for consumption or investment, it is preferable to use an index that reflects changes in prices of the goods and services *purchased*. Since some produced output is exported and some purchased goods and services are imported, the purchase price deflator can differ from the conventional product price deflator if the terms of trade between exported and imported goods (i.e., their relative prices) change over time. To underline our use of a purchase price rather than a product price deflator, we refer to our resulting measure as real net national *income* rather than product.

Finally, we chose to divide real net national income by the total number of hours that people were at work in the economy rather than by the total number of people in the society. The logic of this approach was suggested above. Increases in real income achieved without any increase in work time—i.e., increases in real income per hour of work—are clearly beneficial (assuming no deterioration in working conditions). But increases in real income achieved by increasing average work time—which will show up in increased real income per capita—are not so unambiguously beneficial, for they involve the sacrifice of time for other activities. Dividing by work hours thus provides a better measure of the welfare implications of a rise in real income than does dividing by population.

The three steps just described can be readily applied to convert real GNP per capita into our preferred measure of real net national income per hour of work, or—for short—hourly income.[2] Hourly income is still far from a perfect measure of people's average well-being, but we are convinced that it represents a significant improvement over the conventional measure.

APPENDIX B

The Inadequacy of Conventional Explanations of Stagflation

The puzzling coexistence of rising inflationary pressures with a rising long-term trend in the unemployment rate throughout the 1970s severely taxed the explanatory power of mainstream economic theories. As long as inflation would increase when unemployment declined and would then subside when unemployment rose, economists schooled in the Keynesian tradition could remain confident in their understanding of the workings of a capitalist economy. But the phenomenon of stagflation that has characterized the current economic crisis shook up the conventional Keynesian wisdom and led economists to search through their analytical tool kits for some way to account for what was happening.

Those most wedded to the traditional Keynesian perspective checked first for "demand-pull" forces that could explain the upward pressure on prices by high rates of aggregate demand and capacity utilization. It is true that from 1966 to 1969 the U.S. economy was operating at an unusually high rate,[1] as LBJ sought to fight both the war in Vietnam and the War on Poverty, and this no doubt imparted an initial upward thrust to prices. But since then there has been only one year—1973—of relatively high capacity utilization; and from 1973 on, as we have shown in Chapter 5, U.S. government macropolicy was quite restrictive. The anomaly of stagflation in the 1970s reflects precisely the failure of traditional Keynesian demand-side explanations: inflation continued to spiral upward even though demand pressures were abating.

Many economists therefore shifted their focus to "cost-push" forces at work in the U.S. economy, and the dramatic hike of oil prices in 1973 provided an obvious case in point. But such cost-push explanations can account at most for temporary surges in the level of prices; they do not explain the persistent upward trend in the rate of inflation since the late 1960s. Some economists have called attention to the importance of three-year union contracts, and the growth of cost-of-living adjustments (COLAs) as sources of wage cost-push in the U.S. economy. But three-year contracts have been common since the 1950s, and COLAs remain relatively limited in scope and amount. Moreover, the portion of the U.S. labor force covered by any kind of union contract has been declining steadily since the late 1950s,[2] so a union-based wage cost-push theory is quite unpersuasive.

The weakness of these arguments has led an increasing number of U.S. economists into the "monetarist" camp. This school, dominated by the ideas of Nobel Prize winner Milton Friedman, blames the U.S. Federal Reserve Board (the Fed) for permitting too rapid a rate of growth of the money supply. It is true that the supply of money in the U.S. economy has been growing increasingly rapidly: its average annual growth increased from 7.1 percent in 1959–66 to 8.7 percent in 1966–73 and 10 percent in 1973–79.[3] But this alone is not sufficient evidence.

The monetarists argue that what matters is the rate of growth of the money supply relative to potential output. To the extent that the former grows more rapidly than the latter, monetary policy is considered "inflation-accommodating" because it permits prices to rise. The higher the rate of growth of money relative to potential output, the more rapid inflation is expected to be. For the three successive periods 1959–66, 1966–73, and 1973–79, the data for the U.S. economy show that the *relative* money supply grew at average annual rates of 3.2 percent, 4.9 percent, and 6.5 percent, while prices rose at rates of 1.8 percent, 4.7 percent, and 7.5 percent.[4]

Monetarists are correct that U.S. monetary policy has become more inflation-accommodating over these three periods, and that prices have risen increasingly rapidly. But the monetarist theory cannot explain why prices increased more rapidly than the relative money supply after 1973, while they increased more slowly before then. And it is precisely this kind of upward drift in inflationary tendencies that a good theory of stagflation must be able to explain.

Finally—and most importantly—the monetarists do not *explain*, they merely *observe*, the shift in Fed policy toward inflation-accommodating monetary policy from the mid-1960s through the late 1970s. Surely the governors of the Federal Reserve Board are not robots, responding to economic indicators like thermostats. An adequate analysis must consider *why* policy moves in one direction or another, as well as postulating its effects. And a complete theory of stagflation must explain *why* the Fed allowed the money supply to grow in an increasingly inflation-accommodating way from the 1960s through the 1970s.

APPENDIX C

Multivariate Regression Analysis of the U.S. Economic Crisis

We present in this appendix the details of the multivariate regression analyses with which we have quantified our effort, in Chapters 4 and 6, to account for economic decline in the U.S. economy. Our presentation here will be complete but brief. For a more thorough discussion of our econometric models and empirical findings, and complete documentation of our data sources, readers are referred to two working papers: "Hearts and Minds: A Social Model of Aggregate Productivity Growth in the United States, 1948–1979," Economics Institute of the Center for Democratic Alternatives, Working Paper No. 1, March 1983; and "The Social Structure of Accumulation and the Rate of Profit," Economics Institute of the Center for Democratic Alternatives, Working Paper No. 5, April 1983.

The Productivity Model

Our major task was to formulate a model and estimate a corresponding equation expressing changes in U.S. productivity in terms of changes in a set of "independent" variables that our theoretical approach suggested to be potentially significant determinants of productivity growth. After experimenting with several variations on our main theme, we arrived at a final productivity equation that we estimated by ordinary least squares (OLS) with annual data from 1948 to 1979. The results follow:

1. Productivity

$$\dot{q} = .006 + .441\dot{k} + .562\dot{u} + .038\dot{e} + .051\dot{w} + .023\dot{f} - .058\dot{m}$$
$$(1.34) \quad (4.22)^{**} \quad (10.94)^{**} \quad (6.45)^{**} \quad (2.44)^{**} \quad (2.47)^{**} \quad (-3.38)^{**}$$

$$R^2 = .91 \quad \bar{R}^2 = .89 \quad \text{d.w.} = 1.81$$

where the numbers in brackets refer to t-statistics, ** denotes significance at a 99 percent confidence level, $\dot{x}$ denotes the annual rate of change in variable x, and the variables are defined as follows:

q = *productivity* (real output per hour of production-worker labor in the non-farm private-business sector (NFPBS)

k = *capital intensity* (utilized real capital stock per hour of production-worker labor in the NFPBS)

u = *capacity utilization* (the ratio of actual to potential real GNP)

e = *employer leverage over workers* (the product of the rate of supervision and the cost of losing your job for the nonagricultural labor force, adjusted by weighted earnings inequality and union representation)

w = *quality of working conditions* (the inverse of the accident rate in manufacturing)

f = *business failure rate* (per million listed enterprises)

m = *relative cost of nonagricultural crude materials* (with respect to the price of finished goods)

All of the coefficients on the explanatory variables have the sign predicted by our theoretical reasoning, and all are highly significant. However, the accuracy of these results depends on how fully the variables conform to certain conditions required for the valid application of the conventional ordinary least squares (OLS) regression technique. In particular, we must be assured that the direction of causality in Equation 1 runs predominantly from the variables on the right-hand side to the productivity variable on the left. Careful examination of each variable gives us grounds for confidence on this score.

First of all, the variables k and u are routinely treated as independent causal variables in productivity analyses. e is the product of the rate of supervision and the cost of losing your job; it hardly seems plausible that increases in productivity could cause simultaneous increases in the rate of supervision or in either of the two main components of the cost of losing your job—the average duration of unemployment and the relative income loss associated with job termination. w varies inversely with the accident rate; in so far as higher levels of productivity are associated with speed-ups at the workplace, there might be a positive effect on the accident rate, but such an effect is opposite in sign to our hypothesized effect of the quality of working conditions on productivity. The results shown in Equation 1 support our view; if there were any reverse causality in this instance, it would lead to an understatement of the true magnitude of our hypothesized relationship.

Unlike the other independent variables, f enters into Equation 1 with a different dimensionality than $\dot{q}$: *changes* in productivity are a function of the *level* of the business failure rate. Could a deceleration in productivity growth cause a decline in the failure rate? Quite the contrary. A productivity slowdown—because it is likely to contribute to generalized economic difficulties and growing stagflation—would be far more likely to *increase* business failures than to *decrease* them. As for the remaining right-hand variable c, one would expect that productivity—if it had any causal effect at all—would be positively linked to the cost of nonagricultural crude materials, for raw-materials prices tend to be relatively high in good times and relatively low in bad times. Once again, the expected sign of any reverse causality would be the opposite of what we have hypothesized in our model of the determinants of productivity and the opposite of our regression results. Thus, if anything, our estimates of the coefficients on f and m in Equation 1 understate the true magnitude of the hypothesized effects.

We utilized the numerical results of Equation 1 to develop the explanatory accounting framework displayed in Figures 6.5 and 6.6 in standard fashion. First, from our raw time series data, we calculated the average annual values of each variable shown in Equation 1 for the three periods 1948–66, 1966–73, and 1973–79. In the case of each right-hand variable, we then multiplied these period averages by the coefficient on that variable from Equation 1. For any given period and variable, the resulting product reflects the average annual contribution of that variable to the average annual rate of productivity growth over the same period. The numbers shown in Figures 6.5 and 6.6 were calculated by subtracting these contribution products (and the productivity growth value itself) for the period 1948–66 from the corresponding values for 1966–73 and 1973–79, respectively. The values shown for "work intensity" in Figures 6.5 and 6.6 represent the

398   APPENDIXES

sum of the values obtained, as described above, for the two variables e
and w that together reflect work intensity. The values shown for "innovative pressure" and "popular resistance" are the values obtained, as
described above, for the variables f and m.

The Cold-Bath Models

Our second task was to formulate models and estimate equations
reflecting the cold-bath causal relationships depicted in Figure 6.7. The
results are presented in the following equations; each equation was
estimated with annual data from 1948 to 1979, with the exception of
the fiscal-restrictiveness equation, which was estimated from 1952 to
1979 because of the lag structure of the independent variables.

2. Fiscal Restrictiveness

$$r = -.143 + .149u - .520b - .366c_{vw} - .475c_{kw} + .124i_e$$
$$(-2.16)** \ (2.21)** \ (2.26)** \ (-1.56)* \ (-4.56)** \ (1.80)*$$
$$-.015d_{gd}$$
$$(-4.04)**$$

$$R^2 = 0.83 \quad \bar{R}^2 = 0.76 \quad d.w. = 2.41$$

3. Capacity Utilization

$$\dot{u} = -.009 - 124.99\dot{r} + .0267\dot{v} + 11.03t$$
$$(-3.41)** \ (-2.68)** \ (6.09)** \ (1.86)*$$

$$R^2 = 0.66 \quad \bar{R}^2 = 0.63 \quad d.w. = 1.53$$

4. Capital Intensity

$$\dot{k} = -0.13 - 53.26\dot{r} + .002c_{lk} + .301\dot{p}$$
$$(-1.32) \ (-3.95.)** \ (1.53)* \ (2.85)**$$

$$R^2 = 0.57 \quad \bar{R}^2 = 0.52 \quad d.w. = 2.06$$

The symbols have the same meanings as in Equation 1; * denotes
significance at the 95 percent confidence level; and the new variables
are defined as follows:

r = *fiscal restrictiveness* (the sum of the "high-employment" federal
    budget surplus, the state and local government budget surplus,
    and an estimate of the restrictive impact of the OPEC oil-price
    increase of 1973, all as a percentage of GNP)

b   = *relative income loss* (the difference between an average worker's income when unemployed and when employed, expressed as a percentage of the latter, lagged one business cycle)

c_{vw} = *Vietnam War costs* (additional U.S. government military expenditures attributable to the Vietnam War, as a percentage of GNP)

c_{kw} = *Korean War costs* (additional U.S. government military expenditures attributable to the Korean War, as a percentage of GNP)

i_e = *expected rate of inflation* (for next twelve-month period)

d_{gd} = *government demand dummy* (equal to 1 in years in which demands on the government were escalating—after 1963)

v   = *real investment* (real domestic fixed-capital formation as a percentage of real GNP)

t   = *trade balance* (total U.S. exports minus total U.S. imports as a percentage of GNP)

c_{lk} = *relative factor cost* (the ratio of average production-worker wages to the cost of capital)

$\hat{p}$ = *predicted profit rate* (a three-year moving average of the after-tax profit rate in the U.S. nonfinancial corporate business sector, as predicted by the multivariate regression equation reported below)

Equation 1 was estimated by the OLS technique, but for Equations 2 and 3 it was necessary to apply a two-stage least-squares technique (2SLS) to avoid bias due to the interdependence of the variables r and u.

All of the coefficients on the explanatory variables in Equations 2 to 4 have the expected sign and are significant. Equation 2 clearly supports our hypothesized negative relationship between employer leverage over workers and the degree of restrictiveness in government fiscal policy; declines in b—a major component of e—lead to increases in r in the next business cycle, for example, and the opposite effect holds for increases in b. (The conventional hypothesis linking r to i_e receives some support from Equation 2, but the impact of i_e is much less significant than that of b.) Equations 3 and 4 confirm that both capacity utilization and capital intensity are significantly and negatively affected by the degree of fiscal restrictiveness.

We utilized the numerical results of Equations 2 to 4 to calculate the "cold-bath" effects displayed in Figure 6.6. The variables $\dot{k}$ and $\dot{u}$ in Equation 1 capture the contributions to productivity change of capital intensity change and capacity utilization change, respectively.

The results of Equations 3 and 4 permitted us to determine the extent to which changes in ú and k̇ could be attributed to changes in fiscal restrictiveness (ŕ) and changes in expected profits, using the same method described earlier to attribute changes in productivity to changes in the right-hand-side variables of Equation 1. Similarly, we used the results of Equation 2 to determine the extent to which changes in r could in turn be attributed to changes in employer leverage over workers, as reflected in the variable b. The cold-bath proportions of the contributions of declines in capital intensity and capacity utilization to the second productivity slowdown, as shown in Figure 6.6, represent the proportions accounted for by changes in fiscal restrictiveness due in turn to changes in employer leverage.

The Profit Rate Equations

To provide a systematic quantitative basis for our analysis of the determinants of U.S. corporate profitability at the end of Chapter 4, we formulated a model and estimated parallel equations to explain the behavior of the after-tax profit rate and Tobin's Q in the nonfinancial corporate business (NFCB) sector of the U.S. economy.[1] Each equation was estimated by the OLS technique with annual data from 1948 to 1979. The results follow:

5. After-tax Profit Rate

$$y = -.0532 + .231j + .150t - .009n$$
$$(6.27)^{**} \quad (+4.65)^{**} \quad (+5.70)^{**} \quad (-.74)$$

$$-.329x + .605u$$
$$(-7.32)^{**} \quad (+6.43)^{**}$$

$$R^2 = .81 \quad \bar{R}^2 = .78 \quad d.w. = 1.11$$

6. Tobin's Q

$$z = -2.96 + 1.66j + 1.13t - .63n$$
$$(-4.79)^{**} \quad (+4.59)^{**} \quad (+5.93)^{**} \quad (-6.77)^{**}$$

$$-.90x + 3.66u$$
$$(-2.76)^{**} \quad (+5.33)^{**}$$

$$R^2 = .90 \quad \bar{R}^2 = .88 \quad d.w. = 1.30$$

The symbols have the same meanings as before, and the new variables are defined as follows:

y = *after-tax profit rate* (the sum of NFCB adjusted corporate profits and net interest, minus NFCB corporate profits tax liability, divided by net NFCB fixed capital stock)

j = *cost of job loss* (the product of relative income loss—b—and the average duration of unemployment)

t = *terms of trade* (U.S. export price index divided by U.S. import price index)

n = *relative cost of nature-based inputs* (index of all crude-material prices relative to all finished-goods prices)

x = *corporate profits tax rate* (NFCB corporate profits tax liability divided by unadjusted NFCB corporate profits)

z = *Tobin's Q* (the ratio of the stock-market value to the net replacement cost of capital assets)

Once again, all of the coefficients on the explanatory variables in Equations 5 and 6 have the sign predicted by our theoretical reasoning, and all but one—n in Equation 5—are highly significant.

APPENDIX D

Estimating the Waste Burden

We detail here the methods and sources underlying our estimates of waste presented in Chapter 7 and summarized in Figure 7.2. We present them in order of the components of waste outlined in that summary figure.

Labor Utilization. There were 97.3 million employed, on average, during 1980, working a total of 182.2 billion hours during the year.[1] With a full-employment unemployment rate of 2 percent, we estimate that this total hour pool would have been expanded from three sources:

• Instead of 7.45 million unemployed, there would have been only 2.16 million unemployed—2 percent of the labor force (expanded by the number of discouraged workers estimated below). This would have resulted in 5.39 million additional employed, working a total of 10.09 billion hours (on the assumption of annual hours employed equal to the average for the presently employed in 1980).

- There were 5.53 million not in the labor force in 1980 even though they said they "want a job now." Of these, we estimate that those who were not looking (a) because they "think they cannot get a job"; (b) because of "home responsibility"; and (c) for "all other reasons" would all reenter the labor force under conditions of full employment with publicly supported child care. This would have resulted in 3.33 million additional employed, working a total of 6.1 billion additional hours (assuming that 2 percent were unemployed despite reentering the labor force).
- There were 4.21 million part-time workers who preferred full-time work—the "involuntary part-time" employed. We assume that all of these would be able to work full time; this would have resulted in an additional average of 351.3 hours per year per worker for this group, and an additional total employment of 1.48 billion hours.

Under conditions of full employment as we outline them in Part III, finally, there would be some decline in total hours worked as a result of the elimination of involuntary overtime. We estimate that 15 million worked overtime in 1980; that their median overtime hours worked was 7.5 hours per week; that 47.8 percent of these worked under conditions of involuntary overtime; and that, for the purposes of discussion, half of those exposed to involuntary overtime would reduce their working time to the standard workweek. This would have resulted in a reduction in total annual hours by 1.4 billion.

Summing these four adjustments, we estimate that total annual hours would have been 16.27 billion higher, for an increase of 8.93 percent over actual total annual hours in 1980.[2]

Productive Allocation of Labor. In 1948, 12.1 percent of employees in the private sector were in the nonproduction/supervisory category. In 1980, 18.7 percent of employees fell into that category. We assume that this incremental 6.6 percent could have been transferred to "productive" tasks and thus increase useful output by that proportion.[3]

Work Intensity. A wide variety of empirical studies suggest that more democratic workplace relations would result in levels of worker productivity as much as 30 percent higher than levels in hierarchical organizations. We have picked the minimum end of the range of prevailing estimates: 15 percent.[4] We have further assumed that this dividend would apply not only to those presently employed in 1980 but also to those whose labor was not being utilized or who were working in unproductive jobs. We thus multiply the productivity dividend (15 percent) times the augmented productive-worker labor time estimated in the two previous categories (1.155) to arrive at our final estimate of the additional output resulting from more democratic work relations (17.3 percent).

Productive Efficiency. The economy was operating at much lower efficiency than necessary in 1980 as a result of restrictive fiscal and monetary policy. We estimate the effects of this cold bath through our multivariate regression model detailed in the previous appendix.

Investment and capacity utilization were lower after 1973 as a result of greater fiscal restrictiveness. By applying the coefficients for the fiscal restrictiveness variable in the equations for the rate of growth of capital intensity and capacity utilization, and further by applying the coefficients for the effects of work intensity on expected profits to the equation for the growth of capital intensity, we can estimate that portion of the reduced growth of capital intensity and capacity utilization between 1966–73 and 1973–79 which resulted from fiscal restrictiveness and capital's response to reduced work intensity. (These proportions equaled 51.9 percent of the reduced growth of capital intensity and 95.3 percent of the reduced growth of capacity utilization.)

If hourly-output growth had not been reduced by these cold-bath effects, there would have been six years of more rapid growth in hourly output reflected in the level of productive efficiency of the U.S. economy by 1980. Again seeking a somewhat conservative estimate of these effects, we calculated the arithmetic growth in hourly output over those six years (rather than the compounded growth) by applying the coefficients in our hourly-output growth equation to the incremental increases in capital-intensity growth and capacity-utilization growth which would have resulted if there had not been a cold bath in the economy during those six years.

As in our estimation of the effects of greater work intensity, finally, we also calculated the interaction effect between the potentially higher hourly output and the greater number of production-worker hours which would have resulted from greater labor utilization and more productive allocation of labor.

This resulted in estimates of the direct effects from greater capital-intensity growth and capacity-utilization growth of 2.61 percent and 1.44 percent, respectively, and direct plus indirect effects of 3.02 percent and 1.66 percent, respectively; these latter figures, rounded to the nearest .1 percent, are the estimates reported in the text of Chapter 7 and Figure 7.2.

Military Expenditures. We adopt the estimate by the Boston Study Group that defense expenditures in 1978 need only have been $73 billion; the same real amount of spending in 1980 would have amounted to $86.3 billion in 1980 prices. (See Chapter 7, note 25.)

We further estimate that $4.4 billion could have been saved from reduced waste in military production. (See Chapter 7, note 26.) This suggests the possibility of a total defense budget in 1980 of only $81.9 billion instead of $131.7 billion, for a savings of $49.8 billion.[5]

Energy Production. We estimate that total research and capital costs supporting the development of nuclear plant construction from 1952 to 1980 equaled $96 billion in 1979 dollars. If this potential capital expenditure had been devoted to more productive investment purposes over that entire period, given that the average age of the capital stock in 1980 was 10.1 years, we estimate that the capital stock in 1980 could have been $34.7 billion larger in 1980: $96 billion/(28 years/10.1 average age). Given the output-to-capital ratio in 1980, this would have resulted in an additional output of $32.6 billion in 1980.

Nuclear plants produced 2.7 quads (quadrillion BTUs) of electricity in 1980. We must take into account the cost of doing without this electricity in order to estimate the *net* savings from the past capital costs of nuclear-plant construction. Since 20 percent of electricity-generating capacity in 1980 was unutilized, and since electricity from nuclear plants represented only 11 percent of total production, it might have been possible to get by without any nuclear plants and without any additional costs of replacement. But since some excess capacity must be maintained in electricity-generating systems, and since the regional distribution of excess capacity is quite uneven, we think it more prudent to estimate the costs of substituting for at least some of the nuclear capacity. We could have saved those units of electrical-power capacity through conservation. Existing nuclear capacity totaled 55,000 megawatts and it costs roughly $200 in conservation costs per kilowatt of reduced consumption. This would suggest a maximum cost of replacing nuclear-generating capacity of $11 billion, certainly a high estimate since only about two thirds of nuclear capacity was actually being used. We think it safe to use one half of that figure, thus estimating that it would have cost $5.5 billion in capital expenditures to substitute for nuclear-generating capacity. Thus the net saving in capital costs could have been $34.7 − $5.5 = $29.2 billion.

Applying the average output/capital ratio of .94 in 1980, the net saving in output in 1980 which would have resulted from having avoided wasteful nuclear-power development would have been $27.4 billion.[6]

Food Production. Consumers spent $260.1 billion in 1980. Of this, $178.6 billion covered the "marketing bill"—including intermediate labor costs, packaging materials, transport costs, intermediate profits, and other expenditures. This amounted to 68.7 percent of total food expenditures. In 1948, the marketing bill accounted for only 55.6 percent of total food expenditures. If we had been able to pay only the latter portion in 1980, the food marketing bill would have totaled only $144.6 billion, for a savings of $32 billion on food-consumption expenditures.[7]

Health Care. Our estimates of waste in the health-care system are based on 1974 data on health-care expenditures, since more recent comparative international data are not available. In 1974, the United States ranked fourteenth in infant mortality among the advanced countries. The thirteen countries ranking ahead of the United States averaged $338 per capita per year on health expenditures, while the United States was spending $491 per capita. If the United States health-care system had been as effective as the systems of the other thirteen countries, we would have spent $153 less per capita in 1974. Projecting this savings forward to 1980 (by the index of medical-care costs), we would have saved $61.1 billion in health-care expenditures in 1980.[8]

Crime Control. This estimate is derived simply by applying the figure for total per capita criminal-justice expenditures, including police protection, judicial activities, and correction, which applied in 1966, to the figure which prevailed in 1980. This would have resulted in a projected 1980 expenditure of $15.4 billion—instead of the estimated $27.9 billion—for a net saving of $12.5 billion.[9]

Advertising. In 1948, total expenditures on advertising averaged $33 per capita. If this figure had applied in 1980, adjusted for the price deflator for personal consumption expenditures, we would have spent only $23.9 billion on advertising in 1980. Instead, we spent $54.6 billion. We could thus have saved $30.7 billion.[10]

APPENDIX E

Estimating the Macroeconomic Benefits and Costs of the Economic Bill of Rights

It is notoriously difficult to estimate the benefits and costs of fundamental changes in the economy—at least in part because it is hard to make reasonable conjectures concerning the responses of the major economic actors to economic changes which they have not yet experienced. We do not propose to replicate the simplistic promises of Laffer logic. But we believe that some effort to estimate, however roughly, the benefits and costs of our economic program is essential. We present a basic benefit-cost accounting of the first two years of our program in this appendix; the numbers are obviously approximate, but even if they are off by 5–10 percent, we think that they help to illustrate the basic dimensions of the fiscal and other requirements of our program and demonstrate with substantial plausibility how it could pay for itself.

Four key questions may be raised about the benefits and costs of the Economic Bill of Rights (EBR): Would implementation of the EBR require reductions in personal consumption to allow for increased use of the national product for social or collective ends? The answer is *no;* private as well as public consumption would increase. Would implementation of the EBR require an increase in the average personal tax rate? Again, the answer is *no;* the tax rate necessary to finance the EBR (with a balanced budget) would be substantially lower than the rate required to balance the government budget before the initiation of the program. Would the government control a larger share of total income? The answer is still *no;* total government spending as a share of GNP would decrease in the age of the EBR. Would implementation of the EBR heighten inflationary pressures? Once again, the answer is *no;* by increasing rapidly the supply of available goods and services, the EBR would help to moderate inflationary pressures.

In order to assess the probable short-term macroeconomic benefits and costs of the EBR, we assume that it goes into effect in 1984, and we evaluate the consequent changes in the U.S. economy from 1984 to 1986. This requires that we first estimate the state of the economy in 1984, our benchmark year, using the information available to us in early 1983.

We assume that by 1984 the U.S. economy will have made a moderate recovery from the deep recessionary trough of 1982, returning to a condition similar to that of 1980. More specifically, we assume that in 1984: (1) the real GNP is 5 percent higher than in 1980; (2) total employment and total hours of work are 5 percent higher than in 1980, which, assuming an 8 percent increase in the labor force since 1980, implies an unemployment rate of 9.5 percent; (3) the ratio of production workers to total workers (and hours) remains the same as in 1980; (4) real capital stock is 5 percent higher than in 1980, reflecting the unusually low levels of net investment from 1980 to 1984; (5) officially measured "potential" real GNP is 9 percent higher than in 1980, reflecting the growth of the labor force and the real capital stock as well as a modest rate of technological advance; this implies a decline in the ratio of actual to potential GNP from 95.6 percent in 1980 to 92 percent in 1984; (6) the business failure rate is the same as in 1980; (7) real total nonmilitary government spending is the same as in 1980; (8) real government military spending is 40 percent higher than in 1980; and (9) overall price inflation from 1980 to 1984 is 25 percent.

We express all magnitudes in this appendix in 1984 prices, except where otherwise noted. Our assumptions imply that the GNP in 1984 will be $3,456 billion (though this particular benchmark is not critical to our subsequent calculations) and that total government spending will be $1,201 billion (including $230 billion in military spending). Further, our assumptions imply that real output per hour of work and real capital stock per hour of work are the same in 1984 as they were in 1980.

We cannot assume, of course, that the Economic Bill of Rights would immediately eliminate all or even most of the waste in the U.S. economy which we detail in Chapter 7. Some gains would come relatively quickly, while others would take many years or decades. Our detailed assessment of the gains and losses in useful output is confined to what we think might reasonably be accomplished in two years —from 1984 to 1986—on the assumption that large and politically mobilized majorities favored and actively pushed the program.

Four major waste reclamation gains may be anticipated:

Labor utilization may be expected to grow rapidly in response to full employment, antidiscrimination, public child care, and related policies. By how much might the rate of unemployment decline in two years? During World War II, from 1941 to 1943, it fell from 9.9 percent to 1.9 percent. We think it is conservative to project a decline of roughly half this magnitude, from 9.5 percent in 1984 to 5 percent in 1986. We further estimate, on the basis of the historical evidence, that this 4.5 percent decline in the unemployment rate would lead to an increase in total worker hours of 14 percent. (For comparison, we note that from 1949 to 1951 a 2.6 percent drop in the unemployment rate increased hours by 9.8 percent, and that from 1964 to 1966 a 1.4 percent drop in the unemployment rate increased hours by 6.9 percent.) Offsetting this 14 percent gain in labor utilization would be three effects: There would be an increase in educational enrollments resulting from the EBR, particularly in higher education and other life-long learning activities, amounting to a withdrawal of between one and two million full-time equivalent students from the labor force—a loss of roughly 1.5 percent of the 1984 utilized labor hours. The reduction in work hours associated with the elimination of involuntary overtime and the introduction of flexible work hours might imply a labor utilization loss of another 1.5 percent. Enhanced public support of unions and the reduced threat of unemployment, especially in the face of possible business attempts to disrupt the EBR, would be likely to induce more widespread strike activity and on-the-job slowdown; we estimate this labor utilization loss at 1 percent, an amount of time lost through strike activity equaled only by the record-shattering post–World War II strike wave in 1946. Including all of these effects, we estimate an increase in work hours of roughly 10 percent from 1984 to 1986.

Productive effort per hour worked could go either way, tending to increase in response to heightened worker commitment and motivation, as wages and working conditions improve, and tending to fall in response to the reduction in unemployment and the threat of job loss. Ultimately we expect significant gains from reorganizing workplace relations; but we must be realistic in assuming that many of the carrot-and-stick effects on work intensity associated with current management-labor relations will remain applicable in the short run. To avoid exaggerating the immediate returns to the EBR, we therefore project a *decline* of 2 percent in productive effort per hour worked from 1984 to 1986. (This is *twice* the rate of decline associated with the reduction in employer leverage over workers during the entire decade of the 1960s, according to our productivity model introduced in Chapter 6.) We also assume no decrease by 1986 in the burden of redundant supervisory labor; thus the proportion of total worker hours represented by production workers will remain the same as in 1984 (and 1980).

Productive efficiency will rise in response to increases in capacity utilization, and increases in capital intensity (the ratio of real utilized capital stock to work hours). We project that by 1986 the ratio of actual to (officially measured) "potential" real GNP—our measure of overall capacity utilization—will have risen from 92 to 100 percent (a figure exceeded in 10 years since 1948, most recently in 1973). This gain of 8 percentage points in capacity utilization is only half of that achieved between 1941 and 1943, and compares to a gain of 7.5 points from 1949 to 1951 and 3.9 points from 1964 to 1966. (In both 1951 and 1966 the ratio rose above 102 percent.) As for capital intensity, note that this is equal to the rate of capacity utilization multiplied by real capital stock per production-worker hour. We project an increase in real capital stock of 8 percent from 1984 to 1986, at an annual rate of growth comparable with the 1960s. Since both total and production worker hours are projected to increase by 10 percent, this implies that real capital stock per production-worker hour will decrease by 1.8 percent. Taking into account the increase in the rate of capacity utilization from 92 to 100 percent—up 8.7 percent from its 1984 level—we arrive at an overall increase in capital intensity of 6.7 percent.

What effect will the increases of 8.7 percent in capacity utilization and 6.7 percent in capital intensity have on productivity? To estimate the magnitude of the effect, we again make use of our productivity model. According to the results obtained from the model (as reported in Appendix C), we can expect an increase in nonfarm business productivity from 1984 to 1986 of 4.5 percent on account of increased capacity utilization and 3 percent on account of increased capital intensity. The model also suggests that a rise in the business failure rate would serve to boost productivity growth. Vigorous pursuit of higher minimum wages, antidiscrimination policies, and solidarity wage bargaining can be expected to heighten innovative pressure on firms. If the effect is to raise the business failure rate from roughly .4 percent (in 1980 and 1984) to roughly .6 percent in 1986, our model indicates an additional productivity gain of .5 percent. Taking into account all of these gains, we project an increase of 8 percent in real output per production-worker hour in the nonfarm business sector of the U.S. economy.

Significant gains in *useful output,* our last waste-reclamation project, may also be anticipated. We have included only one in our estimates here: We project a 50 percent cut in military spending from its anticipated level of $230 billion in 1984. Even at $115 billion in 1986, the amount of real resources devoted to national defense would be substantially greater than the amount estimated in 1978 by the Boston Study Group to be fully adequate for national security (see Appendix D). The resultant saving of $115 billion makes available for useful purposes in 1986 an amount equal to 3.3 percent of total GNP in 1984. (Cancellation of all nuclear plants currently under construction and rapid pursuit of relatively easy-to-implement conversation projects would save additional resources, but we have not tried to estimate their magnitudes here.)

Offsetting the gain in useful output from reduced military spending might be some losses incurred through our proposed changes in international economic policy. We make the extreme assumption that we would entirely cease importing goods from some countries on the grounds that the cost competitiveness of those goods is based on the denial of workers' rights. We further assume that these imports constituted 20 percent of our import bill, or 2.4 percent of the total GNP, and that acquiring the same goods elsewhere would be 25 percent more expensive. (Our entire import bill from the non-OPEC countries of Africa, Asia, and Latin America, plus the Soviet Union and Eastern Europe, amounted to a little over 3 percent of the GNP in 1980.) To obtain the goods at higher prices, the U.S. would have to export more U.S.-produced goods, which would therefore not be available for use in the United States. The resulting loss in available output by 1986 comes to .6 percent of the 1984 GNP. Subtracting this from the gain in useful output via reduced defense spending, we project an overall net gain by 1986 of 2.7 percent of the 1984 GNP, or $93 billion.

Bringing together all of our estimated changes in the U.S. economy from 1984 to 1986, we can now estimate the level of GNP and the overall gain in useful output by 1986. For the nonfarm business sector, we have projected an increase in production-worker hours of 10 percent and, subtracting the 2 percent loss in productive effort from the 8 percent increase in productive efficiency, an increase in productivity (real output per production worker) of 6 percent. The overall increase in real output comes to 16.6 percent, which would raise nonfarm business product from its 1984 level of $2,534 billion (assuming the same proportion of GNP as in 1980) to a 1986 level of $2,955 billion (in 1984 prices). Assuming the same 10 percent rate of growth in worker hours outside the nonfarm business sector, but *no* increase in productivity, the output of the rest of the U.S. economy would rise from $922 billion in 1984 to $1,014 billion in 1986. Thus the total GNP would increase from $3,456 billion to $3,969 billion—an increase of 14.8 percent over two years, or an average annual rate of growth of 7.2 percent. This rate of growth is really quite reasonable for a period of economic expansion, especially after an unusually deep recessionary period; the U.S. real GNP increased at an annual rate of 15.2 percent from 1941 to 1943, 8.5 percent from 1949 to 1951, and 6 percent from 1964 to 1966.

The increase in GNP from 1984 to 1986 comes to $513 billion. But the overall gain in useful output from all sources includes also the output released by reduced defense spending, offset by the extra output absorbed by changes in international trade policy; the net gain from these sources was estimated at $93 billion. Thus the overall gain in useful output by 1986 amounts to $606 billion, representing roughly 15 percent of the 1984 GNP.

Not all of this gain in useful output would be available for people's immediate benefit, however, for we have to take into account the possible need for devoting a larger amount of GNP to capital formation in 1986. Consistent with our earlier assumptions about the state of the economy in 1984, we project that real gross private domestic investment—and each major component thereof—will be 5 percent greater in 1984 than in 1980. To estimate required real investment in 1986, we assume that: (1) real replacement investment (capital consumption allowance) must increase at the same rate projected for real capital stock from 1984 to 1986, i.e., 4 percent per year; (2) real net fixed nonresidential investment, as well as inventory investment, must be sufficient to maintain the future rate of growth of the nonresidential capital stock at 4 percent per year; and (3) real net fixed residential investment must be twice its level in 1984 (thus beginning to meet the long neglected housing needs of the nation and restoring real residential investment back to its peak levels of the early 1970s). Under these assumptions, gross private domestic investment will have to rise from $529 billion in 1984 to $674 billion in 1986—an increase of $145 billion.

Our estimated increase in useful output ($606 billion) thus exceeds the estimated increase in investment by $461 billion. This immediate waste-reclamation dividend could be used for a combination of increased personal consumption and government social programs. It amounts to roughly 12 percent of the level of GNP in 1984. It could provide, within two years, additional benefits of nearly $5,000 per household, or alternatively, a reduction in work hours that would allow for at least an extra month of vacation for every working person.

The size of this dividend carries the strong presumption, moreover, that the EBR would relieve inflationary pressure: The rapid expansion of available goods would dampen the fires of the heightened distributional conflict which, according to our account of stagflation in Chapter 5, has been the fundamental impetus for the inflationary surges of the past decade. By itself, of course, the expansion of output will not curb inflation; our program of flexible price controls will also be essential. But the EBR does provide a necessary condition for a politically viable method of controlling prices.

We have confined ourselves thus far to the macroeconomy as a whole. How would the implementation of the Economic Bill of Rights affect the public fisc?

To answer this question, we must first estimate the burden of government taxation in 1984. We begin with our benchmark estimate of $1,201 billion in total government spending in 1984 (see above); this figure represents 34.8 percent of estimated GNP in that year. Next we need to estimate the fraction of GNP represented by the three major categories of government revenue other than personal taxation—contributions to social insurance, indirect business taxes, and corporate profits taxes. We project that by 1984 the corporate profits fraction will have dropped by half, from 3.2 percent in 1980 to 1.6 percent in 1984; the social insurance fraction will have risen by the same 1.6 percent, from 7.8 to 9.4 percent; and the indirect business tax fraction will have remained constant at 8.1 percent. These three sources of revenue would then raise 19.1 percent of GNP, or $660 billion, leaving a deficit of $541 billion to be financed either by the remaining revenue source—personal taxes—or by government borrowing. At the same proportion of GNP as in 1980 (82 percent), we estimate personal income in 1984 as $2,834 billion. Thus to balance the 1984 total government budget, personal taxes would have to be imposed at an average rate of 541/2,834 = 19.1 percent.

Now let us consider the changes in government spending and revenues that we project for 1986, after two years of implementation of the Economic Bill of Rights.

Our EBR would result in the following reductions in expenditure by 1986, as compared with 1984. First, as we noted earlier, military spending would be reduced by $115 billion. The elimination of U.S. foreign military aid would save another $3 billion. Cutting subsidies to the nuclear power industry would save the taxpayer at least $1 billion. Additionally, increased job opportunities and the declining need for unemployment insurance, food stamps, AFDC, and general assistance payments would allow for considerable savings. These payments totalled $38 billion in 1980 (in 1980 prices). Assuming that increased need in 1984 will be balanced by the current administration's policy of reduced provision for the needy, so that the same fraction of GNP is devoted to them, these payments will amount to roughly $50 million in 1984 (in 1984 prices). Taking into account the elimination of all AFDC payments—to be replaced by single-parent-home child payments as costed below—and a 50 percent reduction in the other payments—attributable to the overall improvement in economic conditions, and roughly proportionate to the reduction in the unemployment rate—we project an overall saving by 1986 of $34 billion from these sources. Adding all of the savings together, we arrive at an overall reduction in existing government programs of $153 billion.

But, of course, the new programs of the EBR would also lead to significant increases in government spending from 1984 to 1986. If one half of the projected increase in employment took the form of public

—federal, state, and local—employment, with people working in child-care centers, on conservation projects, as teachers' aides, on infrastructural maintenance, and so on, about 5 million new jobs would be financed from public revenues. (This public employment would make possible, among other benefits, immediate funding of our publicly supported child-care program as proposed in Chapter 12.) At an average yearly salary of $20,000, this would come to a salary bill of $100 billion, with likely additional materials costs of $20 billion. Investment subsidies at all levels might amount to as much as half of the additional investment required by the program ($145 billion, as estimated above); hence we must budget $73 billion for such subsidies.

In 1980, there were 5.8 million single-parent householders with children under 18 years; 3.8 million received AFDC payments. Assuming increases in proportion with the growth of the labor force, we project these figures to 6.3 million and 4.1 million in 1984. How many people would we expect to claim single-parent-home child-care payments under the EBR by 1986? Given the availability of high-quality child care and the increase in job opportunities under the EBR, we might expect many to be attracted into the paid labor force. A reduction below the current numbers of AFDC recipients is quite possible. To be on the safe side, however, we estimate that a number of people equal to all those receiving AFDC payments in 1984, plus one half of the remaining single-parent householders, would choose to receive home child-care payments. This yields an estimate of roughly 5 million recipients. At an average rate of payment of roughly $12,000 (weighted for family size), the total cost of the program would come to $60 billion.

By eliminating all higher education tuition fees at public institutions, the EBR would require increased public expenditure in 1986 both to compensate for tuition receipts foregone from students already enrolled and to cover the *full* costs of educating additional students attracted by the elimination of tuition fees. Extrapolating from the $4.4 billion (in 1979 prices) tuition paid to public institutions in 1979, we estimate that replacing foregone tuition in 1986 would cost roughly $7 billion. Assuming that the elimination of tuition fees attracts an additional two million full-time equivalent students to public higher education (including transfers from private institutions), and estimating the full cost per student at roughly $5,000, we budget an additional total of $10 billion for higher education.

Other smaller expenditure items implied by the EBR would include: education, training, and related costs of promoting workplace democracy ($1 billion); the costs of the public needs inventory ($0.3

billion); expansion of energy research and development in renewable energy sources ($2 billion); and consumer information and food marketing assistance ($0.7 billion). Adding all of these increased expenditures together, we reach an overall increase in government spending of $284 billion.

We can now project the level of total government expenditure in 1986 implied by our EBR. Beginning with a 1984 benchmark government expenditure level of $1,201 billion, we saved $153 billion in spending reductions and budgeted $284 billion in spending increases. With a net increase of $131 billion over 1984, total government expenditure in 1986 would be $1,332 billion. This figure represents 33.6 percent of the projected GNP of $3,969 billion in 1986—a decline of 1.2 percent from the estimated government share of 34.8 percent in 1984. The increase in government spending from 1984 to 1986 ($131 billion) is roughly 25 percent of the increase in overall GNP ($513 billion). The analogous figure for 1980–82, by contrast, was 40 percent.

It remains for us to examine the tax implications of the EBR. How would the $1,332 billion of government spending be financed in 1986? We assume, as before, that contributions to social insurance would rise to 9.4 percent of the GNP, and indirect business taxes would remain at 8.1 percent; thus government revenues from those sources would amount to 17.5 percent of the 1986 GNP—or $695 billion— leaving another $637 billion to be financed. The corporate profits tax, according to our proposals, would have been eliminated and replaced by a personal income tax *sur*charge on property income at the same rate as the standard rate of taxation on wage-and-salary income. Personal income and property income, at the same proportions of 82 percent and 17.8 percent of GNP as in 1980, would amount in 1986 to $3,255 billion and $706 billion, respectively, yielding a taxable income base of $3,961 billion to which the standard tax rate would apply. Thus to balance the 1986 government budget, the standard tax rate would have to be $637/3,961 = 16.1$ percent. This rate is roughly 3 percent lower than the average tax rate required to balance the budget in 1984 (19.1 percent).

To be sure, under the EBR property income would in effect be taxed at twice the standard 1986 rate, or 32.2 percent. But this burden would fall heavily only on the wealthy, and it would be offset to a substantial extent by the elimination of corporate profits taxes. (At 1.6 percent of the GNP, as in 1984, corporate taxes would have amounted to $64 billion in 1986; the property income tax surcharge under the EBR comes to 16.1 percent of $706 billion, or $113 billion.)

Had contributions to social insurance already been incorporated into our proposed Comprehensive Income Tax, the comparison with the benchmark 1984 tax rate of 19.1 percent would be unaffected, since the assumed size of social insurance contributions is proportionately the same in both cases. (The incidence of the Comprehensive Income Tax, however, would be more progressive than the incidence of the combination of taxes in the benchmark comparison.)

We note, additionally, that we have derived tax rates from the assumption of an overall balanced government budget only for the purposes of comparison. Whether or not the budget should be balanced in 1984 or 1986 is an open question, to be answered on the basis of the macroeconomic conditions obtaining at the time. Under any comparable degree of deficit in 1984 and 1986, our conclusion holds that the EBR would allow a reduction in the rate of taxation.

These estimates of the short-term benefits and costs of the Economic Bill of Rights, however favorable, may understate the ultimate benefits of the program. We argued in Chapter 7 that substantial waste in the U.S. economy results from authoritarian and bureaucratic production relations—amounting conservatively to 18.8 percent of useful GNP in 1980. The first two years of implementation of the EBR would not yet begin to reduce this waste burden, but in subsequent years the program would clearly begin to tap those wasted resources. The additional benefits—from both greater productive allocation of labor and rising work intensity—would result from institutional restructuring and not from additional government expenditures; they would constitute net benefits as well as gross benefits.

Similarly, we do not claim in the first two years of the EBR the added benefits from eliminating wasteful production of relatively useless output (except for military spending). These benefits would also not require additional government expenditures beyond those administrative expenditures for government planning which we have already included in the budgets discussed above.

Viewed over the longer term, in sum, the net macroeconomic benefits of the EBR would most likely be greater—and its costs more affordable—than suggested by our estimates for its first two years. And even the first two years, by our illustrative calculations in this Appendix, are clearly worth the effort.

NOTES

Because of their frequent use, we use a simplified reference for the following sources:

U.S. Bureau of the Census, *Historical Statistics of the United States, Colonial Times to 1970* (Washington, D.C.: U.S. Government Printing Office, 1976), 2 vols.; referred to as *Historical Statistics*.

President's Council of Economic Advisers, *Economic Report of the President* (Washington, D.C.: U.S. Government Printing Office, various years); referred to as *Economic Report*.

U.S. Department of Commerce, Bureau of Economic Analysis, *The National Income and Product Accounts of the United States, 1929–1976* (Washington, D.C.: U.S. Government Printing Office, September 1981), and "Revised Estimates of the National Income and Product Accounts," *Survey of Current Business*, July 1982; referred to as *National Income and Product Accounts (NIPA)*.

U.S. Bureau of the Census, *Statistical Abstract of the United States* (Washington, D.C.: U.S. Government Printing Office, various years); referred to as *Statistical Abstract*.

U.S. Department of Labor, *Employment and Training Report of the President* (Washington, D.C.: U.S. Government Printing Office, various years); referred to as *Employment and Training Report*.

U.S. Bureau of Labor Statistics, *Handbook of Labor Statistics* (Washington, D.C.: U.S. Government Printing Office, various years); referred to as *Handbook of Labor Statistics*.

Organization of Economic Cooperation and Development, *National Accounts* (Paris: OECD, various years); referred to as OECD, *National Accounts*.

1: The Slack Economy and the Zero-Sum Illusion

1. From text of Reagan speech, New York *Times*, February 19, 1981, p. B8.

2. Garth, Friedman, Morris, Inc., "America's Economic Challenge— Public Expectations," poll commissioned for and distributed by the New York Stock Exchange, 1981, questions 2–5, 7.

3. Mid-1982 poll results reported by Mark J. Penn and Douglas E. Schoen, "What Democrats Should Do," New York *Times,* August 12, 1982, p. A27. November 1982 poll quotes and quote from Celeste campaign from New York *Times,* November 3, 1982, pp. A1, A21.

4. Lester Thurow's important book *The Zero Sum Society* (New York: Basic Books, 1980) develops the zero-sum argument. But, unlike most adherents of the zero-sum logic, Thurow does not support a redistribution of income toward corporations and the rich.

5. Peter G. Peterson, "No More Free Lunch for the Middle Class," New York *Times Magazine,* January 17, 1982, pp. 40, 41.

6. Daniel Bell, "Models and Reality in Economic Discourse," in D. Bell and I. Kristol, eds., *The Crisis in Economic Theory* (New York: Basic Books, 1981), p. 48.

7. Edward F. Denison, *Accounting for Slower Economic Growth* (Washington, D.C.: The Brookings Institution, 1979), p. 4.

8. For an analysis of the coal example which supports and documents this interpretation, see M. Connerton, R. B. Freeman, and J. L. Medoff, "Productivity and Industrial Relations: The Case of U.S. Bituminous Coal," unpublished paper, Harvard University, December 1979. Our capital-stock figures are from the U.S. Bureau of Labor Statistics.

9. Peter F. Drucker, "Toward the Next Economics," in D. Bell and I. Kristol, eds., *The Crisis in Economic Theory,* p. 11.

10. *Statistical Abstract,* 1981, pp. 790–91, 818.

11. Franklin Fisher, Zvi Griliches, and Carl Kaysen, "The Costs of Automobile Model Changes Since 1949," *Journal of Political Economy,* October 1962.

12. Mark Dowie, "Pinto Madness," *Mother Jones,* September–October 1977.

13. *Historical Statistics,* p. 225.

2: The Arithmetic of Economic Decline

1. Quoted in New York *Post,* January 23, 1978, p. 29.
2. Quoted in *Business Week,* January 15, 1978, p. 64.

3. Quoted in William Bowen, "The Decade Ahead: Not So Bad If We Do Things Right," *Fortune*, October 8, 1979, p. 88.

4. The levels in Figure 2.1 for 1982 are based on estimates from data available in *Survey of Current Business*, November 1982. The inflation figure is based on the rate of increase from the 1981 Consumer Price Index to the average CPI for the months from April through September 1982. The unemployment figure is the average unemployment rate for the months from April through September 1982.

5. Data on 1981 unemployment during the year are from U.S. Bureau of Labor Statistics, "One in Five Persons in Labor Force Experienced Some Unemployment in 1981," USDL 82-255, July 20, 1982.

6. See Institute for Labor Education and Research, *What's Wrong with the U.S. Economy?* (Boston: South End Press, 1982), p. xi and notes, for analysis of the income sources of the bottom 90 percent of U.S. households in 1980. Underlying data are from Internal Revenue Service, *Statistics of Income, Individual Income Tax Returns*.

7. The Bureau of Labor Statistics has traditionally provided a standard statistical series on "real spendable *weekly* earnings." This series was discontinued in December 1981 because it was judged that the average workweek had changed substantially over time (with shifts among part-time and full-time workers) and that the calculations made in the series for taxes were unrealistic. We have been sympathetic with some of these criticisms but also felt that it was essential to be able to provide a continuous statistical series on the purchasing power of the take-home pay of production workers. This has led us to develop our alternative series on real spendable hourly earnings, which is free of the two problems in the weekly earnings series. See the technical paper cited in the source note for Figure 2.2a.

8. Based on *Employment and Training Report*, 1981, p. 213.

9. Some might argue that a series on hours should use adults of working age in the denominator, not total population. We would argue theoretically that our measure is the correct one, since the working responsibilities of employees in the economy as a whole are to provide output for the economy as a whole, not just themselves. If more people within a household must work in order to sustain household living standards, then the welfare of that household has probably declined. For our measure of aggregate hours for 1980–81, see Appendix A, note 2.

10. *Economic Report,* 1982, B-28, B-31.

11. *Business Week,* January 28, 1980, p. 73. Following quote from Rapping is from the same source.

12. Unlike the earnings data in Figure 2.2, which are for *production* workers in the nonagricultural private sector, the hourly income data in Figure 2.3 are based on the hours of *all* people at work (except unpaid family labor).

13. Hourly income—defined as real net national income per hour of work—is very closely related to productivity—defined as real net domestic output per hour of work. The only differences involve three technical distinctions:

    (1) Real net national *income* is the nominal value of net national income/product divided by a *purchased*-output price index, while real *output* is the same nominal value of net national income/product divided by a *produced*-output price index;

    (2) *National* income includes income received by U.S. nationals from their activities abroad (e.g., foreign investment) and excludes income received by foreigners from their activities within the United States; domestic output includes output produced by foreigners in the United States but excludes output produced by U.S. nationals abroad; and

    (3) The denominator in hourly income is hours of work by U.S. nationals anywhere, while the denominator in productivity is hours of work by all people within the United States.

    Distinction 1 is explained more thoroughly in Appendix A.

14. These productivity-growth rates were calculated from annual data tabulated in *Economic Report,* 1982, Table B-40. Note that the productivity figures apply to persons at work in the private business sector, while the hourly-income figures cited earlier apply to the whole U.S. national economy; the difference is accounted for primarily by the government sector.

15. Some scholars question the use of the kind of productivity data presented in Figure 2.4, which are compiled by the U.S. Department of Commerce largely on the basis of information collected by the Bureau of Labor Statistics. It is argued that (1) the index of manufacturing productivity compiled by the Federal Reserve Board (FRB) is more reliable because it is based more fully and directly on physical measures of output growth, as opposed to dollar measures deflated by estimated price indexes, and (2) the measure of hours (in the denominator of productivity estimates) should reflect hours worked by production workers only—not supervisory and other nonproductive personnel. But even if we use

the FRB index of real manufacturing output, and divide it by hours of production workers in manufacturing to arrive at an alternative manufacturing productivity index, we find that productivity growth still shows a definite pattern of slowdown: from 4.3 percent in 1948–66 to 4.1 percent in 1966–73 to 2.8 percent in 1973–79 (as compared with the Department of Commerce figures of 2.9 percent, 3.3 percent, and 1.5 percent). Because FRB data are available only for the manufacturing sector, we could not make use of their series for our analysis of overall productivity growth in Chapter 6. But we have made a point of analyzing productivity in terms of real output per hour of production workers rather than all workers; see Chapter 6 and note 20 to Chapter 6.

16. See Figure 4.7 for evidence on the behavior of the after-tax profit rate in the U.S. nonfinancial corporate sector from 1948 to 1981.

17. OECD, *National Accounts, 1950–1980,* Vol. I (Paris: OECD, 1982).

18. OECD, *National Accounts,* Vol. I (1982), p. 88. The comparisons are in current prices at current international exchange rates.

3: Beyond Scapegoats

1. Quoted in New York *Times,* March 14, 1980, p. D2.
2. The Business Week Team, *The Reindustrialization of America* (New York: McGraw-Hill, 1982), pp. 9–10.
3. U.S. Department of Energy, *Historical Review of Domestic Oil and Gas Exploratory Activity* (Washington, D.C.: U.S. Government Printing Office), October 1979.
4. *Economic Report,* 1980, p. 35.
5. William D. Nordhaus, "Oil and Economic Performance in Industrial Countries," *Brookings Papers on Economic Activity,* 1980, No. 2, p. 375.
6. Congressional Budget Office, "The Effect of OPEC Oil Pricing on Output, Prices and Exchange Rates in the United States and Other Industrialized Countries," 1981.
7. J. R. Norsworthy, Michael J. Harper, and Kent J. Kunze, "The Slowdown in Productivity Growth: Analysis of Some Contributing Factors," *Brookings Papers on Economic Activity,* 1979, No. 2, p. 412.
8. Ernst Berndt, "Energy Price Increases and the Productivity Slowdown in United States Manufacturing," in *The Decline in Produc-*

tivity Growth (Boston: Federal Reserve Bank of Boston, June 1980), p. 86.

9. William E. Simon, *A Time for Action* (New York: McGraw-Hill, 1980), pp. 22–23.

10. The sources of the Sweden-U.S. comparison are: M. Sawyer, "Income Distribution in OECD Countries," *OECD Economic Outlook,* July 1976, p. 19; *Statistical Abstract,* 1980, pp. 902, 903, 906, 912; and Ira C. Magaziner and Robert B. Reich, *Minding America's Business* (New York: Harcourt Brace Jovanovich, 1982), p. 21.

11. OECD, *National Accounts,* Vol. I, p. 88. The comparison is in prices at exchange rates in 1980.

12. U.S. Bureau of Labor Statistics, "Output Per Hour, Hourly Compensation, and Unit Labor Costs in Manufacturing, Eleven Countries, 1950–1980," unpublished data, June 1982, Table 6.

13. *Ibid.,* Table 1.

14. *Economic Report,* 1982, B-21. The average effective corporate-tax rate is calculated simply as the total corporate-profit-tax payments divided by the total pretax corporate profits (without inventory evaluation and capital consumption adjustment).

15. *Economic Report,* 1981, B-26. (Based on calendar-year data.)

16. Office of Economic Policy, Planning and Research of the State of California, "International Economic Performance and Comparative Tax Structure," unpublished report, January 20, 1981.

17. Our measure of the personal-tax rate is the ratio of personal income taxes to gross income for a worker with the average production worker's wages whose spouse earns 66 percent of the average production worker earnings and who has no dependents in the year 1978. Data on this measure are from OECD, *The Tax Benefit Position of Families at Selected Income Levels* (Paris: OECD, 1980). Among the advanced capitalist countries (those with 1980 per capita gross domestic products greater than $4,500), the countries with higher tax rates than the United States averaged a growth rate of per capita gross domestic product from 1970 to 1980 of 2.6 percent annually, compared to 2 for the U.S. and 2.37 for those countries with lower tax rates than the United States. The high-tax countries average more than twice the U.S. rate of growth of output per worker-hour in manufacturing (5.24 percent annually compared to 2.5 percent) and also grew faster than the low-tax-country average (4.4 percent annually). The gross domestic product data are from OECD, *National Accounts;* the data on manufacturing output per hour are from U.S. Bureau

of Labor Statistics "Output Per Hour, Hourly Compensation, and Unit Labor Costs in Manufacturing."

18. For a useful summary of the literature and arguments, see Mark Green and Norman Waitzman, *Business War on the Law: The Benefits of Health/Safety Enforcement* (Washington, D.C.: Corporate Accountability Research Group, 1980).

19. See testimony of Barry Bosworth, director, Council on Wage and Price Stability, before Senate Subcommittee on Banking, Finance, and Urban Affairs, June 21, 1978, based in part on Robert W. Crandall, "Federal Government Initiatives to Reduce the Price Level," *Brookings Papers on Economic Activity*, 1978, No. 12, Table 12; and Data Resources, Inc., "The Macroeconomic Impact of Federal Pollution Control Programs: 1978 Assessment," unpublished report, January 11, 1979.

20. *Statistical Abstract*, 1981, p. 79.

21. Based on OECD, *National Accounts*, and unpublished OECD data.

22. Comparison of workers' rights is based on information reported in Magaziner and Reich, *Minding America's Business*, p. 144.

23. U.S. Bureau of Labor Statistics, "Output Per Hour, Hourly Compensation, and Unit Labor Costs," Table 10. Unit labor costs grew at an average annual rate of 3.7 percent in the U.S. over these years. Measured in U.S. dollars at the going exchange rates, unit labor costs in Japan rose at an average annual rate of 6.6 percent. The analogous rate for Germany was 8.6 percent; for Italy, 7.4 percent. The relatively slow growth of U.S. unit labor costs manifests itself whether other countries' figures are measured in the national currency or converted to dollars at the going exchange rate. The latter is the measure of relevance for discussions of U.S. international competitiveness.

24. To estimate annual rates of change of the share of production-worker compensation in total income generated in the nonfarm-business sector, we calculated indexes for 1948, 1966, 1973, and 1979 as follows. First, we divided the value of the index of nonfarm-business unit labor cost by the index of the nonfarm-business implicit price deflator (both from *Economic Report*, 1982, Table B-40) to obtain an index of the share of total-worker compensation in nonfarm-business income. Then we multiplied the resulting index by the ratio of production-worker compensation to total-worker compensation in the nonfarm-business sector, as estimated by David M. Gordon and reported in "A Statistical Series on Production Worker Compensation," Technical

Note No. 3, Economics Institute of the Center for Democratic Alternatives, 1982. The total-worker and the production-worker compensation shares showed similar time trends over the postwar period.

25. According to data presented in *Economic Report*, 1982, Table B-2, real personal consumption expenditure increased by 39 percent from 1970 to 1980, while real gross private domestic investment increased by only 28 percent and real government purchases by only 15 percent over the same period. The corresponding increases for the period between the business cycle peak years of 1966 and 1979 were 59 percent, 43 percent and 23 percent.

26. William G. Shepherd, "Causes of Increased Competition in the U.S. Economy, 1939–1980," *Review of Economics and Statistics*, November 1982.

27. *Statistical Abstract*, 1980, p. 568.

28. Leslie Ellen Nulty, *Understanding the New Inflation: The Importance of the Basic Necessities* (Washington, D.C.: Exploratory Project for Economic Alternatives, 1977).

29. *Business Week*, October 12, 1974.

30. Herbert Stein, "The Never-Never Land of Pain-Free Solutions," *Fortune*, December 31, 1979, p. 74.

31. C. Jackson Grayson, "Emphasizing Capital Investment Is a Mistake," *Wall Street Journal*, October 11, 1982. Emphasis in the original.

32. The Federal Reserve Board's index of capacity utilization in manufacturing averaged 81.4 percent from 1974 to 1979, as compared with 83.3 percent for 1948–66 and 84.1 percent for 1967–73 (percentages calculated from data in *Economic Report*, 1982, Table B-45). Estimates of the ratio of actual to potential GNP, from the Bureau of Economic Analysis, show a similar pattern.

33. See Peter K. Clark, "Investment in the 1970s: Theory, Performance and Prediction," *Brookings Papers on Economic Activity*, 1979, No. 1; we are grateful to Dr. Clark for providing us with unpublished figures on the rental price of capital services, as described in his Appendix B. We have estimated the figure for 1979 based on trends from 1976 to 1978.

34. See Frederic S. Mishkin, "The Real Interest Rate: An Empirical Investigation," National Bureau of Economic Research, Working Paper No. 622, January 1981, especially Figure A-1. The figures referred to in the text are Mishkin's estimated *ex ante* real interest rates (i.e., the rates based on actual interest rates adjusted by the expected rate of inflation).

35. Barry Bluestone and Bennett Harrison, *The Deindustrialization of America* (New York: Basic Books, 1982), p. 158.

36. It is notoriously difficult to estimate the size of the Eurodollar market, and we have not made an independent effort to do so. The text figure reflects recent estimates by Morgan Guaranty, reported in the New York *Times,* November 8, 1982, p. D1.

37. Capacity utilization and unemployment figures are from *Economic Report,* 1982, B-45, B-30. Estimates of potential output using a 4 percent unemployment rate are from *Economic Report,* 1979, p. 75, extrapolating the 1979 figure from the 1973–78 rate of growth. Net domestic investment figures are from *National Income and Product Accounts,* Table 5.3.

38. William D. Nordhaus, "Policy Responses to the Productivity Slowdown," in *The Decline in Productivity Growth* (Boston: Federal Reserve Bank of Boston, June 1980).

39. William Brainard and George Perry, "Editors' Summary," *Brookings Papers on Economic Activity,* 1981, No. 1, pp. vii–viii.

4: The Rise and Demise of the Postwar Corporate System

1. Samuel P. Huntington *et al., The Crisis of Democracy: Report on the Governability of Democracies to the Trilateral Commission* (New York: New York University Press, 1975), p. 98.

2. *Business Week,* March 12, 1979, p. 36.

3. Quoted in William Appleman Williams, *Americans in a Changing World* (New York: Harper & Row, 1978), p. 339.

4. Quoted in Alan Wolfe, *The Limits of Legitimacy: Political Contradictions of Contemporary Capitalism* (New York: The Free Press, 1977), p. 176.

5. Robert L. Heilbroner, "Does Capitalism Have a Future?," New York *Times Magazine,* August 15, 1982, p. 44.

6. Quoted in Alan Wolfe, *America's Impasse* (New York: Pantheon, 1981), p. 146.

7. Wolfe, *America's Impasse,* p. 147.

8. Richard N. Gardner, *Sterling-Dollar Diplomacy in Current Perspective* (New York: Columbia University Press, 1980), rev. ed., pp. 134, 259.

9. Our account is based on Kermit Roosevelt, *Countercoup: The Struggle for the Control of Iran* (New York: McGraw-Hill, 1979). The quotes are from pp. 2 and ix.

10. This account is from Steven Schlesinger and Stephen Kinzer, *Bitter Fruit* (Garden City, N.Y.: Doubleday, 1982). The quote below is from p. 29. The quote at the end of the vignette is from New York *Times,* June 27, 1982, p. 1.

11. *Historical Statistics,* pp. 868–69.

12. Although there is no single price index reflecting the cost of imported raw materials, the trend in their cost relative to domestic finished goods can be inferred from two available series: (1) the price of imports relative to gross domestic product (GDP) and (2) the price of nonagricultural crude materials relative to GDP. Series (1) declined from 1.28 in 1948 to 1.03 in 1966 and then increased to 1.51 in 1979 (calculated from data in *Economic Report,* 1982, Table B-3); series 2 fell from 1.38 in 1948 to 1.08 in 1966 and rose to 1.78 in 1979 (see Figure 6.4 for a time series graph with data sources).

13. *Economic Report,* 1982, Table B-3.

14. Barry Bluestone and Bennett Harrison, *The Deindustrialization of America* (New York: Basic Books, 1982), p. 132.

15. *Economic Report,* 1982, B-1, B-15; *Historical Statistics,* pp. 1114, 229.

16. Quoted in Wolfe, *The Limits of Legitimacy,* p. 214.

17. Quoted in Jeremy Brecher, *Strike!* (San Francisco: Straight Arrow Books, 1972), p. 228.

18. *Proceedings of the Forty Second Consecutive Constitutional Convention of the United Mine Workers of America,* 1956, Vol. 1, p. 309.

19. Richard Lester, *As Unions Mature* (Princeton, N.J.: Princeton University Press, 1958), p. 102.

20. Strike information from U.S. Bureau of Labor Statistics, "Collective Bargaining in the Bituminous Coal Industry," Report No. 625, December 1980, Table 4; Hill quote from M. Connerton, R. B. Freeman, and J. L. Medoff, "Productivity and Industrial Relations: The Case of U.S. Bituminous Coal," unpublished paper, Harvard University, 1979, p. 54.

21. Connerton, Freeman, and Medoff, p. 1.

22. Account of tobacco workers' union from Bob Korstad, "Those Who Were Not Afraid: Winston-Salem, 1943," in Marc S. Miller, ed., *Working Lives* (New York: Pantheon, 1980).

23. Korstad, pp. 198–99.

24. Claude Brown, *Manchild in the Promised Land* (New York: Macmillan, 1965), p. 8.

25. See Jerry Cohen and William S. Murphy, *Burn, Baby, Burn!* (New York: Dutton, 1966).

426   NOTES

26. Cohen and Murphy, pp. 45, 47.
27. *Handbook of Labor Statistics,* 1978, pp. 323, 175; and *Historical Statistics,* p. 182.
28. *Historical Statistics,* 1978, pp. 508–9.
29. Quoted in William Serrin, *The Company and the Union* (New York: Vintage, 1974), p. 170.
30. *Employment and Training Report,* 1981, p. 212; and data for production and nonproduction workers' share of total employee compensation developed by David M. Gordon, based on *Employment and Training Report* and *Economic Report,* 1981, p. 247, and reported in "A Statistical Series on Production Worker Compensation," Technical Note No. 3, Economics Institute of the Center for Democratic Alternatives, 1982. Not all of the employees designated by official data as "non-production" or "supervisory" personnel are exclusively managers or supervisors, but by far the largest proportion are. In 1980, for example, there were 13.892 million "supervisory" workers on private nonfarm payrolls. In the same year, according to detailed occupational data, there were approximately 11.5 million managers, clerical supervisors, and blue-collar worker supervisors in the private sector. (This is an approximate estimate because detailed data on government supervisory personnel were not available from the census; the number reported here reflects an approximate deduction from the total number of managers and supervisors for those in government, assuming that equal proportions worked in those categories in both the public and private sectors.) All the rest of the 13.9 million certainly have supervisory responsibilities, since it appears that at least 8 million or so employees who are not managers or supervisors *also* supervise other employees. For data, see *Employment and Training Report,* 1981, pp. 152–53, 212; and Institute for Labor Education and Research, *What's Wrong with the U.S. Economy?* (Boston: South End Press, 1982), p. 220.
31. See David M. Gordon, Richard Edwards, and Michael Reich, *Segmented Work, Divided Workers: The Historical Transformation of Labor in the United States* (New York: Cambridge University Press, 1982), Chapter 5; and Peter Henle, "Exploring the Distribution of Income," *Monthly Labor Review,* December 1972.
32. This account of the rise and demise of nuclear power is based primarily on the doctoral research of Stephen Cohn, unpublished doctoral dissertation, University of Massachusetts at Amherst, 1983.
33. See John G. Fuller, *We Almost Lost Detroit* (New York: Reader's Digest Press, 1975).

34. Based on data in Jeffrey Sachs, "The Changing Cyclical Behavior of Wages and Prices," *American Economic Review,* March 1980, Table 2.

35. Frances Fox Piven and Richard A. Cloward, *The New Class War: Reagan's Attack on the Welfare State and Its Consequences* (New York: Pantheon, 1982), p. ix.

36. The shares of U.S. exports in the exports of the advanced nations are calculated from OECD, *National Accounts* using current exchange rates (from the same source). The industry data are from *Business Week,* June 30, 1980, p. 60, based on Commerce Department data.

37. Wolfe, *America's Impasse,* pp. 22–23 and passim.

38. Gordon, Edwards, and Reich, *Segmented Work, Divided Workers,* Figure 5.1A.

39. Gordon, Edwards, and Reich, *Segmented Work, Divided Workers,* Table 5.6.

40. *Handbook of Labor Statistics,* p. 412.

41. As the authors of the Report of a Special Task Force to the Secretary of Health, Education, and Welfare, *Work in America* (Cambridge, Mass.: M.I.T. Press, 1972), concluded: "It may be argued that the very success of industry and organized labor in meeting the basic needs of workers has unintentionally spurred demands for esteemable and fulfilling jobs" (p. 12).

42. The detailed sources and methods of estimating the cost of losing your job are presented in Juliet B. Schor and Samuel Bowles, "The Social Wage and the Labor Process: Measuring Some Influences on Worker Resistance," unpublished paper, Williams College, July 1982.

43. Michele I. Naples and David M. Gordon, "The Industrial Accident Rate: Creating a Consistent Time Series," Institute for Labor Education and Research, December 1981. See also David M. Gordon and Michele I. Naples, "More Injuries on the Job," New York *Times,* December 13, 1981.

44. *Historical Statistics,* p. 607.

45. The rising relative cost of nonagricultural crude materials after the mid-1960s is documented in Figure 6.4. The relative cost of agricultural crude materials also rose from the mid-1960s on, after falling sharply during the previous two decades, according to the annual data on price indexes for "foodstuffs and feedstuff" and "total finished goods" tabulated in *Economic Report,* 1982, Table B-57.

46. *Statistical Abstract,* 1980, p. 616; *Historical Statistics,* p. 827; and

Edison Electric Institute, *Statistical Bulletin* (Washington, D.C.), various years.

47. *Statistical Abstract*, 1980, p. 604.

48. *Statistical Abstract*, 1980, p. 770; and *Historical Statistics*, p. 949.

49. *Statistical Abstract*, 1980, p. 761.

50. Tobin's Q is defined as the ratio of the stock-market value to the current net replacement cost of capital assets (plant, equipment, and inventories); for the U.S. economy, data on Tobin's Q are usually compiled for the aggregate nonfinancial corporate business sector (see *Economic Report*, 1982, Table B-88). Tobin's Q measures roughly how much one would have to pay to *purchase* the average corporation on the stock market, relative to how much it would cost to *build* the firm anew. This is a good indicator of profit expectations, because the more investors are willing to pay to acquire a company (relative to the supply cost of its capital assets), the more optimistic they must be about their ability to use the company's assets to turn a profit in the years ahead.

5: The Missed Recession, the Great Repression, and Spiraling Stagflation

1. Leonard Silk, "The Great Repression," New York *Times*, March 14, 1982, p. D1.

2. *Economic Report*, 1982, B-2.

3. Annual data on (adjusted) corporate profits, corporate-profit-tax liability, and overall GNP (tabulated in *Economic Report*, 1982, Tables B-21 and B-1) enable one to compute the amount of taxes the U.S. federal government would have collected from corporations had the effective tax rate of 1959 been in effect in 1966; this amount exceeded actual corporate taxes collected in 1966 by $6.8 billion, or roughly 1 percent of the 1966 GNP level of $756 billion.

4. *Statistical Abstract*, 1980, p. 366.

5. *Historical Statistics*, p. 340; and *Statistical Abstract*, 1980, p. 329.

6. This measure is preferable to the *actual* budget deficit because the peaks and troughs of the ordinary business cycle have huge effects on the size of the government deficit; one can better track discretionary fiscal decision-making if one controls for such business-cycle effects. For a thorough discussion of the concept of the high-employment budget deficit and the methodology used to estimate

it, see Frank de Leeuw et al., "The High-Employment Budget: New Estimates, 1955–80," *Survey of Current Business,* November 1980.

7. Frank de Leeuw and Thomas M. Holloway, "The High Employment Budget: Revised Estimates and Automatic Inflation Effects," *Survey of Current Business,* April 1982, pp. 21–33.

8. Based on the M-2 definition of the money supply, *Economic Report,* 1982, Table B-61.

9. *Economic Report,* 1982, B-34.

10. The figures on the growth of productivity, unit labor costs, and prices in this and the following paragraph were calculated from data tabulated in *Economic Report,* 1982, Table B-40.

11. *Economic Report,* 1982, B-82. We calculate the effective corporate-profit-tax rate as the total corporate-profit-tax liability divided by pretax corporate profits (with inventory evaluation adjustment and capital consumption adjustment).

12. Quoted in Jeremy Brecher, *Strike!* (San Francisco: Straight Arrow Books, 1972), pp. 266–67.

13. De Leeuw and Holloway, "The High Employment Budget. . . ."

14. Quoted in *New York Times Magazine,* December 20, 1970, p. 50.

15. Alan Blinder, *Economic Policy and the Great Stagflation* (New York: Academic Press, 1981), pp. 143–44.

16. GM profits are from *Fortune,* "The Fortune 500," various years; the profit margin is the ratio of profits to sales.

17. Emma Rothschild, *Paradise Lost: The Decline of the Auto Industrial Age* (New York: Vintage Books, 1974), p. 111.

18. Rothschild, p. 116.

19. Rothschild, p. 121.

20. Rothschild, p. 102.

21. See Michele I. Naples, "The Structure of Industrial Relations, Labor Militance, and the Rate of Growth of Productivity," unpublished doctoral dissertation, University of Massachusetts, 1982.

22. For summaries of much of this tendency, see David M. Gordon, Richard Edwards, and Michael Reich, *Segmented Work, Divided Workers* (New York: Cambridge University Press, 1982), Chapter 5; and Barry Bluestone and Bennett Harrison, *The Deindustrialization of America* (New York: Basic Books, 1982), Chapter 6.

23. Michele I. Naples and David M. Gordon, "The Industrial Accident Rate: Creating a Consistent Time Series," Institute for Labor Education and Research, December 1981.

24. Graham Staines, "Is Worker Dissatisfaction Rising?," *Challenge,* May–June, 1979.

25. *Handbook of Labor Statistics,* 1980, p. 438.

26. *The Economist,* November 17, 1979, pp. 40, 39.

27. See Kenneth Flamm, "Explaining U.S. Multinationals in the Post-war Era," unpublished paper, University of Massachusetts, 1982; Arthur MacEwan, "Slackers, Bankers, Marketers: Multinational Firms and the Pattern of U.S. Foreign Direct Investment," mimeo, University of Massachusetts at Boston, May 1982. MacEwan's calculations are based on U.S. Commerce Department data.

28. Bluestone and Harrison, p. 178.

29. Douglas Fraser, letter of resignation from the Labor-Management Advisory Committee, July 19, 1978, circulated by United Automobile Workers Union.

30. We include estimates of the surplus in state and local budgets in this measure of government high-employment surplus, whereas we excluded them in summaries for the 1960s, because state and local governments did not begin running substantial surpluses until 1972–80. (See *Economic Report of the President,* 1981, B-75.) We assume that these surpluses were steady enough that federal fiscal planners could anticipate the expected fiscal-year surpluses and adjust their desired level of stimulus or restriction by that amount. Our measure of the effect of the OPEC price increase on aggregate demand is based on the initial transfer of purchasing power (the price rise above and beyond the rate of increase in prices of nonfood, nonfuel crude materials, multiplied by full employment oil imports), offset by the second-round expansion of export demand occasioned directly and indirectly by the rise in purchasing power in the oil-producing countries. We assume these second-round export effects distributed as follows: half in the immediately succeeding year, and a quarter each in the next two years. See also *Economic Report,* 1980, pp. 64–65, where a similar calculation is reported.

31. Quoted in Leonard Silk and David Vogel, *Ethics and Profits: The Crisis of Confidence in American Business* (New York: Simon & Schuster, 1976), p. 64.

32. De Leeuw and Holloway, "The High Employment Budget. . . ."

33. *Economic Report,* 1980, p. 51.

34. *Economic Report,* 1979, p. 145. More extended evidence on the "perverse cycle" phenomenon can be found in Samuel Bowles, "The Post-Keynesian Capital-Labor Stalemate," *Socialist Review,*

No. 65 (September 1982), pp. 45–74, and Juliet Schor, "Changes in the Cyclical Variability of Wages," unpublished doctoral dissertation, University of Massachusetts, 1982.

35. See Figure 2.2 and footnote 24 of Chapter 3.
36. This summary of trade effects is based on Robert Z. Lawrence, "Deindustrialization and U.S. International Competitiveness: Domestic and International Forces in U.S. Industrial Performance, 1970–1980," unpublished paper, The Brookings Institution, October 1982.
37. The Business Week Team, *The Reindustrialization of America* (New York: McGraw-Hill, 1982), p. 48.
38. The Korean War period of the early 1950s differed from the Vietnam War period of the late 1960s in that it involved a much more rapid buildup of the U.S. military machine, sharp tax increases, and the imposition of temporary price controls.
39. "Whip Inflation Now" was the so-called WIN policy launched with much fanfare by President Gerald Ford in the summer of 1974, following the acceleration of inflation in the preceding year. The main element of the WIN policy was a sharply restrictive federal government macropolicy that soon plunged the economy into recession.
40. Our model is based on what has been characterized as the "conflict theory of inflation"; for a more thorough treatment, see Sam Rosenberg and Thomas Weisskopf, "A Conflict Theory Approach to Inflation in the Postwar U.S. Economy," *American Economic Review*, May 1981.

6: Solving the Productivity Puzzle

1. Quoted in *Wall Street Journal*, April 12, 1982.
2. Jeffrey J. Hallett, "Productivity—From the Bottom Up," in R. Friedman and W. Schweke, eds., *Expanding the Opportunity to Produce: Revitalizing the American Economy through New Enterprise Development* (Washington, D.C.: the Corporation for Enterprise Development, 1981), p. 406.
3. William Brainard and George Perry, "Editors' Summary," *Brookings Papers on Economic Activity*, 1981, No. 1, p. vii.
4. See Harvey Leibenstein, "Allocative Efficiency vs. X-Efficiency," *American Economic Review*, June 1966, pp. 392–415.

5. C. Jackson Grayson, "Emphasizing Capital Investment Is a Mistake," *Wall Street Journal,* October 11, 1981.

6. Quoted in Emma Rothschild, *Paradise Lost: The Decline of the Auto Industrial Age* (New York: Vintage Books, 1974), p. 110.

7. Quoted in Studs Terkel, *Working* (New York: Avon Books, 1974), p. 263.

8. Recent contributions to this literature include Harry Braverman, *Labor and Monopoly Capital* (New York: Monthly Review Press, 1974); Richard Edwards, *Contested Terrain* (New York: Basic Books, 1979); and Gordon, Edwards, and Reich, *Segmented Work, Divided Workers* (New York: Cambridge University Press, 1982). More specialized treatments may be found in Stephen Marglin, "What Do Bosses Do? The Origin and Function of Hierarchy in Capitalist Production," *Review of Radical Political Economics,* summer 1974; James Devine and Michael Reich, "The Microeconomics of Conflict and Hierarchy in Capitalist Production," *Review of Radical Political Economics,* Winter 1981; Herbert Gintis, "The Nature of the Labor Exchange," *Review of Radical Political Economics,* summer 1976; and Samuel Bowles and Herbert Gintis, "Heterogeneous Labour and the Marxian Theory of Value," *Cambridge Journal of Economics,* June 1977.

9. Braverman, *Labor and Monopoly Capital,* pp. 54, 57 (emphasis in the original).

10. We did not include an index of union membership as a percentage of the labor force, in this group of indicators of the relative employer leverage over workers, because union resistance varies primarily with the policies and militancy of unions, not with the simple fact of union representation. The changes in the attitude of unionized coal miners, illustrated in our vignette in Chapter 4, provide a graphic example of the range of possible outcomes within the unionized context.

11. Ira C. Magaziner and Robert B. Reich, *Minding America's Business* (New York: Harcourt Brace Jovanovich, 1982), p. 66.

12. See, in particular, Joseph A. Schumpeter, *Business Cycles: A Theoretical, Historical, and Statistical Analysis of the Capitalist Process* (New York: McGraw-Hill, 1939), Vols. I–II.

13. "Taft Hartley," from the album *Somebody's Story,* by Charlie King. Lyrics reprinted by permission of Snakebite Records, Leverett, Massachusetts.

14. Quoted in Barry Commoner, *The Closing Circle* (New York: Knopf, 1972), p. 9.

15. William D. Nordhaus, "Policy Responses to the Productivity Slowdown," in *The Decline of Productivity Growth* (Boston: Federal Reserve Bank of Boston, June 1980).

16. Changes in educational attainment cannot help to account for any decline in hourly output growth since 1966, for average educational attainment has actually been rising more or less steadily throughout the postwar period. Thus Edward Denison and John Kendrick have both estimated that the contribution of education to output growth in the United States has gradually increased rather than decreased. On the other hand, changes in the age-sex composition of the labor force may have played some role in accounting for a slowdown in hourly output growth, for the proportion of younger and female workers in the U.S. labor force did rise from the mid-1960s to the mid-1970s. Estimates by Denison, Kendrick, and Martin Baily suggest that this effect reduced the growth of hourly output by at most .3 percent per year between 1966 and 1973, and that from 1973 to 1978 the age-sex composition changes were actually favorable rather than unfavorable for output growth. In any case we find the evidence that women workers are less productive unpersuasive; it seems to us more plausible that women workers (and younger workers as well) are employed in *low-productivity jobs*. Combining the effects of educational and demographic changes, Kendrick estimates that changes in average labor quality reduced the growth of hourly output by about .2 percent per year from 1948–66 to 1966–73 and increased it by .3 percent from 1966–73 to 1973–78. J. R. Norsworthy et al. report similar findings, except that the effects of labor quality changes were even smaller. See Edward Denison, *Accounting for Slower Economic Growth* (Washington, D.C.: The Brookings Institution, 1979); J. R. Norsworthy, M. J. Harper, and K. Kunze, "The Slowdown in Productivity Growth: Analysis of Some Contributing Factors," *Brookings Papers on Economic Activity*, 1979, No. 2; John Kendrick, "Survey of the Factors Contributing to the Decline in U.S. Productivity Growth," in *The Decline in Productivity Growth;* and Martin Baily, "Productivity and the Services of Capital and Labor," *Brookings Papers on Economic Activity*, 1981, No. 1.

17. According to estimates made by the Bureau of Economic Analysis, the ratio of actual to potential GNP averaged 1.001 from 1966 to 1973 as compared with .984 from 1948 to 1966; the ratio was 1.021 in 1966 and 1.016 in 1973.

18. Denison, pp. 123–27.

19. The quote is from Denison, p. 125. After a more thorough analysis of the issue, reported in "R&D and the Productivity Slowdown," *American Economic Review*, May 1980, Zvi Griliches asked,

"Can the slowdown in productivity growth be explained, wholly or in part, by the recent slowdown in the growth of real R&D expenditures?" and answered "probably not" (p. 343). In another study, John Kendrick estimated that "advances in knowledge" (based on accumulated R&D spending as well as other related factors) reduced the rate of growth of hourly output by as much as .3 percent per year from 1948–66 to 1966–73 and by another .3 percent from 1966–73 to 1973–78. But Kendrick's estimates are generally regarded as much too high. Thus William Nordhaus, drawing on all the available studies, attributed only a very small fraction of the slowdown in the growth of hourly output between 1948–65 and 1973–79 to R&D. (Kendrick, "Survey of the Factors . . .", and Nordhaus, "Policy Responses. . . ." For a recent study of the effects of R&D expenditures, which attributes as much as 10 percent of the 1970s decline in growth of total factor productivity to reduced investment in R&D, see Kim B. Clark and Zvi Griliches, "Productivity Growth and R and D at the Business Level: Results from the PIMS Data Base," National Bureau of Economic Research, Working Paper No. 916, June 1982.)

20. The production-worker productivity-growth figures cited here were calculated from the annual index of real output per hour of all persons in the nonfarm private-business sector (*Economic Report,* 1982, Table B-40) divided by the ratio of production workers to all workers in private nonagricultural establishments (*Employment and Training Report,* 1981, Table C-2).

21. Michele Naples' analysis of the relationship between labor militancy, industrial relations, and productivity provides strong corroboration of our emphasis on the social determinants of productivity. See her "The Structure of Industrial Relations, Labor Militance, and the Rate of Growth of Productivity," unpublished doctoral dissertation, University of Massachusetts, 1982.

22. See the sources cited in note 20 for productivity figures in this and the following paragraph.

23. We do not believe that a decline in work intensity was the only possible outcome of the erosion of the postwar corporate system. Had the decline in the cost of job loss, for example, been accompanied by the emergence of forms of workplace organization less reliant on the stick of economic insecurity and more effective in proffering the carrot of workplace commitment, no decline in work intensity need have occurred. Indeed, output per work hour might well have increased. Sweden and other Northern European

countries have experienced rapid productivity growth with systems of labor coordination and allocation which rely very little on unemployment and other market-induced economic anxieties. The productivity-retarding effects of the decline in the cost of job loss thus do not reflect human nature, or even capitalism in general. Rather, the relationship between output per work hour and the cost of job loss is an aspect of the particular system of domination which characterized the U.S. economy in the postwar era. See Samuel Bowles and Herbert Gintis, "The Welfare State and Long-Term Economic Growth: Marxian, Neoclassical and Keynesian Approaches," *American Economic Review,* Vol. 72, No. 2 (May 1982), pp. 341–45.

24. The Reagan administration's economic policy has had a contradictory impact on productivity growth. On the one hand, it has increased the cost of job loss and raised the business-failure rate: both of these developments, according to our analysis, should help boost productivity growth. On the other hand, it has reduced capacity utilization and further retarded capital formation: these developments should slow productivity growth. While the overall effect on productivity growth may eventually be positive, any resulting benefits will be greatly outweighed by the costs of an enormous underutilization of available labor hours. For a more thorough analysis of the impact of the Reagan policy, see Chapter 8.

25. C. Jackson Grayson, "Emphasizing Capital Investment Is a Mistake," *Wall Street Journal,* October 11, 1982.

7: Measuring the Costs of Corporate Power

1. From "A Roundtable: Three Views of the Recession," New York *Times,* April 4, 1982, p. E4.
2. This represents the sum, in 1980, of managers, clerical supervisors, and blue-collar supervisors (traditionally called foremen) in the census occupational tabulations. See *Employment and Training Report,* 1981, pp. 152–53.
3. Walter W. Heller, *New Dimensions of Political Economy* (New York: Norton, 1967), pp. 58, 59–60 (emphasis in the original).
4. U.S. Bureau of Labor Statistics, "Statistical Supplement to International Comparisons of Unemployment," *Bulletin* No. 1979, June 1982.

5. Quoted in Alan Wolfe, *America's Impasse* (New York: Pantheon, 1981), p. 53.

6. Quoted in *Business Week*, June 30, 1980, p. 84.

7. See Raymond A. Katzell and Daniel Yankelovich et al., *Work, Productivity, and Job Satisfaction: An Evaluation of Policy-Related Research* (New York: Harcourt Brace Jovanovich, 1975).

8. James O'Toole, *Making America Work: Productivity and Responsibility* (New York: Continuum, 1981), p. 102.

9. Karl Frieden, "Worker Ownership and Productivity," in R. Friedman and W. Schweke, eds., *Expanding the Opportunity to Produce: Revitalizing the American Economy Through New Enterprise Development* (Washington, D.C.: The Corporation for Enterprise Development, 1981), pp. 412–13.

10. Derek C. Jones and Jan Svejnar, eds., *Participatory and Self-Managed Firms: Evaluating Economic Performance* (Lexington, Mass.: Lexington Books, 1982). See also Juan Espinosa and Andrew Zimbalist, *Economic Democracy: Workers' Participation in Chilean Industry 1970–1973* (New York: Academic Press, 1978), pp. 141–75.

11. The Business Week Team, *The Reindustrialization of America* (New York: McGraw-Hill, 1982), pp. 91–92.

12. See, for example, Richard Edwards, *Contested Terrain* (New York: Basic Books, 1979); Raymond Katzell, Daniel Yankelovich et al., *Worker Productivity Experiments in the United States* (New York: New York University Press, 1977); David Jenkins, *Job Power* (Baltimore: Penguin Books, 1974); and Charles Hecksher, "Worker Participation and Management Control," *Journal of Social Reconstruction*, January–March 1980.

13. Based on Katzell and Yankelovich, *Work, Productivity, and Job Satisfaction*, pp. 114, 109–10.

14. Quoted in Emma Rothschild, *Paradise Lost: The Decline of the Auto Industrial Age* (New York: Vintage Books, 1974), p. 163.

15. Results from a poll by Peter D. Hart Research Associates, reported in Jeremy Rifkin, *Own Your Own Job* (New York: Bantam, 1975), pp. 137, 176.

16. Lester C. Thurow, "Why Productivity Falls," *Newsweek*, August 24, 1981, p. 63.

17. Survey results and quotes from Rourke (in both this and following paragraph) from Boston *Globe*, September 21, 1982, p. 63.

18. These data comparisons are from consistent international data compilations provided in International Labor Organization, *Yearbook of Labor Statistics* (Geneva: International Labor Organi-

zation), 1981, Table II-c. The category included is that of "administrative and managerial employees."

19. See summaries and studies in Jones and Svejnar, eds.

20. Steve Lohr, "Overhauling America's Business Management," New York *Times Magazine*, January 4, 1981, pp. 15, 16.

21. The Business Week Team, p. 111.

22. O'Toole, p. 186.

23. John Z. DeLorean with J. Patrick Wright, "How Moral Men Make Immoral Decisions—A Look Inside GM," in Mark Green and Robert Massie, Jr., eds., *The Big Business Reader* (New York: Pilgrim Press, 1980), p. 39.

24. See Ronald Dellums, "Defense Sense," *The Nation*, August 21–28, 1982.

25. The Boston Study Group, *The Price of Defense: A New Strategy for Military Spending* (New York: New York Times Books, 1979).

26. Study on waste through noncompetitive bidding reported in Mark Green, *Winning Back America* (New York: Bantam, 1982), p. 284. Data on procurement contracts in current defense budget from *Statistical Abstract*, 1981, p. 355.

27. *Statistical Abstract*, 1981, p. 695.

28. This argument is most clearly formulated, although primarily in case-study form, in John Helmer, *Drugs and Minority Oppression* (New York: Seabury Press, 1975).

29. According to the *Economic Report*, 1982, Table B-38, average weekly hours for production workers in private nonagricultural establishments was 35.3 in 1980.

II: The Limits of Trickle-Down Economics

1. Norman Podhoretz, "The Neo-Conservative Anguish Over Reagan's Foreign Policy," New York *Times Magazine*, May 2, 1982, p. 31.

8: Supply-Side Follies

1. William Greider, "The Budget's Bottom Line," *Rolling Stone*, June 24, 1982, pp. 9, 10.

2. See Chapter 2 notes and figures for sources. The data in this paragraph are the most recent available from the Department of Commerce and the Bureau of Labor Statistics at the time of writing. The potential GNP gap figure for the first quarter of 1981 is from Frank de Leeuw and Thomas M. Holloway, "The High Employment Budget: Revised Estimates and Automatic Inflation Effects," *Survey of Current Business,* April 1982; the corresponding figure for the fourth quarter of 1982 was calculated by extrapolating the potential GNP through 1982 at an annual growth rate of 2.9 percent, the same rate assumed by De Leeuw and Holloway for the 1979–81 period.

3. *Economic Report,* 1982, p. 109.

4. Joint Economic Committee, U.S. Congress, "Impact of the 1981 Personal Income Tax Reductions on Income Distribution," December 23, 1981, p. 2.

5. *Wall Street Journal,* January 29, 1982, p. 14.

6. *Wall Street Journal,* January 13, 1982, p. 33.

7. New York *Times,* July 18, 1982, p. D1.

8. U.S. Department of Commerce, Bureau of Economic Analysis, "Business Plans Decrease in 1983 Capital Spending," News Release 83-01, January 12, 1983.

9. We base these estimates on the behavior of the variables in our productivity equation during years which have experienced drops in aggregate output comparable to the change in the macroeconomy between 1981 and 1982.

10. Quoted in William Greider, "The Education of David Stockman," *The Atlantic,* December 1981, p. 54.

11. Quoted in New York *Times,* July 23, 1982, p. D1.

12. A more extended critique of conservative economic policy in the United States can be found in James T. Campen and Arthur MacEwan, "Crisis, Contradictions and Conservative Controversies in Contemporary U.S. Capitalism," *Review of Radical Political Economics,* Fall 1982.

13. The tax rates are for an average production worker whose spouse earns 66 percent of the average production-worker's earnings, with no children, in 1978, from Organization for Economic Cooperation and Development, *The Tax Benefit Position of Families at Selected Income Levels* (Paris: OECD, 1979). Advanced economies are those whose per capita gross domestic product (in current U.S. dollars, at current exchange rates) exceeded $4,500 in 1978. Levels and growth rates of gross domestic product are from OECD, *National Accounts.* Output per worker-hour in manufac-

turing is from Bureau of Labor Statistics, "Output Per Hour, Hourly Compensation, and Unit Labor Costs in Manufacturing, Eleven Countries, 1950–1980," unpublished data, June 1982.

14. See the review of studies and evidence in Campen and MacEwan.

15. Federal Reserve Bank of New York, *Quarterly Review*, Autumn 1980.

16. Alan Auerbach and Lawrence Summers, "The Investment Tax Credit: An Evaluation," National Bureau of Economic Research, Working Paper No. 404, November 1979.

17. Joseph A. Pechman, "Tax Policies for the 1980s," in Joseph Pechman and J. J. Simler, eds., *Economics in the Public Service* (New York: Norton, 1982), p. 152.

18. Committee on Finance, U.S. Senate, *Conference on U.S. Competitiveness: Can the U.S. Remain Competitive?* (Washington, D.C.: U.S. Government Printing Office, 1980), p. 93.

19. Committee on Finance, p. 94.

20. James Tobin, "The Reagan Economic Plan: Supply-Side, Budget and Inflation," Federal Reserve Bank of San Francisco, *Quarterly Review*, May 1981, p. 13.

21. Frank Ackerman, *Reaganomics: Rhetoric and Reality* (Boston: South End Press, 1982), p. 136.

22. James Tobin, "The Reagan Economic Plan," pp. 12–13; Don Fullerton, "On the Possibility of an Inverse Relationship Between Tax Rates and Government Revenues," National Bureau of Economic Research, Working Paper No. 467, April 1980.

23. For a review of the evidence, see Auerbach and Summers.

24. Jerry Hausman, "Income and Payroll Tax Policy and Labor Supply," National Bureau of Economic Research, Working Paper No. 610, December 1980, p. 26.

25. Quoted in Greider, pp. 46, 47.

26. Robert Buchele, "Supply Side Meets the Real World," unpublished paper, Smith College, April 1981, p. 5.

9: Monetarists or Corporatists to the Rescue?

1. Quoted in New York *Times*, October 18, 1979, p. A1.

2. The Business Week Team, *The Reindustrialization of America* (New York: McGraw-Hill, 1982), p. 185.

3. *Newsweek*, July 27, 1981.

4. Kevin Phillips, "Post-Conservative America," *New York Review of Books,* May 13, 1982, p. 27.

5. Phillips, p. 27.

6. James Tobin, "The Reagan Economic Plan: Supply-Side, Budget and Inflation," Federal Reserve Bank of San Francisco, *Quarterly Review,* May 1981, p. 9.

7. New York *Times,* September 4, 1981, p. D2.

8. As quoted in Washington *Post,* March 8, 1981, p. F1.

9. *Historical Statistics,* p. 948.

10. Phillips, "Post-Conservative America," p. 27.

11. Frances Fox Piven and Richard A. Cloward, *The New Class War: Reagan's Attack on the Welfare State and Its Consequences* (New York: Pantheon, 1982), p. 139.

12. Organization for Economic Cooperation and Development, *United Kingdom,* OECD Economic Surveys, July 1981 (Paris: OECD, 1981), p. 32.

13. For review of the British experience, see OECD, *United Kingdom,* and Willem H. Buiter and Marcus Miller, "The Thatcher Experiment: The First Two Years," *Brookings Papers on Economic Activity,* 1981, No. 2. The data reported in the text, the most recent available at the time of writing from official British data sources, have been generously supplied to us by Ian Begg of the Cambridge Economic Policy Group and represent estimates for 1982 as of early November 1982.

14. OECD, *United Kingdom,* July 1981, p. 49.

15. Quoted in *The Guardian* (U.K.), March 30, 1981, p. 1.

16. *The Economist,* April 4, 1981, p. 47.

17. Quoted in Alfred J. Watkins, "Felix Rohatyn's Biggest Deal," *Working Papers,* September–October 1981, p. 44.

18. Charles Maier, *Recasting Bourgeois Europe: Stabilization in France, Germany, and Italy in the Decade After World War I* (Princeton: Princeton University Press, 1975), p. 9.

19. This and subsequent quotes from "The Reindustrialization of America," *Business Week* (special issue), June 30, 1980.

20. Quoted in Watkins, "Felix Rohatyn's Biggest Deal," p. 47.

21. From New York *Times,* April 4, 1982, p. E4.

22. Lester C. Thurow, "How to Rescue a Drowning Economy," *New York Review of Books,* April 1, 1982, p. 4.

23. "The New Industrial Relations," *Business Week,* May 11, 1981, pp. 85, 98.

24. Quoted in Watkins, "Felix Rohatyn's Biggest Deal," p. 51.

25. Quoted in Watkins, p. 50.

26. Quoted in Watkins, p. 50.
27. Quoted in Watkins, p. 50.
28. Ezra F. Vogel, *Japan as Number One: Lessons for America* (Cambridge, Mass.: Harvard University Press, 1979), pp. 54–55.
29. Shuichi Kato, "The Japan Myth Reconsidered," *Democracy,* July 1981, p. 101 (emphasis in the original).
30. Stokes's report in New York *Times,* July 4, 1982. The figures in the paragraph above are also from Stokes's article.
31. Kathleen Molony, "'Contented' Labor: Selective Paternalism," *The Nation,* February 13, 1982, p. 184.
32. The quotes in this and the following paragraph are from Robert B. Reich, "Playing Tag with Japan," *New York Review of Books,* June 24, 1982, p. 40.
33. Chalmers Johnson, *MITI and the Japanese Miracle: The Growth of Industrial Policy,* 1925–1975 (Palo Alto, Calif.: Stanford University Press, 1982), p. 307.
34. Jon Halliday, "High-Tech Militarization: The Road to Rearmament," *The Nation,* February 13, 1982, p. 187.
35. Vogel, p. 254.

10: The World According to Business

1. James Tobin, "Supply-Side Economics: What Is It? Will It Work?," *Economic Outlook USA,* Summer 1981, p. 53.
2. Kenneth Keniston, "The Mood of Americans Today," New York *Times Book Review,* November 8, 1981, p. 44.
3. See, in particular, Peter K. Clark, "Investment in the 1970s: Theory, Performance, and Prediction," *Brookings Papers on Economic Activity,* 1979, No. 1. The as yet unpublished comparative study of investment determinants among the advanced capitalist countries done by a team of OECD economists appears to confirm the overwhelming importance of the overall rate of growth of the economy relative to the cost of capital.
4. Quoted in New York *Times,* January 31, 1982.
5. Mark Shepherd, Jr., "The U.S. Corporation within the Competitive Environment," in U.S. Senate Committee on Finance, *Conference on U.S. Competitiveness: Can the United States Remain Competitive?* (Washington, D.C.: U.S. Government Printing Office, 1980), pp. 65–66.

6. See data reported in Ira C. Magaziner and Robert B. Reich, *Minding America's Business* (New York: Harcourt Brace Jovanovich, 1982), pp. 25, 45.
7. See data reported in source note in Figure 4.2.

11: Profits Before Democracy?

1. Quoted in Howard Zinn, *A People's History of the United States* (New York: Harper Colophon Books, 1980), p. 342.
2. Quoted in William Appleman Williams, *Americans in a Changing World* (New York: Harper & Row, 1978), p. 314.
3. Kevin Phillips, "Post-Conservative America," *New York Review of Books,* May 13, 1982, p. 27.
4. For a discussion of long swings and the literature discussing them, see David M. Gordon, "Stages of Accumulation and Long Economic Cycles," in T. Hopkins and I. Wallerstein, *Processes of the World System* (Beverly Hills, Calif.: Sage, 1980); David M. Gordon, Richard Edwards, and Michael Reich, *Segmented Work, Divided Workers: The Historical Transformation of Labor in the United States* (New York: Cambridge University Press, 1982), Chapter 2; Ernest Mandel, *Long Waves of Capitalist Development* (New York: Cambridge University Press, 1980); and Kenneth Barr, "Long Waves: A Selective, Annotated Bibliography," *Review,* Spring 1979.
5. Quoted in Victor S. Clark, *History of Manufactures in the United States* (Washington, D.C.: Carnegie Institution, 1929), Vol. II, p. 175.
6. See summary of evidence in David M. Gordon, Richard Edwards, and Michael Reich, *Segmented Work, Divided Workers: The Historical Transformation of Labor in the United States* (New York: Cambridge University Press, 1982), p. 234 and accompanying note.
7. See Lawrence Goodwyn, *Democratic Promise: The Populist Movement in America* (New York: Oxford University Press, 1976); and C. Vann Woodward, *Tom Watson: Agrarian Rebel* (New York: Rinehart, 1955).
8. Quoted in Zinn, p. 283.
9. Grant McConnell, *The Decline of Agrarian Democracy* (Berke-

ley: University of California Press, 1959), pp. 5, 8–9 (emphasis in the original).

10. McConnell, p. 3.

11. For some evidence on business attitudes during this crucial period in the 1890s, see Samuel P. Hays, *The Response to Industrialism, 1885–1914* (Chicago: University of Chicago Press, 1957), Chapters 6–7; and Grant McConnell, *The Decline of Agrarian Democracy,* Chapters 1–2.

12. *Historical Statistics,* p. 1081.

13. Samuel P. Hays, *The Response to Industrialism, 1885–1914,* p. 46.

14. Ralph L. Nelson, *Merger Movements in American Industry, 1895–1956* (Princeton: Princeton University Press, 1959), p. 37.

15. Quoted in Zinn, *A People's History of the United States,* p. 290.

16. Quoted in Zinn, p. 344.

17. For detailed evidence on the swings in factors shares and the consumption-to-investment ratio, see Robert R. Keller, "Monopoly Capital and the Great Depression: Testing Baran and Sweezy's Hypothesis," *Review of Radical Political Economics,* Winter 1975, especially Tables 1, 3.

18. Studs Terkel, *Hard Times: An Oral History of the Great Depression* (New York: Pocket Books, 1970), p. 310.

19. Quoted in Alan Wolfe, *The Limits of Legitimacy: Political Contradictions of Contemporary Capitalism* (New York: The Free Press, 1977), p. 130.

20. Quoted in Williams, *Americans in a Changing World,* p. 263.

21. See William Ashworth, *A Short History of the International Economy Since 1850* (London: Longmans, Green, 1962), 2nd ed., p. 259.

22. Alan Wolfe, *America's Impasse* (New York: Pantheon, 1982), pp. 22–23.

23. Quoted in Leonard Silk and David Vogel, *Ethics and Profits: The Crisis of Confidence in American Business* (New York: Simon & Schuster, 1976), pp. 78, 189, 75.

24. Silk and Vogel, p. 43.

25. Quoted in Andre Gunder Frank, *Crisis in the World Economy* (New York: Holmes and Meier, 1980), p. 158.

26. Martin Feldstein, "The Retreat from Keynesian Economics," *The Public Interest,* Summer 1981, p. 104.

27. Mark Shepherd, Jr., "The U.S. Corporation within the Competitive Environment," in U.S. Senate Committee on Finance, *Conference on U.S. Competitiveness: Can the United States Remain*

Competitive? (Washington, D.C.: U.S. Government Printing Office, 1980), pp. 71, 70.

28. John Maynard Keynes, "National Self-Sufficiency," *Yale Review,* Vol. 22, 1932–33, pp. 761–62, 763, 768.

III: An Economic Bill of Rights

1. From Studs Terkel, *American Dreams Lost and Found* (New York: Pantheon, 1981), p. 236.
2. Arthur Okun, *Equity vs. Efficiency: The Big Tradeoff* (Washington, D.C.: The Brookings Institution, 1975), p. 2.
3. The quotes which follow come from Gary Hart, "An Economic Strategy for the 1980s," unpublished working paper, February 6, 1982; Paul Tsongas, *The Road from Here: Liberalism and Realities in the 1980s* (New York: Knopf, 1981); and Bill Bradley, two-part series, New York *Times,* June 23, 24, 1982. See also Thomas Ferguson and Joel Rogers, "Neoliberals and Democrats," *The Nation,* June 26, 1982. The quote from Felix Rohatyn is from the New York *Times,* April 4, 1982, p. E4.
4. We have found the following sources particularly helpful: Martin Carnoy and Derek Shearer, *Economic Democracy* (White Plains, N.Y.: M. E. Sharpe, 1980); Dan Luria and Jack Russell, *Rational Reindustrialization* (Detroit: Widgetripper Press, 1982); and Mark Green, *Winning Back America* (New York: Bantam Books, 1982).

12: The Right to Economic Security and Equity

1. From Studs Terkel, *American Dreams Lost and Found* (New York: Pantheon, 1981), p. 232.
2. Herman Kahn, *The Coming Boom: Economic, Political, and Social* (New York: Simon & Schuster, 1982), p. 52; and New York *Times,* October 10, 1982, pp. iv–1.
3. *Handbook of Labor Statistics,* 1980, pp. 464, 466.
4. Budget levels for 1980 from "Family Budgets," *Monthly Labor Review,* August 1981, p. 56; and updated to 1983 by actual and projected rate of increase in consumer price index.

5. Detailed cost comparisons are provided in "Public Systems Provide Consumers Lower Cost Power," *Public Power*, July–August 1976, pp. 18–20; and "Public Power Costs Less," *Public Power*, May–June 1981, pp. 14–16.

6. For a synthetic presentation of the arguments underlying these paragraphs, see David M. Gordon, *The Working Poor* (Washington, D.C.: Council of State Planning Agencies, 1980).

7. Though simplified, our example is based on an investigation of wages, productivity, and capital stock per worker in five industries: electric and electronic equipment, instruments and related products, textile-mill products, food and kindred products, and apparel and other textile products. We have assumed that the workers will move from the firms with relatively low output per hour in the declining industries to the more advanced firms in the expanding industries. For this reason we have assumed that the productivity gains and the increased capital costs alike will be greater than a simple comparison of industry averages would indicate. All detailed industry data are from the U.S. Bureau of Labor Statistics unpublished series on capital stock for detailed industries and from the U.S. Department of Commerce, Bureau of Economic Analysis, National Income and Product Accounts for detailed industries.

8. See Edward F. Denison, *Why Growth Rates Differ* (Washington, D.C.: The Brookings Institution, 1967).

9. H. J. Habakkuk, *American and British Technology in the Nineteenth Century* (Cambridge, U.K.: Cambridge University Press, 1962).

10. The Swedish Confederation of Trade Unions, *Trade Unions and Full Employment* (Stockholm: Swedish LO, 1951), published in English in 1953, p. 94.

11. Rudolph Meidner, *Employee Investment Funds: An Approach to Collective Capital Formation* (London: George Allen & Unwin, 1978), p. 30.

12. Swedish political economist Villy Bergström further comments on solidarity wage policies in Sweden:

. . . full employment was the absolute and dominant goal of economic policy. Solidaristic wage policy with its structural implications has been pursued in a climate of confidence as to the overall employment opportunities in the country. These important facts explain the oddities of having unions foster restructuring and "mechanization." The solidaristic wage policy started to be successfully implemented in the mid-1960s, and led to a very fast restructuring of the Swedish economy in the last decade. . . .

Bergström, "The Political Economy of Swedish Capital Formation," Department of Economics, University of Uppsala, Working Papers Series No. 3, 1979.

13. Donald J. Treiman and Heidi I. Hartmann, eds., *Women, Work, and Wages: Equal Pay for Jobs of Equal Value* (Washington, D.C.: National Academy Press, 1981), pp. 93 (emphasis in the original), 95.

14. Swedish Confederation of Trade Unions, *Trade Unions and Full Employment,* p. 96.

15. See newspaper reports in New York *Times,* July 6, 1981, p. A8; July 13, 1981, p. A8; and July 14, 1981, p. A12. Quotes from Callahan from *Ms. Magazine,* February 1982, p. 84; and Comparable Worth Project, "Newsletter," July 1981, p. 2.

16. For the Supreme Court Decision, see *County of Washington* v. *Gunther,* 452 US 161, 68 L Ed 2d 751, 101 S Ct 2242; for a useful analysis of the case, see W. Newman and J. M. Vonhof, "Separate But Equal . . . ," *Illinois Law Review,* 1981:2.

17. Data on minority and female incomes from U.S. Bureau of the Census, *Current Population Reports,* Series P-60, No. 59, Tables 33 and 46; and No. 129, Table 37 and 59.

18. Michael Reich, *Racial Inequality: A Political-Economic Analysis* (Princeton, N.J.: Princeton University Press, 1981), Chapters 4, 7.

19. See Bradley Schiller, *Poverty and Discrimination* (Englewood Cliffs, N.J.: Prentice-Hall, 1981), 3rd ed., pp. 175 ff.

20. See Schiller, Chapter 10.

21. Based on summary of recent census data in Andrew Hacker, "Farewell to the Family?," *New York Review of Books,* March 18, 1982.

22. Hacker, p. 37.

23. Data on working hours from W. S. Woytinsky and Associates, *Employment and Wages in the United States* (New York: Twentieth Century Fund, 1953), p. 52; and Sar A. Levitan and Richard S. Belous, *Shorter Hours, Shorter Weeks* (Baltimore: Johns Hopkins University Press, 1977), Chapter 2.

24. U.S. Bureau of Labor Statistics, "Output Per Hour, Hourly Compensation, and Unit Labor Costs in Manufacturing, Eleven Countries, 1950–1981," unpublished data, June 1982, Table 6. The Netherlands data refer to 1980; see also *Handbook of Labor Statistics,* 1974, p. 166.

25. Output per hour will double in thirty-three years if it grows at 2.1 percent annually. If the remaining growth in output per hour (.8 percent annually) is "consumed" in the form of reduced hours, a reduction in the workweek would be possible—from 5 to 3.85 days weekly. The calculation assuming a 50 percent increase in output is made analogously.

26. Institute for Social Research, *Quality of Work Life*, 1977 (Ann Arbor: University of Michigan, 1979).

27. Barry Bosworth, "Re-establishing an Economic Consensus: An Impossible Agenda?," *Daedalus,* Summer 1980, p. 64.

28. Arnold Weber, *In Pursuit of Price Stability: The Wage-Price Freeze of 1971* (Washington, D.C.: The Brookings Institution, 1973), p. 38.

13: The Right to a Democratic Workplace

1. From Studs Terkel, *American Dreams Lost and Found* (New York: Pantheon, 1981), p. 156.

2. Based on report in *Fortune,* July 12, 1982, p. 64; underlying work will appear in Richard Freeman and James L. Medoff, *What Do Unions Do?* (New York: Basic Books, 1983).

3. *Fortune,* December 1, 1980, p. 149.

4. Institute for Social Research, *Quality of Working Life, 1977* (Ann Arbor: University of Michigan, 1979), based on question asked of all nonunion members whether they would vote for or against union representation were there an election.

5. U.S. Bureau of Labor Statistics, "Characteristics of Major Collective Bargaining Agreements," *Bulletin* No. 2095, May 1981.

6. *The Economist,* November 17, 1979, pp. 39, 46.

7. Quoted in Richard Edwards, *Contested Terrain: The Transformation of the Workplace in the Twentieth Century* (New York: Basic Books, 1979), p. 8.

8. Daniel Seligman, "Who Needs Unions?," *Fortune,* July 12, 1982, p. 66.

9. House Democratic Caucus, "Statement of Democratic Economic Principles," U.S. House of Representatives, April 8, 1981, p. 5.

10. Rudolph Meidner, *Employee Investment Funds: An Approach to Collective Capital Formation* (London: George Allen & Unwin, 1978), Appendix II.

11. Martin Carnoy and Derek Shearer, *Economic Democracy* (White Plains, N.Y.: M. E. Sharpe, 1980), p. 136.
12. Martin Slater, "Worker Councils in Italy: Past Development and Future Prospects," in David Garson, ed., *Worker Self-Management in Industry: The West European Experience* (New York: Praeger, 1977), p. 207.
13. "A Roundtable: Three Views of the Recession," New York *Times,* April 4, 1982, p. E4.
14. Meidner, p. 46.
15. Meidner, pp. 84, 85.
16. See R. Friedman and W. Schweke, eds., *Expanding the Opportunity to Produce: Revitalizing the American Economy Through New Enterprise Development* (Washington, D.C.: The Corporation for Enterprise Development, 1981). See also Thomas Peters and Robert Waterman, *In Search of Excellence* (New York: Harper & Row, 1982), and *The Economist,* January 8, 1983, pp. 11–12. *The Economist* reports: "A 1981 study showed that small firms produce about 24 times as many innovations per research-and-development dollar as large firms do. Assemble more than seven researchers, reports another survey, and research efficiency goes down."
17. Neal R. Peirce and Carol Steinbach, "Reindustrialization on a Small Scale," in Friedman and Schweke, p. 8.
18. Neal R. Peirce, "Local Private-Public Enterprise—Context and Trends," in Friedman and Schweke, p. 171.
19. "Community Enterprise: A Decade of Experimentation and Experience," in Friedman and Schweke, p. 164.

14: The Right to Shape Our Economic Futures

1. From Studs Terkel, *American Dreams Lost and Found* (New York: Pantheon, 1981), p. 377.
2. Robert Lekachman, *Greed Is Not Enough: Reaganomics* (New York: Pantheon, 1982), p. 207.
3. For some related conclusions from a different tradition of analysis, see William G. Ouchi, "Markets, Bureaucracies, and Clans," *Administrative Science Quarterly,* March 1980.
4. The Business Week Team, *The Reindustrialization of America* (New York: McGraw-Hill, 1982), p. 148.

5. For a particularly useful review of French planning techniques, see Stephen S. Cohen, *Modern Capitalist Planning: The French Model* (Berkeley: University of California Press, 1977), rev. ed.

6. Quoted in Martin Carnoy and Derek Shearer, *Economic Democracy* (White Plains, N.Y.: M. E. Sharpe, 1980), pp. 269–70.

7. Lester C. Thurow, "How to Rescue a Drowning Economy," *New York Review of Books*, April 1, 1982, p. 4.

8. OECD, *National Accounts, 1950–80*. On public investment in Norway, see Don S. Schwerin, "Groups, Institutions, and Economic Growth," paper presented to the American Political Science Association, New York, September 1978. Schwerin reports: "A significant segment of the capital market (20–30 percent) is . . . directly responsive to governmental criteria for investment. . . . Industrial investment in Norway has not only been exceptionally high, but investment has been systematically channeled into new industries promising productivity gains, at the expense of established economic sectors. . . ." High investment levels in Norway substantially predate the discovery of North Sea Oil. For further data, see the annual OECD country reports on Norway.

9. For brief description of provisions for nationalization of banks in France, see New York *Times*, December 21, 1981, p. D1.

10. Carnoy and Shearer, p. 117.

11. See Governor's Public Investment Task Force, *Final Report*, State of California, October 1981.

12. Lawrence Litvak, *Pension Funds and Economic Renewal* (Washington, D.C.: Council of State Planning Agencies, 1981), p. 136.

13. In 1980, for example, federal expenditures on social-insurance administration totaled $4.4 billion while total federal expenditures for insurance benefits and repayments totaled $170.6 billion. *Statistical Abstract*, 1981, pp. 278–79.

14. Andrew Tobias, *The Invisible Bankers: Everything the Insurance Industry Never Wanted You to Know* (New York: The Linden Press of Simon & Schuster, 1982).

15. Tobias, p. 25.

16. Tobias, p. 21.

17. Jeremy Rifkin and Randy Barber, *The North Will Rise Again: Pensions, Politics, and Power in the 1980s* (Boston: Beacon Press, 1978), p. 203.

18. Rozanne Enerson, "The People's Bank on the Prairie," *Working Papers*, July–August 1982, p. 13.

19. See, for example, Stuart Holland, *Beyond Capitalist Planning* (Oxford: Basil Blackwell, 1979).

20. Stephen A. Marglin, "What Do Bosses Do? Part II," *Review of Radical Political Economics,* Spring 1975.

21. Thurow, p. 3.

22. Carnoy and Shearer, p. 266.

23. Based on Barry Bluestone and Bennett Harrison, *The Deindustrialization of America* (New York: Basic Books, 1982), p. 238.

24. Julia Leighton, Melissa Roderick, and Nancy Folbre, " 'Pick Up Your Tools and Leave, the Mill Is Down': Plant Closings in Maine, 1971–1981," unpublished paper, Bowdoin College, August 1981.

25. Bluestone and Harrison, p. 130 (emphasis in the original).

26. Michael J. Piore and Charles F. Sabel, "Italian Small Business Development: Lessons for U.S. Industrial Policy," Department of Economics, M.I.T., Working Paper No. 288, August 1981, p. 2.

27. Irving Kristol, "The Worst Is Yet to Come," *Wall Street Journal,* November 26, 1979.

28. The Business Week Team, p. 134.

15: The Right to a Better Way of Life

1. Quoted in Richard J. Barnett, *The Crisis of the Corporation* (Washington, D.C.: Institute for Policy Studies, 1975), p. 6.

2. See, for example, the discussions in Marcus G. Raskin, ed., *The Federal Budget and Social Reconstruction* (Washington, D.C.: Institute for Policy Studies, 1978), Chapters 8, 17–18; Mark Green, *Winning Back America* (New York: Bantam Books, 1982), pp. 200–5; and Peter Dreier, "Dreams and Nightmares," *The Nation,* August 21–28, 1982.

3. Quoted in William Greider, "The Education of David Stockman," *The Atlantic,* December 1981, p. 35.

4. James M. Fallows, *National Defense* (New York: Random House, 1981).

5. Cited in Mark Green, *Winning Back America* (New York: Bantam, 1982), p. 97.

6. Daniel Yergin, "Conservation: The Key Energy Source," in Robert Stobaugh and Daniel Yergin, eds., *Energy Future* (New York: Random House, 1979), p. 136.

7. Green, p. 96.

8. President's Council on Environmental Quality, "Solar Energy: Progress and Promise," April 1978.

9. See the discussion, for example, in Stuart Holland, *Beyond Capitalist Planning* (Oxford: Basil Blackwell, 1978). For a more exhaustive treatment of the economic case for public control of energy, see Samuel Bowles and David Kotz, "Oil: Should Government Control the Tap?," Los Angeles *Times*, October 10, 1979.

10. Based on detailed reports in Peter Meyer, "Land Rush," *Harper's*, January 1979, p. 54.

11. See, for example, Land Ownership Task Force, *Land Ownership Patterns and Their Impacts on Appalachian Communities* (New Market, Tenn.: The Appalachian Alliance, 1981), 6 vols.; and "Who Owns Appalachia?," *Southern Exposure*, January–February 1982, pp. 32–48.

12. See review of available data in Meyer, "Land Rush," p. 49.

13. See, in particular, Bruce F. Hall and E. Philip LeVeen, "Farm Size and Economic Efficiency: The Case of California," *American Journal of Agricultural Economics*, November 1978, and B. F. Stanton, "Perspectives on Farm Size," *American Journal of Agricultural Economics*, March 1978.

14. See Walter Goldschmidt, *As You Sow: Three Studies in the Social Consequences of Agribusiness* (Montclair, N.J.: Allanheld, Osmun, 1978), originally published in 1947; Mark Kramer, *Three Farms: Making Milk, Meat and Money from the American Soil* (New York: Bantam, 1981); and Michael Perelman, *Farming for Profit in a Hungry World* (Montclair, N.J.: Allanheld, Osmun, 1977).

15. Cited in New York *Times*, March 29, 1982, p. D11; tax-supported comprehensive national health insurance was favored in this poll by a margin of 48 percent to 42 percent, with the remainder having no opinion.

16. Marilyn A. Elrod, "Comprehensive Health Service: An Alternative Answer to the Health Care Crisis in the United States," in Marcus G. Raskin, ed., *The Federal Budget and Social Reconstruction* (Washington, D.C.: Institute for Policy Studies, 1978), pp. 316–17.

17. Quoted in Elrod, p. 316.

18. For a review of deterrence studies, see Alfred Blumstein, Jacqueline Cohen, and Daniel Nagin, eds., *Deterrence and Incapacitation: Estimating the Effects of Criminal Sanctions on Crime Rates* (Washington, D.C.: National Academy of Sciences, 1978).

The most thoughtful demolition of the rehabilitation theory is still Andrew von Hirsch, *Doing Justice: The Choice of Punishments* (New York: Hill and Wang, 1976).

19. On prison costs, see Douglas McDonald, *The Price of Punishment* (New York: Praeger, 1980), and U.S. National Institute of Justice, *American Prisons and Jails, Volume III: Conditions and Costs of Confinement*, by Joan Mullen and Bradford Smith (Washington, D.C.: U.S. Government Printing Office, 1981).

20. Robert L. Woodson, "Public Policy and the Underclass—New Hope for the Future," in R. Friedman and W. Schweke, eds., *Expanding the Opportunity to Produce: Revitalizing the American Economy Through New Enterprise Development* (Washington, D.C.: The Corporation for Enterprise Development, 1981), p. 163.

21. Quoted in Alexander Cockburn and James Ridgeway, "Why Does the Right Own the Tax Issue?," *Village Voice*, March 30, 1982, p. 6.

16: Toward a Democratic Economy

1. From Studs Terkel, *American Dreams Lost and Found* (New York: Pantheon, 1981), pp. 276–77.

2. From Terkel, p. 312.

3. These estimates are based on straight-line projections of the increase in two categories—those in federal and state prisons and local jails and those on parole and probation—from 1979 to 1981. The data come from Department of Justice, Bureau of Justice Statistics, *Bulletin*, 1982.

4. This projection is based on the assumption that the increase in the concentration of large corporate ownership between now and 1990 will be comparable to the increase after the last two crises, as highlighted in Figure 11.2.

5. These two projections are based on a projection of the trends in Figure 11.3 and of the recent data on the trend in the union membership share of the nonagricultural labor force.

6. These poll results come, respectively, from the New York *Times*, November 8, 1979, p. A16; Jeremy Rifkin, *Own Your Own Job* (New York: Bantam, 1975), p. 176; *In These Times*, April 4–10, 1979, p. 8; and the Gallup Poll, Survey 191-G, Q. 10, conducted March 12–15, 1982.

7. A summary of these and other related results may be found in Daniel Yankelovich, *New Rules* (New York: Random House, 1981), pp. 95 ff.

Appendix A: The Relevance of Hourly Income

1. For an interesting effort along these lines to develop a measure of "net economic welfare," see W. Nordhaus and J. Tobin, "Is Growth Obsolete?," in the National Bureau of Economic Research, *Fiftieth Anniversary Colloquium* (New York: Columbia University Press, 1972), Vol. V.
2. We calculated annual figures for hourly income in the U.S. economy as follows. First, we divided GNP (*NIPA*, Table 1.1) by the implicit price deflator for gross domestic purchases (*NIPA*, Table 7.3). Then we subtracted the constant-price value of capital consumption allowances with capital consumption adjustment (*NIPA*, Table 5.2). Finally, we divided the resulting real net national income by the total hours worked by persons engaged in production (*NIPA*, Table 6.13). The total hours figures for 1980 and 1981 were obtained by extrapolation from the 1979 figure in the same proportion as the "manhours of employed labor force" series published by *BLS*.

Appendix B: The Inadequacy of Conventional Explanations of Stagflation

1. According to estimates made by the Bureau of Economic Analysis, the years 1966–69 and 1973 were the only ones since 1965 in which the ratio of actual to potential GNP exceeded one. And these were also the only years since 1965 in which the Federal Reserve Board's index of capacity utilization in manufacturing exceeded 86 percent. *Economic Report*, 1982, Table B-45.
2. Union membership as a proportion of the total U.S. nonagricultural labor force reached a postwar peak of approximately 35 percent in the mid-1950s and has declined gradually since then, falling nearly to 20 percent by the late 1970s. *Handbook of Labor Statistics*, 1980, Table 165.
3. Our figures on the U.S. money supply refer to the money concept

M-2, as tabulated in the *Economic Report,* 1982, Table B-61. We chose to measure growth over the periods 1959–66, 1966–73, and 1973–79 because each end-point is a business-cycle peak year (in terms of the ratio of actual to potential GNP).

Note that the acceleration in the growth of the *nominal* money supply over the three periods does not contradict our argument (in Chapter 5) that monetary policy became increasingly restrictive after 1973. The restrictiveness of monetary policy depends on the growth of the *real* money supply, relative to potential output, and this was actually negative between 1973 and 1979. Deflating the data on M-2 by the implicit price deflator for GNP (*Economic Report,* 1982, Table B-3), and comparing the resulting figures on the real money supply with estimates of potential output made by the Bureau of Economic Analysis, we find that the relative growth rate of real money was 1.4 percent for 1959–66; .3 percent for 1966–73; and −.9 percent for 1973–79.

4. The figures on the relative growth of the (nominal) money supply were calculated from the data on M-2 and potential output cited in note 3; the figures on price inflation were calculated from the implicit price deflator data cited in the same footnote.

Appendix C: Multivariate Regression Analysis of the U.S. Economic Crisis

1. Data on the after-tax profit rate (y) and Tobin's Q (z) from 1955 to 1980 are available in *Economic Report,* 1982, Table B-88. Values for y before 1955 were calculated directly from the underlying profit data in *NIPA,* Table 1.13, and the fixed capital stock data supplied by the Bureau of Economic Analysis. Values for z before 1955 were obtained from D. Holland and S. Myers, "Trends in Corporate Profitability and Capital Costs," in R. Lindsay, ed., *The Nation's Capital Needs* (Washington, D.C.: The Committee for Economic Development, 1979), Table 2.

Appendix D: Estimating the Waste Burden

1. In order to maintain consistency with published employment data in the *Employment and Training Report,* 1981, we estimate total

annual hours for 1980 by adjusting average weekly hours in the private sector for 1979 (Table C-4) by the implicit average weekly hours for the whole economy from the 1979 data in the National Income and Product Accounts; multiplying that new average hours by 52 weeks a year, for 1,872.3 average hours per year; and then multiplying that by average 1980 employment (Table A-1 of *Employment and Training Report,* 1981).

2. Data sources for the labor utilization adjustments: unemployment, discouraged workers, and involuntary part-time from Tables A-1, A-14, and A-26 of *Employment and Training Report,* 1981. Median weekly hours of the part-time employed, estimated number working overtime, median hours of overtime, and percentage of involuntary overtime come from calculations based on the data tapes of the 1977 Quality of Working Life survey conducted by the Institute for Social Research, University of Michigan. We are grateful to John Evansohn for providing us with these data tabulations.

3. Data from *Employment and Training Report,* 1981, Table C-2.

4. For a full range of studies, see Derek C. Jones and Jan Svejnar, eds., *Participatory and Self-Managed Firms: Evaluating Economic Performance* (Lexington, Mass.: Lexington Books, 1982).

5. Actual defense expenditures in 1980 from *Economic Report,* 1982, B-1, representing total outlays for national defense.

6. Data on total expenditures, 1952–80, for federal support for nuclear power research; capital costs of plants already in operation; capital costs for plants under construction at that time; total electricity production from nuclear and all sources; used capacity; and conservation costs per kilowatt-hour saved are all supplied to us by Leonard Rodberg, energy economist at Queens College of the City University of New York, based on his research and research by Charles Komanoff and Joseph Bowring and data from the Department of Energy, the General Accounting Office, and the Battelle Institute. Data on average age of capital stock from *Statistical Abstract,* 1981, p. 546. Data on total capital stock and total product for nonfarm private (nonresidential) from *Statistical Abstract,* 1981, p. 545, and *Economic Report,* 1981, p. 245.

7. Data on 1948 food expenditures and the marketing ratio from *Historical Statistics,* p. 490. Data for 1980 from *Statistical Abstract,* 1981, p. 678. Note that the columns in the *Historical Statistics* series for farm value and marketing bill are reversed, as is obvious from comparing them to the series on p. 489 and the data from the *Statistical Abstract.*

8. Data on comparative infant mortality rates from *World Health*

Statistics Annual, 1973, 1976. Data on health expenditures from Organization for Economic Cooperation and Development, *Public Expenditures on Health* (Paris: OECD, 1977), p. 10; with the conversion to U.S. dollars at current prices and exchange rates.

9. Data for criminal-justice expenditures from *Historical Statistics,* p. 416; and *Statistical Abstract,* 1981, p. 182. The 1980 expenditure figure is estimated by extrapolating the trend line from 1976–79, since 1980 figures were not yet available. (Given other evidence on the rapid increase in criminal-justice expenditures, this is surely a minimum estimate of 1980 costs.) The price deflator was the GNP deflator for government purchases of goods and services, *Economic Report,* 1981, p. 237.

10. Data on advertising expenditures from *Historical Statistics,* p. 856; and *Statistical Abstract,* 1981, p. 572. Price deflator for personal-consumption expenditures from *Economic Report,* 1981, p. 236.

Appendix E: The Costs of an Economic Bill of Rights

The data utilized in this appendix are based on the following sources: *Economic Report,* 1982; *NIPA; Statistical Abstract; Historical Statistics;* and unpublished data supplied by the Bureau of Economic Analysis.

INDEX

Rockefeller, David, 209, 217
Rohatyn, Felix, 208, 211, 217–18,
   315
Roosevelt, Franklin, 251
Roosevelt, Kermit, 66, 67
Roosevelt, Teddy, 241, 247
Rothschild, Emma, 106
Rourke, Charles K., 166
Rousseau, Jean Jacques, 209

Sabel, Charles, 343, 344
Sadlowski, Ed, 262
Sakamoto, Yoshikazu, 224
Schumacher, E. F., 284
Schumpeter, Joseph, 133, 209
Scott-Stokes, Henry, 222
Securities and Exchange
   Commission, 311–17
Shah of Iran, 66, 67
Shearer, Derek, 341
Shepard, Thomas R., Jr., 136
Shepherd, Mark, Jr., 257
Shepherd, William G., 52
Silk, Leonard, 98, 202, 256
Simon, William E., 37–38
Smith, Adam, 354
Smith, Al, 257
Social Democratic Party
   (Sweden), 316
Social Security Act of 1935, 77
Social Security system, 333
Solidarity wages, 283–85
South Africa, 175
Soviet Union, 175
Spanish-American War, 247
Spillover effects, 233
Stagflation, 21–26, 113–20
Staines, Graham, 107
Steel industry, 53
Stein, Herbert, 54
Stevens (J. P.), 109, 284–85, 307
Stobaugh, Robert, 357
Stockman, David, 183, 189, 196,
   202, 356
Stone, W. Clement, 104
Strauss, Lewis, 75
Supply-side economics, 182–96,
   227, 265
   corporatism distinguished from,
      208–9
   deregulation, 192–95
   investment tax credit, 195

Laffer Curve, 195–96
   monetarism distinguished from,
      201–2
   principle propositions, 189
   tax reduction, 190–92
   See also Probusiness strategies
Sweden, 39–41
   allocation of labor, 167
   cooperative work agreements,
      314
   "management rights" clauses,
      313
   plant closings, 47
   profit sharing, 316
   solidarity wages, 283–84
   suicide rate, 46
   taxation, 196
   trade union movement, 306
   unemployment, 158
Swedish Labor Organization, 316
Switzerland, 46, 190

Taft, Robert, 85
Taft-Hartley Act of 1947, 73, 307,
   309, 310
Taxation
   business taxation, 99, 100, 103
   as cause of economic crisis,
      42–43
   Economic Bill of Rights
      proposals, 373–78
   supply-side economics and,
      190–92
Tax-based incomes policy (TIP),
   297–98, 299
Taylor, Frederick, 306
Tennessee Valley Administration,
   (TVA), 361
Texas Instruments, 232
Thatcher government, 206–8
Thurow, Lester C., 166, 212, 329,
   336, 341
Time for Action, A (Simon),
   37–38
Tobacco Workers Organizing
   Committee (TWOC), 71
Tobias, Andrew, 333, 334
Tobin, James, 95, 194, 195,
   202, 227, 231
Tobin's Q, 95–97
Trade, 346–51
Transfer pricing, 69

INTRODUCTION

read with this book in one hand and your Bible in the other.

This book is not the Bible—it is intended to point you to the Bible. The desire of my heart is that this work will unlock for you the treasure of the truth of God's Word and the insights into that truth that Oswald Chambers explored. May you use this book as a help in meditating on God's Word, and as a help in applying it to your life.

James Reimann
Joshua 1:8